T0328386

Chinese Organizations in Sub-Saharan Africa

Trade between China and Africa is increasing year on year, while the West increasingly debates the nature and implications of China's presence. Yet little research exists at the organizational and community levels. While western press reporting is overwhelmingly negative, African governments mostly welcome the Chinese presence. But what happens at the management level? How are Chinese organizations run? What are they bringing to communities? What is their impact on the local job market? How do they manage staff? How are they working with local firms?

This book seeks to provide a theoretical framework for understanding Chinese organizations and management in Africa and to explore how their interventions are playing out at the organizational and community levels in sub-Saharan Africa. Based on rigorous empirical research exploring emerging themes in specific African countries, this book develops implications for management knowledge, education and training provision, and policy formulation. Importantly it seeks to inform future scholarship on China's management impact in the world generally, on Africa's future development, and on international and cross-cultural management scholarship.

Primarily aimed at scholars of international management, with an interest in China and/or in China in Africa, this important book will also be of great interest to those working in the area of development studies, international politics, and international relations.

Terence Jackson is Emeritus Professor of Cross-Cultural Management, Middlesex University Business School, London, UK, and a visiting professor in the Department of Management, Rhodes University, Grahamstown, South Africa.

Lynette Louw, appointed in the Raymond Ackerman Chair of Management, Department of Management, is the Deputy Dean, Faculty of Commerce at Rhodes University, Grahamstown, South Africa.

Dev K. (Roshan) Boojihawon is Associate Professor of Strategy at University of Birmingham, Business School, Department of Strategy and International Business.

Routledge Studies in International Business and the World Economy

European Born Globals
Job creation in young international businesses
Edited by Irene Mandl and Valentina Patrini

Management Research
European Perspectives
Edited by Sabina Siebert

Global Business Intelligence
Edited by J. Mark Munoz

Confucianism, Discipline and Competitiveness
Chris Baumann, Hume Winzar, and Doris Viengkham

Cases in Critical Cross-Cultural Management
An Intersectional Approach to Culture
Jasmin Mahadevan, Henriett Primecz, and Laurence Romani

Understanding Multilingual Workplaces
Methodological, Empirical and Pedagogic Perspectives
Edited by Sierk Horn, Philippe Lecomte, Susanne Tietze

Self-Initiated Expatriates in Context
Recognizing Space, Time and Institutions
Edited by Maike Andresen, Chris Brewster and Vesa Suutari

Chinese Organizations in Sub-Saharan Africa
New Dynamics, New Synergies
Edited by Terence Jackson, Lynette Louw and Dev K. (Roshan) Boojihawon

For more information about this series, please visit: www.routledge.com/ Routledge-Studies-in-International-Business-and-the-World-Economy/ book-series/SE0358

Chinese Organizations in Sub-Saharan Africa

New Dynamics, New Synergies

Edited by Terence Jackson,
Lynette Louw and
Dev K. (Roshan) Boojihawon

Routledge
Taylor & Francis Group

LONDON AND NEW YORK

First published 2021
by Routledge
2 Park Square, Milton Park, Abingdon, Oxon OX14 4RN

and by Routledge
605 Third Avenue, New York, NY 10017

First issued in paperback 2022

Routledge is an imprint of the Taylor & Francis Group, an informa business

© 2021 selection and editorial matter, Terence Jackson, Lynette Louw and Dev K. (Roshan) Boojihawon; individual chapters, the contributors

Publisher's Note
The publisher has gone to great lengths to ensure the quality of this reprint but points out that some imperfections in the original copies may be apparent.

British Library Cataloguing-in-Publication Data
A catalogue record for this book is available from the British Library

Library of Congress Cataloging-in-Publication Data
A catalog record for this book has been requested

ISBN 13: 978-0-367-62346-3 (pbk)
ISBN 13: 978-1-138-69255-8 (hbk)
ISBN 13: 978-1-315-53209-7 (ebk)

DOI: 10.4324/9781315532097

Typeset in Sabon
by Apex CoVantage, LLC

Terence Jackson
To Alysia

Lynette Louw
*To all those who participated in this project
for their hard work and dedication, and especially
the masters' and Ph.D. graduates in the Department
of Management, Rhodes University.*

Dev K. (Roshan) Boojihawon
To my rays of light: Ameetah, Tejal, Diya and Pavi

Contents

Figures

Tables

Contributors

Editors

Terence Jackson is Emeritus Professor of Cross-Cultural Management, Middlesex University Business School, London, UK, and a visiting professor in the Department of Management, Rhodes University, Grahamstown, South Africa. He has undertaken a number of research projects in sub-Saharan Africa and has published critical articles on areas including the cross-cultural management of international development in Africa, the contribution of the informal sector, and China's engagement in Africa. He has previously published *Management and Change in Africa: A Cross-Cultural Perspective* with Routledge.

Lynette Louw, appointed in the Raymond Ackerman Chair of Management, Department of Management and the Deputy Dean, Faculty of Commerce at Rhodes University in Grahamstown, South Africa. She is a specialist in strategic management, international organisational behaviour and cross-cultural management. Her research in Africa has been published widely both in South Africa and internationally. She is a co-author of *Management: Fourth South African Edition* and the editor and co-author of *Strategic Management: Developing Sustainability in Southern Africa*, 3rd edition.

Dev K. (Roshan) Boojihawon is Associate Professor of Strategy at University of Birmingham, Business School, Department of Strategy and International Business. His research interests span across areas of international strategy and entrepreneurship focusing specifically on organisational and processual variables and influences in managing across borders within SMEs and multinational firms in professional services contexts. He has researched processual, nonmarket and practice-based underpinnings of 'strategy' in diverse organisational settings in Sub-Saharan Africa, and his research has been published widely in international journals including *Journal of World Business, Human Resource Management Review, Business Strategy and the Environment*, and *Journal of International Management and Strategic Change*.

Contributors

Ogechi Adeola, Associate Professor of Marketing and the academic director of the Sales & Marketing Academy at Lagos Business School, Pan-Atlantic University, Lagos, Nigeria [oadeola@lbs.edu.ng]

Abdoulkadre Ado, Assistant Professor in International Business and Global Management, Telfer School of Management, University of Ottawa, Ottawa, Canada. [Ado@telfer.uottawa.ca]

Christian Martin Boness, research partner on the "Chinese Organisations in sub-Saharan Africa: New Dynamics, New Synergies" project in the Department of Management, Rhodes University, Grahamstown, South Africa. [christianboness@gmx.net]

Dev K. (Roshan) Boojihawon, Senior Lecturer in Strategy, Business School, University of Birmingham, Birmingham, UK. [D.K.Boojihawon@bham.ac.uk]

Fungai Chigwendere, Ph.D. graduate, Department of Management, Rhodes University, South Africa. [fungaich@gmail.com]

Robert E. Hinson, Professor, University of Ghana Business School, Accra, Ghana. [hinsonrobert@gmail.com]

Terence Jackson, Emeritus Professor of Cross-Cultural Management, Middlesex University Business School, London, UK, and visiting professor, Department of Management, Rhodes University, Grahamstown, South Africa. [t.jackson@mdx.ac.uk]

Lynette Louw, Raymond Ackerman Chair of Business Administration, Department of Management and Deputy Dean, Faculty of Commerce, Rhodes University, Grahamstown, South Africa. [l.louw@ru.ac.za]

Mattheus J. Louw, Senior Lecturer, Department of Management, Rhodes University, Grahamstown, South Africa. [m.louw@ru.ac.za]

Linda Mabuza, master's graduate, Department of Management, Rhodes University, Grahamstown, South Africa. [c/o Mattheus Louw m.louw@ru.ac.za]

Claude-Hélène Mayer, Senior Research Associate, Department of Management, Rhodes University, Grahamstown, South Africa. [claudemayer@gmx.net]

Charles Mbalyohere, research partner on the "Chinese Organisations in sub-Saharan Africa: New Dynamics, New Synergies" project in the Department of Management, Rhodes University, Grahamstown, South Africa, and Lecturer in Strategic Management, Open University Business School, Milton Keynes, UK. [charles.mbalyohere@open.ac.uk]

Chengcheng Miao, Ph.D. student, Henley Business School, University of Reading, Reading, UK. [chengcheng.miao@pgr.reading.ac.uk]

Ellis L.C. Osabutey, Reader, Business School, University of Roehampton, London, UK. [Ellis.Osabutey@roehampton.ac.uk]

Steven Paterson, master's graduate, Department of Management, Rhodes University, Grahamstown, South Africa. [steven.paterson@live.com]

Zindiye Stanislous, Lecturer in the Department of Management, Rhodes University, Grahamstown, South Africa. [Stanislous.Zindiye@univen.ac.za]

Preface

Chinese presence in Africa is changing things. Trade between China and Africa is increasing year on year, as are the debates in the West on the nature and implications of China's presence. Yet little research and collective knowledge exists at the organizational and community levels. In the press, China's presence is overwhelmingly reported negatively. Mostly, African governments welcome this presence. But what happens at the management level? How are Chinese organizations run in Africa? Do they simply compete with Western firms on costs? Do they compete with African firms on the basis of expertise? What are they bringing to communities? What is their impact on the local job market? How do they manage staff? How are they working with local firms?

There are many more questions that have not been answered in a systematic way, apart from anecdotes and dubious journalism. This book seeks to provide both theoretical frameworks for understanding Chinese organization and management in Africa as well as rigorous empirical research that highlights emerging themes and provides insights into individual African countries. It provides case studies to inform policy, practice and future research. It points to implications and possible impacts on management knowledge, educational and training provision and policy formulation concerning Africa's future development. Importantly, it seeks to inform future scholarship on China in the world generally, on Africa's future development and on international and cross-cultural management scholarship that informs much of the work in this book. As such, the book should appeal mainly to international management scholars and advanced students, Africa and China specialists, as well as those scholars and policymakers concerned with Africa's development.

The rationale for this project stems from the increasing importance of the implications of China's overseas policies and the actions of its major organizations and how this is played out at the management, organizational and community levels in sub-Saharan Africa. It stems from a dearth of serious and critical scholarship at this level, among a sea of literature at the macro-levels of international relations, politics and economics aimed primarily at global business and foreign investment. While this macro-level literature informs our work, there is a serious need to point the way in theory building and empirical research that can start to address a critical analysis of the role of Chinese organizations and how they operate in Africa. There is also a need to examine the implications on management practice, policy and business leadership. The scholarship in this book is largely informed by critical cross-cultural and international management studies, yet there is a need to focus on the way an increasing dominance in the world of South–South interaction could be changing management knowledge and the future of key management disciplines. Hence, we bring to bear other management sub-disciplines that can inform this work.

The basis of this book was an international symposium held over two days at Rhodes University, South Africa as a culmination of two years of a three-year project funded by the Sandisa Imbewu Fund at Rhodes University. A number of the current chapters where developed from papers presented at the symposium, while others were invited from experts in the field. In total, the books aims to: (1) develop critical theories that can interrogate the nature of Chinese organizations in sub-Saharan African countries, and their interactions with partners, staffs and communities, and which can take scholarship in this area forward; (2) examine empirical evidence, as a result of structured and coordinated research in different sub-Saharan countries including case studies of organizations, extracting emerging themes; and (3) discuss the implications of this research to practice, policy and future research.

In Part I, we focus on the context of the Chinese presence in Africa and the implications for organization and management and its importance for the way we study China's engagement in the continent. In Chapter 1, Terence Jackson looks critically at research on China in Africa in its geopolitical context. This context is very different to when theories of international management were first formulated, and he contends that this context changes the way we should look at how we do our research, often putting aside our preconceptions about Africa and the motives of China's presence in Africa. We still have some way to go in understanding Chinese organization and management in Africa, but also some way to go in understanding the implications of this for international management studies as a whole. Some of the issues mooted in Chapter 1 are taken up by Lynette Louw in Chapter 2 when she discusses why the Chinese presence in Africa is important to management scholars. From a comprehensive literature review of the area, she goes into some depth on Chinese motives and their implications and the relevance to Africa's development. She focuses on cultural synergies and divergence between African and Chinese cultures that are important to the way we study this area. The transfer of knowledge and technology is a contentious issue taken up in this chapter, as well as in Chapter 3. Here Osabutey, Hinson and Adeola approach this from a strategic position, outlining policy and investment strategies that enhance symbiotic Sino-Africa relations. They suggest a new research framework for addressing these issues and point the way for better policymaking to enable Africa to take better advantages of the opportunities presented in dealing with Chinese organization.

Chengcheng Miao takes up these issues in the context of human resource strategies of Chinese forms in Africa in Chapter 4. She shows how the strategic motives and characteristic of Chinese foreign direct investment as well as the type of firm ownership influences the nature of human resource management (HRM) in Chinese firms in Africa, alongside the impacts of traditional culture. After outlining these international HRM strategies used by Chinese companies, she goes on to focus on the management of Chinese expatriates in African countries, presenting a conceptual framework for understanding the relationships between ownership, motives and expatriate management and the research opportunities this may present. In Chapter 5, Fungai Chigwendere's work focuses on the contentious issue of communication in Chinese organizations in Africa. By providing a framework for understanding intercultural communication effectiveness, she explores the synergies and differences in Sino-African organizations, suggesting ways forward for appropriate research in this area.

After reviewing the existing knowledge on the context of Chinese organization and management in Africa and drawing out some of the research implications in Part I, Part II focuses on our empirical work and emerging themes in different African countries. In Chapter 6, Abdoulkadre Ado takes up the theme of cross-cultural communication, explored in the previous chapter by Chigwendere, and focuses on its implications for knowledge transfer in China–Africa joint ventures. His empirical work compares anglophone and francophone countries. Although his findings suggest that language is a major barrier handled in different ways in anglophone and francophone countries, this barrier has also acted as a conduit for innovative communication practices. Still on the theme of communication, but that of a different sort, media communication, Zindiye Stanislous in Chapter 7 looks at the way press coverage of the Chinese presence in Zimbabwe has influenced, quite often negatively, perceptions of Chinese firms.

Steven Paterson and Lynette Louw's work in Chapter 8 focuses on employees' commitment in one Chinese multinational enterprise (MNE) in South Africa, identifying the factors that contribute to higher levels of commitment and how this works within this large MNE. Shifting the focus slightly in Chapter 9, Linda Mabuza and Mattheus J. Louw look at how organizational culture in a Chinese firm, also in South Africa, leads to a high-commitment work system. Focusing on the organizational culture of this MNE, their study shows a predominance of a 'market' culture that through its HRM practices has driven performance. Chapter 10 focuses our attention on Tanzania, where Claude-Héléne Mayer and Christian Martin Boness look at differences and similarities in the perceptions of management practices between local and Chinese staffs, concluding that there is a lack of intercultural understanding and making suggestions for both future research and management practice. In Uganda, in Chapter 11, Charles Mbalyohere points to the role of the mediator in facilitating mutual understanding within a Chinese agricultural machinery company. He shows how the nurturing of trust-based relationships with lead Ugandan managers and their subsequent role as mediators can bridge disparities between Chinese managerial behavior and Ugandan employee perceptions.

In Part III, we look at some of the implications of this work. In Chapter 12, Dev K. (Roshan) Boojihawon looks at the implications for building synergies between Chinese and African staffs through hybrid practice-based management partnerships. He looks at the role of Africa-based business schools in co-developing African and Chinese managers. There is a clear failure of such schools to make appropriate impact in view of the reliance on western-based management principles and practices. He points to the need for African management experience to be taken seriously, particularly in the light of the Chinese presence, a necessity that reflects the sentiments in many of the chapters in this text.

Terence Jackson, Middlesex University Business School,
London, UK and Rhodes University, South Africa.

Lynette Louw, Rhodes University, South Africa

Dev K. (Roshan) Boojihawon, University of Birmingham, UK

Acknowledgements

The authors wish to acknowledge, with gratitude, the contributions of the following towards the project *Chinese Organisations in Sub-Saharan Africa: New Dynamics, New Synergies* which led to the publication of this book:

- The Open University Business School, UK, for supporting and funding part of the research fellowship to aid with the data gathering process in this research.
- The Sandisa Imbewu Fund, Rhodes University, Grahamstown, South Africa, for their financial support for this project.
- The National Research Foundation (NRF) of South Africa for the Grant No. 93636.
- Middlesex University Business School, London, UK, for their support.

Part I
The context

1 Current research on Chinese organizations in Africa

What do we know, and what do we need to do?

Terence Jackson

Many articles and chapters on the subject of China's engagement in Africa start with facts and figures that show China's investment and presence in Africa is both substantial and growing. I do not wish to add to those statistics here but simply to affirm that the Chinese presence is significant enough to have substantially worried the western powers, as their pre-eminence in Africa has eroded over the past years (Carmody, 2011; Jackson, 2014). There is now a wealth of literature on China in Africa at the macro level, to which I also do not wish to add. Although growing, the literature and therefore our knowledge of China's presence at the organizational level is still small. This is no longer a result simply of a lack of interest among international management scholars, although this has been a factor. Although many of the researchers in this book have alluded to the difficulty of access to Chinese organizations, most have found a way. Yet this is still a major issue, but it is a methodological one and not necessarily a deliberate obstructive attitude from Chinese managers. Kriz, Gummesson, and Quazi (2014, p. 30) note that in business dealings with Chinese managers '*guanxi* needs to be carefully crafted for those wanting to "step across the door"', yet 'there has been little discussion of its possible methodological implications'. We should be cautious about applying western-centric methodological approaches in researching Chinese organizations in Africa, as we should in applying western values and assumptions to our findings.

Yet, the implications for scholarship in international management and business go deeper than this. It extends to our fundamental assumptions about our subject matter. Overcoming these assumptions is an important part of the way we study China in Africa. It frames our view. Flyvbjerg (2001) asserts that in the social sciences there cannot be a view from nowhere. It always has to come from somewhere. It is perhaps unfortunate that often an implicit view taken by scholars in international management studies is that of modernization theory. This is particularly endemic to the recent upsurge in interest in Africa by international management scholars (Jackson, 2015a, 2015b). The trajectory of development is presumed to be in the model of western, developed economies

(Jackson, 2012). Western management solutions are proposed to counter the perceived unproductive, inefficient and sometimes corrupt 'African' practices (Jackson, 2004; provides a critique). Yet as Raewyn Connell (2007, p. x) asserts in her attempts to establish 'Southern Theory' in the social sciences:

> With anthropology now the designated intellectual container for primitive societies, the rest of social science formed itself on ethnocentric assumptions that amount to a gigantic lie – that modernity created itself within the North Atlantic world, independent of the rest of humanity. Models constructed on the basis of that lie, such as functionalist sociology, modernization theory and neoclassical economics, were then exported to the rest of the world with all the authority of the most advanced knowledge, and all the weight of First World wealth and power.

Yet the critiques of this stance within management and organization studies may be less than helpful when focusing on China's presence in Africa. The fashion in critical management studies for Postcolonial analysis may be flawed in analysing China's role in Africa. This is because geopolitical dynamics have been changing over the last decade or so, as ancient civilizations, certainly via colonial and postcolonial dynamics, have been re-emerging (Jackson, 2012).

This chapter begins with the big picture: the geopolitical one. That is not to revisit the macro aspects of China's presence in Africa but rather to contextualize scholarship at the organizational level and examine the conceptual implications of the dynamics that underline China's organizational engagement with Africa. I then turn towards the nature of Chinese organizations in Africa. What are they doing? How are they engaging? And, related to the big picture, Why are they engaging? Next, it is important to look at what we know about community engagement: What are Chinese organizations bringing to African communities: infrastructure, knowledge, skills, employment? And, what is the nature of such 'gifts' they bring? What do they take back to China? Knowledge or simply repatriated profits? These questions relate to the role of China in Africa's development.

This chapter, overall, attempts to answer the questions, what do we know, and what do we need to know? I therefore turn later in the chapter to the latter question, what do we need to know and what do we need to do in order to advance scholarship in this area? What should we research, and how should we research it? Again, this refers back to the assumptions that scholars (and managers) make about China's engagement and the conceptual and methodological implications of this, whether in the framework of modernization theory, postcolonial critique or other theory that better reflects current geopolitical dynamics.

International management research on China in Africa in its geopolitical context

Management studies, as other branches of the social science, are influenced by the wider socio-economic context. This is because we are human beings studying other human beings and we are social creatures of time and place. Functionalist and positivist social scientists have perhaps tried to deny this by developing paradigms that appear to set scientists apart from their context and subject in order to study a supposed objective reality. This is not the place to go too deeply into this, but perhaps an example of the assumptions made in management studies might suffice.

In recent joint research on Chinese multinational enterprise (MNE) expatriation in Africa (Jackson & Horwitz, 2017), we noted that western MNEs knowledge transfer, from West to East or North to South, is assumed. Hence a literature has arisen around the concept of absorptive capacity of the 'receiving' organization in attempts to transfer knowledge from expatriate staff to local staff, with a critique of African organizations for being weak in this capacity (Kamoche & Harvey, 2006; Osabutey, Williams, & Debrah, 2013). Absorptive capacity is 'the ability to recognize the value of external knowledge, assimilate it, and apply it to subsidiary operations' (Cohen & Levinthal, 1990, p. 128). Yet knowledge transfer appears not to be important for Chinese MNEs operating in Africa. This has been criticized. Whilst a modernization ethos appears prevalent among western MNEs, or at least certainly in international human resource management (HRM) theory, this appears not to be present in Chinese MNEs and how they operate (Osabutey & Jackson, 2019). This unwillingness to get involved in changing host country institutions (at government levels) and organizations (at MNE levels) has gained them a bad press in areas such as human rights. It is likely that in order to understand this approach, a cross-cultural analysis is needed, with a certain paradigm shift in expatriation theory away from the assumptions of modernization in international HRM theory.

An 'objective reality' is difficult to discern when the researcher starts to shed the encumbrance of universal generalization: the belief that management and HRM theory can be generalized from the accepted wisdom of western civilization and applied anywhere in the world. Further, critiques of such assumptions may equally be sited in time and place and have little bearing on new and changing realities. From a western perspective, it must be assumed that China is the new imperialist in Africa (a competitor of the West in terms of postcolonialization and economic domination both in the region and globally). A western stance that China is not interested in knowledge transfer assumes that (western) knowledge is the answer to a pre-modern Africa's lack of technological advancement (outside knowledge is needed for this advancement). It also appears to assume that Africa's weakness in absorptive capacity is evidence of local organizations' and staffs' lack of ability or willingness to absorb outside knowledge, and that China's unwillingness to share knowledge is indicative of their purely extractive intentions. Whereas, a lack of absorptive capacity may indicate the lack of appropriateness of (western) knowledge to African enterprise. Chinese unwillingness to share outside knowledge may be indicative of a lack of modernizing motive that may be assumed from a western perspective. This is certainly reflected in China's apparent unwillingness to dictate terms of aid, loans and inward investment to African governments.

My argument here is that if researchers are in the mindset of western modernization theory when approaching the subject of China's engagement in Africa, they may make theoretical assumptions that go beyond 'objective reality'. But what of the antidotes to the type of modernization assumption endemic to international management and international HRM theory? Most typically, Postcolonial Theory, which is critical of modernization assumptions that have gained traction in critical management theory has been seen as antidotes to the perceived universalization of management theory. When focusing on western interactions with 'the orient' or 'the South' this has relevance, but may not be relevant to the South on South interactions of China in Africa

Postcolonial Theory grew out of and developed within a specific historical and global context, dealing with North–South (or West–East) dynamics. It provided a critique of why African local or indigenous knowledge has been disparaged and often ignored in favour of a dominant (modernizing) management knowledge (Jackson, 2012). For example, it could be argued that the motives for (western) colonialism, the need to subjugate peripheral countries, and even the task of ruling a country with a minimum colonial army (Ferguson, 2003), the motive to impose a 'civilizing' religion (Thomson, 2000) and more latterly the neocolonial motives to impose a western liberal democratic governance structure and universal human rights (Schech & Haggis, 2000), all add up to a pejorative portrayal of local knowledge and values that appears to be reflected in the modernizing project in management and organization.

As a result of an increased Chinese organizational and management presence in Africa, the combined influences on management and organizational knowledge in Africa and the way these influences come together in different hybrid forms of managing and organizing may be changing. Hence, within Postcolonial Theory, Bhabha's (1994) elucidation of 'mimicry' of the colonizer by the colonized, part of a process giving rise to cultural 'third spaces', may have to be reconsidered from a perspective of a South on South relationship, rather than one where the 'North' dominates the 'South' in terms of both process and content.

Critical theory within international management studies has therefore not only come of age, but the age from which this grew has now been superseded with a global dynamic that reflects different realities and needs different theories to understand it. But I do not want to throw the baby out with the bathwater. The main importance of Postcolonial Theory to the current work is its critical perception that indigenous knowledge is somewhat elusive given the historical circumstances of colonialism, decolonization and neocolonialism and the associated power relationships in constituting resultant hybrid forms of knowledge. Indeed, if 'Africa' is a colonial invention that colours contemporary discussion, then interpreting the 'indigenous' and indigenous knowledge, and making it available and understandable to an 'international' body of scholarship is a western project. Through a lens of Postcolonial Theory, we should rightly be critical of this project. Yet this critique is premised on a North–South dynamic and does not take account of South–South (or more accurately South–North–South) dynamics, which although they have been present for many years have recently come to the fore and appear to be reshaping geopolitical relations (Campbell, 2008).Wider geopolitical dynamics have a major impact on the nature of knowledge, the way knowledge is transferred internationally and the nature of local knowledge resulting from and contributing to these dynamics. This includes scholarly knowledge and the way we study China in Africa specifically, but also international management generally. This is why it is so important for scholars to understand this new dynamic and the way it impacts on their work. Postcolonial Theory's implicit assumption, which the current work takes as a premise, that wider geopolitical dynamics have a major impact on the nature of knowledge must also be applied to Postcolonial Theory itself, which is both time and space limited. Hence, it is unlikely that these theories, which challenge the hegemony of western imperialism and globalization discourse, are still applicable to understanding China's engagement with Africa and indeed emerging South on South relations and concomitant management and organizational knowledge from the South?

That Postcolonial Theory alerts researchers to the necessity to be critically aware of wider geopolitical dynamics also means that it is now time to move on from this critical theory and develop new theory.

This is mainly because the current relationship of China with African countries clearly appears not to have been built on a colonial or imperial history. In fact, this appears as quite the antithesis, as these relationships appear to be based on anti-colonial discourse and geopolitics. It is therefore unlikely that Postcolonial Theory can adequately explain the current geopolitical dynamics of China in Africa. That it is not a postcolonial relationship has implications for the way we might conceptualize and study relationships at the organizational level, and indeed for the way international and cross-cultural management scholars should begin to conceptualize the wider and changing geopolitical context, and how this should be incorporated into their scholarship.

The first aspect of this is to develop a conceptual and methodological framework for interrogating China's engagement with African countries.

The second aspect is to explore and understand the content of China's engagement and the way it is changing management and organizational knowledge and practices in Africa. This involves exploring synergistic relations between China and Africa, where these may not have existed in the relationship between the western powers and African countries. It also involves investigating what emerges in the crossvergence between Chinese and African approaches to managing, organizing, staffing and so on. In Postcolonial Theory parlance this is Bhabha's (1994) 'Third Space' as mentioned before. Connected with this is the extent to which China's engagement in Africa is giving greater voice to African local management knowledge. Because this may have been disparaged by western managers (as Postcolonial Theory would have it), is there greater respect for indigenous African voices by Chinese managers? The greater the voice, the more influence African parties have in co-creating this Third Space. This co-creation also stems from the greater cultural synergies between, for example, the Confucian concept of *ren* (a virtue or capacity of benevolence and compassion: humanity) (Ip, 2009) and *ubuntu* (see my extended discussion, Jackson, 2012). It may be possible that Chinese management knowledge and organization may be more synergistic with, or appropriate to, community- and humanistic-oriented local knowledge and values that appear to pertain in African community values, in distinction to western colonial-imposed and more recent western institutions and values.

Starting from a historical perspective, there is no doubt that China's engagement with African countries is quite different to that of the western colonial powers. China appears to have been an anti-colonial ally. It is therefore difficult to take up a critical stance from a Postcolonial Theory perspective, partly because there appears not to be a modernizing ethos involved in China's presence in Africa. Likely, the presence of cultural and other synergies between China and Africa provides a different dynamic and outcome through crossvergence within organizations and perhaps with local communities that may have different outcomes to the concept of a Third Space provided by Postcolonial Theory. Modernization theory, and its antidote Postcolonial Theory, appear outmoded. Any theory dealing with China's engagement with Africa at the organizational level specifically and with international management generally in these new geopolitics is emergent. Yet it is a project, because of modernization theory's assumption of cultural universalism and association with neocolonialism and Postcolonial Theory's outdatedness, that needs to be undertaken if we are to better understand China's engagement with Africa.

The nature of Chinese organizations in Africa

I have alluded prior to the quite different histories of Sino-African engagement to that of the western powers' engagement with Africa. Unlike the trajectory of the western modernizing project that informs much of the

management literature on Africa, underpinned by centuries of colonialism and critiqued among others by Postcolonial Theory, the coming to
Africa of China has been quite different. One could logically expect the
outcomes also to be different. Yet the processes that lead to the nature of
Chinese organization are, of course, quite complex. This is mainly because
of the nature of globalization, the dominance of western influence and
the emerging political, cultural and economic influence of nations such
as China. This is connected to China's motives for being in Africa and
how this filters down from the official government policy level to the
organizational level. In addition, the before-mentioned cultural synergies
between China and Africa, and how these are acted out, are also factors
in the nature of Chinese organizations in Africa.

Following the China–Russia split in 1956, much of the anti-colonial
struggles in the Third World had ideologically allied themselves with
China as a result of its

> apparently disinterested substantive support to liberation movements
> or hard-pressed front line . . . states, particularly in Mozambique,
> South Africa, Southwest Africa, Zambia and Zimbabwe, its populist
> orientation towards the peasantry and the need for an agrarian revo-
> lution, towards struggle from below, and its emphasis on guerrilla
> warfare and armed struggle against imperialism.
>
> (Young, 2001, p. 188)

Its role in the decolonization of Africa was significant (Thiam & Mulira,
1999). Yet Alden and Alves (2008) view somewhat cynically China's diplomatic use of this historical involvement with Africa.

China's current motives for being in Africa, described by Gill, Huang,
and Morrison (2007) as resources-seeking to fuel China's development
goals, market-seeking to sustain its growing economy and political-
seeking to support its aspirations to be a global influence, must also
be seen within this recent historical context. It may also be possible
that Gill et al.'s (2007) three types of motives may be too restrictive in
terms of hypothesizing the connection between the reasons for China's
being in Africa and the approach that Chinese MNEs have towards
people policies and practices. Also, there may not be a direct relationship between wider strategic motives professed by Chinese government
policies and their manifestations in intergovernmental relations with
African governments and actions at the organizational level. Yet just
as the way that the West's resource-seeking motives for being in Africa
may have been modified by a historical civilizing and proselytizing
ethos and a present-day modernizing ethos, so China's resource-seeking
motive may be moderated by the nature of its sociopolitical engagement. For example, Kaplinsky (2008) suggests the existence of a sense
of 'Third World Solidarity' in China's relations, drawing on its socialist

heritage and anti-imperialist discourse, and as a reaction to the International Monetary Fund's (IMF's) neoliberal policies and government alignment with the United States. These other influences on the nature of China's resource seeking should be considered in theorizing China's engagement with Africa. Analyses based purely on resource and market seeking may be erroneous in not considering the overall influences on the nature of China's engagement and the consequent nature of how Chinese organizations engage with other stakeholders, staff and community. Bound up with this is what Chinese organizations actually take with them to African counties.

Although China was never fully colonized by the West, western civilization up to the current day has had an impact. Western management has influenced organization and management in China (Jackson & Bak, 1998; Warner, 2010; Cooke, 2004). Yet this is tempered by Chinese characteristics. An understanding of the way that people are managed in China necessitates an understanding of the balance in China between individual human rights and national development. This is the context in which the adoption of western HRM, for example, should be understood. China, like the African Union, has challenged the West's interpretation of human rights. As in China, and many parts of Africa, community is important above individual rights. Hence the main area of contention is the emphasis on the individual as the holder of certain rights, and the extent to which this may override the needs of the collective, and in the case of the Chinese nation, the responsibility of the state to put first the need for economic and social development to ensure the livelihood and well-being of people as a whole. In the Chinese view, this may not be seen as being at the expense of individual rights, the pursuit of which are not necessarily recognized as a legitimate objective.

How is this then applied to HRM in organizations, particularly as Cooke (2011, p. 198) reports, 'The interests of the state, the enterprise and the work-force are assumed to be unified'? Cooke (2011) goes on to describe the patriotic and paternalistic foundations of people management in China, including principles of unity, congruence and harmonization. This reflects Confucian philosophy. Despite economic liberalization and reforms in state-owned enterprises and commercial considerations in private enterprises, this is still a main guiding influence. This encourages social harmony and cohesion, focusing on social relations, collectivism and self-sacrifice for the collective good.

Such people management practices as company-sponsored employee-oriented activities reflect this, seeking to embed societal and company values (Cooke, 2008; Jackson & Bak, 1998). This also appears reflected in the continuing role of the sole labour organization, the All-China Federation of Trade Unions (ACFTU). This is led by the state/communist party and focuses on a welfare role rather than protecting workers' rights, which logically do not have to be protected where the interests of state, company and workforce are perceived as one; where a different concept of human rights exists.

Similarly, workers' participation is very much aligned to the ACFTU, supplemented by legislation by the Workers' Representative Congress, which is guided by the trade union. Cooke (2011) suggests that even with a more recent trend for private-sector firms to set up a workers' congress, this is normally in compliance with legislation and serves as an extension to the company's HRM function. Hence when China's apparent anti-union stance in African countries is criticized, it should perhaps be analysed in this light.

Even with reform within China and the adoption of some western practices, Warner (2010) asserts a much larger emphasis in today's China on harmony and Confucian values and a turning away from simply economic efficiency. So, what Chinese firms may go armed with to Africa would be a mixture of western and Chinese influences. The nature of Chinese firms may also be influenced by a combination of Chinese state motivation (e.g. friendship and mutual learning) and the way this is interpreted by state-owned enterprises and private firms and individual organizations' own motivations for being in Africa (e.g. profit).

Yet, combined with what Chinese firms bring to Africa, and what they hope to get out of the engagement, is the host environment within which they are working, and their interaction with this context. Do Chinese organizations, when they go out in the world, do things differently from 'developed' to 'developing' host country and from country to country in Africa?

Although Chinese management practices are informed by home-country practices, MNE managers cannot assume a simple transfer of systems to overseas subsidiaries because of political, legal, economic and sociocultural differences. This applies in the field of international HRM as Shen's (2007) study of eleven Chinese MNEs with subsidiaries in a range of developed and developing nations suggests. This research indicated that the companies generally paid higher rates than the market average in developed countries to compensate for the lack of training and development opportunities which the MNEs were weak in as well as employment participation and involvement, and these higher wages attracted host country nationals while those 'soft' aspects rarely caused labour disputes. Yet subsidiaries in developing countries (including in those in Africa) paid low wages with poor working conditions. This was in contrast to the generally good working conditions they operated in developed countries. Employment standards were therefore localized, yet standards appeared to be lower than comparable western MNEs in developing countries. Shen (2007) also suggested that labour standards in developing countries were influenced by the low standards in China. Also, attitudes towards unions taken by Chinese managers from their home country tended to be reflected in their apparent negative attitudes towards union recognition in host developing countries.

This is reflected in the research undertaken across African countries by Baah and Jauch (2009, p. 14) on behalf of the African Labour Research Network, when they write:

> Although working conditions at Chinese companies in Africa differ across countries and sectors, there are some common trends such as tense labour relations, hostile attitudes by Chinese employers towards trade unions, violations of workers' rights, poor working conditions and unfair labour practices. There is a virtual absence of employment contracts and the Chinese employers unilaterally determine wages and benefits. African workers are often employed as 'casual workers', depriving them of benefits that they are legally entitled to.

Yet this needs some qualification. Within the Chinese companies Baah and Jauch (2009) surveyed, it appears that only workers with strong union representation achieved pay rates above the national average. Yet, they explain, following the structural adjustment programmes of the 1980s and 1990s with wide-scale privatizations and mass retrenchments, Africa's trade unions became weak as they struggled to recruit non-permanent workers and those in the informal economy. Hence, 'Employers, including the Chinese, take advantage of flexible labour markets and undermine collective bargaining' (Baah & Jauch, 2009, p. 14).

There are also differences among countries, sectors and individual companies that they observe in this study: 'In Nigeria, for example, there were Chinese companies with exemplary working conditions and labour relations alongside others where workers rights are frequently abused' (Baah & Jauch, 2009, p. 66). Yet some studies of local African firms indicate that Chinese standards are no worse or better than those of these local companies. Hence in Mozambique, although labour laws have been changed in areas such as strengthening minimum wages 'these have been widely ignored by employers' according to Wood (2011, p. 316). In Nigeria, according to Ovadje and Ankomah (2001, p. 180), 'Given salaries are very poor, a pay rise occurs only after hard bargaining and sometimes violent strikes'. Debra (2001, p. 202) reported that 'in spite of the influential role of the trade union movement in Ghana, many employers still treat trade unions with suspicion'. Baah and Jauch (2009) suggest that reported suspicious attitudes of Chinese managers towards unions appear in line with local attitudes generally.

What Chinese firms actually bring to African countries, and how they ultimately contribute to African development (and to Chinese development) can be seen in the nature of Chinese engagement with African communities.

Chinese engagement with African communities

Chinese companies operating in African countries appear to contribute to employment within African communities, although that employment may not be of high quality. The lack of jobs is an issue in many African countries where 'the failure of African labor markets to create good paying jobs has resulted in excess labor supply in the form of either open unemployment or a growing self-employment sector' (Kingdon, Sandefur, & Teal, 2005).

Yet there is some dispute as to the way the Chinese presence in Africa is influencing this situation. Gadzala (2010) argues that in Zambia, the practice of employing Chinese co-nationals is forcing more Zambians into the informal economy. Here they face competition from Chinese small businesses, and this has a detrimental effect on the local economy and local employment prospects. Yet Kragelund (2009) argues that China's investment in Zambia is beneficial to the local economy. For example, Africa Monitor (2010) provides evidence that the creation of special economic zones in Zambia and elsewhere has contributed to further employment. It gives the example of the Chambishi multi-facility economic zone in Zambia which has encouraged a range of sub-industries to develop around the original copper smelter. A previous report by Africa Monitor (2010, p. 7) also suggests, in Zambia, that because of China's policy of diversification from the extraction industries towards manufacturing, infrastructure and agriculture, 'FDI pledges in the other three sectors are substantial at around US$625 million combined, and are directly responsible for the creation of around 13,000 jobs'.

Bräutigam (2011a), who has been responsible for disabusing a number of western negative assumptions about the effects of the Chinese presence on African communities, addresses the assumption that 'companies bring in all their own workers and refuse to hire Africans' (pages 4–5). This, she says, mainly applies to oil-rich countries where local labour is expensive. Otherwise fieldworkers have largely reported Chinese projects having a majority of Africans in their workforce. Chen, Goldstein, and Orr's (2009) study of Chinese construction firms also reports that on average Chinese firms employ half and half Chinese and local employees, and that these firms see themselves committed to a long relationship with local communities. Further, Davis et al. (2008) report that the use of Chinese labour was dependent on the availability of skills in the local market. There is a tendency not to bring in Chinese manual labourers but only skilled labourers where there is a local skills shortage.

Yet contributing to the local labour market is only half of the story. To what extent are Chinese firms contributing to developing skills and importing knowledge that can upskill the local community? Although, again, there are varying reports on this, the general picture appears to be a focus on upskilling and knowledge transfer at the wider community level but not at the firm level. For example, Business Africa (2010) reports a lack of skills transfer to African workers, with the bulk of Chinese-financed projects implemented by Chinese teams and making small use of the domestic workforce. But at the wider level, Bräutigam (2011b) reports a commitment by the Chinese to provide short-term training to 15,000

Africans over three years in poverty reduction, new leather technologies and other areas not specifically linked to projects and to train 1,500 principals and teachers and 1,000 doctors, nurses and health sector managers in the 30 countries receiving new hospitals. She also contends that vocational training figures highly in China's aid-financed construction, with centres being opened in Ethiopia, Uganda and Angola. Although a clear strategic goal of China's overall engagement with Africa, the extent to which Chinese MNEs are involved directly in such capacity building remains to be investigated.

Although China appears to be contributing to Africa's skills development at the wider level, what of direct engagement with the communities within which they are situated?

As noted previously, China's official policy is one of mutual trust and mutual learning. From the Chinese Ministry of Foreign Affairs: China will 'unswervingly carry forward the tradition of China–Africa friendship, and, proceeding from the fundamental interests of both the Chinese and African peoples, establish and develop a new type of strategic partnership with Africa featuring political equality and mutual trust, economic win-win cooperation and cultural exchange' (MOFA, 2006). This certainly is reflected strategically, but not necessarily at the organizational and interpersonal level reflected in employment relations.

Chinese government aid, unlike from many western donors, is spread evenly across countries in Africa with only oil-rich Libya and Swaziland with official connections with Taiwan not having been recipients. The nature of this aid also appears different from that of western donors, as it appears to be built on China's own experience of combating poverty through developing infrastructure and production. Influenced by the requests of recipient countries, it emphasizes business and downplays official development assistance, providing loans for infrastructure intended to reduce the high cost of production and subsidies for joint ventures to create employment and local capacity. It also does appear to be creating demand for Chinese machinery and equipment; encouraging trade with preferential loans for buyers of Chinese goods and tariff-free access for commodities by low-income African countries (Bräutigam, 2011b). Hence, strategically, China does appear to be engaging with the needs of African communities through infrastructure projects and agricultural initiatives for example.

It is unlikely from the available evidence that there is any deliberate attempt of Chinese managers to engage directly other than for recruitment. Chinese expatriates tend to live in compounds in a frugal way and appear not to have much connection with the local community (Bräutigam, 2011a). However, Mohan and Tan-Mullins (2009) contend that this applies specifically to technical and less skilled Chinese on fixed-term contracts.

Apart from this apparent isolation from local communities, there is another isolation issue: that of language. Chinese expatriates' reported lack of English (Chen et al., 2009; Baah & Jauch, 2009) is of course not just a potential problem in engaging with local communities but has the more direct effect of militating against mutual learning and cross-fertilization in Chinese organizations. Part of this deficit in mutual learning may be a lack of understanding about the shared nature of cultural characteristics between Chinese expatriates and their African hosts. Making use of synergies between cultures does not appear to be a feature of China–Africa relations at the organizational level. Language is an obvious factor preventing this. Yet it should not be automatically assumed that the issue is with the English language use of Chinese expatriates (in anglophone African countries). For example, the Baah and Jauch (2009) study for the African Labour Research Network recommended that 'union organisers dealing with the Chinese must learn the Chinese language'(p. 74).

As a result of possible isolation issues of Chinese expatriates in physical and language terms, the potential of cultural synergies from a relational point of view may simply remain a potential rather than an actual factor in community relations between Chinese nationals and their African hosts.

As noted prior, the Chinese value of *ren* (humanity) (Ip, 2009) appears close to the African value of *ubuntu* (humanity) (Mbigi, 1997). Ip (2009) points out that the Confucian concept of the person is essentially a social one, through familial collectivism. The person is defined by his or her relationships. A person's identity cannot be understood as something separate from his or her social attachments and place in the hierarchy of social relationships. A person is shaped by this social embeddedness in terms of their interests and goals and also constrained by the same relationships. The social bonds thus created are a source of indebtedness and obligations. This explains well 'the modern day version of Confucian relationalism': *guanxi* according to Ip (2009, p. 465). This appears similar to the communalism of African cultures and contrary to western individualistic cultures that may be at variance to African community cultures (Jackson, 2004; Horwitz & Budhwar, 2015).

However, the possibility exists that *ren* does not apply to African employees. They may be considered members of outgroups and not part of Chinese *guanxi*; and Chinese managers and employees are outgroup members as far as African *ubuntu* is concerned. However, Mutabazi (2002) points out that his research indicates *ubuntu* does apply to outgroup members (strangers to African communities). It is unlikely that Chinese MNEs recruit from the local African community on the basis of *guanxi*, but because senior personnel staff are often locals, employees may well be recruited on the basis of local social networks. Cultural synergy and community relations is an area needing more research as I discuss later.

Interaction with local communities is, presumably, a two-way process. In a spirit of mutual learning, the question of what does Africa get from

China's engagement has a corresponding question: what do Chinese firms, and staff, take back to China in terms of mutual learning? The reported western modernizing ethos in Africa (Bräutigam, 2011a) may militate against reverse diffusion or 'the transfer of practice from foreign subsidiaries to operations in the country of origin' discussed by Zhang and Edwards (2007, p. 2147). In contrast, one might expect the professed mission of mutual learning (MOFA, 2006) would facilitate reverse diffusion in Chinese MNEs operating in Africa. Development through knowledge transfer (I would prefer the term 'knowledge sharing') is not a one-way process.

Zhang and Edwards (2007) suggest that MNEs from emerging economies learn (through their expatriates) from operations in advanced economies by taking back knowledge learned in the host country to their home country. The theory suggests that this probably does not work the other way around: MNEs from advanced economies do not take expertise back through knowledge learned in their operations in developing economies. Yet the official intention from the Chinese government of mutual learning and friendship with African countries, and indeed a history of China in Africa being different to the West's engagement (Bräutigam, 2011b), as well as possible greater cultural synergies between China and Africa (Jackson, Louw & Zhao, 2013), may suggest otherwise. Again, this is an under-researched aspect of China's engagement in Africa.

At the community level, and the level of organizational engagement with local staffs and the wider community, mutual learning appears to be the key issue. At the wider level, Africa's development is the main issue, and the nature of China's engagement with this. As a South-on-South engagement, it is also important to consider the benefits to China's ongoing development. With North-on-South engagement, the benefits, in colonial and postcolonial times, appeared to accrue mostly to the colonizers, rather than to African countries. Accusations that China is the new colonizer may indicate that the benefits are (as with western countries' engagement) accruing to China in terms of benefits through extracting resources for their own industry, finding new markets and political seeking in the world. This not only negates the argument for reverse diffusion (China learning from Africa), it also negates the argument for mutual developmental benefits to all partner countries. These are important issues that must be addressed in any future research agenda.

What do we still need to know about China's engagement at the organizational level?

It is obvious from the preceding discussion that there is still much to know and understand about China's engagement in Africa at the organizational level. Above all, there are conceptual considerations. These are two-fold. Not only is the theoretical orientation of the researcher important in terms of how China's engagement is conceptualized, the implications for China's engagement in the geopolitical scheme of things and how international management studies are taken forward are also key. My contention is that changes in geopolitical dynamics over the last decade or two have necessitated a rethink of how we conceptualize international management studies.

Understanding the theoretical implications for international management studies

Critical analysis of modernization through postcolonial theory has perhaps had its day, and this becomes manifest when studying China in Africa at the organizational level. Although a good starting point, it seems not to be relevant in understanding the motivations for China being in Africa. This has implications for studying management in Chinese organizations. From a modernization theory perspective, for example, absorptive capacity is seen as a weakness in African organizations, where an alternative explanation is that western management knowledge and technology transfer is not appropriate. China's lower technology operating practices may be more appropriate. Seeing China's lower priority for transferring knowledge and technology may be seen in the light of perceptions of protectionist attitudes, or may be seen through the lens of a lack of modernizing ethos. Such reconceptualization is in its infancy, particularly where much of extant international management studies is conservative and noncritical anyway. To study the engagement of Chinese organizations in Africa, this reconceptualization is necessary. Its theoretical bases need to be constructed and scrutinized against available evidence. Its critical lens needs to be integrated into the mainstream of international management studies, as the analysis of Chinese organizations in Africa has implications beyond this geographical boundary.

Appropriate research methodologies

There is a need to heed the warnings of Kriz et al. (2014, p. 30) in order to 'step across the door' and successfully engage with Chinese managers and staff, who may be rightfully suspicious of western and Africa researchers knocking on their door and asking to interview them: not least because of the negative reporting in the press, as well as prior assumptions manifesting in published research in this area. Rethinking methodological approaches follows reformulations of prior theoretical assumptions. As noted before, theoretical formulations in international management studies based on modernization theory and its main critical antidote postcolonial theory need to be rethought in the context of South on South relations. Social science becomes problematic if our studies are assumed to be objective in a way that denies that our epistemology comes from somewhere. We make human judgements about other human beings, and this needs to be made explicit in our methodology. Not only must the motivations of Chinese firms, through their managers and staff, be interrogated, but our motivations and roles as investigators must be made clear. The work of Linda Tuhiwai Smith (1999) on decolonizing methodologies comes to mind in this regard when looking at South on South relations. This work is about researching indigenous people and knowledge and is premised on the predominance of western concepts of rationality dismissing other knowledge systems as primitive and irrational. 'Indigenous' systems of knowledge and rationality are only seen to apply in a particular place or time and not seen as relevant and contributing to global knowledge and debate. This is why it is necessary not only to incorporate knowledge of Chinese motivations for being in Africa, but to integrate Chinese and African knowledge and thought processes into our research and to clarify for whom the research is being undertaken and why. Is it being undertaken to make western firms more competitive against Chinese firms? Is it intended to make Chinese firms more competitive, or African firms? Or, is it focused on Africa's development? If the latter, modernization theory may again encroach on this debate, informing our conceptualization and methodology.

From motivation to action

The reason for Chinese firms being in Africa will influence what they do. Yet we still know little directly about what motivates firms and their managers and how official Chinese policy is interpreted by Chinese managers. There is dispute about what Chinese firms contribute to employment. Yet there are indications, and some consensus, that they do contribute to employment but jobs are not of high quality, with employment conditions sometimes being poor (Baah & Jauch, 2009). The nature of Chinese employment needs far more investigation. Upskilling is seen in some investigations as not a priority (Business Africa, 2010). If this is the case, reasons should be investigated. This stems back to the motivation of Chinese firms in Africa. What are they there for? Knowledge and technology transfer is connected with this and has been researched in more detail (Osabutey et al., 2013). It is important to approach these issues from a non-modernization perspective, as well as understanding the motivation of Chinese managers in their attitudes and actions in transferring knowledge.

Motivation also translates into engagement with local communities, which may be mainly through employment, and the level of contribution to upskilling and employability in the local community. Isolationism appears to be an issue discussed in the literature (Bräutigam, 2011a), with Chinese staffs living in compounds for the duration of their expatriate assignment. Language skills also appear to isolate Chinese staffs (Chen et al., 2009; Baah & Jauch, 2009). This may prevent cultural exchange and a shared knowledge of the similarities between Chinese and African cultures. Again, there is a need for more research into cultural synergies and how this may be used more successfully by Chinese and African partners and whether better community integration may be more beneficial for both partners.

Connected with this is mutual learning, what African communities get from this, and very much under-researched, what do Chinese firms take back from Africa to China in terms of knowledge and understanding.

Chinese firms and their contribution to Africa's development

What Chinese firms contribute to Africa's development, over and above infrastructure projects, and how this contributes to China development, over and above feeding industrial growth through China's extraction industry in Africa, are questions that provide answers to research that is of course particularly motivated towards Africa's and the South's development issues. This is an orientation that is not often taken in research into international management involving North–North (or West–West) interaction or in research that focuses on North–South interaction, for example investigating western firms in Africa. Questions on development, and what development means in a non-modernizing context, are more to the fore when researching South on South relations. The historical background to China being in Africa is quite different to that of the West's engagement with African countries. Modern Chinese firms do not have a national and cultural heritage of the slave trade and colonization in Africa, whereas it could be argued that western firms carry this ideological burden, through a modernization ethos. The lack of critical research in this area has hampered our understanding of Chinese and western firms in Africa. It is difficult to understand organizational and managerial interaction in Africa without understanding and integrating this important background.

References

Africa Monitor. (2010). More diverse FDI from China to smooth relations. *Africa Monitor: Southern Africa, 15*(9), 7.

Alden, C., & Alves, A. C. (2008). History & identity in the construction of China's Africa policy. *Review of African Political Economy, 35*(115), 43–58.

Baah, A. Y., & Jauch, H. (Eds.). (2009). *Chinese investments in Africa: A labour perspective*. Johannesburg: African Labour Research Network.

Bhabha, H. K. (1994). *The location of culture*. New York: Routledge.

Bräutigam, D. (2011a). *China in Africa: What can Western donors learn?* Oslo: Norwegian Investment Fund for Developing Countries (Norfund).

Bräutigam, D. (2011b). *The dragon's gift: The real story of China in Africa*. Oxford: Oxford University Press.

Business Africa. (2010). China syndrome. *Business Africa*, 19(5), 1–3.

Campbell, H. (2008). China in Africa: Challenging US global hegemony. *Third World Quarterly*, 29(1), 89–105.

Carmody, P. (2011). *The new scramble for Africa*. Cambridge: Polity Press.

Chen, C., Goldstein, A., & Orr, R. J. (2009). Local operations of Chinese construction firms in Africa: An empirical survey. *International Journal of Construction Management*, 11, 75–89.

Cohen, W. M., & Levinthal, D. A. (1990). Absorptive capacity: A new perspective on learning and innovation. *Administrative Science Quarterly*, 35, 128–152.

Connell, R. (2007). *Southern theory*. Cambridge: Polity.

Cooke, F. L. (2004). HRM in China. In P. S. Budhwar (Ed.), *Managing human resources in Asia-Pacific* (pp. 35–60). London: Routledge.

Cooke, F. L. (2008). Enterprise culture management in china: An 'insider's' perspective. *Management and Organization Review*, 4(2), 291–314.

Cooke, F. L. (2011). Employment relations in China and India. In M. Barry & A. Wilkinson (Eds.), *Research handbook of comparative employment relations* (Chapter 8, pp. 184–213). Cheltenham, UK: Edward Elgar.

Davies, M., Edinger, H., Tay, T., & Naidu, S. (2008). *How China delivers development assistance to Africa*. Centre for Chinese Studies, University of Stellenbosch.

Debrah, Y. A. (2001). Human resource management in Ghana. In P. Budhwar & Y. A. Debrah (Eds.), *Human resource management in developing countries* (Chapter 12, pp. 190–208). London: Routledge.

Ferguson, N. (2003). *Empire: How Britain made the modern world*. London: Penguin.

Flyvbjerg, B. (2001). *Making social science matter*. Cambridge: Cambridge University Press.

Gadzala, A. W. (2010). From formal- to informal-sector employment: Examining the Chinese presence in Zambia. *Review of African Political Economy*, 37(123), 41–59.

Gill, B., Huang, C.-H., & Morrison, J. S. (2007). Assessing China's growing influence in Africa. *China Security*, 3(3), 3–21.

Horwitz, F. M., & Budhwar, P. (Eds.). (2015). *Handbook of human resource management in emerging markets* (pp. 1–19). Cheltenham: Edward Elgar Publishing.

Ip, P. K. (2009). Is confucianism good for business ethics in China? *Journal of Business Ethics*, 88, 463–476.

Jackson, T. (2004). *Management and change in Africa: A cross-cultural perspective*. London: Routledge.

Jackson, T. (2012). Postcolonialism and organizational knowledge in the wake of China's presence in Africa: Interrogating South-South relations. *Organization*, 19(2), 181–204.

Jackson, T. (2014). Employment in Chinese MNEs: Appraising the dragon's gift to sub-Saharan Africa. *Human Resource Management*, 53(6), 897–919.

Jackson, T. (2015a). Management studies from Africa: A cross-cultural critique. *Africa Journal of Management*, 1(1), 78–88.

Jackson, T. (2015b). Modernization theory in international management studies and the role of cross-cultural management scholarship. *International Journal of Cross Cultural Management*, 15(2), 131–133.

Jackson, T., & Bak, M. (1998). Foreign companies and Chinese workers: Employee motivation in the People's Republic of China. *Journal of Organizational Change Management*, 11, 282–300.

Jackson, T., & Horwitz, F. M. (2017, February). Expatriation in Chinese MNEs in Africa: An agenda for research expatriation in Chinese MNEs in Africa: An agenda for. *The International Journal of Human Resource Management*, *5192*, 1–23.

Jackson, T., Louw, L., & Zhao, S. (2013). China in sub-Saharan Africa: Implications for HRM policy and practice at organizational level. *International Journal of Human Resource Management*, *24*(13), 2512–2533.

Kamoche, K., & Harvey, M. (2006). Knowledge diffusion in the African context: An institutional theory perspective. *Thunderbird International Business Review*, *48*, 157–181.

Kaplinsky, R. (2008). What does the rise of China do for industrialization in sub-Saharan Africa? *Review of African Political Economy*, *115*, 7–22.

Kingdon, G., Sandefur, J., & Teal, F. (2005). *Labor market flexibility, wages and incomes in sub-Saharan Africa in the 1990s*. Centre for the Study of African Economies, Department of Economics, University of Oxford.

Kragelund, P. (2009). Knocking on a wide-open door: Chinese investments in Africa. *Review of African Political Economy*, *122*, 479–497.

Kriz, A., Gummesson, E., & Quazi, A. (2014). Methodology meets culture: Relational and Guanxi-oriented research in China. *International Journal of Cross Cultural Management*, *14*(1), 27–46.

Mbigi, L. (1997). *Ubuntu: The African dream in management*. Randburg, South Africa: Knowledge Resources.

Ministry of Foreign Affairs of The People's Republic of China (MOFA). (2006). *China's African policy*, January 2006. Retrieved December 4, 2019 from www.fmprc.gov.cn/zflt/eng/zgdfzzc/t463748.htm

Mohan, G., & Tan-Mullins, M. (2009). Chinese migrants in Africa as new agents of development? An analytical framework. *European Journal of Development Research*, *21*, 588–605.

Mutabazi, E. (2002). Preparing African leaders. Chapter 15 in C. B. Derr, S. Roussillon, & F. Bournois (Eds.), *Cross-cultural approaches to leadership development* (pp. 202–223). Westport, CT: Quorum Books.

Osabutey, E. L. C., & Jackson, T. (2019). Technological forecasting & social change the impact on development of technology and knowledge transfer in Chinese MNEs in sub-Saharan Africa: The Ghanaian case. *Technological Forecasting & Social Change*, *148*(November 2018), 119725. https://doi.org/10.1016/j.techfore.2019.119725

Osabutey, E. L. C., Williams, K., & Debrah, Y. A (2013). The potential for technology and knowledge transfers between foreign and local firms: A study of the construction industry in Ghana. *Journal of World Business*, *49*, 560–571.

Ovadje, F., & Ankomah, A. (2001). Human resource management in Nigeria. In P. Budhwar & Y. A. Debrah (Eds.), *Human resource management in developing countries* (Chapter 11, pp. 174–189). London: Routledge.

Schech, S., & Haggis, J. (2000). *Culture and development: A critical introduction*. Oxford: Blackwell.

Shen, J. (2007). Approaches to international industrial relations in Chinese multinational corporations. *Management Revue*, *18*(4), 410–426.

Smith, L. T. (1999). *Decolononizing methodologies: Research and indigenous peoples*. London: Zed Books.

Thiam, I. D., & Mulira, J. (1999). Africa and the socialist countries. In A. A. Mazrui (Ed.), *General history of Africa, Vol. VIII: Africa since 1935* (pp. 798–828).

Paris, France: UNESCO; Oxford: James Curry; Berkeley, CA: University of California Press.

Thomson, A. (2000). *An introduction to African politics*. London: Routledge.

Warner, M. (2010). In search of Confucian HRM: Theory and practice in Greater China and beyond. *International Journal of Human Resource Management*, *21*, 2053–2078.

Wood, G. (2011). Employment relations in South Africa and Mozambique. In M. Barry & A. Wilkinson (Eds.), *Research handbook of comparative employment relations* (Chapter13, pp. 303–321). Cheltenham: Edward Elgar.

Young, J. C. (2001). *Postcolonialism: An historical introduction*. Malden, MA: Blackwell.

Zhang, M., & Edwards, C. (2007). Diffusing "best practice" in Chinese multinationals: The motivation, facilitation and limitations. *International Journal of Human Resource Management*, *18*(12), 2147–2165.

2 Why is the Chinese presence in Africa important to management scholars?

Lynette Louw

China's presence in Africa has led to a new form of geopolitics which incorporates and consolidates South–South relations (Anshan, 2007, p. 70; Asongu & Aminkeng, 2013, p. 261; Jackson, Louw, & Zhao, 2013, p. 2512). There is increasing interest in understanding the dynamics of international relations between China and Africa, with several studies seeking to understand the reasons for and the basis of China's presence in Africa, as well as Africa's perceptions of and reactions to China (Ado & Su, 2016, p. 40; Alden & Davies, 2006; Park & Alden, 2013; Wang & Elliot, 2014, p. 1012). However, literature on China's engagement with Africa is largely negative with criticism of China's presence in Africa being accompanied by accusations of China undermining Africa (Ado & Su, 2016, p. 41; Wang & Elliot, 2014, p. 1022). On the other hand, China's increasing presence in Africa, especially in business-related activities since the 1990s, suggests that China is positively perceived and received by Africans. The reality is that there is a relationship between China's presence in Africa and the growing challenges and obstacles faced by countries in Africa (Wang & Elliot, 2014, pp. 1012–1013). It is therefore not surprising that in the past ten years China's growing engagement and relationship with various African countries has raised concerns amongst policy analysts, the media and economists (Ado & Su, 2016, p. 41; Sun, 2014, p. 1). These concerns relate to China's economic approach towards Africa which has been criticised for its impact on the sustainability of African countries (Wang & Elliot, 2014, p. 1022) despite China's role in funding infrastructural projects in these countries (Ado & Su, 2016, p. 44; Sun, 2014, p. 1; Wang & Elliot, 2014, p. 1024). An example is the multi-billion resource loans offered by China to finance and ensure infrastructural development in African countries such as Sudan and Angola (Bräutigam, 2011) – countries still recovering from recent conflicts.

Ado and Su (2016, p. 41) caution that the overwhelmingly negative outlook on China's relationship with Africa is based mainly on speculation and is aggravated by research that lacks scientific rigor and empirical evidence. Sun (2014, p. 1) and Wang and Elliot (2014, p. 1022) assert that China's engagement with Africa can be best understood from two perspectives – a moral and a so-called "virtuous" perspective. From a moral perspective, China is viewed as taking advantage of some of the countries in Africa by exploiting their resources and China's presence in Africa is viewed as impacting negatively on the African continent (Ado & Su, 2016, p. 41). Conversely, China is viewed as "virtuous" when providing funds to African countries to aid infrastructural development and boost social and economic development. It is within the context of balancing these complex and diverse views of Africa's relationship with China that this chapter seeks to explore the dynamic nature of this relationship while highlighting important issues for consideration by management scholars by citing issues within current theories and debates within the realm of international management studies.

It is accepted that the presence of Chinese organisations in Africa has contributed positively to Africa in terms of well-coordinated trade, foreign investment, infrastructural development, foreign aid and debt cancellation (Adisu, Sharkey, & Okoroafo, 2010, p. 7; Ado & Su, 2016, p. 50; Wang & Elliot, 2014, p. 1016; Ayodele & Sotola, 2014). Ayodele and Sotola (2014) assert that China's presence in Africa presents the continent with significant growth opportunities. Nonetheless, the presence of China in Africa has influenced and changed the geopolitical and economic relationships in a South–South context. At the economic level, African organisations are frequently unable to compete with Chinese organisations' competitive advantage of low production costs (Wang & Elliot, 2014, p. 1026; Adisu et al., 2010, p. 5) and their importation of inexpensive inferior quality products from China (Wang & Elliot, 2014, p. 1030). Furthermore, China's influence is also manifested at the organisational level (Alden & Davies, 2006; Park & Alden, 2013). At this level, as happened during the era of western engagement when there was suppression of Africa's culture, knowledge and values related to organisation and management, it can be questioned whether a similar situation will recur with Chinese business culture, values and knowledge being imposed on the management of Chinese organisations in Africa. As asserted by Jackson (2012, p. 182), the presence of Chinese organisations may change management style and ethos. This is particularly important given that there are already conscious efforts by China to influence Africa's perceptions and views in order to gain a greater acceptance in Africa (Wang & Elliot, 2014, p. 1019). An example of this is the 2013 plan of President Xi of the People's Republic of China (PRC) to promote personnel exchanges, involving ideas on governance and the education and training of young Africans to promote and protect China–Africa relations. Additionally, China funds various educational and cultural centres across Africa (Wang & Elliot, 2014, p. 1019). Differences in cultural practices, values and work ethics may result in Chinese managers favouring the employment of Chinese workers at the expense of local workers (Adisu et al., 2010, p. 5). This could potentially lead to conflict. It is therefore important for management scholars to investigate how engagement with Chinese organisations in Africa influences management knowledge and practices (Jackson, 2012, p. 194).

The main challenges and sources of conflict in the relationship between Africa and China are to be found in the areas of cultural differences (Mayer, 2019), the negative impact on local trade and commerce and the presence of a diverse workforce owing to an influx of Chinese workers (Adisu et al., 2010, p. 7). Despite the influence and impact on China–Africa relations at both the economic and organisational level, it is at the organisational level that there is a dearth of research on how China–Africa engagement affects organisations and how managers ought to respond (Jackson et al., 2013; Smith, 2012). Therefore, in the light of the business scenario in modern-day Africa, it is essential for management scholars to understand how Africa's engagement with China influences Africa's management and organisational knowledge and values (Jackson, 2012, p. 182). Furthermore, China's continued presence in Africa has intensified existing concerns regarding the reliability and relevance of the current theories on cross-cultural management and international studies which attempt to explain China's engagement with the continent, not only at the organisational level but also at the community level (Jackson, 2012, p. 181). It is within this context that this chapter seeks to provide insights for management scholars to gain an in-depth understanding of the cross-cultural dynamics in South–South relations and to develop theories to explain the implications of this growing relationship (Jackson, 2012, p. 181). These insights will allow for a better understanding of the motives (reasons) for China's presence in Africa (Drogendijk & Blomkvist, 2013); how the changing geopolitical dynamics influence the contribution of the critical development theories in international and cross-cultural management studies (Jackson, 2012; Jackson et al., 2013; Kamoche & Siebers, 2015; Pickett, 2017, p. 10; Von Kimakowitz, 2016, p. 7); the extent to which cultural synergy (convergence and cross-vergence) and divergence occur and the implications for understanding China–Africa exchanges at the organisational level (Bird & Fang, 2009; Guo, 2015; Jackson & Aycan, 2006); how the transfer of technology and knowledge (Wang & Blomstrom, 1992) between Chinese and African partners is changing management and organisational knowledge and practices in Africa (Ostabutey & Jackson, 2019); and the implications for management practices, particularly human resource management (HRM) (Kamoche & Siebers, 2015; Meibo & Peiqiang, 2013; Ngo, Turban, Lau, & Lui, 1998; Nyambegera, Kamoche, & Siebers, 2016; Xing, Liu, Tarba, & Cooper, 2016).

The first section of this chapter will focus on the motives for China's presence in Africa. The second section will examine the influence of changing geopolitical dynamics on critical development theories in international and cross-cultural management studies. The third section will investigate the extent to which cultural synergy (convergence and crossvergence) and divergence occurs and its implications for understanding China–Africa exchanges at the organisational level. The factors influencing the extent to which and the way the transfer of technology and knowledge is changing will be discussed in section four. The fifth section focuses on the influence of Chinese and African cultural philosophies and practices on management and organisational knowledge and HRM practices.

Motives of Chinese foreign direct investment (FDI) in Africa

In recent years, the motives for China's presence in Africa have come under serious scrutiny (Ayodele & Sotola, 2014; Jackson, 2012, p. 198; Mlambo, Kushamba, & Simawu, 2016, p. 257). There have been mixed opinions on China's presence in Africa, leading to uncertainty as to whether China's engagement is beneficial for Africa or not (Mlambo et al., 2016, p. 257). China has been blamed for targeting resource-rich unstable African countries (Kolstad & Wiig, 2012, p. 26) and has been accused of the destruction of manufacturing industries in Africa, the exploitation of natural resources without any benefits for African countries and of neocolonialism. (Ado & Su, 2016, p. 50; Malone, 2008, p. 2; Mlambo et al., 2016, p. 257). Additionally, China stands accused of contributing to over-indebtedness by the granting of unrestricted loans or resource-backed loans, ultimately weakening the IMF's efforts to regulate Africa's borrowing (Campbell, 2008, pp. 92–93). On the other hand, as previously mentioned, China is regarded as a development partner of Africa, largely because of its support and facilitation of infrastructural development (Mlambo et al., 2016, p. 257) and financial and technical aid assistance (Ado & Su, 2016, p. 49).

While China's relationship with Africa dates back to the 1950s (Ayodele & Sotola, 2014), the current engagement with Africa is markedly different to earlier engagement. An analysis of China's current engagement with Africa identifies five main motives which are: to seek natural resources (*resource-seeking*) needed in China (Drogendijk & Blomkvist, 2013, p. 78; Jackson et al., 2013, p. 2516; Jackson & Horwitz, 2018, pp. 1861–1862); to exploit the sizeable export market in Africa, (*market-seeking*) (Drogendijk & Blomkvist, 2013, p. 78; Jackson et al., 2013, p. 2516; Jackson & Horwitz, 2018, pp. 1861–1862); to garner political support for China (*political-seeking*) (Jackson et al., 2013, p. 2516; Jackson & Horwitz, 2018, pp. 1861–1862); to benefit from a global network of foreign subsidiaries (*efficiency-seeking*) (Drogendijk & Blomkvist, 2013, p. 78); and to take advantage of value added activities for growth and to maintain competitiveness (*strategic asset-seeking*) (Rugman & Verbeke, 2004). Considering the focus of this chapter, the three FDI motives of Chinese organisations in Africa of resource-seeking, market-seeking and political-seeking will be elaborated upon since efficiency-seeking and strategic asset-seeking are considered an extension of the market-seeking motive. The former pertains to market growth of large multinational corporations, implying cultural convergence based on the parent organisation. The latter pertains to market growth through strategic alliances and joint ventures, implying that cultural crossvergence takes place where synergies are created by combining existing organisational knowledge with new knowledge (Rugman & Verbeke, 2004).

China's engagement with Africa is mainly to extract natural resources, gain support in international spheres, to trade and to invest. Africa, on the other hand, engages with China to access funds to finance infrastructural projects, to obtain affordable loans and foreign aid and to gain diplomatic support (Gallagher & Irwin, 2014, p. 12; Mlambo et al., 2016, p. 271). When considering the benefits of China and Africa's engagement, the key question is whether the benefits for China and Africa are equal (Mlambo et al., 2016, p. 271). Statements by some African leaders suggest that Africa is not reaping enough from this relationship. For example, the former Deputy Prime Minister of Zimbabwe, Professor Arthur Mutambara, stated that Africa needs to re-evaluate this relationship and transform it into a significant developmental opportunity for Africa. A former president of the Republic of South Africa, the Honourable Mr Mbeki, emphasised that the relationship between Africa and China is unsustainable in the long term. Trade deficits with China, coupled with the exportation of cheap goods to Africa and China's stance of non-interference on issues of human rights and governance, all raise concerns regarding the sustainability of the relationship (Mlambo et al., 2016, p. 271). It should be noted that China has been heavily criticised for its non-interference policy when investing in Africa (Mlambo et al., 2016, p. 271). Mlambo et al. (2016, p. 271) argue that the blame rests not only with China but also with African leaders.

Even though it is asserted that the relationship presents Africa with more opportunities and benefits than threats (Van de Walle, 2016, p. 171), the relationship appears to be more beneficial for China (Mlambo et al., 2016, p. 271). From careful observation of the relationship between Africa and China, it is evident that China is clear on what it hopes to achieve from engagement with Africa and has an unambiguous strategy on how it hopes to achieve this objective. While Africa may be clear on its political reasons for engaging with China, the economic reasons for Africa's relationship with China are unclear (Mlambo et al., 2016, p. 271). In other words, Africa lacks an economic vision and strategy for its engagement with China. Africa has, therefore, a long way to go to ensure that its relationship with China also benefits Africa, both economically and politically (Mlambo et al., 2016, p. 271). To strive for a balanced relationship with China, Africa must focus on its own growth and implement reform and policies to ensure that the current inequalities in its relationship with

China are identified and addressed (Mlambo et al., 2016, p. 271). African leaders should provide clear guidelines for bilateral, fair and balanced cooperation with China (Ado & Su, 2016, p. 47).

The literature on China's presence in Africa argues that in return for its investment in Africa, China needs Africa's materials and oil to sustain its development (Ado & Su, 2016, p. 42), indicating a *resource-seeking* motive. China's resource-seeking motive in Africa includes natural resources and location-specific factors such as suitable labour, proper institutional frameworks, technology and high-quality infrastructure (Drogendijk & Blomkvist, 2013). The extent to which an organisation's motive is primarily that of resource-seeking may be evident if there is minimal use of local employees with the required skills compared to the number of Chinese employees and if working conditions fail to meet the local required operating standards in the host country (Baah & Jauch, 2009, cited in Jackson, 2012). The motive of resource-seeking may require the migration of scarce engineering skills to African countries and researchers may find evidence that employment and opportunities for the development of local skills are being created. While the resource-seeking motive may imply a lower predisposition to transfer technology and knowledge to African countries, China's investment in Africa positively influences development in these countries (Osabutey & Jackson, 2019, p. 3). Chinese FDI in Africa which is motivated by *market-seeking* involves organisations establishing themselves in export markets in African countries to benefit from trade barriers and attractive cost and investment factors (Drogendijk & Blomkvist, 2013, p. 78). Since slow growth has been experienced in some domestic markets such as the USA (Fernald & Charles, 2014, p. 3; Mehta, Larsen, Rosenbloom, & Ganitsky, 2006, p. 156; Sharma, 2017, p. 104) and intense competition has been experienced in certain domestic markets such as China (Kragelund, 2009, p. 494; Mutlu, Zhan, Peng, & Lin, 2015, p. 572; Song & Wang, 2018, p. 189), there is an accelerated search for foreign markets abroad, not merely as an option but as an imperative for most organisations to ensure sustained competitive advantage (Mehta et al., 2006, p. 156). In addition, Chinese organisations regard Africa as a growth opportunity for their products. This motive fosters growth as Chinese organisations interact with the domestic organisations, acquire local market knowledge (Drogendijk & Blomkvist, 2013, p. 78) and provide employment opportunities for locals. To secure their competitive advantage, it is unlikely that Chinese organisations in Africa would transfer technology and knowledge to host organisations and employees in Africa (Osabutey & Jackson, 2019, p. 3). If it appears that this motive is more attractive to private FDI and entrepreneurial activities rather than to Chinese state-owned enterprises (SOEs), Gu (2009) asserts that the roles and significance of private FDI have been under-researched.

Chinese organisations may also adopt a *political-seeking* model if their motive is that of gaining political support. In this case, organisations may adopt a friendship approach that involves establishing close ties with local needs, as well as adopting an informed and engaging approach by Chinese managers towards their African employees. The political-seeking motive in encouraging Chinese organisations to invest abroad is supported by China's "going out" strategy underpinned by its foreign policy (Drogendijk & Blomkvist, 2013; Wang & Hu, 2017, p. 820). This strategy is characterised by "active, harmonised and innovative financing approaches between the government, banks and business associations" (Osabutey & Jackson, 2019, p. 3).

Jackson (2012, p. 198) cautions researchers against focusing exclusively on a single motive and neglecting additional alternate motives for China's engagement in Africa. For example, the motive of resource-seeking, in addition to knowledge-sharing through local skills development, also requires market-seeking.

In summary, to fully understand the motives of Chinese FDI in Africa, management scholars should investigate how these motives are integrated into the business model of various Chinese organisations. Management scholars should be cautious when drawing conclusions from their findings as different motives may manifest in ways that appear to be similar within organisations. Motives will also be different for state-owned – supported by the Chinese government (Drogendijk & Blomkvist, 2013) – compared to privately owned Chinese organisations in Africa. Furthermore, Jackson (2012, p. 197) hypothesises that the motives of Chinese organisations may also influence the way in which management knowledge is developed and implemented in Chinese organisations as well as in the way it is incorporated with local knowledge. Motives of Chinese organisations can also be used to test the influence on HRM policies and conditions of employment. (Jackson et al., 2013, p. 2530). However, validation of any hypotheses requires empirical evidence on the nature of the motives and the management practices, systems and styles within the organisation. In order to develop such studies, it is important to draw on critical development theories within cross-cultural and international studies, and to test their relevance within the current debates.

Critical development theories: relevance for international and cross-cultural management studies

To understand how the presence of China in Africa is changing the geopolitical dynamics, the contribution of the critical development theories in international and cross-cultural management studies should be consulted. Two notable theories seek to explain the development in Africa – the modernisation and dependency theories (Pickett, 2017, p. 10; Von Kimakowitz, 2016, p. 7). Other important theories for consideration, especially in the context of Africa–China relations, are the postcolonial (Kamoche & Siebers, 2015) and Connell's (2014) southern theory.

The issue of African development in the 21st century has raised concerns and has led to the questioning of the reliability of critical development theories to explain the current nature, patterns and conditions of development in Africa (Dode & Cletus, 2019, p. 85; Jackson, 2012, p. 18). Other continents, such as Asia and South America, which were once at the same development level as the African continent have since surpassed Africa (Dode & Cletus, 2019, p. 85). Furthermore, Africa is now looking to the Asian continent, especially China, for development assistance (Mlambo, 2019, p. 1; Xue, Ding, Chang, & Wan, 2019, p. 2). While the modernisation and dependency theories seek to explain the development in Africa (Pickett, 2017, p. 10; Von Kimakowitz, 2016, p. 7), they do not debate whether Africa is underdeveloped or developing, but rather examine the reasons for the underdevelopment in Africa (Agbebi & Virtanen, 2017, p. 430; Dode & Cletus, 2019, p. 86). Postcolonial theory proposes that the "developing world is represented in the eyes of the developed world" (Kamoche & Siebers, 2015, p. 2723), providing an opportunity for the emergence of a hybrid of new viewpoints from the North and South, and for reframing South–South geopolitical dynamics at the organisational and community levels.

Modernisation theory is driven by the North–South (developed–developing world) geopolitical power relationships and is entrenched in the benefits of promulgating capitalism in modernisation. Contrary to dependency theory, modernisation theory refutes that external factors are responsible for underdevelopment in Africa. It rather focuses on the importance of endogenous factors (Von Kimakowitz, 2016, p. 32) and suggests that Africa is responsible for its own underdevelopment, and that prevailing situations in African countries promote or hinder development (Dode & Cletus, 2019, p. 86). Modernisation theory, therefore, suggests that Africa should be responsible for its own development and not rely on other developed continents (Dode & Cletus, 2019, p. 86). In addition, proponents of modernisation theory argue that it promotes a system of democracy by enforcing a system of inclusion and an attitude of empathy (Sarfati, 2017, p. 397). Even though modernisation theory is not without criticism, especially from Africa and other Third World countries, it provides reasons for the underdevelopment of Africa and suggests ways to enhance development (Dode & Cletus, 2019, p. 90). Agbebi and Virtanen (2017, p. 445) agree, asserting that China's presence in Africa presents Africa with an opportunity to become self-reliant by adopting an approach of self-interest in its engagement with China to ensure that any dealings are beneficial for the development of Africa. Furthermore, considering that China itself is experiencing advances in industrialisation, it might be considered a model for Africa. Also, bearing in mind the previous discussion on the motives for China's presence in Africa, and that China's policies are fundamentally anti-capitalistic and anti-colonialist, it seems unlikely that China would exploit Africa. This remains to be disputed or supported. According to Jackson et al. (2012, p. 201) "modernization theory appears to have been implicit in much of the extant scholarship in international and cross-cultural management theory, and this is particularly apparent in the literature on organizational and management in Africa" painting a pejorative picture. However, based on the discussion in this section, it is doubtful whether a pejorative picture of management in Africa will be painted in the new South–South relationship. As such, it is doubtful if African partners will be considered as being subordinates, whether predominantly western knowledge and expertise will be shared and whether local traditions and knowledge needs to be modernised (Jackson et al., 2013, p. 2521).

On the other hand, dependency theorists, critical of the modernisation theory, argue that underdevelopment in Africa is as a result of its history of the slave trade, colonialism and neocolonialism by Europe and North America and the imposition of their capitalist systems (Von Kimakowitz, 2016, p. 40; Agbebi & Virtanen, 2017, p. 430; Dode & Cletus, 2019, p. 85). Dependency theorists further argue that trade between the developed and the underdeveloped (developing) countries is characterised by trade deficits which perpetuate the dependency (Agbebi & Virtanen, 2017, p. 430; Pickett, 2017, p. 12). In an attempt to investigate the complexities of China's engagement with Africa, Agbebi and Virtanen (2017, p. 430) applied dependency theory by examining whether China's engagement with Africa creates a new form of dependency which is attributable to neocolonialism or which is based on "self-reliance or unity of thought process". They suggest that the application of this approach raises several important points of interest, which either agree or disagree with certain elements of dependency theory. For example, China does not have a sovereign history in Africa but rather shares a similar history with Africa, as both continents were suppressed under the era of western sovereignty. Thus, the South–South cooperation is motivated by apparent similarities between China and Africa (Agbebi & Virtanen, 2017, p. 441). Additionally, China's historical relations with Africa have expressed China's reproach of imperialism and colonialism and have indicated China's support for an independent African continent, as was emphasised by Chinese Premier Zhou Enlai in 1964 (Agbebi & Virtanen, 2017, p. 441). However, the huge trade deficits for African countries trading with China are similar to the trade deficits under the North–South era, a situation which provides support for the dependency theory. Other similarities include those of African countries simply being suppliers of raw material in the North–South relations (Kolstad & Wiig, 2012, p. 26) and the intense competition in the manufacturing sector which led to the demise of most manufacturing organisations (Amin, 2015, p. 173). It is argued that the 377 manufacturing projects approved by China in 2014 are an indication that the China–Africa relationship does not relegate Africa to merely being a supplier of raw materials but provides an opportunity for African countries to be manufacturers (Agbebi & Virtanen, 2017, p. 441). Agbebi and Virtanen (2017, p. 446) suggest that analysing the relationship from the dependency theory perspective suggests an interdependence. Van de Walle (2016, p. 171) argues that supporters of China's approach in Africa unfavourably differentiate Chinese pragmatism and the West by exaggerating and presenting the West's influence on Africa's democracies as autocratic and unwarranted. Considering the similarities in the South–South relationship between China and Africa, it seems unlikely that an analysis of this relationship should be based on the dependency theory. While this theory is well-researched within development studies, the opposite applies to international management. (Jackson et al., 2013, p. 2519).

Dependency theory has, however, long been criticised, particularly the claims of foreign investment and aid as reasons for slow economic growth and inequalities. Other cases, such as Taiwan, have proven otherwise (Barret & Whyte, 1982, p. 1064). In addition, Dode and Cletus (2019, p. 85) argue that while the factors identified as being responsible for Africa's underdevelopment cannot be eliminated within the context of the dependency theory, they question the responsibility of these factors for Africa's underdevelopment in the 21st century. The dependency theory is particularly useful in addressing the role of power dynamics and cultural dominance in organisations, the extent to which local knowledge and practices are considered and the impact of cost-saving on wages and working conditions (Jackson et al., 2013, p. 2521).

Postcolonial theory, on the other hand, explains the effects of colonisation on societies and the societies' responses. As mentioned previously, the "developing world is seen through the eyes of the developed world". Pertinent to Africa is the development of a body of management theory and practice from the North to the South (developing world) in which, for example, "African management is seen in a derogatory manner" (Jackson et al., 2013, p. 2519). The developing world can internalise such representations in two ways. First, there is "both an acceptance and challenging of these representations that constitute hybrid forms of presentation of the nature of people of the Third World" (Jackson et al., 2013, p. 2519). Secondly, in challenging these representations, the developing world cannot refer back to an "authentic identity" in the precolonial period (Jackson et al., 2013, p. 2519). Consequently, the local viewpoint is either poorly articulated or has not been elicited. However, a hybrid of new viewpoints can emerge when viewpoints from the North and South are challenged and co-created in an ongoing conflictual process. In this sense, the Third World emerges. Postcolonial theory has thus contributed towards a better understanding of the "subtle implications of power in international relations mainly through cultural transmission and the way knowledge is transferred internationally" (Jackson, 2012, p. 186). Likewise, postcolonial theory provides a basis for a better understanding of the co-creation of management knowledge by learning from each other, and the reverse diffusion of knowledge between the Chinese and African counterparts which provides insights into cultural interaction. Closely aligned with the postcolonial theory is Connell's (2014, p. 211) concept of southern theory where geopolitical assumptions embedded in northern social theory uncover leading thoughts from the colonial and postcolonial eras (Connell, 2014, p. 211).

It is thus imperative to understand how the changing geopolitical dynamics of China's presence in Africa interact with the critical development theories and to understand the perspectives that the dependency theory and postcolonial theories provide on institutional dynamics and cultural interaction, respectively. Furthermore, it is important in understanding the nature of China's engagement in Africa, and the implications for China–Africa relations and exchanges, to position this within the context of extant cross-cultural theory. There are many studies of China in Africa that fail to consider cultural interaction, and this is a serious deficit. The following section discusses cultural synergy (convergence and crossvergence) and divergence theories and their implications for international management and for understanding China–Africa exchanges at organisational level.

Cultural synergy and divergence: implications for management scholars

The origins of cross-cultural studies date back to the research of Edward Burnett Tylor (1832–1917) who attempted one of the first definitions of culture. This has been well-cited within the literature. According to Berry, Poortinga, and Pandey (1997, p. 18), Tylor defined culture as a complex concept which constitutes the various habits and capabilities acquired by man as a member of any society, such as knowledge, belief, art, morals, laws and customs. Tylor's research focused on an examination of the differences between the various world societies during the Second Industrial Revolution (1870–1920) in terms of cultural achievements, political organisations, kinship organisations and ideology (mind or spirit) (Jorgensen, 1979, p. 309).

In the international management literature, the theories of convergence, divergence (at national and organisational levels) and crossvergence are debated. Largely driven by increased trade, travel and interconnectedness of markets (Wu, 2006, p. 35), the convergence theory advances that the values, attitudes and behaviours of individuals are becoming similar to those common in western countries (Guo, 2015) and that the value systems, management and organisational practices of different countries are also becoming similar (Jackson et al., 2013; Ralston, Holt, Terpstra, & Kai-Cheng, 1997). The similarities imply that because of the standardisation of management practices and principles across cultures, particularly from the Anglo-American perspective, cultural differences are reduced. On the other hand, divergent theory suggests that individuals from a society will retain the specific value systems, attitudes and behaviours which are the norm in their national cultures (Guo, 2015). At the national level, the seminal research studies of Hofstede (1980), Kluckhohn and Strodtbeck (1961) and Trompenaars and Hampden-Turner (1998) assert that national culture influences local management and organisational practices. Sarala and Vaara (2010) caution that the differences that exist between national cultures could inhibit knowledge transfer because national identity is often perceived as being obstructive to cooperation and is therefore viewed negatively. Such negative perspectives contribute to conflict, pose a threat to the existence of other cultures (Arnett, 2002, p. 779; Bird & Fang, 2009, p. 139; Kastanakis & Voyer, 2014, p. 425; Vaara, Sarala, Stahl, & Björkman, 2012, p. 1) and hinder the understanding and investigations of the various ways in which organisations can benefit from cultural differences in various contexts (Stahl & Tung, 2015). Contrary to the negative perspectives, cultural differences may, in fact, lead to some cultures learning from and being inspired by others (Bird & Fang, 2009, p. 139). Similarly, at the organisational level, differences in organisational culture are often associated with resistance to change, lack of trust (Sarala & Vaara, 2010) and decreased organisational learning and transfer of knowledge (Kamoche, 1997). The lack of trust is apparent when people from one cultural group regard members of another cultural group as being the out-group, as is explained in this chapter in the section on knowledge transfer. These differences can, however, be surmounted by fostering an organisational culture which promotes intercultural understanding and competence (Mayer, 2019).

According to Jackson et al. (2013, p. 2518), however, the convergence and divergence theories ignore wider geopolitical power dynamics – assumed by convergence but ignored by the divergence perspective. In support of convergence, there is evidence that western management models have influenced Chinese management practices (Jackson et al., 2013, p. 2519). Similarly, for divergence, there is evidence that China has "developed its own models of managing organizations up to and throughout its path to industrialization, developing a market economy, integrating with the global economy and entering global markets" (Ip, 2009 in Jackson et al., 2013, p. 2519). Theories regarding Chinese management can be developed by considering two sources of indigenous constructs including primarily the philosophies of Chinese traditional wisdom such as "Confucianism, Taoism, Legalism, the Art of War, as well as Chinese modern thought, such as Maoism and Deng Xiaoping Thoughts" (Li, Leung, Chen, & Luo, 2012, p. 10) and, secondly, traditional and contemporary Chinese practices. Traditional practices including paternalistic leadership, network of *guanxi, mianzi* (face), interpersonal harmony (Li et al., 2012; Liu, 2019) and contemporary practices such the internationalisation pattern of Chinese multinational firms, Chinese *shanzhai* (imitative innovation), a migrant labour force, the generation of single children born in the 1980s and 1990s, and the gaping inequality and fragmentation in society experienced since the beginning of China's reform, should all be considered by management scholars when generating theories for Chinese management.

Instead, the cultural crossvergence theory, implicit within postcolonial theory (Jackson et al., 2013, p. 2519), is more appropriate in understanding cross-cultural management. Postcolonial theory has contributed towards a better understanding of the "subtle implications of power in international relations mainly through cultural transmission and the way knowledge is transferred internationally" (Jackson, 2012, p. 186). The crossvergence theory advocates that the dynamic sociocultural interaction of individuals with business ideology leads to the development of a new and unique value system (Ralston, 2008) that is different to the prevailing national culture (Guo, 2015). This theory implies that a new and different organisational value system can be co-created with mutual understanding and trust. It implies that the partnerships between Africa and China foster mutual learning with reverse diffusion of knowledge and learning from each other. But, is this case based on empirical evidence?

Consideration of the theories mentioned above raises the following questions for management scholars. Firstly, to what extent does cultural synergy (convergence and crossvergence) and divergence take place in Chinese organisations in Africa? Secondly, what are the implications of cultural synergies (convergence and crossvergence) and divergence for effective and appropriate management of Chinese organisations in Africa?

In addressing these questions, management scholars should be cognisant of the dynamic interaction between local and global cultural contexts and should consider the implications of South–South interaction while probing the nature of indigenous thought, values and practices (Jackson, 2015, p. 9). Yet, before further consideration of the issues of intercultural understanding and the influence of Chinese and African cultural philosophies and practices on HRM practices, a key related issue must be examined. This is the issue of technology and knowledge transfer in local–global exchanges and how this is affected by cross-cultural understanding within Sino-African relationships at the organisational level.

Factors influencing the transfer of technology and knowledge: implications for management practices

There are several other factors – aside from cross-cultural understanding – involved in technology and knowledge transfer that should be considered when focusing on Sino-Africa exchanges at the organisational level. At the macro level, and driven by globalisation, there is no doubt that FDI is a key player in the transfer of technology and knowledge (Audretsch,

Lehmann, & Wright, 2014, p. 301; Osabutey & Jin, 2016, p. 5391). Technological advancement and the sharing of knowledge are important for the enhancement of economic development and growth, global competitiveness and the trade performance indices of a country (Wang & Blomstrom, 1992, p. 137). Given the importance of successfully transferring technology and knowledge in a host country, management scholars should clearly understand the measures that a host country organisation should implement to facilitate and ensure the effective transfer of technology and knowledge (Wang & Blomstrom, 1992, p. 137).

The presence of FDI organisations in emerging economies is associated with the expectation of a transfer of technology and knowledge to local organisations in the host country. However, this perception might be flawed as there are a number of factors that influence the transfer of technology and knowledge, such as the appropriateness of the transfer, cultural synergy, the absorptive capacity of the organisation in the host country (Ostabutey & Jackson, 2019), the motives for China's presence in Africa and the influence of geopolitical relationships.

The question can be posed as to whether the technology and knowledge transfer from North to South is as appropriate as the transfer from South to South? Recent literature suggests that the transfer from South to South is more appropriate since the markets in the South are smaller and less attractive to the North and operations in the South are more labour-intensive (Osabutey & Jackson, 2019, p. 2). As such, the technology from the North might not be appropriate owing to a skills deficit and poor dynamic capabilities of employees and organisations in the South. It is further suggested by Osabutey and Jackson (2019, p. 2) that the transfer of technology and knowledge in South–South relationships is likely to be more successful and appropriate when the host country's technologies, capabilities, endowments and management practices are similar to those of the transferring country. Despite this similarity, since the interaction between multinational organisations and local contexts are embedded in the various organisational practices and cultural values, the managerial practices in organisations at various levels will be influenced (Meyer, Mudambi, & Narula, 2011, p. 239). Literature also supports that differences in cultural beliefs, norms and values have a significant influence on the transfer of technology and knowledge in organisations (Boh, Nguyen, & Xu, 2013, p. 1; Castellano, Davidson, & Khelladi, 2017, p. 263). If the differences in cultural perceptions between employees in the Chinese organisations in Africa are large – divergence – the transfer of technology and knowledge will be impacted negatively. However, the opposite is true if mutual learning and diffusion of knowledge takes place – crossvergence (Sarala & Vaara, 2010).

Emerging literature suggests that in the context of Chinese organisations in Africa, the cultural influences on managerial practices may be compatible as Chinese management practices are often informed by the synergies between Africa's *"ubuntu"* and China's *"Confucianism"* (Jackson, 2012; Xing et al., 2016, p. 34). *Ubuntu* means "a person is a person through others" *(umuntu ngumuntu ngabantu)* in Nguni languages (Hadebe & Nkomo, 2019, p. 43) and advocates respect for human dignity through sharing and honesty before profits, systems and procedures. Employees in organisations are thus regarded as human beings rather than merely as resources (Jackson et al., 2013, p. 2526). In Confucianism, a person is defined by harmonious interpersonal relationships of *ren* (benevolence and compassion), *yi* (moral righteousness) and *li* (etiquettes or norms), *zhi* (wisdom, knowledge, integrity) and *xin* (trustworthiness) (Gan, 2014, p. 109; Wang, Wang, Ruona, & Rojewski, 2005, p. 314). Hence, an organisation's goals strategies, structures, processes and relationships with stakeholders must conform to the principles of *ren-yi-li* while leaders adhere to *junzi* (moral person) and *he* (familial collectivism) (Jackson et al., 2013, p. 2527; Liu, 2019). The *ren-yi-li* values are based on helpfulness, encouragement and friendliness when working collectively towards a goal (Liu, 2019, p. 21) and are particular to an "in-group". Since social relationships are important for both *ubuntu* and Confucianism, in both philosophies the identity of an individual is embedded in their social networks and associations. In traditional Chinese practices, the obligation in such a network is referred to as *guanxi* (Fang & Faure, 2011; Li et al., 2012, p. 10). However, in *guanxi*, if a person is not a member of an "in-group" network they will be treated as someone from an "out-group" and not be part of the Chinese *guanxi*. Therefore, it is possible that the Chinese will consider an individual from Africa as being a member of the "out-group". From an African perspective, *ubuntu* applies to the "out-group" (Jackson & Horwitz, 2018, p. 1864). As reiterated by Mayer (2019, p. 7), culture is a "construct through which individuals and groups create boundaries, as well as in-groups and out-groups which are dynamic and changeable". It has been argued that while the potential cultural synergies which exist between Chinese and African people could facilitate the transfer of technology and knowledge, the concepts of "in-group" and "out-group" may hamper such a transfer and thereby compromise mutual understanding. In support of cultural synergies, the study of Xing et al. (2016, p. 34) found that the similarity between *ubuntu* and *guanxi* is apparent at three levels – relationships with others, time and productivity. Relationships are reciprocal and familial, time is not a finite commodity and productivity is achieved in a harmonious manner.

Furthermore, Ostabutey and Jackson (2019, p. 1) assert that the transfer is low largely because of the "Chinese government's professed policy of friendship and mutual learning" and a relationship that is anti-imperialist. This begs the question to what extent knowledge transfer is taking place or whether mutual learning and knowledge diffusion is taking place instead. Mutual learning implies that knowledge is shared rather than being transferred (Jackson & Horwitz, 2018, p. 1859), as suggested by cultural crossvergence theory.

Furthermore, the absorptive capacity of the host organisation also influences the effective transfer of technology and knowledge. Absorptive capacity is "the capacity to recognize the value of new external information, assimilate it and apply it to commercial ends" (Cohen & Levinthal, 1990, p. 128). In turn, the absorptive capacity is highly influenced by culture (Lee, Trimi, & Kim, 2013, p. 27; Leidner & Kayworth, 2006, p. 357; Vance, Elie-Dit-Cosaque, & Straub, 2008, p. 75). Leidner and Kayworth (2006, pp. 365–366) state that the specific aspect of culture that determines how people from different cultures adopt and diffuse technology and knowledge transfer can largely be attributed to the degree of uncertainty avoidance in a culture. More specifically, avoidance of technology is driven by the fact that technology is generally perceived as risky. For this reason, cultures with high levels of uncertainty avoidance are less likely to adopt technology (Leidner & Kayworth, 2006, pp. 365–366; Vance et al., 2008, p. 81). Therefore, if technology is perceived as risky, trust becomes an important determinant of the adoption of technology, and this is also highly influenced by culture (Vance et al., 2008, p. 81). The different levels of trust within cultures will therefore influence the adoption of technology (Vance et al., 2008, p. 94).

In organisations, the assimilation and use of external technology and knowledge are influenced by both internal and external factors. Internal factors refer to the knowledge and capabilities of employees, diversity, organisational structures, communication, and HRM while external factors refer to the national culture of a host country and the organisation's stance within cultural knowledge networks (Noblet, Simon, & Parent, 2011, p. 369). For example, poor knowledge and capabilities within an organisation will negatively impact on technology and knowledge transfer implying that training will be required at the host organisation to facilitate the transfer process. In this regard, Osabutey and Jackson (2019, p. 3) assert that "lack of absorptive capacity among African employees may be seen as a barrier".

The adoption of technology and knowledge is influenced not only by a country's national culture but also by the technology adoption stage of the country (Lee et al., 2013, pp. 27–28). For example, in order to facilitate the transfer and adoption of technology and knowledge in countries like Australia and Canada which are in a mature stage of technology adoption, organisations must focus on the innovative aspects of technology such as the perceived ease of use, perceived usefulness and the quality of the output. For countries such as Brazil, Japan and Thailand, however, organisations need to depend on social factors to facilitate the transfer and adoption of technology and knowledge, given that people in these cultures depend largely on recommendations from others to adopt technology and knowledge (Lee et al., 2013, pp. 27–28). Based on these findings, it is suggested that management scholars investigate the national culture in African countries, bearing in mind the stage of adoption of technology in these countries, as this can also impact the transfer and adoption of technology.

In addition, the motives for China's presence in Africa also influence technology and knowledge transfer, as discussed in the first section of this chapter headed "Motives of Chinese foreign direct investment (FDI) in Africa".

It is thus important for management scholars to conduct further research to gain a better understanding of the factors that influence technology and knowledge transfer and to what extent this transfer between Chinese organisations and organisations in Africa takes place and, if not, what the obstacles are.

Besides the influence of the factors discussed in this section, and specifically the influence of cultural values on the transfer of technology and knowledge, geopolitical relationships also influence this transfer (Connell, 2014, p. 212; Frenkel, 2008, p. 924). Geopolitical relations determine the technology, knowledge and management practices that are relevant for the FDI (Frenkel, 2008, p. 924; Jackson, 2012, p. 197). The role of geopolitics is frequently ignored in research, especially between developed and developing countries when determining the overall undertakings of organisations and the process of knowledge transfer within organisations (Frenkel, 2008, pp. 938–939). Connell (2014, p. 212) argues that with reference to Africa, indigenous knowledge is often neglected, and western knowledge is imposed. Furthermore, Connell (2014, p. 212) emphasises that to understand the prevalent asymmetrical nature of knowledge between Africa and the West is to understand what brought about its existence which is attributed largely to colonialism and postcolonialism, in which various types of neocolonialism emerged. Frenkel (2008, p. 937) argues that current research tools and methodologies do not reveal how the transfer process is embedded in geopolitics nor do they elaborate on the opinions that managers might have on the practices that are transferred or that they are required to implement. Also, the tools and methodologies that draw inferences chiefly from interviews with managers do not provide an opportunity for the opinions of the weak – the lower-level employees, especially from developing countries – to be heard. It is suggested that to provide a better view and understanding of the transfer of knowledge and practices, studies should adopt a research design that is interpretive and focuses on multiple levels within organisations (Frenkel, 2008, pp. 937–938). By focusing research on multiple levels within an organisation, the western countries' aspirational and ideological standards could be counteracted (Bräutigam, 2011). Senior managers' opinions of the relevance and significance of transferred practices as well as the circulation of the transferred practices should be investigated in terms of organisational identity. Of equal importance to consider is the identity of those who will be recipients of the knowledge transfer practice. Lastly, it is also suggested that the decision of whether or not to transfer knowledge should be given equal strategic consideration by all parties and both options should be evaluated equally. Neglecting to do so will exacerbate geopolitical influence, prevent appropriate censure and impede the implementation of corrective measures (Frenkel, 2008, p. 939). Furthermore, such negligence leads to a misrepresentation of the realities of the technology and knowledge transfer process and may create additional shortcomings in the transfer system within an organisation (Frenkel, 2008, p. 939). This is likely to be counterproductive to the organisational aim of ensuring optimal performance of the FDI.

An additional factor related to the importance of geopolitics in China–Africa research is Jackson's (2012, p. 197) suggestion that even though Chinese management knowledge and organisations may be supportive of community- and humanity-oriented values in Africa, it is only by means of sound research within the context of geopolitics and accurate empirical evidence that such assumptions can be validated.

A significant factor in the way Chinese firms handle and design their HRM strategies and systems is their motivation for deciding to invest in Africa. The motive will determine the objectives of the firm, their need to employ local staff and their need to bring in Chinese nationals to achieve these objectives. This will depend largely on the skills available locally as well as their willingness to develop local talent and to transfer and share knowledge and skills. The next section will provide information on how Chinese and African cultural philosophies and practices influence management and organisational knowledge and Chinese HRM practices.

Influence of Chinese and African cultural philosophies and practices on Chinese HRM practices

With increased pressure from global competition, workforces need to be mobile and are perforce diverse. In the midst of this growing globalisation, organisations are faced with a hybridisation of management and organisational knowledge, HRM policy implications, challenges of designing HRM systems and processes and of implementing HRM practices that are appropriate in both local and global contexts (Aycan, 2005, p. 1083; Briscoe & Schuler, 2004, p. 26). To enhance organisational competitive advantage, the main challenge is to manage a diverse workforce by implementing appropriate management and HRM practices that are considerate of employees from different cultural backgrounds (Briscoe & Schuler, 2004, p. 29; Noruzi & Westover, 2010). Over the last two decades, despite the protracted argument between the integration of HRM practices (convergence) and local HRM differences (divergence) having dominated most research on HRM, the concept remains extremely complex (Aycan, 2005, p. 1083) and research to address this issue remains sparse because of continued reliance on several assumptions and theoretical arguments with scant empirical evidence (Xing et al., 2016, p. 29). The complexity of this type of research is exacerbated by the multiple embeddedness of organisations within the political, legal and economic environments, together with the internal organisational environment and inherent sociocultural differences (Shen, 2007) and fluctuating South–South geopolitical dynamics. Because of this embeddedness, it is particularly difficult to empirically research the "nature of indigenous inputs, contributions and knowledge" (Jackson et al., 2013, p. 2520). Jackson (2015) cautions on the contentiousness of constructing indigenous management scholarship. He further asserts that, while concepts such as *ubuntu* and *guanxi* in the African and Chinese cultures are generally considered as "indigenous" and "local", the critical aspect of studying indigenous knowledge may be lost. Instead, creating "indigenous" knowledge emerges from dynamic cross-cultural interactions, creating new knowledge and social forms (Jackson, 2015) thus creating a "third space". In this "third space", hybrid systems of management and organisational knowledge and values emerge at the organisational level through mutual sharing, learning and co-creation of new knowledge. Since the interactions in this "third space" will always be influenced by the geopolitically dominant partner, Jackson et al. (2013, p. 2520) propose that integrating geopolitical dynamics with crossvergence theory, supported by postcolonial theory, is particularly useful for scholars in understanding management and organisational knowledge and Chinese HRM policy and practices in Africa (Jackson et al., 2013, p. 2520).

While cultural synergies in humanism, paternalism (although varying in perspectives), communalism, collectivism and belonging are evident between the African and Chinese cultures (Jackson et al., 2013, pp. 2523–2525), the question for management scholars is whether these conceptualised similarities have the propensity to drive crossvergence of Chinese and African management and HRM practices in Africa – a hybrid system? For instance, in a study done by Mabuza (2015) in a Chinese multinational corporation (MNC) in South Africa, the Chinese managers were perceived as being concerned about the well-being of their employees, likened to being part of a "big family" and "getting to know co-workers". This illustrates the association with the *ubuntu* value system in which humanness, caring and familial group belonging is important (Khoza, 2006; Mangaliso, 2001) and motivational for the African employees.

While synergies exist between these cultures, the engagement between the Chinese and local employees is still constrained by cultural differences (Kamoche & Sieber, 2015, p. 2718), such as the "out-group" perspective inherent in *guanxi*. Making sense of and understanding the implications of these cultural differences would be key for the co-creation of a hybrid system of management and organisational knowledge and Chinese HRM practices within the "third space". This could be particularly valuable considering the current scarcity of empirical findings.

In probing the implications for Chinese HRM practices and the current scant empirical evidence, it is suggested that management scholars probe the influence of the different cultural philosophies on HRM practices as they relate to the role of trade unions and human rights; the influence of organisational strategy and structure on decision-making; the contentious nature of employment; job creation in the local context; and training and development. This section provides a brief overview of the implications for the relevant HRM practices and poses questions for management scholars to consider.

The role of trade unions is critical in managing labour relations and in influencing HRM practices in Africa (Wood & Glaister, 2008). Irrespective of the various national differences, trade unions in Africa are very powerful owing to "collective employee participation and involvement" (Xing et al., 2016, p. 30). Unions in Africa are independent and concerned with employees' rights and interests. In contrast, the All-China Federation of Trade Unions (ACFTU), led by the state/communist party in the People's Republic of China dominates Chinese unions (Zhu, Warner, & Feng, 2011) and impacts on Chinese HRM practices in Africa, particularly Chinese SOEs (Xing et al., 2016, p. 36). ACFTU focus on national well-being rather than on protecting workers' rights, as is the case in Africa. The difference in the perception of a trade union poses the question whether the role of unions could drive the divergence of Chinese managers' HRM practices in Africa or whether the cultural synergies could drive convergence in practices.

Within any organisation, strategy and organisational structure influence how decisions are made and determine the HRM practices. In an intercultural setting, the impact of strategy and structure is more challenging because of the intercultural interactions amongst diverse employees, as is the case with engagement of Chinese organisations in Africa. In accordance with the hierarchical structure of Chinese SOEs, employees are expected to respect authority (Xing et al., 2016, p. 37) and there is a strict divide between workers and Chinese managers – illustrating the principle of paternalistic hierarchy and filial piety. In Chinese culture, filial piety pertains to a family patriarch who exercises enormous power over their children or in other relationships which are considered unequal (Gan, 2014, p. 10). This contrasts with African employees' expectations of equality, embracing familial, brotherhood-type relationships with their managers. In Chinese SOEs, there is the tendency for authority to be retained in the hands of Chinese managers at the top level and to localise middle to lower level employees.

Even though HRM policy and practices are often informed by the home country, Chinese MNEs and SOEs should consider the local cultural philosophies and practices in the host country. Baah and Jauch (2009, p. 13) share their findings on the nature of employment in Chinese organisations across 10 countries in Africa as follows, "Chinese employees have a hostile attitude towards trade unions; there is evidence of violation of workers' rights and unfair labour practices; poor working conditions; the absence of appointment contracts; low remuneration rates; hiring of contract employees to avoid paying benefits". Chinese organisations are also accused of paying the lowest wages in Africa, especially in comparison with developed countries (Shen, 2007). In another study of a Chinese MNE in Kenya, Mpafa and Mlotshwa (2015) found that there were no formal recruitment and selection policies and procedures, labour turnover was high and Kenyan employees were appointed in the lower levels in the organisation. Horwitz, Kamoche, and Chew (2002, p. 1030) confirm that Chinese employees unilaterally determine wages and benefits. Chinese employees generally have a predisposition to equity, in contrast to Africans who prefer equality and redistribution. In contrast, the opposite was found in a Chinese MNE in South Africa, where the remuneration was considered fair and competitive and the organisation was perceived as having "egalitarian practices with regard to status, income and culture" (Mabuza, 2015, pp. 139, 145). From these examples, the nature of employment in different countries is guided by the legal requirements and the sociocultural context in different countries. Furthermore, in terms of job creation in the local market, the following questions can be posed: "At which level in the organisation are locals being employed?" "How many locals are being employed compared with Chinese employees?" and "What is the nature of employment contracts?" Another concern in terms of HRM practices is the extent to which Chinese organisations in Africa have implemented training and development programmes. Within this context, the following questions are posed to management scholars: "To what extent do the Chinese bring employees from China?" "To what extent are the local, largely unskilled, employees upskilled through training and development?" and "What is the impact of this on learning and sharing knowledge?

Summary

China's engagement with Africa encompasses multiple complex issues at many levels. While the relationship has historically been portrayed as an ideal win–win relationship, almost all studies have shown a win–lose relationship between China and Africa. While the findings of studies portraying China–Africa relations as a win–lose relationship are sometimes valid, most tend to generalise the findings across African countries, without sufficient empirical evidence. There is also a lack of transparency in Chinese state-owned enterprises. Additionally, many studies have been conducted using inappropriate methodologies. As is the case in any relationship, Africa's relationship with China is subject to both risks and benefits, and it is incumbent on Africa to minimise the risks and maximise the benefits.

This chapter highlighted concerns related to cultural issues and their various impacts on management of the intercultural interaction of Chinese organisations in Africa, the motives for Chinese FDI in Africa, the relevance of critical development theories for international and cross-cultural management studies, the implication of cultural synergy and divergence at the organisational level, factors influencing the transfer of technology and knowledge and its implications for management practices and the influence of Chinese and African cultural philosophies and practices on HRM practices.

In recent years, the motives of China in Africa have come under serious scrutiny. There have been mixed opinions on China's presence in Africa, with increasing ambivalence on whether China's engagement is beneficial for Africa or not. In this chapter, in addressing the motives of Chinese FDI in African countries, three motives appear to be relevant – resource-seeking, market-seeking and political-seeking. To fully understand the motives of Chinese FDI in Africa, management scholars should investigate how these motives are integrated into the business models of various Chinese organisations. They should also seek to understand the power dynamics underpinned in the critical development theories and to test their relevance for international and cross-cultural studies, investigate how technology knowledge is transferred and examine the prevalent influences on employment and HRM strategies and systems. In addition, management scholars should be cautious when drawing conclusions from their findings as different motives may manifest subtly in ways that appear to be similar within organisations.

Three critical development theories and their relevance to cultural interactions were discussed. Firstly, modernisation theory was discussed, explaining how Sino-African relations can enhance the development of African countries. Secondly, the usefulness of dependency theory was discussed as it addresses the role of power dynamics in organisations and the extent to which local knowledge and practices are considered. Thirdly, postcolonial theory was discussed in terms of the effects of colonisation on societies and the responses of these societies, assisting researchers in understanding the subtle implications of power in international relations and the way in which knowledge is transferred internationally. In the field of international HRM and cross-cultural management, a paucity of research on these critical development theories is evident. Thus, management scholars should scrutinise the impact of these critical theories on the Sino-African relationship. The research should strive to provide the foundation of knowledge upon which the transformation of the African continent can be built.

Cultural synergy was explained in terms of convergence and crossvergence theories, while the cultural differences were considered through divergence theories. Consideration of cultural synergy and divergence raises the following concerns for management scholars to consider. Firstly, to what extent does cultural synergy (convergence and crossvergence) and divergence take place in Chinese organisations in Africa? Secondly, what are the implications of cultural synergies (convergence and crossvergence) and divergence for effective and appropriate management of Chinese organisations in Africa? Thirdly, to what extent are the South–South synergies or divergences influenced by western management education and the multinational organisations in Africa and China? Furthermore, for management scholars to understand the meaning and implications of cultural synergy and divergence in Sino-African relationships and exchanges, their research should be positioned within the context of extant cross-cultural theory.

An exposition of the factors that influence the transfer of technology and knowledge, such as the appropriateness of the transfer, cultural synergy, the absorptive capacity of the organisation in the host country, and Chinese FDI motives was provided in this chapter. Considering the geopolitical context, Chinese FDI motives and the intricate interrelationship between the factors that influence the transfer of technology and knowledge between China and Africa, management scholars should be concerned with conducting further research to better understand whether the transfer of technology and knowledge between Chinese organisations and organisations in Africa takes place and, if not, what the hindrances are considering any prevailing power dynamics.

Despite considerable research in this field, HRM for organisations in Africa remains a very complex process since it is inextricably integrated with culture and identity. In this chapter, the extent to which Chinese and African cultural philosophies and practices influenced selected Chinese HRM practices was discussed. The selected HRM practices included the role of the trade union and human rights, the impact of strategy, the structure on decision-making, the nature of employment, job creation in the local context and training and development. The implications of these HRM practices in organisations in Africa for learning and knowledge sharing need to be empirically verified. Furthermore, the extent to which cultural synergies have the propensity to drive convergence and crossvergence of Chinese managers' HRM practices in Africa should be investigated by management scholars.

As outlined in this chapter, there are many challenges associated with the search for a comprehensive understanding of the nature of China's involvement in Africa. The effective resolution of these challenges will determine Africa's future foreign policy with China and influence future development on the African continent. As outlined in this chapter, it is essential for management scholars to undertake appropriate research to enable in-depth discussions to take place on the various aspects and implications of the China–Africa relationship. However, it should be noted that such research cannot be done without considering the impact of the geopolitical relations and the scholar's rigorous reflection on the scientific validity and reliability of their research.

It is hoped that this chapter will be the catalyst for management scholars to interrogate the motives for Chinese FDI in Africa, the effect of the changing South–South geopolitical dynamics and the influence of the critical development theories – in particular, postcolonial theory – in relation to their research at the organisational level. The contribution of future Sino-Africa research in generating a body of scholarship in international and cross-cultural management, particularly at the organisation and society levels, can be threefold. Firstly, this can be done by further development of conceptual frameworks and hypothesised assumptions at a theoretical level. Secondly, the existing conceptual papers, frameworks and assumptions (such as Ado & Su, 2016; Connell, 2014; Horwitz, 2017; Jackson, 2002a, 2002b, 2012, 2014, 2015; Jackson & Horwitz, 2018; Jackson et al., 2013; Li, et al., 2012) need to be empirically verified, if such verification has not yet been done. Lastly, the recommendations for further research provided by contemporary empirical studies (such as Chigwendere, 2017; Chodokufa, 2018; Handley, 2016; Jackson, 2004; Nyambegera et al., 2016; Mabuza, 2015; Mayer, Boness, & Louw, 2017; Osabutey & Jackson, 2019; Paterson, 2013; Ralston et al., 1997; Xing, Liu, Tarba, & Cooper, 2016; Wang & Elliot, 2014) should be considered by management scholars.

References

Adisu, K., Sharkey, T., & Okoroafo, S. C. (2010). The impact of Chinese investment in Africa. *International Journal of Business and Management, 5*(9), 3.

Ado, A., & Su, Z. (2016). China in Africa: A critical literature review. *Critical Perspectives on International Business, 12*(1), 40–60. https://doi.org/10.1108/cpoib-05-2013-0014

Agbebi, M., & Virtanen, P. (2017). Dependency theory – A conceptual lens to understand china's presence in Africa? *Forum for Development Studies, 44*(3), 429–451. https://doi.org/10.1080/08039410.2017.1281161

Alden, C., & Davies, M. (2006). A profile of the operations of Chinese multinationals in Africa. *South African Journal of International Affairs, 13*(1), 83–96. https://doi.org/10.1080/10220460609556787

Amin, J. A. (2015). Sino-Cameroon relations: A foreign policy of pragmatism. *African Studies Review, 58*(3), 171–189.

Anshan, L. (2007). China's engagement in Africa: Singular interest or mutual benefit. *Expert roundtable on resource governance in Africa in the 21st century*, Heinrich Böll Foundation, Berlin.

Arnett, J. J. (2002). The psychology of globalization. *American Psychologist, 57*(10), 774.

Asongu, S. A., & Aminkeng, G. A. A. (2013). The economic consequences of China – Africa relations: Debunking myths in the debate. *Journal of Chinese*

Economic and Business Studies, 11(4), 261–277. https://doi.org/10.1080/147
65284.2013.838384

Audretsch, D. B., Lehmann, E. E., & Wright, M. (2014). Technology transfer in
a global economy. *Journal of Technology Transfer*, 39, 301–312. https://doi.
org/10.1007/s10961-012-9283-6

Aycan, Z. (2005). The interplay between cultural and institutional/structural
contingencies in human resource management practices. *The International
Journal of Human Resource Management*, 16(7), 1083–1119. https://doi.org/
10.1080/0958519050014395

Ayodele, T., & Sotola, O. (2014). *China in Africa: An evaluation of Chinese
investment*, IPPA Working Paper Series. Initiative for Public Policy Analysis
(IPPA). Retrieved from www.ippanigeria.org/articles/China%20Africa%20
relation_Workingpaper_final.pdf

Baah, A. Y., & Jauch, H. (Eds.). (2009). *Chinese investments in Africa: A labour
perspective*. Johannesburg, South Africa: African Labour Research Network.

Barrett, R. E., & Whyte, M. K. (1982). Dependency theory and Taiwan: Analysis
of a deviant case. *American Journal of Sociology*, 87(5), 1064–1089.

Berry, J. W., Poortinga, Y. H., & Pandey, J. (1997). *Handbook of cross-cultural
psychology: Theory and method* (2nd ed.). Boston, MA: Allyn and Bacon.

Bird, A., & Fang, T. (2009). Cross cultural management in the age of globalization. *International Journal of Cross Cultural Management*, 9(2), 139–143.

Boh, W. F., Nguyen, T. T., & Xu, Y. (2013). Knowledge transfer across dissimilar
cultures. *Journal of Knowledge Management*, 17(1), 29–46.

Bräutigam, D. (2011). *The Dragon's gift: The real story of China in Africa*. Oxford:
Oxford University Press.

Briscoe, D. R., & Schuler, R. S. (2004). *International human resource management: Policy and practice for the global enterprise* (2nd ed.). London and New
York: Rutledge Taylor & Francis.

Campbell, H. (2008). China in Africa: Challenging US global hegemony. *Third
World Quarterly*, 29(1), 89–105. https://doi.org/10.1080/01436590701726517

Castellano, S., Davidson, P., & Khelladi, I. (2017). Creativity techniques to
enhance knowledge transfer within global virtual teams in the context of
knowledge-intensive enterprises. *The Journal of Technology Transfer*, 42(2),
253–266. [e-journal].

Chigwendere, F. (2017). *Achievement of intercultural effectiveness in multicultural Chinese/African organisations*. Unpublished PhD thesis. Grahamstown,
South Africa: Rhodes University, Grahamstown, NRF Funded.

Chodokufa, K. (2018). *Stakeholder relationships within Chinese mining companies in Southern Africa: A cross cultural perspective*. Unpublished thesis. Grahamstown, South Africa: Rhodes University.

Cohen, W. M., & Levinthal, D. A. (1990). Absorptive capacity: A new perspective
on learning and innovation. *Administrative Science Quarterly*, 35(1), 128–152.

Connell, R. (2014). Using Southern theory: Decolonizing social thought in theory,
research and application. *Planning Theory*, 13(2), 210–223. DOI: 10.1177/
1473095213499216

Dode, R. O., & Cletus, E. C. (2019). Modernization theory and African development in the 21st century. *KIU Journal of Social Sciences*, 5(1), 85–94. Retrieved
July 2, 2020, from https://www.ijhumas.com/ojs/index.php/kiujoss/article/
view/479

48   *Lynette Louw*

Drogendijk, R., & Blomkvist, K. (2013). Drivers and motives for Chinese outward foreign direct investments in Africa. *Journal of African Business, 14*(2), 75–84. https://doi.org/10.1080/15228916.2013.804320

Fang, T., & Faure, G. O. (2011). Chinese communication characertistics: A Yin Yan perspective. *International Journal of Intercultural Relations, 5*, 320–333.

Fernald, J. G., & Charles, I. J. (2014). *The future of U.S. economic growth*, NBER Working Paper No. 19830. National Bureau of Economic Research. Retrieved from www.nber.org/papers/w19830

Frenkel, M. (2008). The multinational corporation as a third Space: Rethinking international management discourse on knowledge transfer through Homi Bhabha. *The Academy of Management Review, 33*(4), 924–942.

Gallagher, K. P., & Irwin, A. (2014). Exporting national champions: China's outward foreign direct investment finance in comparative perspective. *China & World Economy, 22*(6), 1–21.

Gan, S. (2014). *How to do business with China: An inside view of Chinese culture and etiquette*. London: Authorhouse.

Gu, J. (2009). China's private enterprises in Africa and the implications for African development. *European Journal of Development Researh, 21*, 570–587. https://doi.org/10.1057/ejdr.2009.21

Guo, C. (2015). Cultural convergence, divergence and crossvergence. Volume 6. *International Management*. Retrieved January 14, 2020 from https://onlinelibrary.wiley.com/doi/abs/10.1002/9781118785317.weom060049

Hadebe, S., & Nkomo, D. (2019). African cultural concepts and their influence on management. In C. H. Mayer, L. Louw, & C. M. Boness (Eds.), *Managing Chinese-African business interactions – Growing intercultural competence in organisations* (Palgrave Studies in African Leadership Series, Pp. 37–57). Cham, Switzerland: Palgrave Macmillan.

Handley, R. C. (2016). *Impact of organisational culture and leadership styles on the quality of work life: An exploratory study of Chinese organisations in South Africa*. Unpublished Masters thesis. Grahamstown, South Africa: Rhodes University, Grahamstown.

Hofstede, G. (1980). *Culture's consequences: International differences in work-related values*. London: Sage Publications.

Horwitz, F. M. (2017). International HRM in South African multinational companies. *Journal of International Management, 23*, 208–222. https://doi.org/10.1016/l.intman.2017.01.005

Horwitz, F. M., Kamoche, K., & Chew, I. K. H. (2002). Looking East: Diffusing higher performance work practices in Southern Afro-Asian context. *International Journal of Human Recource Management, 13*(7), 1019–1041.

Jackson, T. (2002a). Reframing human resource management in Africa: A cross-cultural perspective. *The International Journla of Human Resource Management, 13*(7), 998–1018.

Jackson, T. (2002b). The management of people across cultures: Valuing people differently. *Human Resource Management, 41*(4), 455–475.

Jackson, T. (2004). *Management and change in Africa: A cross-cultural perspective*. London: Routledge.

Jackson, T. (2012). Postcolonialism and organizational knowledge in the wake of china's presence in Africa: Interrogating south-south relations. *Organization, 19*(2), 181–204.

Jackson, T. (2014). Employment in Chinese MNESs: The Dragon's gift to sub-Saharan Africa. *Human Resource Management, 53*(6), 879–919. https://doi.org/10.1002/hrm.21565

Jackson, T. (2015). Management studies from Africa: A cross cultural critique. *Africa Journal of Management, 1*(1), 78–88. https://doi.org/10.1080/23322373.2015.994425.

Jackson, T., & Aycan. Z. (2006). Editorial: From cultural values to cross cultural interfaces. *Internal Journal of Cross Cultural Management, 6*(1), 5–13.

Jackson, T., & Horwitz, F. M. (2018). Expatriation in Chinese MNEs in Africa: An agenda for research. *The International Journal of Human Resource Management, 29*(11), 1856–1878. https://doi.org/10.1080/09585192.2017.1284882

Jackson, T., Louw, L., & Zhao, S. (2013). China in sub-Saharan Africa: Implications for HRM policy and practice at organizational level. *The International Journal of Human Resource Management, 24*(13), 2512–2533. https://doi.org/10.1080/09585192.2012.725067

Jorgensen, J. G. (1979). Cross-cultural comparisons. *Annual Review of Anthropology, 8*, 309–331. Retrieved from www.jstor.org/stable/2155622

Kamoche, K. (1997). Knowledge creation and learning in international HRM. *International Journal of Human Resource Management, 8*(2), 213–225, DOI: 10.1080/09585199700000049

Kamoche, K., & Siebers, L. Q. (2015). Chinese management practices in Kenya: Toward a post-colonial critique. *The International Journal of Human Resource Management, 26*(21), 2718–2743. http://doi.org/10.1080/09585192.2014.968185

Kastanakis, M. N., & Voyer, B. G. (2014). The effect of culture on perception and cognition: A conceptual framework. *Journal of Business Research, 67*(4), 425–433.

Khoza, R. J. (2006). *Let Africa lead: African transformational leadership fo 21st century business.* Johannesburg: Penguin.

Kluckhohn, F., & Strodtbeck, F. L. (1961). *Variations in value orientations.* Evanston, IL: Peterson.

Kolstad, I., & Wiig, A. (2012). What determines Chinese outward FDI? *Journal of World Business, 47*(1), 26–34.

Kragelund, P. (2009). Knocking on a wide-open door: Chinese investments in Africa. *Review of African Political Economy, 36*(122), 479–497.

Lee, S., Trimi, S., & Kim, C. (2013). The impact of cultural differences on technology adoption. *Journal of World Business, 48*(1), 20–29.

Leidner, D. E., & Kayworth, T. (2006). A review of culture in information systems research: Toward a theory of information technology culture conflict. *MIS Quarterly, 30*(2), 357–399.

Li, P. P., Leung, K., Chen, C. C., & Luo, J.-D. (2012). Indigenous research on Chinese management: How and what. *Management and Organizational Review, 8*(1), 7–24. https://doi.org/10.1111/j.1740-8784.2012.00292.x

Liu, Z. (2019). Chinese cultural concepts and their influence on management. In C. H. Mayer, L. Louw, & C. M. Boness (Eds.), *Managing Chinese-African business interactions – Growing intercultural competence in organisations* (Palgrave Studies in African Leadership Series, pp. 19–35). Cham, Switzerland: Palgrave Macmillan.

Mabuza, L. T. (2015). *The influence of organisational culture on a high commitment work system and organisational commitment – The case of a Chinese multinational corporation in South Africa*. Unpublished Master or Commerce theis, Grahamstown, South Africa: Rhodes University.

Malone, A. (2008). *How China's taking over Africa, and why the West should be very worried*. Mailonline. Retreived from www.dailymail.co.uk/news/article-1036105/How-Chinas-taking-Africa-West-Very-worried.html

Mangaliso, M. P. (2001). Building competitiave advantage from "Ubuntu": Management lessons from South Africa. *The Academy of Management Executive*, 15(3), 23–34.

Mayer, C.-H., Boness, C. M. & Louw, L. (2017). Perceptions of Chinese and Tanzanian employees regarding intercultural collaboration. *South African Journal of Human Resource Management*, 15(0), a921. DOI: https://doi.org/10.4102/sajhrm.v15i0.921

Mayer, C.-H. (2019). Introduction. In C.-H. Mayer, L. Louw, & C. M. Boness (Eds.), *Managing Chinese-African business interactions – Growing intercultural competence in organisations* (Palgrave Studies in African Leadership Series, pp. 3–17). Cham, Switzerland: Palgrave Macmillan.

Mehta, R., Larsen, T., Rosenbloom, B., & Ganitsky, J. (2006). The impact of cultural differences in US business-to-business export marketing channel strategic alliances. *Industrial Marketing Management*, 35(2), 156–165.

Meibo, H., & Peiqiang, R. (2013). A study on the employment effect of Chinese investment in South Africa. *Centre for Chinese Studies Discussion Paper*, 5, 2013.

Meyer, K. E., Mudambi, R., & Narula, R. (2011). Multinational enterprises and local contexts: The opportunities and challenges of multiple embeddedness. *Journal of Management Studies*, 48(2). https://doi.org/10.1111/j.1467-6486.2010.00968.x

Mlambo, C., Kushamba, A., & Simawu, M. B. (2016). China-Africa relations: What lies beneath? *The Chinese Economy*, 49(4), 257–276.

Mlambo, V. (2019). Exploitation dressed in a suit, shining shoes, and carrying a suitcase full of dollars: What does china want in Africa? *Journal of Public Affairs*, 19(1), e1892.

Mpafa, A., & Mlotshwa, M. P. (2015). *Employer and employee perceptins of management practices in the aviation industy – The case of a Chinese multinational corporation in Kenya*. Unpublished Bachelor of Commerce Honours thesis. Grahamstown, South Africa: Rhodes University.

Mutlul, C. C., Zhan, W., Peng, M. W., & Lin, Z. J. (2015). Competing in (and out of) transition economies. *Asia-Pacific Journal of Management*, 32, 571–596. https://doi.org/10.1007/s10490-015-9419-y

Ngo, H. Y., Turban, D., Lau, C. M., & Lui, S. Y. (1998). Human resource practices and firm performance of multinational corporations: Influences of country origin. *International Journal of Human Resource Management*, 9(4), 632–652. https://doi.org/10.1080/095851998340937

Noblet, J. P., Simon, E., & Parent, R. (2011). Absorptive capacity: A proposed operationalisation. *Knowledge Management Research and Practice*, 9, 367 377. https://doi.org/10.1057/kmrp.2011.26

Noruzi, M. R., & Westover, J. H. (2010). Exploring successful international human resource management: Past, present, and future directions. *Timisoara Journal of Economics*, 24(8), 163–168.

Nyambegera, S. M., Kamoche, K., & Siebers, L. (2016). Integrating Chinese and African culture into human resource management practice to enhance employee job satisfaction. *Journal of Language, Technology & Entrepreneurship in Africa*, 7(2), 118–139.

Osabutey, E. L. C., & Jackson, T. (2019). The impact on development of technology and knowledge transfer in Chinese MNEs in sub-Saharan Africa: The Ghanaian case. *Technological Forecasting & Social Change*, 148, 119725. https://doi.org/10.1016/j.techfore.2019.119725

Osabutey, E. L. C., & Jin, Z. (2016). Factors influencing technology and knowledge transfer: Configurational recipes for Sub-Saharan Africa. *Journal of Business Research*, 69(11), 5390–5395. https://doi.org/10.1016/j.jbusres.2016.04.143

Park, Y. J., & Alden, C. (2013). Upstairs and downstairs dimension of China and the Chinese in South Africa. In U. Pillay, J. P. Jansen, F. Nyamnjoh, & G. Hagg (Eds.), *State of the nation: South Africa 2012–2013*. Pretoria, Zimbabwe: HSRC.

Paterson, S. (2013). *The factors influencing local employee commitment in selected Chinese organisations in South Africa*. Unpublished Masters in Commerce thesis. Grahamstown, South Africa: Rhodes University. Sandisa Imbewu and NRF Funded.

Pickett, C. D. (2017). *French political economic interests in francophone Africa: Weighing the merits of dependency theory and modernist theory in the political and economic relations between France and her former African colonies*. Senior Honours Projects, 2010-current, 331. Retrieved from https://commons.lib.jmu.edu/honors201019/331

Ralston, D. (2008). The crossvergence perspective: Reflections and projections. *Journal of International Business Studies*, 39, 27–40. https://doi.org/10.1057/palgrave.jibs.8400333

Ralston, D., Holt, D., Terpstra, R., & Kai-Cheng, Y. (1997). The impact of national culture and economic ideology on managerial work values: A study of the United States, Russia, Japan, and China. *Journal of International Business Studies*, 28(1), 177–207. Retrieved January 14, 2020 from www.jstor.org/stable/155453

Rugman, A., & Verbeke, A. (2004). A perspective on regional and global strategies of multinational enterprises. *Journal of International Business Studies*, 35, 3–18. https://doi.org/10.1057/palgrave.jibs.8400073.

Sarala, R., & Vaara, E. (2010). Cultural differences, convergence, and crossvergence as explanations of knowledge transfer in international acquisitions. *Journal of International Business Studies*, 41, 1365–1390. https://doi.org/10.1057/jibs.2009.89

Sarfati, Y. (2017). How turkey's slide to authoritarianism defies modernization theory. *Turkish Studies*, 18(3), 395–415.

Sharma, R. (2017). The boom was blip: Getting used to slow growth. *Foreign Affairs*, 96(3), 104–115.

Shen, J. (2007). Approaches to international industrial relations in Chinese multinational corporations. *Management Revue*, 18, 1255–1270.

Smith, P. B. (2012). Chinese management theories: Indigenous insights or lessons for the wider world. *Handbook of Chinese Organizational Behavior*, 502–512.

Song, M., & Wang, S. (2018). Market competition, green technology progress and comparative advantages in China. *Management Decision*, 56(1), 188–203. https://doi.org/10.1108/MD-04-2017-0375

Stahl, G. K., & Tung, R. L. (2015). Towards a more balanced treatment of culture in international business studies: The need for positive cross-cultural scholarship. *Journal of International Business Studies*, 46(4), 391–414.

Sun, Y. (2014). *Africa in China's foreign policy*. John L. Thornton China Center and Africa Growth Initiative. Retrieved from file:///D:/New%20folder/Africa-in-China-web_CMG7.pdf

Trompenaars, F., & Hampden-Turner, C. (1998). *Riding the waves of culture: Understanding cultural diversity in business*. London: Nicholas Brealey Publishing.

Vaara, E., Sarala, R., Stahl, G. K., & Björkman, I. (2012). The impact of organizational and national cultural differences on social conflict and knowledge transfer in international acquisitions. *Journal of Management Studies, 49*(1), 1–27.

Vance, A., Elie-Dit-Cosaque, C., & Straub, W. D. (2008). Examining trust in information technology artifacts: The effects of system quality and culture. *Journal of Management Information Systems, 24*(4), 73–100. https://doi.org/10.2753/MIS0742-1222240403.

Van de Walle, N. (2016). Conclusion: Democracyfatigue and the ghost of modernization theory. In T. Hagmann & F. Reyntjens (Eds.), *Aid and authoritarianism in Africa: Development without democracy*. London: Zed Books Ltd.

Von Kimakowitz, E. (Ed.). (2016). The evolution of development thinking, theories, policy, implementation. *St. Gallen*. Retrieved from http://humanisticmanagement.network/wpcontent/uploads/2018/08/Short_Papers_Development_Course_St_Gallen_2016.pdf

Wang, F.-L., & Elliot, E. A. (2014). China in Africa: Presence, perceptions and prospects. *Journal of Contemporary China, 23*(90), 1012–1032. http://doi.org/10.1080/10670564.2014.898888

Wang, H., & Hu, X. Y. (2017.) China's "going-out" strategy and corporate social responsibility: Preliminary evidence of a "boomerang effect". *Journal of Contemporary China, 26*(108), 820–833. https://doi.org/10.1080/10670564.2017.1337301

Wang, J.-Y., & Blomstrom, M. (1992). Foreign direct investment and technology transfer: A simple model. *European Economic Review, 36*,137–155. https://doi.org/10.1016/0014-2921(92)90021-N

Wang, J.-Y., Wang, G. G., Ruona, W. E. A., & Rojewski, J. W. (2005). Confucian values and implication for international human resource development. *Human Resource Development Internatinal, 8*(3), 311–326.

Wood, G., & Glaister, K. (2008). Union power and new managerial strategies: The case of South Africa. *Employee Relations, 30*(4), 436–451.

Wu, M. (2006). Hofstede's cultural dimensions 30 yearss later: A study of Taiwan and the United States. *Intercultal Communication Studies, 15*(1), 33–42.

Xing, Y., Liu, Y., Tarba, S. Y., & Cooper, C. L. (2016). Intercultural influences on managing African employees of Chinese firms in Africa: Chinese managers' HRM practices. *International Business Review, 25*(1), 28–41.

Xue, C. Q. L., Ding, G., Chang, W., & Wan, Y. (2019). Architecture of "Stadium diplomacy" – China-aid sport buildings in Africa. *Habitat International, 90*, 101985. https://doi.org/10.1016/j.habitatint.2019.05.004.

Zhu, Y., Warner, M., & Feng, T. (2011). Employment relations with Chinese characteristics: The role of trade unions in China. *International Labour Review, 150*(1–2), 127–143.

3 Potential symbiotic Sino-African relations and policymaking

Underexplored, under-researched or clearly misunderstood?

Ellis L.C. Osabutey, Robert E. Hinson and Ogechi Adeola

The presence of Chinese organisations in sub-Saharan African countries is expected to be associated with the interactions between Chinese firms and host country firms, employees and communities. Nevertheless, current studies have not adequately incorporated research at the organisational and community levels to explore related nuances and how good host country policymaking could enhance symbiotic relations. The internationalisation of Chinese firms and the increased engagement between China and Africa has received considerable attention in the international business and development literatures (Alden, 2007; Kaplinsky & Morris, 2009; Davies, Draper, & Edinger, 2014; Shen, 2015; Ojo, 2016). The burgeoning Chinese investments in Africa have attracted a lot of attention with views and opinions from the media and academia disjointed and often polarised (Shen, 2015). As prominent donors in Africa, China, in particular, has intricately intertwined trade, aid, FDI, migration and geo-political influence (Alden & Alves, 2008; Jackson, 2012; Jackson, Louw, & Zhao, 2013; McCormick, 2008; Tull, 2006). China's growing footprint in Africa's political and economic landscape is undeniable (Carmody, 2009; Jenkins & Edwards, 2006; Naidu & Mbazima, 2008). China's increasing influence represents a shift in globalisation, with developing African countries preferring to deal with China rather than the West because of mutually beneficial business relationships and China's commitment to building long-term partnerships without political preconditions (Yin & Vaschetto, 2011).

The scale of rapidly growing engagement between China and Africa brings into question the motivations and implications for both parties (Tull, 2006; Alden, 2007; Davies, Edinger, Tay, & Naidu, 2008; Gu, 2009). Jackson et al. (2013) observed that China's presence in Africa is upsetting geopolitical power dynamics, with the IMF and the World Bank concerned about the implications of China's non-conditionality of loans and aid to Africa. Kaplinsky (2008) also indicated that China's relations are an extension of anti-imperialist discourse. While the Chinese government emphasises non-intervention and mutual benefit, the argument from the Global North is critical. The counter view is that China's foreign policy has been of great assistance to Africa in many ways including conflict resolution (Davies et al., 2014). So, whilst the Global North appears to be somewhat against the increasing presence of China in Africa, others, especially the African political elite, welcome China's presence as an unprecedented source of cooperation and economic development (Mohan & Lampert, 2012).

Existing literature has highlighted the potential gains and challenges of FDI inflow from China to Africa (Adisu, Sharkey, & Okoroafo, 2010; Kaplinsky & Morris, 2009). The evident and predicted outcomes appear mixed. On the one hand, there are studies that suggest that the economic and development consequences on Africa have so far not been positive (Chemingui & Bchir, 2010; Elu & Price, 2010; Wang, 2010); others suggest positive consequences (Wu & Cheng, 2010; Yin & Vaschetto, 2011). Although results are mixed, China presents Africa with an opportunity for increased participation and stake in the global economy. However, at the same time, there are questions about Africa's capacity and capability to fully harness opportunities to reduce poverty and improve economic development (Zafar, 2007).

Increasing Chinese presence is having significant effects on African workers in Chinese firms with respect to expectations in terms of work practices and remuneration (Hess & Aidoo). Such issues have implications for HRM policies and practices (Jackson, 2014; Cook, 2014). The historical, cultural and institutional closeness and relatedness between China and Africa also bodes for closer interaction and potential knowledge transfer (Jackson, 2012; Cook, 2014). Jackson (2012, 2014) develops the argument further to conceptualise the possible synergies between Chinese and African management knowledge. Despite these potential synergies, the majority of the evolving literature, to a larger extent, predicts poor long-term outcomes for Africa. A strand of the literature reveals that China has a policy for Africa with little emphasis on specific policies for China from the African side. In addition, existing studies fail to evaluate policy options that could engender a symbiotic win–win situation. In this regard, relevant studies that critically evaluate the research process and outputs to reveal policy options are extremely scarce, to the detriment of good policymaking.

The key research questions that we pose in this chapter are: what are the trade and policy frameworks that define the relationship between China and Africa? How does Chinese presence influence technology transfer, capacity building and economic growth potential in Africa? Is the relationship symbiotic and how can good research contribute to defining a symbiotic relationship? Addressing such questions requires an examination of the evolving China–Africa narrative and a scrutiny of the research processes. Context-specific research could play a role in advancing evidence-based policymaking to achieve economic and development objectives in Africa. In addition, policy could enhance symbiotic relationships with foreign investments and development partners operating on the continent.

The remainder of the chapter is organised as follows: First, we synthesise the literature on Sino-African relationships to understand the tensions between existing scholarly works. Second, we review the literature on China–Africa trade and investment policy. Third, we examine the technological and innovative capacity building potential. Fourth, we review Chinese investments in Africa and the potential symbiotic benefits. Fifth, we examine emerging literature and a new research framework. Finally, we conclude by discussing the implications and then set an agenda for future research.

Existing scholarly work on Sino-African relations

Following the establishment of the Forum on China–Africa Cooperation (FOCAC) in 2000, trade and business relations have increased. Consequently, researchers have become engaged in studying the presence of China in Africa (Ado & Su, 2016). Although the emerging scholarly debate suggests the potential benefits of a South–South relationship, most appear to be placing too much focus on comparing China–Africa relations to Africa's historical relations with the Global North (Lumumba-Kasongo, 2011). Such work also gives little recognition to the role of African agency and views African partners as passive players in the relationship. In a sense, the narratives appear narrow and are, largely, restricted to state-to-state engagement (Mohan & Lampert, 2012). Gu (2009) observe that the bulk of studies focus on state-owned Chinese enterprises and extractive industries with much less attention given to private Chinese enterprises. This has led to a misunderstanding or misrepresentation of the impact, positive or negative, of Chinese involvement. In most cases, the research approaches rely on data from government departments from China and Africa and also use isolated cases which are, methodologically, inadequately representative (Yin, 2009; Ado & Su, 2016) with too much focus on state actors and ignoring the African agency (Mohan & Lampert, 2012). Some of the evidence emerging from countries such as Botswana, Nigeria and Zambia appears to paint a picture of mounting anti-Chinese sentiments as a result of poor working conditions and labour force agitations in a number of Chinese-owned firms (Hess & Aidoo, 2014). There is a degree of diversity of the perspectives in framing the wider implications of the Sino-African relationship for the continent's economic development (Ojo, 2016). It is pertinent for African governments, and their wider policymaking community, to develop policy frameworks that could help ensure that FDI makes a net positive contribution to their economies and societies (Gu, 2009).

Dependency theory explains how the continued underdevelopment of the developing world fuels the development of the more developed (Schech & Haggis, 2000). This raises a question about the possible continuing development of China at the expense of Africa. Jackson (2012) argues that such theories, previously used to study the development of China, could not be adopted to understand the Sino-African relations and African development. Jackson draws on Dependency Theory to argue that the wealth of the developed world is a consequence of the exploitation of the underdeveloped world. Advocates of dependency theory assume that economic domination runs across North–South geo-economic patterns. However, Sino-African relations represent a distinct South–South dialectic occurring in an emerging new global economic configuration marked by a technology gap. To this end, even though synergies may exist between China and Africa (Jackson, 2012, 2014), Africa needs to generate its own technological and innovative capacities to reap benefits from the relationship (Maswana, 2009). Following the argument that various levels of actors shape Chinese engagements in Africa in important ways (Mohan & Lampert, 2012), our conceptual framework stresses the importance of technological and innovative capacity and the role of African researchers and other stakeholders in the evolving debate and policymaking. In addition, it allows us to explore a deeper understanding of the Sino-African relationship, recognising how scholarly work could bridge the knowledge gaps to enhance evidence-based policymaking. This approach needs to review trade and investment policies and how that could influence technological and innovative capacity building to create a symbiotic relationship.

China–Africa trade and investment policy review

The total volume of Chinese trade and investment in Africa has been growing rapidly even though, compared to other regions and nations, Africa's share is relatively small. Africa ranks in importance only slightly higher than Latin America with respect to China's foreign policy (Sun, 2014). Notwithstanding this assessment, the efforts from both sides to enhance cooperation portrays a burgeoning relationship that could be beneficial to both China and Africa. Since the inauguration of FOCAC, China has effectively and consistently implemented 3-year Africa engagement plans (Davies et al., 2014). China's growing influence, *inter alia*, has resulted in African nations preferring to deal with China rather than the West (Yin & Vaschetto, 2011). China's involvement in Africa is part of a long-term strategic commitment driven by economic needs as well as transmitting its development experiences through effective cooperation (Alden, 2007). Although Africa is not China's top policy priority, and economic ties to the continent constitute only a small percentage, China has become Africa's largest trading partner and African governments rely on and attach extreme importance to Chinese foreign investment (Sun, 2014). At the beginning of 2006, the Chinese government published 'China's African Policy', which outlined a new era of Sino-African cooperation across political, economic and sociocultural realms.

Through FOCAC, China's Ministries of Foreign Affairs and Commerce effectively coordinate and implement foreign and aid policy toward Africa. The resource-rich countries of Angola, Sudan, Nigeria and Zambia as well as the more politically strategic countries of South Africa, Ethiopia and Egypt are priority countries in China's broader African engagement (Davies et al., 2008). This means that China does not have one policy framework across Africa; rather, it takes different policy approaches for each country. Regional leaders with international political and economic influence, such as South Africa and Kenya, tend to receive higher levels of policymaking attention (Sun, 2014). China's policies on contracted engineering projects in Africa are generally perceived as following the state-driven strategy of exchanging infrastructure development for natural resources (Cheung, de Haan, Qian, & Yu, 2014). Forster, Butterfield, Chen, and Pushak (2009) suggested that several infrastructure projects in Africa, between 2001 and 2007, were paid for by natural resources. In addition, Dreher and Fuchs (2011) argue that political considerations influence China's allocation of aid as countries that vote in line with China in the United Nations General Assembly, who do not also recognise Taiwan as an independent country, receive more aid. Thus, although China does not rank Africa among its high policy priorities, its engagement with Africa provides leverage on the international scene and satisfies important resource requirements for fulfilling development objectives.

It is germane to note that some Chinese analysts advocate that China's Africa strategy is not long-term and well-thought-out because there are no clear identification and prioritisation between economic and political interests. This has resulted in the proliferation of central-level, state-owned enterprises, provincial governments and private companies (Sun, 2014). Since Africa has no deliberate policies and lacks the regulatory framework to deal with these different types of Chinese firms and institutions, the potential for exploitation is high. Meanwhile, not all the configuration of Chinese firms operating in Africa can be argued as being state controlled. Available state support does not mean that the state is complicit in all the activities, good or bad, of Chinese firms in Africa. It would be naïve to think that Chinese state or provincial governments can also monitor the activities of all its firms abroad. Arguably, it would be misplaced to level criticisms at the Chinese establishment as a whole when some private firms, for example, misbehave. Private firms are only likely to take advantage of the poor institutional arrangements in Africa for private gain. The impact of China's presence in Africa therefore needs to be managed by both sides. Kaplinsky and Morris (2009) assert policy challenges with regards to Africa's potential to maximise gains and minimise losses. They argue that contributions on the subject of China's presence in Africa point to the consensus that, whilst China has a strategy for Africa, Africa lacks a deliberate strategy or policy for China.

Hence, the trade and policy frameworks that define the relationship at the moment are one sided and characterised by a strong and purposively proactive initiative driven from the Chinese side and rather passive African partners. The deliberate policy initiatives from China to Africa point to the importance attached to the relationship. Since African countries operate independently it is not expected that there would be an Africa-wide China–Africa policy. However, countries in Africa could also demonstrate the importance of the relationship by developing trade and investment policies that would enhance the potential gains from the cooperation. Some of the potential gains from foreign presence in host country development relate to potential technological and innovative capacity building through FDI.

Technological and innovative capacity building through FDI

The FDI theory suggests that one of the key contributions of economic growth is the technological and innovative capability and capacity building potential for the recipient host country. Technological change is the main source of long-term economic growth for developing countries (López, 2008). International technology and knowledge transfers are integral, particularly in business operations that combine products and services (Osabutey, Williams, & Debrah, 2014). Knowledge acquisition from foreign firms has an impact on the capabilities and innovativeness of host country firms (Simona & Axèle, 2012). This suggests that Chinese presence would bring potential transfer of technological knowledge to the host countries in Africa. Governments play an important role in technological development by establishing an environment that stimulates firms and specialised technological agents to engage in technological efforts (Dahlman, Ross-Larson, & Westphal, 1987).

Whilst some studies found that firms in sectors with a relatively high MNE presence tend to experience better productivity increase via technology and knowledge transfer (Kokko, Tansini, & Zejan, 1997), other studies indicate that host country firms do worse with increasing foreign presence in a given industry sector (Aitken & Harrison, 1999). Since foreign presence does not guarantee technology transfer, the presence of Chinese firms could improve the capability of African firms or make them worse. Resource constraints, *inter alia*, make technological development challenging for developing countries (Dahlman et al., 1987) and technologies from the North may not always be appropriate for the developing South, but technologies developed in comparable labour-rich emerging economies could be more appropriate (Fu, Pietrobelli, & Soete, 2011).

This supports the argument that there is a higher potential for technology transfer from China to Africa compared to what would accrue from the countries in the Global North.

Technical and managerial expertise is expected from the Chinese because they are considered more advanced in technological processes than their African counterparts (Jackson, 2012). Such expectation could be achieved if African partners take deliberate initiatives to harness burgeoning Chinese capabilities. China's share of global manufacturing value-added, for example, has increased considerably because of extensive innovative and technological capabilities built over the last few decades (Kaplinsky, 2013). They have also learned a lot from foreign firms since catching up technologically, *inter alia*, occurs through 'learning by doing', 'learning by adaptation' and 'learning by capacity expansion' (Bell, 2007). In addition, China's share of global R&D has been increasing steadily (Bruche, 2009). These acquired capabilities could be passed on through the trade and investment relationships with African countries.

As China is progressing quickly from a developing country towards a developed one, Africa can learn a lot from China's experiences. As cited earlier, Fu et al. (2011) argued that the technologies developed in labour-rich emerging economies such as China would be more appropriate to the factor endowment mix in the developing world in Africa. This suggests that for some developing countries, South–South technology and knowledge transfers may be more effective. China's technological progress is spurred by demand from low-income consumers and lower labour costs with poor or less sophisticated infrastructure, thus making China a source of appropriate technology suitable for low-income countries (Kaplinsky, 2013) in Africa. Arguably, potential technology and knowledge transfer from China should be higher than what would be expected from the advanced West.

Absorptive capacity and competitive deployment of international technology depends on an adequate supply of engineering and managerial skills, making host country education and training policies important (Hoekman, Maskus, & Saggi, 2005; Osabutey & Debrah, 2012). Africa's capacity to produce engineering skills through educational effectiveness is lacking (Osabutey & Jin, 2016), but cooperation with China could support the development of required engineering and technological skills. This could be achieved if the notable increase in African citizens attending Chinese universities (Kim, 2013) is structured to fill the technological skills gaps. Since potential synergies between African and Chinese values present opportunities for Sino-African knowledge sharing (Jackson, 2014), it is likely for more technology transfer to occur through interactions between China and Africa, not only at the political and business levels but also with respect to education and training.

There have been increasing collaborative engagements between China and Africa with respect to agricultural technology transfer and development. For example, Tugendhat and Alemu (2016) discuss Chinese training courses for African officials and observe that the overall impact on African agricultural development is limited. They contend that the training programmes are often fragmented and are aimed more at development cooperation that achieves more policy influence for China. Xu, Li, Qi, Tang, and Mukwereza (2016) also evaluated agricultural technology demonstration centres as an alternative model of Chinese foreign aid to African countries and discerned that the demonstration centres could be used as important avenues for negotiations over knowledge and politics. They stressed the need for an integrated link between aid, investment and development. But Gu, Chuanhong, Vaz, and Mukwereza (2016) note that China's engagement with Africa with respect to agriculture, and more generally, involves a multiplicity of agencies, often with contrasting goals, operating with different structures and at different levels. They note that state and business interaction is fragmented from both the Chinese and African organisations and this adds more complexity to the China–Africa engagement on an important sector such as agriculture.

It is no wonder that such South–South cooperation often fails to achieve grand set objectives (Amanor & Chichava, 2016). Even though such programmes have huge potential to pass on technological and innovative capabilities, the fragmented nature of the initiatives often leads to poorer results. Institutional and regulatory inadequacies on the African side also mean expected outcomes are not achieved. Despite this trend of lost technology transfer opportunities, the African side has rarely been seen expressing related disappointments because, perhaps, such benefits have not been a priority. None of the studies have shown an initiative that has been designed and driven from the African side. In order to achieve benefits to both sides, such programmes need an active involvement from both sides. There is no evident initiative or study that demonstrates measurable and desirable outcomes over a given period. The literature lacks measured, timed objectives and outcomes of initiatives resulting from the relationship. Africa needs to set up institutions that can monitor development objectives achieved as a result of China–Africa relations.

Chinese investments in Africa and the potential symbiotic benefits

There is a growing body of literature that suggests that China's presence in Africa is characterised by a selection or combination of resource-seeking, market-seeking and political-seeking motivations (Gill & Reilly, 2007; Wang, 2010). Ramasamy, Yeung, and Laforet (2012) affirm that some of the location motivations among state-owned Chinese firms are inconsistent with existing theories. For example, the existing international business literature has the tendency to view undemocratic countries nega-tively in terms of long-term investments, because they are characterised by weak institutions which are unable to offer required legitimacy and rights (Globerman & Shapiro, 2002). But Ramasamy et al. (2012) rightly observe that the majority of Chinese investments are from state-owned enterprises which are less susceptible to contract failures because of more reliance on government–government relationships. However, Gu (2009) observed that more private entities from China are operating in Africa because of the market potential. Adem (2010) argues that the impact of Sino-African relations may be viewed along a spectrum from optimism to pessimism and suggests that although China, a stronger partner, would benefit more, Africa could also benefit through policies that incorporate a sense of foresightedness. Various studies have evaluated the social, trade, competitive and unemployment effects (Adisu et al., 2010; Alden, 2005; Ashnan, 2007; Kaplinsky, McCormick, & Morris, 2007). Even though most cases appear to show a disadvantaged Africa, studies leading to policy implications and prescriptions are scarce.

There is also an emerging literature that suggests that Chinese invest-ments can also be beneficial to private firms and economies in Africa (Maswana, 2009; Shen, 2013). The increasing dependence of Africa on investments from China also presents potential opportunities and threats. Bandara (2012) observes that FDI from China impacts on growth in Africa and that export to China from Africa influences economic growth in countries with more Chinese FDI. Drummond and Liu (2013) note that an increase in China's domestic investment growth is associated with an equivalent increase export growth from Africa. As expected, the impact is more significant for resource-rich countries. They note that whilst Africans diversify more trade towards China and reduce trading with advanced economies, the phenomenon is likely to lead to more suscepti-bility of Africa to both positive and negative spillovers from China. Ruch (2013) provided evidence that there were industrial production spillovers from China to South Africa. Busse, Erdogan, and Mühlen (2012) used panel data to find a negative impact on economic growth. Such mixed results could have sector-specific nuances and would vary from one Afri-can country to the other. Some aspects of the benefits also point to an increasing dependence of Africa on Chinese engagement not for develop-ment in particular but for economic survival more generally.

Power relations between partners determine bargaining power. Mohan and Lampert (2012) observe that most analyses of China's recent engage-ment with Africa portray China as the dominant force and give a rela-tively insignificant power and role to African agency. They note that such studies tend to focus on Chinese and African state actors and political relationships (Large, 2009; Alden & Large, 2011; Carmody & Krage-lund, 2016). This often gives China a stronger bargaining power. It also appears that China is thriving more in countries with weak democracies considered unattractive for investments and support from the traditional multilateral agencies as well as western firms and governments. This further weakens the bargaining power of such African countries because they have limited options. Countries, such as Angola and Sudan (Alden, 2007), who are unable to meet stringent requirements from traditional investors and donors rely on China for their development. Nevertheless, African governments can make some efforts to enhance their bargaining power. For example, Mohan and Lampert (2012) show how the Angolan state used state-engineered institutional frameworks to broker Chinese investment projects.

This shows that it is possible for the states in Africa to create institutions specifically geared towards dealing with Chinese investment. Chinese engagements go beyond government–government interactions. (Gu, 2009) and Mohan and Lampert (2012) further argue that, at various levels, African actors have also shaped and driven engagement with Chinese firms and migrants. They noted how social actors have influenced and derived benefits from activities of Chinese migrants in some parts of Africa. African traders in countries such as Ghana and Nigeria have predisposed the interests of Chinese firms.

Increasingly, the existing literature describes two types of beneficiaries; government/political elites and individual entrepreneurs. Whilst this trend is not necessarily bad, more could be done to ensure that the Chinese engagement enhances general development across communities and sectors within countries. A wider stakeholder engagement with the aim of fostering a longer-term development agenda is required.

Bilateral relationships and business interactions between countries or international firms often aim for a win–win outcome. However, outcomes are often expected to be judged along a win–win to a win–lose continuum. Most authors engaged in the narrative related to the China–Africa relations and interaction either portray the outcome as win–win or win–lose. For example, Wu and Cheng (2010); Zhao (2008) and Pratt and Adamolekun (2008) suggest a win–win relationship, whilst McKinnon (2010); Elu and Price (2010); Chemingui and Bchir (2010) point to a win–lose outcome. Conclusions therefore drawn from the existing literature on China's presence in Africa are mixed (Ado & Su, 2016). Some of the conclusions appear too simplistic and do not critically reveal the antecedents and implications. A few authors critically evaluate the mutual or symbiotic benefits by suggesting conditional antecedents within short- or long-term periods. Yin and Vaschetto (2011), for example, suggest a mutually beneficial cooperation, provided Africa has learnt from previous experiences with the West. Others suggest that in the long term Africa will benefit (Morris & Einhorn, 2008) but China gains more even in the long term than Africa would (Ademola, Bankole, & Adewuyi, 2009).

One other interesting suggestion by Gu (2009) was that although Africa potentially gains new technology and knowledge, the African elites, unlike their Chinese counterparts, do not evaluate related long-term objectives. Perhaps the political elite do not consider the short- to long-term possible positive or negative spillovers. Such long-term implications are rather lost to the African parties. A notable observation in the extant literature is that none suggests that there is a potential short- to long-term win–lose situation in favour of Africa. For a sustainable short- to long-term win–win situation, Africa needs to have its own policy towards the cooperation with China (Elu & Price, 2010). China cannot be blamed for Africa not being able to explore or exploit the full benefits of the cooperation. Therefore, in order for Africa to derive maximum benefits from the engagement with China, Africa needs to, at least, be involved to some extent in defining the terms of the relationship. If Africa does not get adept in policymaking then foreigners cannot be blamed for unfavourable outcomes from bilateral or multilateral governmental or business level interactions. The attitude of 'taking what we are given without questions asked' is symptomatic of outcomes that are bound to benefit the party with a policy and strategy.

This emphasises that African countries lack policies and strategies to fully benefit from the relationship. Africa woefully failed with regard to policymaking in the early postcolonial days (Decker, 2011; Manu, 2003). This means that Africa has not learned from mistakes made in terms of experiences with the West. Manu (2003) suggests that African partners lack negotiation skills. Arguably, five decades on such negotiation skills remain elusive to the African political elite. Industrialisation and development require the involvement of the state in shaping and influencing the process (Gunnarsson, 1985). Such processes require good negotiation and policymaking skills. Observed weaknesses among the political elite in this respect constrain host country development and independence. Therefore, involving African political elites in the process of internationalisation has rather reinforced politically and economically dependent relationships (Carmody & Kragelund, 2016). Since Amsden (2003) suggests that when foreign capital becomes more important in a country's growth, dependency tends to increase, it is important to evaluate Africa's dependence on Chinese capital. This should give an opportunity to explore China–Africa opportunities against that backdrop of exploitation, development and dependency. Even though Alden (2007) and Taylor (2010) call for a focus on the African state when analysing the impact of China in Africa: Placing the political elite in Africa alone in charge of setting the development agenda may not work (Carmody & Kragelund, 2016).

Emerging literature and a new research framework

As indicated earlier, the majority of studies focus on data from government departments from China and Africa (Yin, 2009; Mohan &

Lampert, 2012; Ado & Su, 2016) even though, as suggested by Gu (2009), there are a considerable number of private Chinese firms operating in Africa. Mohan and Lampert (2012) observe that even those studies that attempt to interrogate bilateral issues often end up focusing on the state elite. Such state level analyses often miss nuances that could lead to a more detailed understanding of the impact of the Chinese presence. More research is required to improve our understanding of the implications of Chinese firms in Africa on international business, management practices and economic development. Perhaps more analyses from institutions or firms at all levels could instigate better policymaking. On the existing literature, anecdotal evidence also suggests that the majority of authors of Chinese origin argue that the relationship is largely symbiotic and see more win–win than win–lose outcomes. Authors of non-Chinese and non-African descent have perspectives where the win–lose outcomes outweigh the win–win. But the African authors, who are generally in the minority, even see the win–lose situation to a larger extent.

This discursive trend was also observed by Ojo (2016). This phenomenon may not be deliberate but could be the result of data that researchers are able to access. In addition, whilst Chinese state and public institutions have published numerous policy documents on China's relationship with Africa, African institutions have done relatively less. With the limited participation of the African stakeholder (including academics and researchers) in the telling of the 'African Story', how can lessons be learned? How can Africa improve its policymaking more generally with respect to dealing with foreign investors? There is the need for more stakeholder involvement in research on the China–Africa relations to evaluate short- and long-term symbiotic benefits. More involvement of African stakeholders could enhance our understanding of the potential benefits. This has some relevance on stakeholders ensuring that research outputs are not a reflection of origins and inadvertent biases of the authors but a demonstration of a deeper stakeholder participation in generating and reporting the 'African story'.

There are reported difficulties in conducting China–Africa research. Shen (2015) clearly outlined the challenges involved in gathering official data and conducting interviews at the firm level on Chinese investments in Africa in both China and Africa. For example, he noted that FDI data from the Ministry of Commerce in China were generally lower than data from investment promotion agencies in the host countries. Whilst official data from the Chinese side may have some limitations, the data from the African side is generally uneven and poor. The challenge to collect firm-level data on both sides is extremely difficult. On the issue, Ado and Su (2016) note that Chinese businesses in both their home and host countries are reluctant to provide accurate primary and secondary data about their activities to researchers. Collaborative research by Chinese and Africans may help if the parties have good networks in their respective countries. This could ensure the collection of good and accurate contextual data.

Although Shen (2015) observed that it was easier for a Chinese researcher to get information from Chinese firms, he also acknowledges that such data generally lacks perspectives from African stakeholders. Arguably, in much the same way, African researchers would also find it difficult to obtain data from Chinese firms in the host countries and perhaps more so in China. Moreover, collaborative research efforts are likely to enhance the quality of data and analyses when a research team is made up of individuals who understand the institutional and cultural settings. Since institutions govern politics, regulatory, social-cultural and economic activities (Peng, Wang, & Jiang, 2008) and establish the basis for firm activities (North, 1990). Understanding institutional and cultural underpinning is crucial for generating good research outputs. Given that the extant literature suggests that developing economies are generally characterised by weak institutions (Khanna & Palepu, 1999, 2006), the interpretation of secondary and primary data as well as the related results should be interpreted with an in-depth understanding of the institutional and cultural arrangements. This means that 'outsiders' may wrongly interpret research data and results. Research on the 'China in Africa' story needs to be more comprehensive but contextual. To achieve that, this chapter proposes that for developing countries such as China and Africa, where institutions may be weak and markedly different from those in developed countries, data and results require more critical contextual analyses to produce accurate and relevant research outcomes.

Researchers need to have a good understanding of both their research subjects and audience for the research outputs to reflect the contexts more succinctly so as to be acceptable to all stakeholders. This chapter proposes the international research communication framework represented by Figure 3.1.

Figure 3.1 attempts to integrate the dynamic interactions between research subjects (empirical focus), research data and results, and research outputs (with the research audience in mind). A good synthesis of issues occurring at organisational and community levels requires local knowledge and in-depth understanding. The interactions between the various elements of the framework occur within institutional and cultural settings and could be influenced by the researchers' own personal biases stemming from origins and social programming. This means that the researchers' role in eliciting policies that could enhance potential symbiotic Sino-African relations must be founded on research outcomes and communications void of biases that do not adequately incorporate cultural and institutional dynamics.

Figure 3.1 suggests that researchers on Africa, for example, have not adequately contextualised findings to reflect the unique research context. The meaningful way to pursue research on Africa is to ensure that the

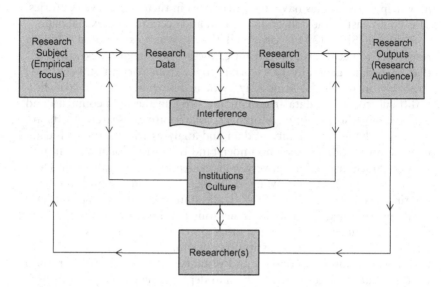

Figure 3.1 International research communication framework

researcher(s) understand both the research subjects and the audience. For example, in our review of the literature in this chapter, the origins and connections of researchers, inadvertently, influence the research data, results and narrative. This could possibly be owing to each group of researchers viewing the research data and results through different cultural and institutional lenses. A'Zami (2014) stressed the importance of culture in understanding the 'China in Africa' phenomenon. It is important to evaluate how researchers can ensure that a good understanding of the institutional and cultural underpinnings reflect on the data and results, as well as how the outputs are communicated to both the audience and subjects. Research findings can only be useful when they are relevant to the subjects for host country policymaking and indeed for the audience, which includes bilateral and multilateral organisations that are also involved in policymaking. This could suggest that policies may fail to work if they are derived from research without active stakeholder involvement and clearer institutional and cultural understanding.

Whether researchers collaborate with stakeholders or not, there should be a tried and tested method that ensures the story is told without the 'interference' or 'noise' resulting from cultural and institutional misinterpretation or misrepresentation (Mohan & Lampert, 2012; Ado & Su, 2016). Indeed, the challenge is for researchers to understand all stakeholders. Good research, when fed back to the research subjects, must make sense (see Figure 3.1). Unfortunately, African stakeholders such as institutions, scholars, researchers and policymakers have not actively participated in research that would enhance understanding and also create the opportunity for evidence-based policymaking.

One other aspect of the 'China in Africa' story is that there appears to be more engagement with the policymakers in China than in Africa. This could be because, as seen earlier, the African side has yet to actively engage in 'China in Africa' policymaking. Research that engages with policymakers in Africa in particular could stimulate this evidence-based policymaking that the continent lacks and needs urgently. Assuming that the policymakers in Africa have the required skill set, the challenge to researchers and academics is to produce research outputs that could provoke African policymakers, not only to understand that policy matters, but to equip them with the necessary tools for making evidence-based policies. This re-echoes the suggestion by Osabutey and Debrah (2012) that the reason why Africa is not doing well with gaining the full benefit from the presence of foreign firms is because of policy lacunae. If it becomes clear, however, that Africa lacks the requisite depth and breadth of policymaking skills then deliberate efforts to train a new brand of policymakers and negotiators should be viewed as critical to realising the full potential benefits from foreign investors. But good policymaking requires good research evidence.

Conclusion

The chapter has pulled together relevant existing literature on the China–Africa interactions at both the political and economic levels, seeking an intersection between international business and host country development. The chapter notes the need for more research that focuses on actors at the organisational and community levels. The broad spectrum of aid, trade, FDI and development has been explored. The trade and policy frameworks are defined and dictated from China, suggesting that like Africa's relationship with the West, the China–Africa relationship is defined with less involvement of the African partners. The literature suggests that the Chinese presence could influence technology transfer, capacity building and economic growth potential in Africa.

The empirical evidence points to a mixture of positive and negative short- to long-term outcomes for the Africans from China–Africa interactions. These outcomes range from a win–win to a win–lose situation with Africa, arguably, being disadvantaged in the long run. The relationship is not deemed to be symbiotic and research outputs, which do not adequately focus on local organisations and communities, lack adequate stakeholder involvement to provide the evidence to support symbiotic policymaking. Africa needs its own strategic policy initiatives to derive technology transfer, capacity building and economic development from this potential South–South cooperation. Perhaps each country should set its own objectives within the context of its existing cultural and institutional arrangements and development agenda. The few success stories that portray short- and long-term benefits in some African countries can be adapted and improved. If Africa is to harness short- and long-term benefits from the engagement, whilst at the same time reducing dependency, its policymakers need to support their governments to undertake more symbiotic development agendas. More research at the organisational and community levels are also required.

Africa, apparently, does not know, has not learned and has failed to develop the capacity and capability to develop policies that enhance the benefits from the presence of foreign firms; so, inadvertently, it fails to explore or exploit, satisfactorily, the potential symbiotic relationship with China. Africa's political elite, on the one hand, may be naïve, myopic or selfish and have lacked foresightedness. They have also lacked requisite negotiation skills with regard to dealing with foreign investors. Africa's institutions, scholars, researchers and policymakers, on the other hand, are not also positioned to develop requisite policies. So, the rhetoric on 'China in Africa' is underexplored, under-researched and clearly misunderstood. Africa must come to grips with policymaking within the context of complex interactions between diplomacy, international business and development. This agrees with the assertion by Carmody and Kragelund (2016) that African countries ought to be able to adopt a strategy that integrates trade, aid, financing and development.

This chapter contributes to the literature by highlighting potential long-term benefits that could be achieved through evidence-based policymaking. Such policies must be developed from research that does not neglect actors at the organisational and community levels. In addition, there is the need for China–Africa policies that are developed and driven from active participation from the African side. Our unique international research communication framework contributes to a need to interrogate research outputs that may not be built on a deeper understanding of institutional and cultural settings. Another worthy contribution of this Chapter is that we emphasise that symbiotic policymaking would require involvement from stakeholders from both China and Africa. Such policies need to be derived from research evidence also generated with the involvement of researchers from both China and Africa. Joint research that involves Chinese and African universities and institutions working with other institutions around the world are necessary. Research that can unearth how poor policymaking in Africa could be improved to augment benefits from dealing with international organisations is urgent. Research outputs with increased African stakeholder involvement are required to help create a culture of evidence-based policymaking. The implications are that researchers need to be interested in conducting studies at the interface between 'International Business' and 'Development'. Studies that show the development of African companies and countries as a result of the presence of foreign entities over a given period are needed. More impact assessment studies are required to allow the replication of success stories. African countries should understand that it is not the responsibility of foreign governments to ensure that Africa benefits fully from bilateral relations or transactions. It is high time Africa learned how to do as China has done from its strategic engagement with more advanced economies.

Acknowledgement

The preliminary version of this chapter was presented at the 3rd Annual Conference of the Academy of International Business (Sub-Saharan Africa Chapter) in 2016.

References

Adem, S. (2010). The paradox of China's policy in Africa. *Africa and Asian Studies*, *9*, 334–355.

Ademola, O., Bankole, A., & Adewuyi, A. (2009). China-Africa trade relations: Insights from AERC scoping studies. *European Journal of Development Research*, *21*(4), 485–505.

Adisu, K., Sharkey, T., & Okoroafo, S. C. (2010). The impact of Chinese investment in Africa. *International Journal of Business and Management*, *5*(9), 3–9.

Ado, A., & Su, Z. (2016). China in Africa: A critical literature review. *Critical Perspectives on International Business*, *12*(1), 40–60.

Aitken, B. J., & Harrison, A. E. (1999). Do domestic firms benefit from direct foreign investment? Evidence from Venezuela. *American Economic Review*, *89*(3), 605–618.

Alden, C. (2005). China and Africa. *Survival*, *47*(3), 147–164.

Alden, C. (2007). *China in Africa*. London: Zed Books.

Alden, C., & Alves, C. (2008). History and identity in the construction of China's Africa policy. *Review of African Political Economy*, *35*(115), 43–58.

Alden, C., & Large, D. (2011). China's exceptionalism and the challenge of delivering differences in Africa. *Journal of Contemporary China*, *20*(68), 21–38.

Amanor, K. S., & Chichava, S. (2016). South-South cooperation, agribusiness, and African agricultural development: Brazil and China in Ghana and Mozambique. *World Development*, *81*, 13–23.

Amsden, A. H. (2003). Comment: Good-bye depency theory, hello depency theory. *Studies of Comparative International Development*, *38*(1), 32–38.

Ashnan, L. (2007). China and Africa: Policy and challenges. *China Security*, *3*(3), 69–93.

A'Zami, D. (2014). "China in Africa": From unders-researched to under-theorised? *Millenieum: Journal of International Studies*, *43*(2), 724–734.

Bandara, A. (2012). *Growth spillovers: Do China's trade and investment matter for African growth?* Tanzania: United Nations Development Programme. Retrieved July 7, 2016 from www.undp.org/content/dam/tanzania/Growth Spillovers.pdf

Bell, R. M. (2007). *Technological learning and the development of productive and innovative capacitgies in the industry and infrastructure sectors of least development countries: What roles of ODA?* Paper prepared for UNCTAD Division of Africa, Least Developed Countries and Special Programmes, SPRU-Science and Technlogy Policy Research, University of Sussex, Brighton.

Bruche, G. (2009). A new geography of innovation: China and India rising. *Columbia FDI Perspectives No 4*, 29 April. New York: Vale Columbia Centre. Retrieved from www.vcc.columbia.edu/content/new-geography-innovation-china-and-india-rising

Busse, M., Erdogan, C., & Mühlen, H. (2012). *China's impact on Africa – The role of trade and FDI.* Retrieved July 7, 2016 from www.etsg.org/ETSG2014/Papers/319.pdf

Carmody, P. (2009). An Asian-driven economic recovery in Africa? The Zambian case. *World Development, 37*(7), 1197–1207.

Carmody, P., & Kragelund, P. (2016). Who is in charge? State power and agency in Sino-African relations. *Cornell International Law Journal, 49*(1), 1–23.

Chemingui, M., & Bchir, M. (2010). The future of African trade with China under alternative trade liberalisation schemes. *African Development Review, 22*(SI), 562–576.

Cheung, Y.-W., de Haan, J., Qian, X. W., & Yu, S. (2014). The missing link: China's contracted engineering projects in Africa. *Review of Development Economics, 18*(3), 564–580.

Cook, F. L. (2014). Chinese multinational firms in Asia and Africa: Relationships with institutional actors and patteerns of HRM practices. *Human Resource Management, 53*(6), 877–896.

Dahlman, C. J., Ross-Larson, B., & Westphal, L. E. (1987). Managing technological development: Lessons from the newly industrialised countries. *World Development, 15*(6), 759–775.

Davies, M., Draper, P., & Edinger, H. (2014). Changing China, changing Africa: Future contours of an emerging relationship. *Asian Economic Policy Review, 9*, 180–197.

Davies, M., Edinger, H., Tay, N., & Naidu, S. (2008). *How China delivers development assistance to Africa: A research undertaking by the centre for Chinese studies.* Prepared for the Department of International Develolopment (DFID). Centre for Chinese Studies, University of Stellenbosch, Beijing.

Decker, S. (2011). Corporate political activity in less developed countries: The Volta River Project in Ghana, 1958–66. *Business History, 53*(7), 993–1017.

Dreher, A., & Fuchs, A. (2011). *Rogue aid? The determinants of China's aid allocation (September 22, 2011).* CESifo Working Paper Series No. 3581. Retrieved from SSRN: https://ssrn.com/abstract=1932086Drummond, P., & Liu, E. (2013). *Africa's rising exposure to China: How large are spillovers through trade?* IMF Working Paper WP/13/250. Washington, DC: International Monetary Fund.

Elu, J., & Price, G. (2010). Does China transfer productivity enhancing technology to Sub-Saharan Africa? Evidence from manufacturing firms. *African Development Review, 22*(SI), 587–598.

Forster, V., Butterfield, W., Chen, C., & Pushak, N. (2009). *Building bridges: China's growing role as infrastructure financier for Sub-Saharan Africa.* Washington, DC: World Bank.

Fu, X., Pietrobelli, C., & Soete, L. (2011). The role of foreign technology and indigenous innovation in the emerging economies: Technological change and catching-up. *World Development, 39*(7), 1204–1212.

Gill, B., & Reilly, J. (2007). The tenuous hold of China Inc. in Africa. *The Washington Quarterly, 30*(3), 37–52.

Globerman, S., & Shapiro, D. (2002). Global foreign direct investment flows: The role of government infrastructure. *World Development, 30*(11), 1899–1919.

Gu, J. (2009). China's private enterprises in Africa and the implications for African development. *European Journal of Development Research, 21*(4), 570–587.

Gu, J., Chuanhong, Z., Vaz, A., & Mukwereza, L. (2016). Chinese state capitalism? Rethinking the role of the state and business in Chinese development coperation in Africa. *World Development, 81*, 24–34.

Gunnarsson, C. (1985). Development theory and third world industrialisation. *Journal of Contemporary Asia, 15*(2), 183–206.

Hess, S., & Aidoo, R. (2014). Charting the roots of anti-Chineses populism in Africa: A comparison of Zambia and Ghana. *Journal of Asian and African Studies, 49*(2), 129–147.

Hoekman, B. M., Maskus, K. E., & Saggi, K. (2005). Transfer of technology to developing countries: Unilateral and multilateral policy options. *World Development, 33*(10), 1587–1602.

Jackson, T. (2012). Postcolonialism and organisational knowledge in the wake of China's presence in Africa: Interrogating South-south relations. *Organisation, 19*(2), 181–204.

Jackson, T. (2014). Employment in Chinese MNES: Appraising the Dragon's gift to Sub-Saharan Africa. *Human Resource Management, 53*(6), 897–919.

Jackson, T., Louw, L., & Zhao, S. (2013). China in sub-Saharan Africa: Implications for HRM policy and practice at organisational level. *The International Journal of Human Resource Management, 24*(13), 2512–2533.

Jenkins, R., & Edwards, C. (2006). The economic impact of China and India on Sub-Sahran Africa: Trends and prospects. *Journal of Asian Economics, 17*, 207–225.

Kaplinsky, R. (2008). What does the rise of China do for the industrialisation in Sub-Saharan Africa? *Review of African Political Economy, 115*, 7–22.

Kaplinsky, R. (2013). What contribution can China make to inclusive growth in Sub-Saharan Africa. *Development and Change, 44*(6), 1295–1316.

Kaplinsky, R., McCormick, D., & Morris, M. (2007). *The impact of China on sub-Saharan Africa*, Working Paper 291, Institute of Development Studies.

Kaplinsky, R., & Morris, M. (2009). Chinese FDI in Sub-Saharan Africa: Engaging with large dragons. *European Journal of Development Research, 21*(4), 551–569.

Khanna, T., & Palepu, K. G. (1999). Policy shocks, market intermediaries, and corporate strategy: The evolution of business groups in Chile and India. *Journal of Economics and Management Strategy, 8*, 271–310.

Khanna, T., & Palepu, K. G. (2006). Emerging giants: Building world-class companies in developing countries. *Harvard Business Review, 84*(10), 60–70.

Kim, Y. (2013). *Chinese-led SEZs in Africa: Are they a driving force of China's soft power?* Discussion Paper No. 1, Centre for Chinese Studies, University of Stellenbosch.

72   *Ellis L.C. Osabutey et al.*

Kokko, A., Tansini, R., & Zejan, M. (1997). *Trade regimes and spillover effects of FDI: Evidence from Uruguay* (Manuscript). Stockholm School of Economics, Stockholm.

Large, D. (2009). China's Sudan engagement: Changing northern and southern political trajectories in peace and war. *The China Quarterly, 199,* 610–626.

López, R. A. (2008). Foreign technology licensing, productivity, and spillovers. *World Development, 36*(4), 560–574.

Lumumba-Kasongo, T. (2011). China-Africa relations: A neo-imperialism or a neo-colonialism? A reflection. *African and Asian Studies, 10,* 234–266.

Manu, F. (2003). Negotiating with foreign investors. *Journal of African Business, 4*(1), 5–35.

Maswana, J. (2009). Can China trigger economic growth in Africa? *Chinese Economy, 42*(2), 91–105.

McCormick, D. (2008). China and India as Africa's new donors: The impact of aid on development. *Review of African Political Economy, 35*(115), 73–92.

McKinnon, R. I. (2010). China in Africa: The Washington concensus versus the Beijing concensus. *International Finance, 13*(3), 495–506.

Mohan, G., & Lampert, B. (2012). Negotiating China: Reinserting African agency into China-Africa relations. *African Affairs, 112*(446), 92–110.

Morris, M., & Einhorn, G. (2008). Globalisation, welfare and competitiveness: the impacts of Chinese imports on the South African clothing and textile industry. *Competition and Change, 22*(4), 355–376.

Naidu, S., & Mbazima, D. (2008). China-African relations: A new impulse in a changing continental landscape. *Futures, 40,* 748–761.

North, D. C. (1990). *Institutions, institutional change, and economic performance.* Cambridge: Cambridge University Press.

Ojo, T. (2016). Framing of the Sino-Africa relationship in diasporic/pan-African news magazines. *Chinese Journal of Communication, 9*(1), 38–55.

Osabutey, E. L. C., & Debrah, A. Y. (2012). Foreign direct investment and technology transfer policies in Africa: A review of the ghanaian experience. *Thunderbird International Business Reveiw, 54*(4), 441–456.

Osabutey, E. L. C., & Jin, Z. (2016). Factors influencing technology and knowledge transfer: Configurational recipes for Africa. *Journal of Business Research, 69,* 5390–5395.

Osabutey, E. L. C., Williams, K., & Debrah, A. Y. (2014). The potential for technology and knowledge transfers between foreign and local firms: A study of the construction industry in Ghana. *Journal of World Business, 49*(4), 560–571.

Peng, M. W., Wang, D. Y. L., & Jiang, Y. (2008). An institution based view of international business strategy: A focus on emerging economies. *Journal of International Business Studies, 39,* 920–936.

Pratt, C., & Adamolekun, W. (2008). The People's Republic of China and FAPRA: Calalyst for theory building in Africa's public relations. *Journal of Public Relations Research, 20*(1), 20–48.

Ramasamy, B., Yeung, M., & Laforet, S. (2012). China's outward foreign direct investment: Location choice and firm ownership. *Journal of World Business, 47,* 17–25.

Ruch, F. (2013). The impact of international spillovers on the South African Economy. *South African reserve bank working paper,* May.

Schech, S., & Haggis, J. (2000). *Culture and development: A critical introduction.* Oxford: Blackwell.

Shen, X. (2013). How the private sector is changing Chinese investment in Africa. *Columbia FDI perspectives,* No 93, 15 April.

Shen, X. (2015). Private Chinese investment in Africa: Myths and realities. *Development Policy Review, 33*(1), 83–106.

Simona, G.-L., & Axèle, G. (2012). Knowledge transfer from TNCs and upgraading of domestic firms: The Polish autotmotive sector. *World Development, 40*(4), 796–807.

Sun, Y. (2014). *Africa in China's foreign policy.* John L. Thornton Centre China Centre and Africa Growth Initiative Brookings. Retrieved July 7, 2016 from www.brookings.edu/~/media/Research/Files/Papers/2014/04/africa%20china%20policy%20sun/Africa%20in%20China%20web_CMG7.pdf

Taylor, I. (2010). *The international relations of sub-Saharan Africa.* London: Continuum.

Tugendhat, H., & Alemu, D. (2016). Chinese agricultural training courses for African officials: Between power and partnerships. *World Development, 81,* 71–81.

Tull, D. M. (2006). Chinese engagement in Africa: Scope, significance and consequence. *Journal of Modern African Studies, 44*(3), 459–479.

Wang, M. (2010). Empirical study on African energy resources and China's outflow of foreign direct investment 2002–2007. *International Journal of Business Research, 10*(6), 195–201.

Wu, Z., & Cheng, E. (2010). Poverty alleviation in the People's Republic of China: The implications for Sino-African cooperation in poverty reduction. *African Development Review, 22,* 629–643.

Xu, X., Li, X., Qi, G., Tang, L., & Mukwereza, L. (2016). Science, technology, and the politics of knowledge: The case of China's agricultural technology demonstration centers in Africa. *World Development, 81,* 82–91.

Yin, J., & Vaschetto, S. (2011). China's business engagement in Africa. *Chinese Economy, 44*(2), 43–57.

Yin, R. K. (2009). *Case study research: Design and methods* (4th ed.). Washington, DC: Sage.

Zafar, A. (2007). The growing relationship between China and Sub-Saharan Africa: macroeconomic, trade, investment, and aid links. *The World Bank Research Observer, 22*(1), 103–130.

Zhao, H. (2008). China-US oil rivalry in Africa. *Copenhagen Journal of Asian Studies, 26*(2), 97–119.

4 International human resource management strategies of Chinese firms in Africa

Chengcheng Miao

China has become the largest investor in Africa in terms of foreign direct investment (FDI) flow (Panitchpakdi, 2010), with its investment crowding out that of Africa's traditional partners, such as the USA and Germany (Donou-Adonsou & Lim, 2018). Over the past decade, the China-Africa Development Fund has encouraged into Africa many enterprises in agriculture, manufacturing, mining, infrastructure and industrial parks (Finance.sina.com.cn, 2017). China's FDI in Africa increased from US$7.48 million in 2003 to US$2.112 million in 2010 (Xu, 2014). According to Gill, Huang, and Morrison (2007, p. 9), 'China needs Africa': for resources to achieve its development goal, for markets to sustain its fast-growing economy, and for political alliances to support its ambition to be influential globally.

China's involvement with Africa dates back to the 1950s when China tried to win recognition in the international arena by supporting African countries as an element of its government aids projects (Mlambo, Kushamba, & Simawu, 2016). From the mid-1990s, large state-owned enterprises (SOEs) and private companies started entering the manufacturing sector in Africa, involving resource-based and infrastructure investments (Gu, 2009). The Sino-Africa relationship had a breakthrough in 2000, after the first Tri-annual Forum on China-Africa Cooperation, a Ministerial Conference that was held in Beijing, and this led on to the first declaration of China's African Policy (Ministry of Foreign Affairs of the People's Republic of China, 2015). Almost ten years later, a new edition was published in 2016 to enhance Sino-Africa cooperation (Ministry of Foreign Affairs of the People's Republic of China, 2015). It is believed that the Belt and Road Initiatives (Finance.sina.com.cn, 2017) announced in 2015 will continue to encourage cooperation between China and Africa. Understanding these historical ties between China and Africa helps us draw a clear and complete picture of why China invests in Africa, which we will argue is closely related to management strategies and practices.

China's increasing presence in Africa has aroused intense debates about its motivations and its impacts, particularly on the host countries. Does China harbour colonial ambitions (Jauch, 2011) or is it a win–win cooperation (Morris & Einhorn, 2008)? Does China's FDI have a positive effect on standards of living in Africa (Donou-Adonsou & Lim, 2018) or has it done too little to increase local employment (Adisu, Sharkey, & Okoroafo, 2016)?

Even though there are controversial issues about China's investment in Africa, it is undeniable that China has become an important player in Africa, economically and socially. Chinese outward FDI, in general, has attracted great attention in academia (Kaplinsky & Morris, 2009; Kolstad & Wiig, 2012; Ramasamy, Yeung, & Laforet, 2012). However, international business (IB) journals seem to have shown little interest in China in Africa (Ado & Su, 2016). In contrast, a substantial number of works on this topic can be found in development-related journals (e.g. *The European Journal of Development Research*, *African Development Review*). On the other hand, with the growing influence of China as a key player in outward FDI, academics have begun to show increasing interest in topics related to international human resource management (IHRM) in Chinese multinationals. However, most of these studies link IHRM in Chinese multinational enterprises (MNEs) to comparisons based on the WEIRD (western, educated, industrialised, rich, developed) countries (Henrich, Heine, & Norenzayan, 2010), and even to Anglophone countries: the UK (Fu, Sun, & Ghauri, 2018; Khan, Wood, Tarba, & Rao-Nicholson, 2018; Shen & Edwards, 2004; Shen, Edwards, & Lee, 2005; Zheng & Smith, 2018), Australia (Fan, Zhang, & Zhu, 2013; Zhang & Fan, 2014; Zhu, 2018) and the USA (Peng et al., 2017). Thus, there is a significant gap in the literature, as little is known about Chinese MNEs and their HRM policies and practices in developing countries. China's presence in Africa is still an underexplored area, which remains full of mysteries. Among a limited number of studies, attention has been drawn to approaches to international staffing (Cooke et al., 2018), knowledge transfer and reverse knowledge transfer (Peng et al., 2017), and management of both expatriates and local employees (Cooke, 2012; Wood et al., 2014) and we summarise and develop thinking in this controversial area by setting it within a framework of Chinese investors' international business strategies in Africa.

This chapter takes the following form: we start with Chinese FDI and its purpose and effect in Africa, arguing that strategic motives and types of companies (ownerships) might affect how Chinese companies manage their employees in subsidiaries. Then we examine their IHRM policies and subsequently narrow our focus to examine expatriation. Finally, we summarise what we know so far and suggest potential research trajectories.

Chinese FDI

The strategic motives of Chinese FDI

Location advantages in host countries attract MNEs to engage in FDI (Verbeke, 2013). There is a common perception that rich natural resources such as oil and other minerals are the main driving forces for FDI in Africa (Asiedu, 2006). China has experienced three decades of economic growth and the expected growth in the future indicates an increasing demand for natural resources (Davies, 2009). Data from 2003 to 2007 also show that the resources-seeking motive of Chinese FDI in Africa is quite distinct, with statistical significance in energy and mineral output variables (Cheung, de Haan, Qian, & Yu, 2012). Ramasamy et al. (2012) explained that since 2009, China has become the largest market for passenger cars, which means oil and energy are urgently required for the development of the industry. By studying the correlation of Chinese FDI flows and natural resources investment, Wood and his colleagues (2014) found that Chinese MNEs invest in Africa in order to secure access to natural resources to meet domestic Chinese demands. It is interesting to note that China is a latecomer in the resource-extractive industries in Africa compared to western investors. One interpretation from Cheung and his colleagues (2012) is that China is trying to catch up with other foreign investors in the resources extraction sector in Africa.

Africa is endowed with rich natural resources, but it is a continent with uncertainties and risks. One question that has frequently been asked by scholars is why China holds a perverse attitude to risk (Buckley et al., 2007). Even though Cheung and Qian (2009) found Chinese investment is not affected by risk characteristics, Ramasamy and his colleagues (2012) argued that Chinese FDI seems to be attracted to countries which are politically risky or have a weak political system. Some scholars argue that MNEs from emerging markets might have competitive advantages over western companies in African markets.

Corruption has been argued to have a negative influence on FDI (Habib & Zurawicki, 2002). More specifically, corruption might be responsible for the withdrawal of some western companies from countries with weak institutions, as it creates pressure and difficulties (Desai, Foley, & Hines, 2004). According to Khanna and Palepu (2006), MNEs from developing countries might have experienced and survived similar bureaucratic pressures, and they are more experienced and more flexible in dealing with corruption and political constraints (Khanna & Palepu, 2006). Wood and his colleagues' findings support such approaches as they suggest that Chinese MNEs are more competitive in highly corrupt markets and understand that corruption is a double-edged sword that might give the company the chance to buy their way out of some burdensome regulations (Wood et al., 2014). In Cooke and her colleagues' study of Chinese stated-owned mining companies in Africa, interviewees confirmed that in order to build good relationships with local authorities for business development they give them money, place their friends or relatives in management positions, build roads and schools, lend transportation and even bring them gifts (Cooke, Wang, et al., 2015). Local contacts believe it is 'normal' to bribe in the Chinese culture. Another reason, according to Buckley and his colleagues (2007), is that the political connection between China and other developing countries gives Chinese MNEs bargaining powers in those host countries.

But the value of generalisation about Chinese investment being attracted to politically risky countries is inevitably limited because of the overlap of countries which are both corrupt and have natural resources. There are many cases of western MNEs operating in countries with a high level of corruption (Wood et al., 2014). Kolstad and Wiig (2012) argue that weak institutions should be discussed alongside large natural resources when talking about Chinese outward FDI. They criticise the credibility of the data on FDI from Buckley et al. (2007) and Cheung and Qian (2009) as those data only reflect approved investments rather than actual investment. That means those data might be biased; there are believed to be some different characteristics between publicly approved investment and less visible investment. Further, Kolstad and Wiig (2012) argue that Buckley's findings on weak institutions cannot capture reality as the effect is unconditional. Instead, their results indicate that the weaker the institutions are in the host country, the more Chinese investment is attracted by that country's natural resources; conversely, the larger the county's natural resources, the more Chinese investment is attracted to weak institutions. That is to say, weak institutions and large natural resources interactively affect Chinese outward FDI (in non-Organisation for Economic Co-operation and Development countries). But what if it is because China is the latecomer in FDI and only has access to natural resources from poorly governed countries? Kolstad and Wiig (2012) argue that their findings rule out this possibility.

While some scholars believe Chinese firms invest in Africa primarily to get access to natural resources (Frynas & Manuel, 2007), others do not find substantial evidence for that proposition (Cheung & Qian, 2009). An alternative explanation for Chinese FDI, in particular, might be to promote domestic exports – market-seeking (Buckley et al., 2007). Apart from the co-effect of rich resources and weak institutions, another important result suggested by Kolstad and Wiig's (2012) finding is that Chinese FDI is attracted to large markets. China's fast-growing export industry requires new markets beyond the developed economies, and Africa appears to have a huge but undeveloped market with great potential (Cheung et al., 2012). However, Wood's finding suggests that MNEs from emerging markets are less likely to use Africa as an export base and when they target less competitive markets they focus on local market share (Wood et al., 2014). For example, the presence of Chinese telecom giants Huawei and ZTE (Zhongxing Telecommunications Equipment) in Africa follows China's 'go-out' policy to gain local markets as part of their strategy for competing in the global market (Agbebi, 2018). Besides, they found that the local market might not be the only interest of emerging MNEs in Africa, they might also be interested in exporting their African products to other non-Chinese markets.

Some scholars challenge the idea of a single motive for Chinese FDI in Africa. It is believed that multiple motives, multiple strategies and multiple players led China to the continent (Brautigam, 2009). Africa has a huge but undeveloped consumer market combined with rich natural resources, which offers a great complement to China (Xu, 2014). Gill et al. (2007) argue that China is looking for resources to achieve its development goal, for markets to sustain its fast-growing economy and for political alliances to support its ambition to be influential globally. More specifically, investment has been used as a commercial and political channel for the Chinese government to build diplomatic bridges to countries that will benefit other projects that might be in China's national interest (Brautigam & Tang, 2011). This is also why there is a huge debate about the involvement of the Chinese government in FDI in Africa, as it arouses concerns about national security risks for host countries (Deng, 2013).

Companies' strategic motives are important yet easily overlooked when discussing their management policies and practices. We argue that companies with different motives might adopt different HRM strategies. For example, motivation might affect the level of pre-departure training (Jackson & Horwitz, 2018) for expatriates:[1] When a firm is more market-seeking, it is likely that expatriates will need to interact more with local communities and so more pre-departure training may be necessary. Similarly, a politically motivated firm might encourage interaction with local communalities for mutual learning and cooperation, which will also lead to a higher demand for pre-departure training. In contrast, firms who are seeking natural resources might pay less attention to the cross-cultural adjustment of their expatriates as limited interaction with local culture is required.

The characteristics of Chinese FDI in Africa

There are four main characteristics of Chinese investment in Africa (Liu & Ge, 2018). First, China's investment base in the continent is low but is growing rapidly. Especially from 2010 to 2014, the average annual growth rate of China's investment in Africa was 25%, while the growth rate of western countries in the same period was about 10%. Second, various industries are represented. Construction, mining and manufacturing are the major sectors. In terms of the number of firms, up to 2014, China had established 3,031 foreign companies in Africa, of which 1,029 were involved in manufacturing projects (Ministry of Commerce, 2017). However, Gu (2009) argued that those figures might not capture reality. According to a senior Chinese official she interviewed, a lot of private companies do not register with local governments, and this number could be ten times more than the published figure. Third, the proportion of investment in resource-based economies has dropped significantly, and investment in non-resource-based economies has grown more rapidly. This supports the argument that China's investment in Africa does not just focus on natural resource extraction (Liu & Ge, 2018). Fourth, private enterprises have become the mainstay of China's investment in Africa. In 2002, only four out of the 21 Chinese companies investing in Africa counted by the Ministry of Commerce were private companies. In 2013, the proportion of private companies investing in Africa reached 53%. In 2017, according to a survey from the McKinsey Group, of the total Chinese investments in more than 10,000 companies in eight host countries, 90% of them were private companies (Sun, Jayaram, & Kassiri, 2017).

Types of firm ownership

Ownership has been discussed by many scholars trying to understand the nature of Chinese multinational enterprises. The simple dichotomy, SOE versus private firms, does not capture the possible options (Chen, Firth, & Xu, 2009; Gu, 2009; Ramasamy et al., 2012; Wegenast & Schneider, 2017; Xu, 2014). Chen et al. (2009) group China's listed companies into four types by tracing the identity of large shareholders: firms controlled by State Asset Management Bureau, SOEs affiliated to the central government, SOEs affiliated to local government, and private investors.

Ramasamy et al. (2012) merged state asset managed bureaux with SOEs affiliated to local government on the grounds that the former includes FDI by provincial or city governments. Furthermore, Kaplinsky and Morris (2009) argued that nuanced qualifications are required for the terms 'state-owned' and 'private' as the boundary between them is not clear, a unique feature of Chinese economic development. They explain that many 'state-owned enterprises' act as channels for private gain: profits are partially captured by key individuals who are not official owners of the companies. Similarly, the returns and decisions of many apparent 'private' companies reflect the direct decision-making power of national institutions, especially provincial governments. It is noteworthy that in China, 'private' means the state holds less than 50% of the shares. Another reality is that government officials might also have their own companies but in a 'private capacity' (Kaplinsky & Morris, 2009, p. 552). They make use of *guanxi* (关系) connections (Ip, 2009) through their government positions. Nolan uses 'ownership maze' and 'vaguely defined property rights' to explain the characteristics of such a situation (Nolan, 2004, p. 169). This inevitably increases the difficulties for scholars who are not used to such arrangements when studying Chinese enterprises.

Chinese state-owned companies were the pioneers in entering Africa. They are usually larger and enjoy greater support from the central or local government compared to private companies. It is easy to overlook the fact that the 'state' is not a single entity (Xu, 2014). Several government agencies promote China's participation in Africa, each with its own mission. For example, the Ministry of Foreign Affairs in Africa identifies the national interest and makes a connection with the local government, cooperating with the Ministry of Commerce. The State-owned Assets Supervision and Administration Commission was established in 2003 to be responsible for managing and increasing the value of state assets. It is also the owner of central SOEs. State banks such as the China Development Bank and the Export-Import Bank are charged with assisting Chinese enterprises to expand overseas. Apart from helping with infrastructure projects, China Development Bank also created an independent subsidiary in 2007 to encourage and support Chinese enterprises to invest in Africa: the China–Africa Development Fund. This Fund's investments include in agriculture, infrastructure, manufacturing, industrial park and resource development.

Some scholars believe that state ownership is harmful to listed companies (Wei, Xie, & Zhang, 2005). However, according to Chen et al. (2009), SOEs actually have better performance. There are, of course, all sorts of problems about the definition and measurement of performance. Given this caveat, their research suggests that SOEs owned by central government perform best, followed by SOEs owned by local giovernment. Private firms are not superior to SOEs but are slightly better than state asset management bureau organisations. But SOEs also have relatively more operational constraints compared with private companies (Chen et al., 2009): For example, while private companies usually pay attention to immediate interests and ignore their social responsibilities, central SOEs are usually required to incorporate 'corporate social responsibilities' (CSR) into their plans (Xu, 2014). So why are there complaints about the 'bad' behaviours of Chinese SOE – such as corruption, human and labour rights violations, environmental pollution and even crimes? Compared with the central government, the provincial and local governments seem to pay less attention and are less enthusiastic about China–Africa relations (Gu, 2009).

To understand the contradiction between inappropriate behaviours and the objectives of the central government, Xu (2014) examined large central SOEs in the resources and infrastructure sectors. Surprisingly, she found that the central government in Beijing seems to have limited control of large SOEs, let alone those small enterprises affiliated to provincial or local government. When competing with large SOEs for projects, provincial SOEs may conflict with Beijing's strategic goals, but the central government has limited capacity to even monitor, let alone control, provincial or local enterprises. Besides, the commitment of large SOEs relies on small public and private contractors. Even though the central government encourages SOEs to 'go out', it has only tenuous control over those contractors (Xu, 2014).

Unlike large SOEs, private companies usually enter the African market by following their own path. Market-seeking motives drive them to maximise their interests (Zhang & He, 2015). According to Gu (2009), Chinese private companies in Africa usually have a 'Three-Jump' pattern of enterprise growth: Trading – Investing – Building industrial parks.

Most companies started trading with Africa, and it gradually led them to make the decision to invest there. From her fieldwork, Gu (2009) learned that most of these private companies initially established contacts with the Chinese diaspora in Africa before investing. Because of weak infrastructure and supply systems, some firms had to source their equipment from China or other countries, which promoted the interaction between trading and investing. Eventually, the spillover from gatherings of other Chinese enterprises encourages the decision to establish industrial parks. So far, there are more than 100 industrial parks built by Chinese firms in Africa, most of them still in construction (Zhang & Wang, 2017).

China's FDI in Africa does not come equally from all regions of the country. 'China's private firms are highly concentrated in origin, as the majority come from several Chinese provinces and coastal regions: primarily Zhejiang, Guangdong, Fujian, Jiangsu, and Shandong' (Gu, 2009, p. 575). Among all the provinces in China, Zhejiang ranks first in investing in Africa. Up to 2014, there were 464 enterprises from Zhejiang province invested in Africa with 459 projects. The total investment was more than $1.4 billion (US dollars). As mentioned previously, private firms establish contacts with the Chinese diaspora in Africa before investing. This gives firms from Zhejiang province an advantage since they have traditionally had a large number of business merchants in both China and abroad, called *zheshang* (浙商) in Chinese. It is also one of the five provincial business groups (Zhejiang, Guangdong, Fujian, Jiangsu and Shandong) in China. In Europe, people adopting a racist stereotype call them 'Eastern Jews' (Li, 2016, p. 7). Building an industrial park is one of their important business modes for large enterprises in Africa. In addition, they also form a strategic alliance with African companies by technology transfer. Entrepreneurial spirit might be the internal cause for the *zheshang*'s success, but it is also because of the external support from the provincial government. The Department of Commerce in Zhejiang province provides strategic consulting, personnel training and legal aid to support firms to 'go out'. For example, in the 'Outline of the 13th Five-Year Plan for the National Economic and Social Development of the Province' published by the Zhejiang government in February 2016, it emphasises its participation in giant projects in Africa such as Congo-Brazzaville Potash Fertilizer Production Base and China Strategy Holdings/Nigeria Oregon Industrial Park.

Voices about Chinese FDI in Africa

National leaders and opinion leaders in Africa generally embrace the Chinese model and welcome Chinese investment in Africa (Adisu et al., 2016), encapsulated by Nigerian human rights activist Ndubisi Obiorah:

> Ndubisi told me that part of him welcomed China's interest: "You remember," he said, "a few years ago, the Economist did a cover story

on Africa: 'The Failed Continent.' My friends and I, we talked about that for weeks. It was depressing: 'Africa, the failed continent!' And now China comes, and they are talking about business, about investment, about win-win cooperation." He smiled a bit ruefully: "Who knows? Maybe this change will be good for Africa."

(Brautigam, 2009, p. 2)

China wins a great amount of credibility among African authorities for two reasons. First, as a developing country, it shows the world its success in fast economic development and reduction of poverty (Brautigam, 2009). Second, from the perspective of locals 'China has an advantage of not having a colonial hangover' (Brautigam, 2009, p. 10). Overall, there seems to be no conclusion to the debate about whether the cooperation of China and Africa is win–win or win–lose. However, partly owing to the deep involvement of the Chinese government in FDI in Africa, there is increasing concern about the nature of Chinese investment in Africa. Ado and Su (2016) critically assessed 41 academic journal papers examining China's presence in Africa from 2001 to 2011 and found that a great deal of work shows negative results, particularly with regard to the local economic development and social development. For example, China is selling manufacturing products with very competitive prices in African markets which, it has been argued, has contributed to the deindustrialisation of Africa (Mlambo et al., 2016). Specifically, it leads to the closure of factories, unemployment and low-income issues. According to Alden (2006), in South Africa, because of Chinese competition in the textile sector, 60,000 workers are unemployed directly and 200,000 indirectly. In Nigeria, such numbers reach 350,000.

In addition, 'bad behaviour' on the part of Chinese SOEs in Africa has been reported, such as labour rights violations, environmental pollution, and criminal activity (Xu, 2014). Other critiques have focussed on aid projects; with a noninterference policy from the Chinese government, they have been accused of ignoring human rights abuses in some countries (Mlambo et al., 2016). Chinese MNEs have been accused of using prison labourers or bringing a great number of unskilled Chinese labourers to Africa, leaving limited job opportunity for local employees (Ajakaiye, 2009). Although such information might be anecdotal and biased (Ajakaiye, 2009), some academics and western media tend to perceive China's presence in Africa as neocolonial (Jauch, 2011).

However, Ado and Su (2016) argue that there seems to be a lack of empirical evidence to support such negative views. Most of those views come from low-quality journals and journalists in the business press or magazines (Wang, 2012). According to Ado and Su (2016), at that date no specialised IB journal had published any paper with interest in China's presence in Africa. Instead, most papers are published in Chinese or African journals with no international ranking nor worldwide accessibility. Reports from journalists are argued to be prejudicial and unreliable and based on anecdotal information. They are mainly western-centre writing for those audiences who feel threatened by the Chinese economy (Ademola, Bankole, & Adewuyi, 2009).

Few studies have identified any positive effects from China's presence in Africa. Donou-Adonsou and Lim (2018) found that Chinese FDI improved the standard of living in Africa between 2003 to 2012. In terms of income, the effect of Chinese FDI in Africa is nearly twice as large as that of American FDI. While some scholars claim that Chinese MNEs use large numbers of expatriates and rarely employ local workers or offer training to local staff, Agbebi (2018) found positive results from an in-depth qualitative study of Huawei. As a part of its CSR policies, Huawei has launched education and training programmes for both employees and non-employees in African countries: for example, *1000 Girls in ICT* and *ICT For Change-Nigeria 2000 Youth ICT Training*. In the former programme, successful trainees at the final stage were sent to the headquarters in Shenzhen, China, for a one-week training session. So far, more than 50,000 people have been trained at Huawei's training centre in Abuja, Nigeria. It is important to note that, as a telecommunication giant, Huawei is not representative of most of Chinese MNEs in Africa. However, it at least shows us the determination of Chinese firms to engage in local development by following the central government's initiatives.

There also remains contrary opinions of China's presence in Africa among locals, especially among local governments, local academics and media. Makoye (2014) warns African countries to be careful, as China is using them as testing grounds for products they might not be able to sell elsewhere. Local consumers complain about the poor quality of Chinese goods. They label those goods 'Zhing Zhong' and 'Fong Kong' in Zimbabwe and South Africa, respectively (Agbebi, 2018). A study by Manyeruke (2006) revealed that Chinese goods of poor quality have higher replacement rates than local products from the perspective of Zimbabwean female consumers, with some products even asking for 'no guarantee', 'no refund' and 'no return'.

Companies with different ownerships embrace different motives when they enter new markets. Ownerships of Chinese companies are complex but crucial for understanding firms' overall strategies. Van Tulder (2015) also pointed out that different ownership structures create different questions to those who manage the organisations, which are poorly addressed in academia. Motives are inevitably associated with the companies' internationalisation, such as why and how IB activities are organised and operated (Benito, 2015). To understand companies' strategic motives will help us to gain a deeper understanding of Chinese organisations and their activities in Africa. Having focused on China's FDI in Africa and the nature of firms engaging in Africa and their motivations, we now turn to cultural aspects that may impact on the nature of this engagement and the implications for HRM policies and practices.

The impacts of traditional culture on HRM in China and Africa

Confucianism has received attention in the management literature related to China (Xing, Liu, Tarba, & Cooper, 2016; Yang, 2012; Yao, Arrowsmith, & Thorn, 2016). Influenced by Confucianism, China embraces a high collectivism culture (Hofstede, 2001). It works together with particularism, paternalism and authoritarianism to shape a Chinese style of people management (Farh & Cheng, 2000; Ip, 2009). Since group and collective interests are above individual interests, individual well-being is only realised as a family, or as group goals are fulfilled. In this sense, equality of employees might not be recognised in a firm since collectivism denies independent value to the individual (Ip, 2009). Firms might sacrifice employees' rights for the interests of the company (Xu, 2014). Family collectivism indicates similar ideas of self-sacrifice for family needs.

Externally, bids for public projects, big commercial deals or loans from state banks may be won through *guanxi* (Ip, 2009). Internally, paternalism is associated with authoritarianism: transferred from the family to the firm level, it reflects the authority of leaders in a hierarchical relationship, reflecting high power distance (Hofstede, 2001; House, Hanges, Javidan, Dorfman, & Gupta, 2004). In this situation, employees may find it difficult to express their ideas freely and honestly (Ip, 2009).

Scholars have compared Confucianism with *ubuntu* in the African tradition, arguing that the two cultures share some similarities, which might have significant implications for HRM practice (Horwitz, 2015; Jackson & Horwitz, 2018; Xing et al., 2016). *Ubuntu* is an old practice but one that has been introduced as a new management concept to improve labour coordination in organisations since the 1990s (Mbigi, 1997). Its core ideology is *ubuntu ungamntu ngabanye abantu*, which means people are people through other people (Karsten & Illa, 2005; Mbigi, 1997). It indicates that people are defined through community and society, providing a solid philosophical base for the community concept of management (Karsten & Illa, 2005; Khoza, 1994). The humaneness of *ubuntu* appears to be close to *Ren* (仁, humanity) of Confucianism (Jackson, 2014; Jackson & Horwitz, 2018). 'Treating others as you would like to be treated; never imposing upon others what you dislike yourself (己所不欲, 勿施于人)' (The Analects, 论语). Both cultures evince high collectivism (Horwitz, 2015; Xing et al., 2016) and both emphasise the importance of connection (*guanxi*, 关系) within groups and communities. If African and Chinese traditions share similar values, Chinese MNEs in Africa may confront fewer problems in people management.

But the reality is that Chinese enterprises in Africa have been criticised by both media and scholars for their ignorance of humanity (Jackson & Horwitz, 2018). One possible reason might be that the group boundary has been ignored in such a situation. *Ren* might only apply to in-group members and those with Chinese *guanxi*; in the African *ubuntu* tradition, Chinese managers and colleagues are conceived as out-group members as well (Jackson & Horwitz, 2018), although Mutabazi (2002) argues that *ubuntu* applies to strangers to African communities as well. Also, *Ren* is just one aspect of Confucianism. Chinese managers might choose to sacrifice local employees' interests and needs for the benefits of the company when there are conflicts between *Ren* and other ideologies. It is still unclear whether or not the cultural synergies between Chinese expatriates and African employees proposed by Jackson and Horwitz (2018) strengthen friendship and cooperation and lead to mutual cooperation and learning at the organisational level.

While culture may be reflected in managerial philosophy and practice (Yang, 2012), it is important to note that culture is dynamic. Chinese contemporary culture is more than Confucianism. It is a combination of traditional and modern ideologies (Yao et al., 2016) resulting from Confucianism, socialism and capitalism (Yang, 2012). It is not surprising to observe strong capitalist influences in cosmopolitan cities such as Beijing and Shanghai or more individualistic values from young employees because of the 'culture invasion' from western countries (Yang, 2012). Similarly, *ubuntu* itself is not able to represent modern African culture (Horwitz, 2015; Horwitz, Kamoche, & Chew, 2002). Despite the influence of colonialism, Africa is also a continent with many diverse cultures. Both Confucianism and *ubuntu* are helpful for us to understand part of the story but are not able to show the whole picture.

IHRM strategies of Chinese companies

Within this complex and dynamic framework of Chinese investment in Africa, we focus on the controversial HRM strategies of Chinese investors. In order to understand these, we need to review briefly the development of HRM in China. HRM in China is a hybrid of modern and traditional management practices (Warner & Warner, 2008), which has undergone several transitional stages (Zhao & Du, 2012). A wide variety of ownership patterns emerged in the transition from a planned (command) economy to a market socialist one, generating significant changes in HRM (Shen & Edwards, 2004). One of the most notable changes was moving away from central job allocation and lifetime employment: the 'iron rice bowl' (铁饭碗) (Shen & Edwards, 2004; Warner, 2008; Zhu, 2018). There has been a transformation towards strategic HRM policies on the part of many businesses, achieved by learning and adapting western HRM systems to the context of China (Zhao & Du, 2012), but the degree of adaptation varies depending on the ownership and size of the organisation (Warner & Warner, 2008).

International staffing approach

These changes have impacted the highly controversial issue of labour in China's investment in Africa. There have been complaints, in particular, about SOEs importing Chinese employees rather than creating job opportunities for locals. This seems to be the case for about half the labour in the construction industry (Xu, 2014). This issue attracted the attention of the central government. Former President Hu Jintao promised that the Chinese MNEs in Africa would increase the employment of local labour at the 5th Ministerial Conference of the Forum of China–Africa Cooperation in 2012. However, it is unclear to what extent the promise has been kept considering the central government's limited control capacity (Xu, 2014).

The high usage of local employees does not necessarily lead to high-quality human resource management. Some small firms pay local employees less than suggested by the Chinese government (Xu, 2014). Such profit-maximisation behaviour creates negative images of Chinese firms in Africa. As one Chinese businessman in Africa described it, most local African people could not distinguish between state-owned companies or private companies; they only know you are Chinese (Gu, 2009). But private companies also expressed their embarrassment. Theoretically, the Chinese government is willing to work with private sectors in Africa to implement their policies. But few private firms feel included in reality in the overall project and strategy (Gu, 2009).

The paradox is that private firms are usually accused of not following the central government's strategic goals, neither paying attention to China–Africa relations nor interested in embracing CSR (Gu, 2009; Xu, 2014). However, compared to SOEs, they seem to have a much higher rate of employing local people. Some of them have more than 90% Africans in their workforces. For example, Haitian Suitcase and Baggage Company in Nigeria has around 93% of local employees, and the Songlin Company in Ghana has 91% (Gu, 2009). Considering the high costs of bringing workers from China, such as the higher wages, visa fees, accommodation, passages home, etc., these investors do not believe it is a wise decision to use a large number of Chinese expatriates (Kamoche & Siebers, 2015).

For managerial positions, of course, they are more willing to deploy Chinese employees because of the required level of skills, cultural differences, language issues and their ability to bridge subsidiary-headquarters relations. Chinese MNEs tend to adopt an ethnocentric approach to international staffing, with all of the key positions being filled by parent company nationals (PCNs) in both parent companies and subsidiaries (Zhong, Zhu, & Zhang, 2015). The number of expatriates in Chinese MNEs is considerably larger than those in American and European MNEs and even exceeds the number in Japanese MNEs, which are known for their ethnocentric approaches (Zheng & Smith, 2018). Gadzala (2010) points out that Chinese MNEs usually adopt ethnocentric approaches which place PCNs in key executive positions in subsidiaries (Horwitz et al., 2002; Zhong et al., 2015).

The major advantage of using such an approach is the convenience of communication with, and control of, the subsidiaries it provides. Since most Chinese firms have limited experience in foreign countries, it is difficult for them to trust local people, with different languages, culture and habits (Feng & Jacques, 2016). Thus, they assign a number of expatriates to manage their subsidiaries abroad. But this practice might arouse discontent among host country nationals (HCNs) and lead to a high turnover in subsidiaries as few management development opportunities are provided for local employees (Shen, 2006; Shen & Edwards, 2004).

Shen (2006) argues that changes in international staffing approaches, especially a change from the ethnocentric approach to the polycentric approach, are influenced by international experience, with international experience acting in a catalytic role rather than a determinate one. MNEs with some international experience might give certain decision-making autonomy to subsidiaries and hire predominantly HCNs: a polycentric approach. Zhu (2018) found her case-study subsidiary of a Chinese bank in Australia officially adopted a polycentric approach to staffing, but in practice the locals it employed were primarily from a Chinese ethnic background. Khan et al. (2018) found a similar thing for Chinese MNEs in the UK. These boundary spanners, ethnic locals or self-initiated expatriates living in the host country (Furusawa & Brewster, 2018), play an intermediary role between headquarters (HQ) and the subsidiaries, facilitating coordination and ensuring more adaptable HRM systems in the subsidiaries. The strategy avoids problems of unfamiliarity with culture and language, high labour cost of PCNs and potentially high turnover of HCNs. But it might also create a communication gap between HQ and subsidiaries (Shen & Edwards, 2004). There are fewer such potential boundary-spanning Chinese in Africa than there are in Australia or the UK.

Another frequently used approach in Chinese MNEs is an ethnocentric staffing approach but with a strong polycentric tendency (Shen & Edwards, 2004). Companies assign expatriates to fill executive management positions in subsidiaries but fill middle-management roles with HCNs (see Figure 4.1). This approach can be viewed as a result of the transition identified by Shen (2006).

One problem in expatriation studies is that there is no clear boundary of levels among expatriates. Most scholars refer only to those who possess

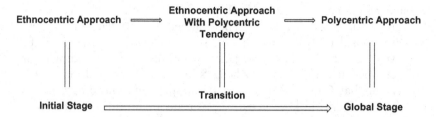

Figure 4.1 Possible transition of international staffing policy in Chinese MNEs

managerial positions as expatriates; others include highly qualified specialists. Since most of the research has been conducted on assigned expatriates, who usually possess senior positions or high pay, it is taken for granted that expatriates are high status. McNulty and Brewster (2019) categorised three levels of expatriates, namely high-status expatriates (top management), middle-status expatriates (professionals) and low-status expatriates (such as construction workers and drivers) and that may be relevant, given the larger numbers of expatriates in some Chinese operations in Africa.

Chinese expatriates in subsidiaries

There is an extensive literature on the roles that expatriates play in the internationalisation of MNEs. Much of it repeats, or is based on, the three main objectives identified in the classic text by Edström and Galbraith (1977): filling skills gaps, coordination and control, and employee development. Cooke (2014) argues that Chinese MNEs use expatriates in Africa, rather than HCNs, because they share similar culture and language with Chinese managers; they are more willing to work long hours or work overtime in order to finish tasks before a deadline; they are generally highly skilled and can deal with multiple tasks; they are easy to manage as they usually live in the same compound; and they are less likely to quit the job or adopt a confrontational approach when handling disagreements with the management.

Shen (2006) concluded that Chinese MNEs in the United Kingdom usually localised HRM practices such as training, performance appraisals and employee relations while centralising recruitment, selection and reward, and compensation. In contrast, Cooke (2012) found Huawei is good at using local agencies for recruitment in its overseas operations. This outsourcing enables Huawei to leverage the expertise needed to effectively recruit local employees. Moreover, subsidiaries are able to develop rapidly without the need to build a full in-house HRM department. Similarly, ZTE uses agencies to help design HRM strategy, policies, procedure, performance management and even the employee Handbook (Cooke, 2012).

Subsidiaries usually adopt distinct management approaches for expatriates and local employees. For example, expatriates' performance is assessed by HQ with assistance from subsidiaries, while HCN's performance is assessed by the subsidiary HRM department (Zhu, 2018). The selection criteria for PCNs focuses on morality and peer opinion, but the one for HNCs is mainly concerned with technical skills and experience (Shen et al., 2005). This is easy to understand as most PCNs are assigned expatriates, and they are already employees in the parent companies, which means they should already meet the requirements for hard skills. Shen et al. (2005) found companies in the UK provided a higher salary to local employees than competitor businesses but fewer training and development opportunities. However, Zhu (2018) observed that MNEs in Australia use significant amounts of in-house and external training, because government policy in Australia demands 1.5% to 2% of payroll be spent on training. Zhu explained that a host country effect together with a dominance effect (global best practice) shapes the HRM practices of emerging market MNEs operating in developed countries, which can override the country-of-origin effect. We examine four issues related to Chinese expatriates that have been debated in the literature: family, selection, compensation and training and development.

Family. One important element affecting international assignments is the family (Yao, 2014). On the one hand, Chinese people accepting an international assignment may sometimes be motivated by the family's welfare and reputation; on the other hand, the responsibility of taking care of parents, especially for the generation under the 'One Child' policy (Yao, 2014; Yao et al., 2016) may make it difficult for people to accept international assignments. The Chinese pension system is weak, parental investment in offspring is a major expense in today's China (Yao et al., 2016) and it is socially expected that those offspring will take care of aged parents. For couples, most assignments in Africa require the expatriate to leave their partner and any children behind in China, so they may not be together for many months or even years.

Selection. Chinese MNEs favour internal recruitment and promotion and usually adopt preselection processes rather than post advertisements openly (Shen & Edwards, 2006). Otherwise, Chinese MNEs follow the same selection method for expatriates as their western counterparts. They use both internal and external recruitment, but the latter only happens when there is difficulty in finding suitable candidates inside the company (Feng & Jacques, 2016). Personal relationships, rather than individual ability and qualification, the phenomenon of *guanxi* (关系) (Ip, 2009), explain why nepotism and cronyism are not unusual among Chinese firms. In fact, Feng and Jacques (2016) find there seems always to be more candidates who are willing to be assigned to industrialised countries than is required. This is because of the attraction of the high salary, better living environment, high food safety, and so on. In addition, young employees are often ready to work in countries with 'bad conditions' in exchange for the potential improvement of both salary and position after repatriation. International assignments are usually compulsory when employees are asked, and employees who refuse might have to leave the company. However, this does not mean Chinese MNEs have no problems with selecting candidates with the right capabilities, such as the ability to speak host country languages and to adapt to the local environment. In the majority of the cases, the selection is made before the interview during 'work meetings' and the formal interview is just for assignment arrangement (Shen & Edwards, 2004), reflecting the 'coffee-machine' system that Harris and Brewster (1999) suggest is common in western MNEs.

Compensation. In terms of compensation, there is no distinct difference between Chinese MNEs and western MNEs (Feng & Jacques, 2016). Chinese MNEs usually follow a home-based policy, and the salary structure contains the base salary, foreign service inducement or hardship premium, and allowances and benefits including pension plans, medical insurance and so on (Shen, 2004). More specifically, the basic salary is determined by the parent company in China based on the number of years of employment and hierarchical levels. Foreign service inducements vary from (host) country to country, and accommodation allowances are associated with local standards (Feng & Jacques, 2016). Less commonly, a contracted package approach is used for some international assignments; a diplomatic-based approach is more hierarchy-focused; and some organisations use host-based plus home-salary policies, where expatriates receive dual salaries from both home and host countries (Shen, 2004).

Training and development. Training expenses are regarded as costly and have been tightly controlled in Chinese enterprises (Zhu, 2018). Chinese MNEs may include language and professional knowledge development in pre-posting training but rarely offer intercultural skills, even though they are seen as potentially very helpful by expatriates (Feng & Jacques, 2016). For those who are sent to dangerous countries, safety training is also provided. Generally, Chinese managers prefer learning by observing or doing on the job (Zhang & Fan, 2014), rather than through indoor seminars.

Managing Chinese expatriates in Africa

Expatriate management has always been an outstanding issue for Chinese enterprises in Africa. In the beginning, as Zhang and Wang (2017) describe, in TEDA (Tianjin Economic-Technological Development Area)/ Suez Economic and Trade Cooperation Zone, the management team tended to use assigned expatriates. The contract for working abroad was usually three years long. After three years, they would return to work for the company in China, and new expatriates would be hired. But this is very costly, and work transfer between old and new expatriates causes some inefficiencies. Later, they adopted a rotation system. Two groups of people are hired to do similar jobs both in China and Egypt. Cooperation and communication between them are enhanced. For a certain period of time, the employees from China and Egypt exchange jobs. To some extent, this helps sustain the stability of employees, but other problems appeared at the same time. Employees have to rotate between China and Africa frequently, and they do not have a stable working environment, which causes problems in both individual health and families. In the long term, staff turnover increases under such circumstance. Meanwhile, the rotation system limits the promotion of local employees and, inevitably, Egyptian staff are not satisfied with this system.

In general, Chinese expatriates are socially isolated, living in a compound and even being equipped with a chef from China to take care of their diet, so they have few contacts with local people (Cooke, Wang et al., 2015). Such discriminant treatment not only makes it harder for expatriates to adjust but also creates more conflicts between HCNs and PCNs. One senior manager reported by these authors also expressed his helplessness in such a situation:

> We do believe that integration and harmonization are important between the expatriates and the local workforce. But our priority at this stage is our expatriates' personal safety. If any serious [security] accidents happen to our expatriates, then the Chinese government and international media will make a big fuss about it. That will have a very bad impact on our overseas operations.
>
> (Cooke, Wang et al., 2015, p. 2755)

So, some Chinese MNEs tend to adopt semi-military management with centralised control and strict disciplines (Cooke, Wang et al., 2015; Rui, Zhang, & Shipman, 2017). For example, there are checks on the time that expatriates return to their accommodation every night, to prevent them from drinking or gambling, which might affect working attitudes and productivity (Rui et al., 2017). Moreover, companies might transfer money and bonuses directly to the account of their partners or other family members, so that they have little money for gambling (Rui et al., 2017). It is believed that such a management style will not help these firms to attract, manage and retain the younger generation, who can find good jobs at home and might not be willing to work in harsh conditions, sacrificing their family life, though perhaps, influenced by western culture, the younger generation is more individualised and might challenge traditional corporate culture or 'inhuman' traditions (Rui et al., 2017).

One reason for the different narratives about expatriate management styles is that scholars rarely differentiate the level of expatriates. The two distinctive expatriate management styles mentioned above (semi-military management vs non-semi-military management) may be applied to different hierarchical levels of expatriates. For example, the rotating system is usually adopted to management middle-status and high-status expatriates, such as technicians and top management teams, while centralised control and strict disciplines are only applied to low-status expatriates such as factory workers.

Labour issues are challenging for Chinese MNEs in Africa. Skill shortages seem to be a constant problem in nearly all industrial parks and economic zones, for both managerial talents and front-line staff (Zhang & Wang, 2017). Most Chinese companies lack talent cultivation and supply systems. Thus, Huajian Group is trying to build a vocational school in its industrial park in Ethiopia. In addition, they also organise visits for key technical staff from China to Ethiopia, giving instruction and training for local employees (Zhang & Wang, 2017). Most of the African countries lack effective education systems, and training local employees for work is expensive. Usually, it takes months or even longer to train them before they can start the job. Meanwhile, there are always shortages of training centres and even trainers in host countries. In addition, African employees have a strong awareness of safeguarding rights and in some countries trade unions have a significant influence (Wood & Brewster, 2007), which leads to a higher cost in the promotion, salary increase and dismissal systems compared to the same situations in China.

One of the most serious critiques of Chinese enterprises in Africa is related to labour issues. It has been argued, for instance, that Chinese MNEs bring large numbers of semi-skilled and unskilled workers from home, decreasing the employment rate of local people (Cooke, 2014; Cooke, Wood, & Horwitz, 2015); and that they provide minimum labour standards or violate national employment laws in Africa (Cooke, Wang et al., 2015). Whether anecdotal or real, such stories are easily found in the western media. But there are few scholarly empirical studies that allow us to develop any deep understanding of the phenomena. For Chinese MNEs in Africa, their HRM is usually less strategic and more administrative: focused on low-cost policies and short-term plans (Cooke, Wood et al., 2015; Horwitz, 2015; Wood et al., 2014). This might be attributed to the fact that China is a latecomer in internationalisation and lacks requisite experience. Thus, they usually adopt a trial-and-error manner; even at the risk that it might destroy their reputation (Cooke, Wang et al., 2015). It is unclear whether Chinese subsidiaries are any different from western MNEs' subsidiaries in this regard.

It could be argued that the lack of qualified workers from host countries gives Chinese MNEs no choice but to use expatriates in some cases.

In general, the shortage of human resources in Africa exists at various levels from craft skilled workers to managers, while the few skilled and well-educated ones often seek opportunities abroad because of the limited choices in their domestic markets (Cooke, Wood et al., 2015). From the perspective of some Chinese firms, their main interest in Africa is to overcome tariff barriers, so they have less interest in accessing existing human and material resources (Wood et al., 2014).

As emerging economies, India and Brazil take a completely different approach to FDI in Africa, which leads to different HRM practices. Driven by market-seeking motives, India seems to make greater use of local workers and unskilled workers (Wood et al., 2014; Jackson & Horwitz, 2018). Brazil is considered to be the best example of contributing to education programmes and infrastructure development in Africa (Wood et al., 2014). In addition, Brazilian expatriates have considerable advantages in adjustment and social connections in Lusophone Africa because of the strong cultural affinities (Wood et al., 2014).

Towards a conceptual framework of Chinese expatriation in Africa

Based on our analysis of the literature, we offer a framework of expatriate management of Chinese MNEs in Africa (Figure 4.2). In general, three main motives have been identified: natural resource-seeking, political alliances, and market-seeking (Dunning, 1993; Dunning & Narula, 1995). Two other potential motives for MNEs to invest in a new country were also identified by Dunning, namely strategic asset-seeking (Meyer, 2015), specifically applied to emerging market MNEs, and efficiency seeking. It does seem that Chinese MNEs invest in Africa to gain strategic assets, such as increasing their managerial expertise or ability to operate internationally (Drogendijk & Blomkvist, 2013), and that this is more important for Chinese SOEs (Ramasamy et al., 2012). Scholars (Buckley, Cross, Tan, Xin, & Voss, 2008; Drogendijk & Blomkvist, 2013) generally believe, however, that the efficiency-seeking motive is less relevant to Chinese MNEs than to more mature and larger global MNEs. Since China is not short of low-cost labour, the efficiency-seeking motive might be of less importance. Such statements from nearly ten years ago might not be applicable to today's China and today's Chinese MNEs and need further investigation.

Even through both SOEs and private companies invest for natural resources, the private companies seem to be more likely to offer value-added services (Ramasamy et al., 2012). It is interesting to note that despite the fact that provincial SOEs are controlled by local governments, their motivations are more diversified and similar to the private sector. We argue that both ownership and strategic motives fundamentally decide HRM strategies of expatriates from all levels.

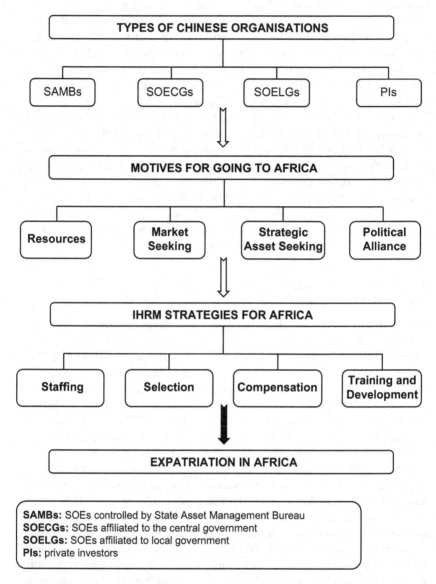

Figure 4.2 Expatriate management of Chinese MNEs in Africa associated with ownership and motive

Research opportunities

The establishment of the Forum on China-Africa Cooperation (FOCAC) as well as the announcement of The Belt and Road Initiatives indicate that the ties between China and Africa will be tighter in the future. With an increasing number of Chinese firms investing in Africa, it is believed that the underexplored phenomenon of China's presence in Africa will attract more attention from scholars and particularly IHRM scholars. So far, excluding those in the current volume, there have been only a few qualitative studies (Agbebi, 2018; Cooke, 2014; Kamoche & Siebers, 2015; Rui et al., 2017; Xing et al., 2016) and quantitative studies (Nabil Khodeir, 2016) examining HRM related issues in Africa. Others are conceptual discussion or review work (Jackson, 2014; Jackson & Horwitz, 2018; Jackson, Louw, & Zhao, 2013). We suggest future research opportunities.

Firstly, at the organisational level, company ownership and FDI motivation should be taken into consideration, alongside industry, in understanding firms' HRM practice and policies, including selection, compensation, training, and so forth. Ownerships of Chinese companies are complex but crucial for understanding firms' overall strategies. For example, as noted, there are three types of SOEs, and each might carry different motivations and have different strategies. In particular, SOEs directly managed by provincial governments are generally more profit-driven than other types. For future research, scholars might consider a more detailed division of ownership rather than making a generalisation of all SOEs.

Secondly, country-specific studies are appropriate to investigate Chinese MNEs in Africa. Much of the existing literature focuses on Africa at a macro level, rather than paying attention to its regional or national differences. Adisu and his colleagues (2016) suggest that country-based analyses might be necessary as each African country has its own unique history and culture. Chinese firms might have different driving forces or investment strategies in different regions of Africa, and there might be key motivational differences that vary from country to country.

Thirdly, at the individual level, future research will benefit from differentiating the different status levels of expatriates. Management practices are different for top management teams, professionals and lesser skilled labours. Low-status workers, in particular, are frequently overlooked in current research. Identity-related investigations will be helpful to study how expatriates from different status levels adjust in a foreign culture.

Fourthly, there is more research needed in the wider expatriate field on expatriates from the new generation. Pereira, Malik, Howe-Walsh, Munjal, and Hirekhan (2017) conducted a longitudinal study of Generation Y expatriates, young, highly qualified and mobile, in an Indian MNE. This may be a more practical problem for HRM in Chinese MNEs. In particular, Chinese society has undergone tremendous changes economically with the reform and opening-up policy. Those who were born post-80 (八零后) and post-90 (九零后) may, it is argued, be fundamentally different from their parents as they have grown up in a socialistic market economy and are strongly influenced by western countries with their individualistic values (Yang, 2012). In addition, the challenges of globalisation and new technology development might lead the new generation to have a different perception of their jobs (Zhu & Warner, 2018). So far, there have only been limited numbers of papers on these new generation employees in China (Ren, Xie, Zhu, & Warner, 2018; Zhu & Warner, 2018), and none that have considered their role in MNEs. Future research could focus on how such people perceive international assignments in Africa; what they might bring to the future relationship and cooperation between Africa and China; and how they might be dfferent from previous generation expatriates in Africa.

In-depth qualitative studies are strongly suggested at this stage of our understanding of the HRM strategies of Chinese MNEs in Africa. Empirical studies are urgently needed to explore what is happening there. Ethnography, which has now built a relatively well-established record for researching business organisations (Garsten & Nyqvist, 2013), might offer unique advantages for such work. There are two reasons ethnography becomes valuable in business studies: contextual-orientation and emic positioning, or providing an insiders' point of view (Ladner, 2016). The unwritten rules about how things work in practice are usually not verbalised and can only be discovered by patient observation in actual sites (Myers, 2013). So, ethnographic studies might help researchers to gain a deeper understanding of how Chinese MNEs manage their employees in Africa and how their expatriates manage their work and life in that context.

Note

1 We adopt here the definition of expatriates in McNulty and Brewster (2017, p. 46): expatriates are: "legally working individuals who reside temporarily in a country of which they are not a citizen in order to accomplish a career-related goal, being relocated abroad either by an organization, by self-initiation or directly employed within the host-country".

References

Ademola, O. T., Bankole, A. S., & Adewuyi, A. O. (2009). China-Africa trade relations: Insights from AERC scoping studies. *European Journal of Development Research*, 21(4), 485–505.
Adisu, K., Sharkey, T., & Okoroafo, S. (2016). The impact of Chinese investment in Africa. *International Journal of Business Management*, 5(9), 3.
Ado, A., & Su, Z. (2016). China in Africa: A critical literature review. *Critical Perspectives on International Business*, 12(1), 40–60.
Agbebi, M. (2018). Exploring the human capital development dimensions of Chinese investments in Africa: Opportunities, implications and directions for further research. *Journal of Asian and African Studies*, 1(22), 189–210.
Ajakaiye, O. (2009). China in Africa: A relationship in transition. *European Journal of Development Research*, 21(4), 479–484.
Alden, C. (2006). *Through African eyes: Representations of China on the African continent*. Paper presented at the SciPo/Fudan/LSE conference, London, October 2006.

Asiedu, E. (2006). Foreign direct investment in Africa: The role of natural resources, market size, government policy, institutions and political instability. *Journal of World Economy, 29*(1), 63–77.

Benito, G. R. (2015). Why and how motives (still) matter. *The Multinational Business Review, 23*(1), 15–24.

Brautigam, D. (2009). *The Dragon's gift: The real story of China in Africa.* Oxford: Oxford University Press.

Brautigam, D., & Tang, X. (2011). African Shenzhen: China's special economic zones in Africa. *Journal of Modern African Studies, 49*(1), 27–54.

Buckley, J. P., Clegg, L. J., Adam, R. C., Liu, X., Hinrich, V., & Ping, Z. (2007). The determinants of Chinese outward foreign direct investment. *Journal of International Business Studies, 38*(4), 499–518.

Buckley, J. P., Cross, R. A., Tan, H., Xin, L., & Voss, H. (2008). Historic and emergent trends in Chinese outward direct investment. *Management International Review, 48*(6), 715–748.

Chen, G., Firth, M., & Xu, L. (2009). Does the type of ownership control matter? Evidence from China's listed companies. *Journal of Banking & Finance, 33*(1), 171–181.

Cheung, Y.-W., de Haan, J., Qian, X., & Yu, S. (2012). China's outward direct investment in Africa. *Review of International Economics, 20*(2), 201–220.

Cheung, Y.-W., & Qian, X. W. (2009). The empirics of China's outward direct investment. *Pacific Economic Review, 14*(3), 312–341.

Cooke, F. L. (2012). The globalization of Chinese telecom corporations: Strategy, challenges and HR implications for the MNCs and host countries. *International Journal of Human Resource Management, 23*(9), 1832–1852.

Cooke, F. L. (2014). Chinese multinational firms in Asia and Africa: Relationships with institutional actors and patterns of HRM practices. *Human Resource Management, 53*(6), 877–896.

Cooke, F. L., Wang, D., & Wang, J. (2018). State capitalism in construction: Staffing practices and labour relations of Chinese construction firms in Africa. *Journal of Industrial Relations, 60*(1), 77–100.

Cooke, F. L., Wang, J., Yao, X., Xiong, L., Zhang, J., & Li, A. S. (2015). Mining with a high-end strategy: A study of Chinese mining firms in Africa and human resources implications. *International Journal of Human Resource Management, 26*(21), 2744–2762.

Cooke, F. L., Wood, G., & Horwitz, F. (2015). Multinational firms from emerging economies in Africa: Implications for research and practice in human resource management. *International Journal of Human Resource Management, 26*(21), 2653–2675.

Davies, K. (2009). While global FDI falls, China's outward FDI doubles. *Transnational Corporations Review, 1*(4), 20–23.

Deng, P. (2013). Chinese outward direct investment research: Theoretical integration and recommendations. *Management and Organization Review, 9*(3), 513–539.

Desai, M. A., Foley, C. F., & Hines Jr, J. (2004). A multinational perspective on capital structure choice and internal capital markets. *The Journal of Finance, 59*(6), 2451–2487.

Donou-Adonsou, F., & Lim, S. (2018). On the importance of Chinese investment in Africa. *Review of Development Finance, 8*(1), 63–73.

Drogendijk, R., & Blomkvist, K. (2013). Drivers and motives for Chinese outward foreign direct investments in Africa. *Journal of African Business, 14*(2), 75–84.

Dunning, J. H. (1993). *Multinational enterprises and the global economy.* Workingham: Addison Wesley.

Dunning, J. H., & Narula, R. (1995). The R&D activities of foreign firms in the United States. *International Studies of Management and Organization, 25*(1–2), 39–73.

Edström, A., & Galbraith, J. (1977). Transfer of managers as a coordination and control strategy in multinational organizations. *Administrative Science Quarterly, 22*(2), 248–263.

Fan, D., Zhang, M. M., & Zhu, C. J. (2013). International human resource management strategies of Chinese multinationals operating abroad. *Asia Pacific Business Review, 19*(4), 526–541.

Farh, J. L., & Cheng, B. S. (2000). A cultural analysis of paternalistic leadership in Chinese organizations. In J. T. Li, A. Tsui, & E. Weldon (Eds.), *Management and organizations in the Chinese context* (pp. 84–127). London: Palgrave Macmillan.

Feng, W., & Jacques, J. (2016). Expatriation policies of Chinese emerging MNCs. In T. Robert & A.-O. C. Bernadette (Eds.), *Emerging Asian economies and MNCs strategies* (pp. 155–170): Chichester: Edward Elgar Publishing.

Finance.sina.com.cn. (2017). 中非发展基金总裁石纪杨:中国和非洲合作高度互补 (The China Africa Development Fund President Shiji Yang: Chinese and Africa cooperation are highly complementary). Retrieved from http://finance.sina.com.cn/meeting/2017-11-01/doc-ifynfvar5683488.shtml?cre=financepagepc&mod=f&loc=5&r=9&doct=0&rfunc=6

Frynas, J. G., & Manuel, P. (2007). A new scramble for African oil? Historical, political, and business perspectives. *African Affairs, 106*(423), 229–251.

Fu, X., Sun, Z., & Ghauri, P. N. (2018). Reverse knowledge acquisition in emerging market MNEs: The experiences of Huawei and ZTE. *Journal of Business Research, 93*, 202–215.

Furusawa, M., & Brewster, C. (2018). Japanese self-initiated expatriates as boundary-spanners in Chinese subsidiaries of Japanese MNEs: Antecedents, social capital, and HRM practices. *Thunderbird International Business Review, 60*(6), 911–919

Gadzala, A. W. (2010). From formal- to informal-sector employment: Examining the Chinese presence in Zambia. *Review of African Political Economy, 37*(123), 41–59.

Garsten, C., & Nyqvist, A. (2013). *Organisational anthropology: Doing ethnography in and among complex organisations.* London: Pluto Press.

Gill, B., Huang, C.-H., & Morrison, J. S. (2007). Assessing China's growing influence in Africa. *China Security, 3*(3), 3–21.

Gu, J. (2009). China's private enterprises in Africa and the implications for African development. *European Journal of Development Research, 21*(4), 570–587.

Habib, M., & Zurawicki, L. (2002). Corruption and foreign direct investment. *Journal of International Business Studies, 33*(2), 291–307.

Harris, H., & Brewster, C. (1999). The Coffee-machine system: How international selection works. *International Journal of Human Resource Management, 10*(3), 488–500.

Henrich, J., Heine, S. J., & Norenzayan, A. (2010). The weirdest people in the world? *Behavioural Brain Sciences, 33*(2–3), 61–83.

Hofstede, G. (2001). *Culture's consequences: Comparing values, behaviors, institutions and organizations across nations.* Thousand Oaks, CA: Sage publications.

Horwitz, F. M. (2015). Human resources management in multinational companies in Africa: A systematic literature review. *International Journal of Human Resource Management, 26*(21), 2786–2809.

Horwitz, F. M., Kamoche, K., & Chew, I. K. H. (2002). Looking East: Diffusing high performance work practices in the Southern Afro-Asian context. *International Journal of Human Resource Management, 13*(7), 1019–1041.

House, R. J., Hanges, P. J., Javidan, M., Dorfman, P. W., & Gupta, V. (2004). *Culture, leadership, and organizations: The GLOBE study of 62 societies.* London: Sage Publications.

Ip, P. K. (2009). Is confucianism good for business ethics in China? *Journal of Business Ethics, 88*(3), 463–476.

Jackson, T. (2014). Employment in Chinese MNEs: Appraising the Dragon's gift to Sub-Saharan Africa. *Human Resource Management, 53*(6), 897–919.

Jackson, T., & Horwitz, F. M. (2018). Expatriation in Chinese MNEs in Africa: An agenda for research. *International Journal of Human Resource Management, 29*(11), 1856–1878.

Jackson, T., Louw, L., & Zhao, S. (2013). China in Sub-Saharan Africa: Implications for HRM policy and practice at organizational level. *International Journal of Human Resource Management, 24*(13), 2512–2533.

Jauch, H. (2011). Chinese investments in Africa: Twenty-first century colonialism? *New Labor Forum, 20*(2), 49–55.

Kamoche, K., & Siebers, L. Q. (2015). Chinese management practices in Kenya: Toward a post-colonial critique. *International Journal of Human Resource Management, 26*(21), 2718–2743.

Kaplinsky, R., & Morris, M. (2009). Chinese FDI in Sub-Saharan Africa: Engaging with large Dragons. *The European Journal of Development Research, 21*(4), 551–569. https://doi.org/10.1057/ejdr.2009.24

Karsten, L., & Illa, H. (2005). Ubuntu as a key African management concept: Contextual background and practical insights for knowledge application. *Journal of Managerial Psychology, 20*(7), 607–620.

Khan, Z., Wood, G., Tarba, S. Y., & Rao-Nicholson, R. (2018). Human resource management in Chinese multinationals in the United Kingdom: The interplay of institutions, culture, and strategic choice. *Human Resource Management,* Special issue, 1–15.

Khanna, T., & Palepu, K. G. (2006). Emerging giants: Building world-class companies in developing countries. *Harvard Business Review, 84*(10), 60–69.

Khoza, R. (1994). *The need for an Afrocentric approach to management.* Centre for Business Studies, Graduate School of Business Administration, University of the Witwatersrand.

Kolstad, I., & Wiig, A. (2012). What determines Chinese outward FDI? *Journal of World Business, 47*(1), 26–34.

Ladner, S. (2016). *Practical ethnography: A guide to doing ethnography in the private sector.* Abingdon: Routledge.

Li, W. B. (2016). 浙商对非洲创业行为研究 (Entrepreneurial Behavioural Study on Zhejiang Merchants in Africa). 北京: 经济科学出版社.

Liu, C., & Ge, S. Q. (2018). 中国企业对非洲投资:经济增长与结构变革 (Chinese companies invest in Africa: Economic growth and structural change). 国际经济评论, *5*, 9–32.

Makoye, K. (2014). *Tanzanian traders seek rescue from Chinese*. Retrieved from www.ipsnews.net/2013/08/tanzanian-traders-seek-rescue-from-chinese/

Manyeruke, C. (2006). The impact of Chinese products on Zimbabwean women. *Eastern Africa Social Science Research Review*, *22*(2), 85–106.

Mbigi, L. (1997). *Ubuntu: The African dream in management*. Cape Town: Knowledge Resources.

McNulty, Y., & Brewster, C. (2017). Theorizing the meaning(s) of "expatriate": Establishing boundary conditions for business expatriates. *International Journal of Human Resource Management*, *28*(1), 27–61.

McNulty, Y., & Brewster, C. (2019). *Working internationally: Expatriation, migration and other global work*. Chichester: Edward Elgar Publishing.

Meyer, K. E. (2015). What is "strategic asset seeking FDI"? *Multinational Business Review*, *23*(1), 57–66.

Ministry of Commerce. (2017). *2016 年度中国对外直接投资统计公报 (2016 China Foreign Direct Investment Statistics Bulletin)*. 北京: 中国统计出版社

Ministry of Foreign Affairs of the People's Republic of China. (2015). *China's African Policy《中国对非洲政策文件》*. Retrieved from www.fmprc.gov.cn/web/zyxw/t1321556.shtml

Mlambo, C., Kushamba, A., & Simawu, M. B. (2016). China-Africa relations: What Lies beneath? *The Chinese Economy*, *49*(4), 257–276.

Morris, M., & Einhorn, G. (2008). Globalisation, welfare and competitiveness: The impacts of Chinese imports on the South African clothing and textile industry. *Competition & Change*, *12*(4), 355–376.

Mutabazi, E. (2002). Preparing African leaders. In C. B. Derr, S. Roussillon, & F. Bournois (Eds.), *Cross-cultural approaches to leadership development* (pp. 202–223). Westport, CT: Quorum Books.

Myers, M. (2013). *Qualitative research in business and management*. London: Sage Publications.

Nabil Khodeir, A. (2016). The impact of Chinese direct investments on employment in Africa. *Journal of Chinese Economic Foreign Trade Studies*, *9*(2), 86–101.

Nolan, P. (2004). *Transforming China: Globalization, transition and development*. London: Anthem Press.

Panitchpakdi, S. (2010). World investment report 2010: Investing in a low-carbon economy (Overview) – Key messages: FDI trends and prospects. *Transnational Corporations*, *19*(2), 63–106.

Peng, Z., Qin, C., Chen, R. R., Cannice, M. V., & Yang, X. (2017). Towards a framework of reverse knowledge transfer by emerging economy multinationals: Evidence from Chinese MNE subsidiaries in the United States. *Thunderbird International Business Review*, *59*(3), 349–366.

Pereira, V., Malik, A., Howe-Walsh, L., Munjal, S., & Hirekhan, M. (2017). Managing yopatriates: A longitudinal study of generation Y expatriates in an Indian multinational corporation. *Journal of International Management*, *23*(2), 151–165.

Ramasamy, B., Yeung, M., & Laforet, S. (2012). China's outward foreign direct investment: Location choice and firm ownership. *Journal of World Business*, *47*(1), 17–25.

Ren, S., Xie, Y., Zhu, Y., & Warner, M. (2018). New generation employees' preferences towards leadership style in China. *Asia Pacific Business Review*, 24(4), 437–458.

Rui, H., Zhang, M., & Shipman, A. (2017). Chinese expatriate management in emerging markets: A competitive advantage perspective. *Journal of International Management*, 23(2), 124–138.

Shen, J. (2004). Compensation in Chinese multinationals. *Compensation & Benefits Review*, 36(1), 15–25.

Shen, J. (2006). Factors affecting international staffing in Chinese Multinationals (MNEs). *International Journal of Human Resource Management*, 17(2), 295–315.

Shen, J., & Edwards, V. (2004). Recruitment and selection in Chinese MNEs. *International Journal of Human Resource Management*, 15(4–5), 814–835.

Shen, J., & Edwards, V. (2006). *International human resource management in Chinese multinationals*. London: Routledge.

Shen, J., Edwards, V., & Lee, G. (2005). Developing an integrative international human resource model: The contribution of Chinese multinational enterprises. *Asia Pacific Business Review*, 11(3), 369–388.

Sun, I. Y., Jayaram, K., & Kassiri, O. (2017). *Dance of the Lions and Dragons*. Washington, DC: Mckinsey Global Institute.

Van Tulder, R. (2015). Getting all motives right: A holistic approach to internationalization motives of companies. *The Multinational Business Review*, 23(1), 36–56.

Verbeke, A. (2013). *International business strategy*. Cambridge: Cambridge University Press.

Wang, M. (2012). Empirical study on african energy resources and China's outflow foreign direct investment. *Journal of International Business Research*, 11(1), 19–27.

Warner, M., & Warner, M. (2008). Reassessing human resource management "with Chinese characteristics": An overview. *International Journal of Human Resource Management*, 19(5), 771–801.

Wegenast, T., & Schneider, G. (2017). Ownership matters: Natural resources property rights and social conflict in Sub-Saharan Africa. *Political Geography*, 61, 110–122.

Wei, Z., Xie, F., & Zhang, S. (2005). Ownership structure and firm value in China's privatized firms: 1991–2001. *Journal of Financial and Quantitative Analysis*, 40(1), 87–108.

Wood, G., & Brewster, C. (Eds.). (2007). *Industrial relations in Africa*. Basingstoke: Palgrave Macmillan.

Wood, G., Mazouz, K., Yin, S., & Cheah, J. E. T. (2014). Foreign direct investment from emerging markets to Africa: The HRM context. *Human Resource Management*, 53(1), 179–201.

Xing, Y., Liu, Y., Tarba, S. Y., & Cooper, C. L. (2016). Intercultural influences on managing African employees of Chinese firms in Africa: Chinese managers' HRM practices. *International Business Review*, 25(1, Part A), 28–41.

Xu, Y.-C. (2014). Chinese state-owned enterprises in Africa: Ambassadors or freebooters? *Journal of Contemporary China*, 23(89), 822–840.

Yang, B. (2012). Confucianism, socialism, and capitalism: A comparison of cultural ideologies and implied managerial philosophies and practices in the P. R. China. *Human Resource Management Review*, 22(3), 165–178.

Yao, C. (2014). The impact of cultural dimensions on Chinese expatriates' career capital. *International Journal of Human Resource Management, 25*(5), 609–630.

Yao, C., Arrowsmith, J., & Thorn, K. (2016). Exploring motivations in Chinese corporate expatriation through the lens of confucianism. *Asia Pacific Journal of Human Resources, 54*(3), 312–331.

Zhang, H. M., & Wang, H. Y. (2017). 非洲发展报告 No. 19 (2016–2017) – 非洲工业化与中国在非洲产业园区建设 (Annual report on development in Africa No.19 <2016–2017> – African industrialization and China's construction of industry parks in Africa). 北京：社会科学文献出版社.

Zhang, M. M., & Fan, D. (2014). Expatriate skills training strategies of Chinese multinationals operating in Australia. *Asia Pacific Journal of Human Resources, 52*(1), 60–76.

Zhang, X. F., & He, S. L. (2015). 中国民营企业走入非洲:发展历程、影响因素及未来走向 (Chinese private enterprises enter Africa: Development process, influencing factors and future trends). *国际经济评论, 3*, 120–130, 127–128.

Zhao, S., & Du, J. (2012). Thirty-two years of development of human resource management in China: Review and prospects. *Human Resource Management Review, 22*(3), 179–188.

Zheng, Y., & Smith, C. (2018). Tiered expatriation: A social relations approach to staffing multinationals. *Human Resource Management*, Special issue, 1–14.

Zhong, Y., Zhu, C. J., & Zhang, M. M. (2015). The management of Chinese MNEs' expatriates: The current status and future research agenda. *Journal of Global Mobility, 3*(3), 289–302.

Zhu, J. S. (2018). Chinese multinationals' approach to international human resource management: A longitudinal study. *International Journal of Human Resource Management*, 1–20.

Zhu, Y., & Warner, M. (2018). Managing "New generation" employees in China and beyond: Summing-up. *Asia Pacific Business Review, 24*(4), 578–584.

5 Towards intercultural effectiveness in Sino-African organisations

Exploring synergies and differences in communication culture

Fungai Chigwendere

The global workplace is a microcosm of wider society (Nair-Venugopal, 2015) and one of the most important contexts of intercultural interaction in the 21st century (Martin & Nakayama, 2015; Ladegaard & Jenks, 2015). The global outlook of many businesses therefore makes the notion of intercultural communication effectiveness (ICE) increasingly relevant as home and host countries interact in organisations with the need for managers to learn to function effectively in other cultures (Dean & Popp, 1990; Hammer, Gudykunst, & Wiseman, 1978). For instance, in a foreign environment, "Knowing how to listen, how to interrupt, how to praise, and how to scold, are more important to a foreign manager than learning the language" (Berger, 1987, in Dean & Popp, 1990, p. 405). It can be assumed that the same principles apply to the host country's organisational incumbents who also strive to interact in a way that is effective for meeting their goals and maintaining their comfort and harmony.

The intercultural encounter plays out in Chinese organisations in Africa where Chinese and African counterparts bring to the organisation their espoused values and norms, developed over time, as appropriate ways to manage their specific environments (Schein, 1990). This creates a unique set of challenges and highlights the assertion that what works in one setting may not achieve similar levels of success in another (Hofstede, 1980).

Despite an abundance of theories that should serve as prescriptive guidelines for effectiveness in intercultural contexts, the continuing challenges and barriers to effectiveness raise the need to find out what being interculturally effective in different contexts involves. That said, in discussions centred on effectiveness, the International Business Trend Report (Training & Development, 1999, cited in Liu, Volcic, & Gallois, 2011) singles out intercultural communication skills, problem-solving ability and global leadership as three highly essential competencies in the global workplace. Communication has long been identified as the basis of human interaction (Samovar & Porter, 1995), and its value is evident in organisational settings in which it plays a critical role in processes from negotiation to conflict resolution, to name only a few.

China in Africa: the situation and the challenges

Illustrative of the extent of China's involvement with Africa is the fact that only two countries in Africa have not benefited from Chinese aid (Brautigam, 2011). In addition, China's non-discriminatory approach to financing development and infrastructure projects in various sectors has had positive spin-offs for African economies (Baah & Jauch, 2009) to the extent that today both South Africa for instance and China regard each other as "strategic partners" (Guliwe, Mkhonta, & Vickers, 2009, p. 300). This is evidenced by a strong Chinese commitment to strengthening ties, symbolised by its sponsorship of South African membership to BRICS (Park & Alden, 2013). However, as China's presence in Africa continues to grow, so too have the complexities of the engagement. Park and Alden (2013) use the metaphor of a double storey to describe the engagement, where engagement "upstairs" involves the bilateral, multilateral, political and economic engagement between South Africa, China and other international partners, while the "downstairs" level is seen to involve processes taking place at the level of small businesses and ordinary people (Park & Alden, 2013).

The organisational context is situated at the downstairs level, where the challenges faced include a harsh business environment characterised by uncertainty of supply, dynamics of negotiation, resolving disputes, communication, a negative public image, coexistence, religion, personnel management (Laryea, 2010; Feng & Mu, 2010), trust, power distances and goal orientation (Men, 2014, in Giese, 2014). Scholars who have sought to investigate the cause and solutions for challenges report differences in cultural, behavioural and social norms as major challenges for both managers and employees (e.g. Men, 2014, cited in Giese, 2014). Illumination on the challenges faced within Chinese organisations in Africa is provided by Zhong Jianhua, China's ambassador to South Africa from 2007 to 2012, who points out that even stable Chinese organisations with years of experience in Africa occasionally struggle with labour and social issues because of the wide gap between Chinese culture and the varied cultures of Africa's diverse population. Dietz, Orr, and Xing (2008) concur, viewing the combination of Chinese and foreign forms of communication and cultural norms as one of the biggest challenges facing Chinese companies going abroad.

Interestingly, in a recent study in Tanzania, Men (2014) reports that Chinese people see dual adaptation by interactants as a possible solution. The Chinese should adapt to local needs and the Tanzanians should adapt to the Chinese work ethic and goals (Men, 2014, in Giese, 2014). This contrasts with the view that the extent to which Chinese employers develop an understanding and acceptance of local practices determines the nature of the relationship they enjoy with local employees. This is because, "local employees simply view the Chinese as different people occupying a strangely familiar role as their bosses" (Arsene, 2014, in Giese, 2014, p. 7). The perspectives presented here differ, with the Chinese perspective advocating dual adaptation while the African perspective is seemingly more one-sided. The African perspective seems to be that onus is placed on the Chinese to understand local African practices. The view presented in this chapter is that, owing to the long-term nature of the engagement, a dual consideration – each of the *other* – may be more profitable.

In all the challenges, a key concern highlighted by Zhong Jianhua is the inadequacy of basic in-depth research of the African market, making it impossible for the Chinese to avoid potential cultural complications (Von Schirach, 2012). Therefore, it appears that more suitable approaches are needed to achieve desired communication outcomes with minimal misunderstandings. Such approaches can only be created with the benefit of knowledge and understanding. With this in mind, a "multi-view" approach (Chigwendere, 2016) to understanding communication in Chinese and African cultures is engaged. Using this approach, the synergies and differences in African and Chinese communication cultures are explored, resulting in a theoretical framework for communication between Western, Chinese and African cultures. The next section briefly presents a conceptual framework for understanding intercultural communication in African and Chinese cultures.

A multi-view conceptual framework

A multi-view approach is proposed here as one where interactants seek a reciprocal understanding of communication effectiveness within and across cultures (Figure 5.1). It is characterised by an inquiry into the home country and host country's perspectives of their communication culture in order to establish intercultural awareness. In the case of Chinese organisations in Africa, inclusion of Western cultures provides a context, given the significant role Western countries have played in the emergence of the formal economic organisation. Engaging Western theory, however, does not underplay or negate the strides made in the development of more indigenous theories of communication such as Afrocentricity (Asante, 1999, 2012) or Asia-centricity (Miike, 2007).

It is argued that adopting a multi-view in the Sino-African context allows for a "dialectical approach" (Martin & Nakayama, 2010) where meaningful intercultural communication can be built on non-Western and Western perspectives of ICE, and on "awareness of difference as much as similarity and of uncertainty as much as certainty" (Xu, 2013, p. 387). The multi-view perspective opens up new possibilities for researchers to

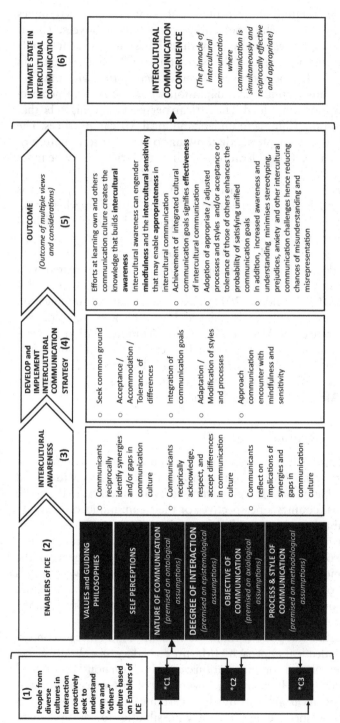

*C1, *C2 and *C3 represents the multiple cultures in interaction
Authors construction

Figure 5.1 A conceptual framework for understanding intercultural communication effectiveness (ICE) – (congruence)

Source: Chigwendere, 2016

look for values and beliefs about communication that cross boundaries (Chen & Starosta, 2003).

According to Narh (2013), different societies are founded on different paradigmatic assumptions influencing their worldviews. Values and assumptions that shape the way individuals view and relate to the world also affect how they express themselves and understand each other (Huang, 2010). In this light, a multi-view approach is deemed appropriate. In Hall's words, "communication is culture" (Hall, 1959, p. 159).

Within the multi-view framework and using a cross-cultural approach, intercultural communication is viewed in terms of "enablers" of ICE. "Enablers are those considerations that enable the understanding of communication in different cultures for the purposes of understanding intercultural communication effectiveness" (Chigwendere, 2016). The resulting understanding is the basis for intercultural awareness – "a state of knowing the distinct characteristics of one's own culture and that of one's counterparts" (Chen, 2015, p. 466). Refer to Enablers of ICE (2) in Figure 5.1 following. These enablers are: values and guiding philosophies, self-perceptions, nature of communication, degree of interaction, objective of communication, and process and style of communication.

As Figure 5.1 indicates, a multi-view approach to conceptualising and understanding ICE is broad. Column 1 is a depiction of people from different cultures (labelled C1, C2 and C3) in interaction. Each cultural group actively seeks to understand self and other as shown by the interlinking reverse arrows connecting all cultural groups together. In this analysis, the groups refer to Western, African and Chinese cultures.

Column 2 represents the enablers for understanding communication, both within and across cultures. The enabler-based understanding of communication is simultaneous and reciprocal in giving clues to what ICE might look like. It is envisaged that this kind of proactive and participative approach results in intercultural awareness (Column 3). A state of intercultural awareness provides the foundation from which suitable strategies and approaches to the intercultural communication encounter can be developed and implemented. Possible ways of improving the effectiveness of the intercultural communication encounter are listed in Column 4. A positive spin-off of intercultural awareness is greater intercultural sensitivity in interaction, thereby enhancing ICE.

Potential outcomes of the multi-view approach are listed in Column 5 in terms of increased understanding, greater sensitivity, achievement of integrated goals, adaptation of styles and greater effectiveness and appropriateness in communication. This creates a "win/win" for all involved. This perspective is in tune with other theoretical approaches aimed at achieving win/win scenarios in communication such as the Grunig and Grunig (1992) two-way symmetrical model for public relations (PR) excellence. PR practitioners are called to adjust or adapt their behaviours with emphasis being placed on reciprocity and mutual understanding.

In the intercultural encounter, increased awareness and understanding ultimately serve to minimise stereotyping and anxiety among other challenges that hamper ICE. Increased awareness also enables the optimising of existing communication synergies.

Finally, Column 6 represents the hypothetical ultimate state of intercultural communication – *intercultural communication congruence* (ICC) – where communication is both effective and appropriate. Such a state is achievable when the cultures of all interacting parties are considered because, "there is no culture that is greater or lesser than the other" (Asante in Asante & Miike, 2013, p. 4). One cannot speak of effectiveness without considering appropriateness in intercultural encounters.

In the multidimensional concept of ICC, approaching communication between people from different cultures from a point of equality and respect breeds a state of congruence where harmony and agreement prevail. Agreement exists in the sense that all parties acknowledge the need for mutual achievement of their ultimate communicative goals. Harmony, on the other hand, is a consequence of the tolerance, accommodation, acceptance or adjustments that may be made over the process of the intercultural communication encounter (Chen, 2015). In other words, this analysis argues that intercultural effectiveness in a multicultural context should not be understood on the basis of monocultural views.

Although the multi-view approach may be criticised for perhaps oversimplifying or overgeneralising distinct cultural characteristics in its application, it is practical and provides a starting point for understanding Sino-African interactions. It is a synthesis of insights derived from existing approaches to form a holistic framework with both practical and scholarly implications. The multi-view is based on combining the perspectives of those involved in interaction, and not on predetermined standards from other cultures, as is the case with existing approaches. Its specificity ensures more accurate culturally relevant understanding. Essentially the multi-view approach is alive and interactive in nature, deriving meaning and insights from active "self and other" reporting by those in the intercultural encounter. In the next section, the multi-view is applied in a synthesis of literature aimed at identifying the synergies and differences in communication culture.

Exploring synergies and differences in Western, African and Chinese communication culture

In seeking to understand similarities and differences in communication, a cross-cultural approach allows for the pooling together and juxtaposition of existing communication literature on different cultures leading to both knowledge creation and insights. Collier, Ribeau, and Hetch (1986) assert that, in addition to culture differences, differences in communication may be attributable to different worldviews and philosophies. Ono

(2013, p. 92) concurs, stating that "without an understanding of world-views, without an understanding of cultural complexity and cultural syncretism, without an in-depth understanding of cultural difference, not much of value can be said about people by outsiders". It can therefore be inferred that differences in guiding philosophies lead to differences in communication practices and characteristics. The findings of Yum (1988) support this claim, where East Asian and North American patterns of communication were compared. East Asian cultures were seen to emphasise social relationships while North American culture placed emphasis on individualism.

In this section, insights developed from a synthesis of literature on culture and communication in Western, African and Chinese cultures are presented. The synthesis of literature is carried out on the basis of the conceptual framework for understanding ICE as presented in Figure 5.1. A cross-section of empirical, non-empirical and philosophical literature was synthesised, resulting in a theoretical view of communication within the different cultures which brings to light the communication synergies and/or gaps in Western, African and Chinese cultures. The final outcome is the development of a theoretical framework depicting communication in Western, African and Chinese cultures which can be validated empirically.

Western, African and Chinese cultures are considered in a synthesis of literature pertaining to ICE in Chinese organisations in Africa. As mentioned, the inclusion of Western cultures is critical in view of the influence that the West has had on the very emergence of the formal economic organisation in Africa. In addition, it provides a point of comparison that may enhance the understanding of non-Western cultures. It is important to highlight that when speaking of African, Chinese or Western cultures, the aim is not to "essentialise" these cultures or "gloss over the heterogeneity and diversity that resides within them" (Martin & Nakayama, 2010, p. 91). Essentialism is the tendency to view human life as having central defining features (Nussbaum, 1992). In the current analysis, the aim is therefore not to imply that all Africans are the same, nor that all Chinese are the same. While there is acknowledgement that Chinese and African cultures may not exist in their purest form because of historical and other influences, there is consensus that in both Chinese and African cultures certain core values endure and continue to form the guiding principles for day-to-day living (Narh, 2013; Salo-Lee, 2006). In Chinese cultures, core values are principally based on Confucianism, while African culture has communalism and Ubuntu at its heart.

Figure 5.2 presents a comparative theoretical framework of communication in Western, African and Chinese cultures. This has been developed on the basis of the enablers of ICE as perceived in the different cultures. The framework is inspired by the work of Chen (2015) who compares the

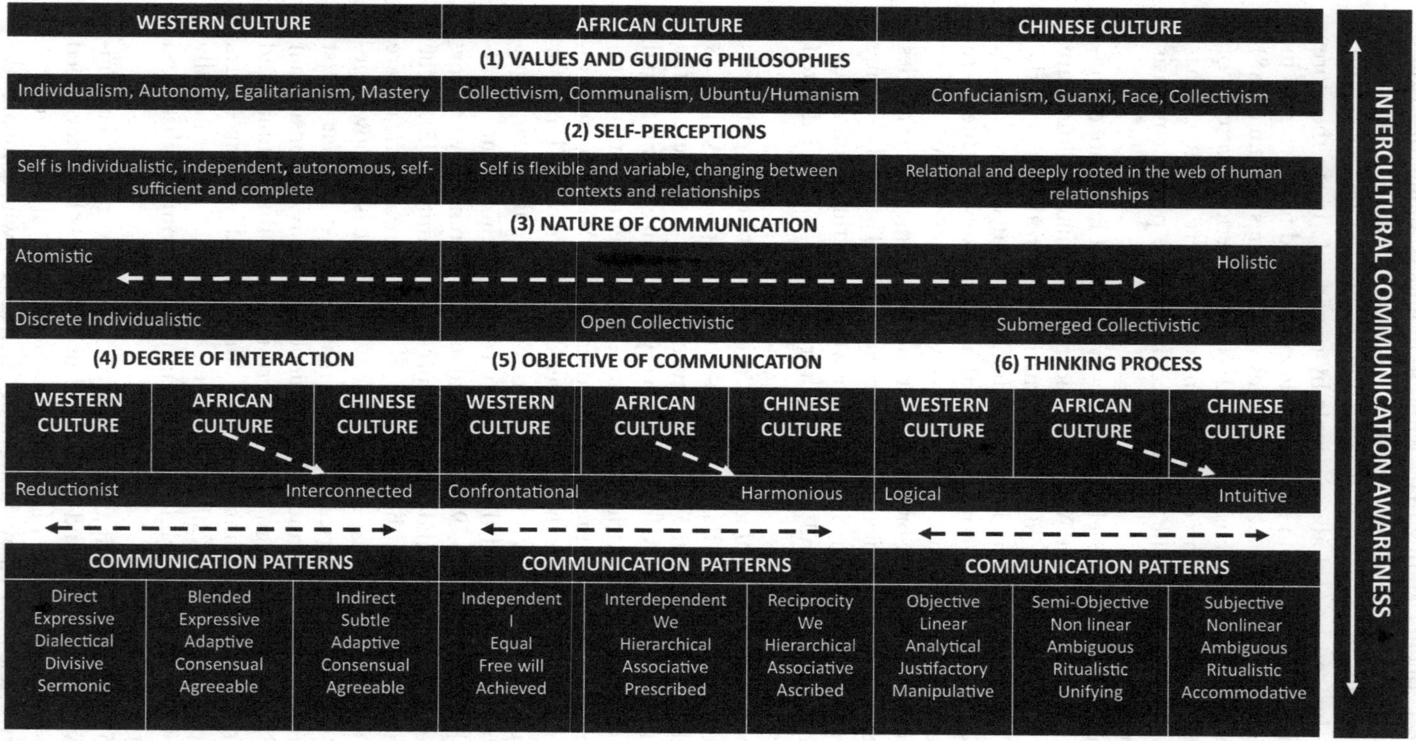

INTERCULTURAL COMMUNICATION AWARENESS

(1) VALUES AND GUIDING PHILOSOPHIES

WESTERN CULTURE	AFRICAN CULTURE	CHINESE CULTURE
Individualism, Autonomy, Egalitarianism, Mastery	Collectivism, Communalism, Ubuntu/Humanism	Confucianism, Guanxi, Face, Collectivism

(2) SELF-PERCEPTIONS

WESTERN CULTURE	AFRICAN CULTURE	CHINESE CULTURE
Self is Individualistic, independent, autonomous, self-sufficient and complete	Self is flexible and variable, changing between contexts and relationships	Relational and deeply rooted in the web of human relationships

(3) NATURE OF COMMUNICATION

Atomistic ←→ Holistic

Discrete Individualistic	Open Collectivistic	Submerged Collectivistic

(4) DEGREE OF INTERACTION

WESTERN CULTURE	AFRICAN CULTURE	CHINESE CULTURE
Reductionist		Interconnected

COMMUNICATION PATTERNS

WESTERN CULTURE	AFRICAN CULTURE	CHINESE CULTURE
Direct	Blended	Indirect
Expressive	Expressive	Subtle
Dialectical	Adaptive	Adaptive
Divisive	Consensual	Consensual
Sermonic	Agreeable	Agreeable

(5) OBJECTIVE OF COMMUNICATION

WESTERN CULTURE	AFRICAN CULTURE	CHINESE CULTURE
Confrontational		Harmonious

COMMUNICATION PATTERNS

WESTERN CULTURE	AFRICAN CULTURE	CHINESE CULTURE
Independent	Interdependent	Reciprocity
I	We	We
Equal	Hierarchical	Hierarchical
Free will	Associative	Associative
Achieved	Prescribed	Ascribed

(6) THINKING PROCESS

WESTERN CULTURE	AFRICAN CULTURE	CHINESE CULTURE
Logical		Intuitive

COMMUNICATION PATTERNS

WESTERN CULTURE	AFRICAN CULTURE	CHINESE CULTURE
Objective	Semi-Objective	Subjective
Linear	Non linear	Nonlinear
Analytical	Ambiguous	Ambiguous
Justifactory	Ritualistic	Ritualistic
Manipulative	Unifying	Accommodative

*In all cultural groups there exist opposite value orientations in each set of paradigmatic assumptions along a continuum, with cultures tending to lean to one extreme over the other in interaction.

**African cultures tend to be more similar to Chinese cultures though a complete overlap is not posited. This position is inferred from literature reviewed.

Figure 5.2 A theoretical framework for understanding ICE (congruence) in Western, African and Chinese cultures.

Source: Chigwendere, 2016

paradigmatic assumptions of American culture (herein taken to represent Western cultures) and Chinese culture. Chen's framework is adapted to incorporate the assumptions of African cultures, also reflecting patterns of communication as inferred from literature. Figure 5.2 is columnar and flows from top to bottom, left to right.

Values and guiding philosophies (1): comparison and implications for communication

Reflected in Figure 5.2 at Subheading 1 are values and guiding philosophies in Western, African and Chinese cultures. Values represent the deepest manifestation of culture (Francesco & Gold, 2005; Trompenaars & Hampden Turner, 1993; Hofstede, 1991) and broad tendencies to prefer certain states over others. These are the ingrained, unwritten rules of a society that bring to the fore things that humans see as being important in their lives (Schwartz, 2012; Trompenaars & Hampden Turner, 1993). They are, "desirable trans-situational goals, varying in importance and serving as guiding principles in the life of a person or social entity (Schwartz, 1994, p. 21). In other words, values are intimately intertwined with moral and ethical codes which determine what people think ought to be done, and how they should behave (Schwartz, 2012). While differences in values are acknowledged in the analyses, cognisance is taken of the view that all cultures potentially share the same value orientations, only differing in the extent to which each culture tends to one extreme of orientation over the other (Chen, 2015; Gudykunst et al., 1996).

A review and synthesis of literature reveals that Western cultures are guided by individualistic values while African cultures are guided by communalistic values embodied in Ubuntu. However, while Ubuntu is opposed to the rugged extremes of individualism, it is not its opposite, neither is it synonymous with collectivism (Khoza, 2011). In Chinese culture on the other hand, Confucianism is the principle guiding philosophy espoused in the values of *jen, yi* and *li*. Qualities representing *jen* include, *yi* (righteousness or justice) and *li* (propriety). *Yi* is concerned with righteousness, faithfulness and justice in social interaction while *li* is concerned with the proper way of interaction and encompasses propriety, rite and respect for social norms (Gan, 2014; Chen & Chung, 1994). What can be discerned from the Confucian principle of *jen* is that relationships and all they stand for in Chinese culture are regulated by a code of ethics. The purpose of adhering to the principles of *jen, yi* and *li* is to ensure the maintenance of social order through the observance of hierarchy and role relationships (Gan, 2014).

Comparatively, African and Chinese cultures are reportedly collectivistic and this could be a potentially useful synergy for enhancing ICE. At face value, it can be inferred that communication emphasis could be similar in the two cultures. However, this may or may not be so, given that research has established that although cultures may be described as collectivistic, there may exist differences in the direction at which collectivism is directed.

African communalism and Ubuntu place an emphasis on the interdependence of the individual and the community at large, including the living, the dead and the spiritual (Narh, 2013; Higgs, 2010; Van der Colf, 2003; McFarlin, Coster, & Mogale-Pretorius, 1999; Maomeka, 1989). Confucianist principles, on the hand, place an emphasis on interconnectedness and relationships between people, honouring their roles in those relationships (Yum, 1988; Lockett, 1988). Particularly, Ubuntu in African culture advocates hospitality, respect and acceptance of all, including sojourners (Bell & Metz, 2011) while under Confucianism, communitarianism does not extend to strangers but is more insider-focused as a result of the "insider vs outsider" distinctions in Chinese culture (Salo-Lee, 2006; Gao & Ting Toomey, 1998).

The sense of community therefore appears to be more universal in African cultures, with application to all in the community, while in Chinese culture, community would tend to be more particularistic, based on the context and the relationship status. What would be interesting to determine is the extent to which the insider vs outsider aspect of Chinese culture can be extended to the collective members in an organisational setting. Would the insider principle apply to the collective members of the organisation despite their different national cultural backgrounds? Having discussed the collectivism/communitarianism of African and Chinese cultures, mention is also made here of the individualism of Western cultures seen in the individual's pursuit of own goals and primary concern with the self, power, achievement and self-direction (Kim, 2007; Miike, 2002; Eaton & Louw, 2000; Gao & Ting-Toomey, 1998; Schwartz, 1992).

Analysing the communal or collectivist aspect of both Chinese and African cultures also reveals another point of divergence in the powers ascribed to the community. In African cultures, the community reigns supreme over all individuals, who in turn have value in themselves as highly valued components of the community (Maomeka, 1989; Metz, 2015). In Chinese culture, however, powers are not ascribed to the community but rather to elders or those sitting higher in the hierarchy of relationships (Chen, 2015; Gan, 2014; Gao & Ting Toomey, 1998; Chen & Chung, 1994; Lockett, 1988; Yum, 1988). In addition, while equality and consensus is valued in African culture (Maomeka, 1989; Traber, 1989), the rule of hierarchy prevails in traditional Chinese cultures (Chen, 2015; Ding, 2006; Gao & Ting-Toomey, 1998; Chen & Chung, 1994).

To say that equality is valued in African culture does not mean that the value of the respect accorded to elders is diminished. People are equal in the sense that they all subscribe to the rules of the community which they all contribute to as individuals. A consultative and consensus orientation resulting in harmony is evident in African cultures, while a more resigned orientation may be seen to exist in Chinese culture. People are resigned to the fact that those in higher positions are the most knowledgeable and this is accepted as one of life's truths. Harmony in Chinese culture therefore "does not consist of uniformity or conformity but rather of a variety of basic elements that form a unity in the interests of all its parts" (Metz, 2015, p. 89).

Furthermore, in the comparison, interesting parallels can be drawn between Chinese and African cultures in terms of concern for people, respect for elders, adherence to social norms, respect for truth, and social justice (Matondo, 2012; Maomeka, 1989; Traber, 1989; Myers, 1987, Bell & Metz, 2011; Metz, 2015). Evidence for this is provided by Matondo (2012) and Metz (2015) who both compare the philosophies of Confucianism and Ubuntu and conclude that Ubuntu and Confucianism share important similarities with regard to value of the community, value of harmony, proper relationships, role of partiality in moral thinking and heightened respect accorded to elders.

An additional point of similarity between Ubuntu and Confucianism is the extent to which personal achievement is underplayed in favour of group achievement, as reported by Shonhiwa (2008), and the preference for modesty in achievement in Chinese cultures. This contrasts with the self-advancement and enhancement motives of Western cultures (Gao & Ting Toomey, 1998). This may serve to highlight the distance between Western worldviews and non-Western worldviews, hence affecting views on communication.

In the midst of synergies, there also exist differences between Confucianism and Ubuntu. Metz (2015) for instance notes the lack of reference to God or indeed an afterlife in Confucianism. This contrasts with African beliefs and Ubuntu where belief in God or a higher being is one of the prominent characteristics of Ubuntu (Metz, 2015). Under Confucianism, there is an emphasis on the physical life – the here and now – as opposed to the spiritual aspect of life (Metz, 2015). This contrasts with the resiliently religious characteristic of Ubuntu (Khoza, 2011). So while Ubuntu and Confucianism may be seen to represent similar values in many respects, these subtle differences remind one of the idiom: "the devil is in the details".

Other subtle differences exist between Confucianism and Ubuntu with potential implications for communication. These include the extent and direction of the status accorded to elders. For instance, while Confucianism holds the belief that people improve morally and get wiser with age (Gao & Ting-Toomey, 1998), in African society, age alone is not a sufficient condition for social wisdom (Bell & Metz, 2011). One has to earn respect by virtue of one's behaviour and contribution to the community over time. Elders must be seen to be "human" through the display of ethical behaviour (Metz, 2015). It is possible, then, that in African culture it is only those elders who have proven their "humanness" who are considered wise and worth listening to. Such contrasts, though seemingly insignificant in themselves, may cause difficulty in Sino-African intercultural communication encounters.

Further on the aspect of subtle differences, although both Chinese and African cultures are reportedly humanist, there may be differences in the nature of humanism. In African culture, humanism attributes self-worth to the individuals who have value in themselves albeit in relation to others (Faniran, 2014, p. 151; Khoza, 2011; Igboin, 2011, p. 99; Jackson, 1999; Maomeka, 1989), while in Chinese culture, the focus is on reciprocity and the relationship that is important between people (Yum, 1988, p. 374). It could be inferred therefore that in African culture, no matter how small the contribution, the individual is "*heard*". The African community member is entitled to make a contribution to the community whether or not their suggestions are ultimately accepted (Maomeka, 1989).

In contrast, in Chinese culture, talking is discouraged as it is thought to bring misfortune (Gao & Ting Toomey, 1998). Discussion is the preserve of the most experienced older community members. In addition, rather than affording the individual a voice, humanism in Chinese culture focuses on people treating each other in the right way as per societal expectations. To an extent, the common sayings "you scratch my back and I'll scratch yours" and "do unto others as you would have them do to you" reflect the humanism of Chinese culture. Aspects of humanism are also reflected in the face-giving and face-saving behaviours of Chinese culture (Ting-Toomey, 1988; Ting-Toomey & Kurogi, 1998).

To complete the picture of the Western vs African vs Chinese comparison of humanism at this point, an allusion is made to Western humanism. According to Khoza (2011), Western humanism differs from African and Chinese humanism on the basis of its view of humankind as the apex of the evolutionary process (Khoza, 2011, p. 433). Here, humankind is seen as self-sufficient, as an adequate reason for its own existence, with the supernatural playing no part in the course of events. As such, Western humanism is characterised by individualism and atheism (Khoza, 2011).

A comparative analysis of values would not be complete without reference to the characterisations of different cultures based on the work of scholars such as Hofstede (1980), Hall (1976), Schwartz (1992, 1994), and Gan (2014). Gan postulates that "traditionally the Chinese people worship the collective while Westerners revere individualism" (Gan, 2014, p. 76). Looking at the intended countries of study in terms of Hofstede's (2011) characterisations, a significantly higher level of individualism is reported in South Africa than in China. In other words, China could be viewed as more collectivist than South Africa. Interestingly, while both countries are considered collectivist, there are differences in the direction of the collectivism. In African cultures, collectivism is directed at the community at large, while in Chinese cultures it is directed to the "*in-group*". This aspect of differentiation has been previously mentioned in this discussion.

Further advancing the analysis of Chinese culture from Western perspectives, the collectivism of Chinese cultures has been equated to Schwartz's (1992) value of embeddedness, while power distance has been equated with the values of hierarchy. Embeddedness epitomises a concern for protection of one's public image and the social order, while hierarchy is reflected in humility and the respect for authority. These values have considerable similarity to those of African culture where authority and respect for elders are highly esteemed communalistic principles. Another interesting emerging characterisation of Chinese people using Schwartz's value orientations is "mastery", which portrays the Chinese people as successful and ambitious (Leung, 2008), thus potentially showing the influence that Western-style education may be having on Chinese culture.

According to Hofstede and Bond (1988), the Chinese people place emphasis on hard work, thrift and the long term. This aspect of Chinese culture presents a point of difference with the Africans, as found by Westropp (2012). Following a cultural analysis of sub-Saharan Africa and China, Westropp (2012) reports a short-term orientation in Africans and a long-term orientation in the Chinese with these differences presenting a potential source of conflict (Westropp, 2012). In addition, the Chinese are seen to be comfortable with uncertainty and ambiguity, hence their characterisation as being relatively low in uncertainty avoidance (Hofstede, 1980). This is explained as a situation where truth may be generally relative and only a major concern in immediate social circles where rules are adopted as they suit the actual situation.

Although the uncertainty avoidance factor has not been researched exhaustively, in view of the literature accessed, there appears to be a divergence with African cultures where communalistic values dictate that all individuals, including leadership, adhere to rules and laws agreed upon by the community. The Hofstede studies give support to this speculation with South Africa scoring higher on the uncertainty avoidance scale. South Africans therefore are shown as having a preference for more structured and predictable outcomes compared to the Chinese.

Hall's (1976) cultural factors also provide a premise upon which to differentiate cultures. As with African culture, the Chinese culture tends to have a polychronic time orientation where a person can do more than one thing at once. Time is controlled by man and is to be programmed into cultural norms of human behaviour and how people relate to each other. However, Chinese culture differs from African culture, in that while in African culture the death of a person for instance can change appointments previously made without a thought, the Chinese are generally speaking punctual and will honour their appointments (Matondo, 2012). They suggest that the Chinese are inclined to focus first on the business at hand and attend to any eventualities later. Western cultures, on the other hand, have a monochronic orientation to time where schedules and appointments are adhered to strictly (Francesco & Gold, 2005).

Furthermore, while touching is common between conversationalists in African culture, it is only accepted among in-group members in Chinese culture. In Western cultures, there exist unsaid acceptable space limits depending on the nature of the relationship between the people interacting. While it may be acceptable to get very close to someone in communication in African culture, the degree of acceptance differs across other cultures.

To conclude this brief and by no means exhaustive discussion on cultural differences, reference is made to the Yin Yang perspective on culture popularised by Fang (2011). The Yin Yang perspective highlights the paradoxical nature of Chinese culture in which paradox is viewed as interdependent opposites rather than as exclusive variables as perceived by the West (Fang, 2011), and this is testimony to the holistic nature of Chinese culture (Chen, 2015; Chen, 2011; Littlejohn & Foss, 2008; Chen & Starosta, 2003; Miike, 2002). The Yin Yang philosophy of Chinese culture may have parallels in the "di-unital logic" of African culture where dichotomies seldom exist (Ani, 2013; Ajei, 2007) and "everything is interrelated through human and spiritual networks" (Myers, 1987, p. 74). When compared to Western culture, however, differences are notable in the Western propensity to dichotomise and emphasise distinctions and the separateness of things. Chinese people's ability to manage paradox is therefore a fact that all cultures in communication with people from the Chinese culture need to be acutely aware of (Faure & Fang, 2008).

It can be concluded that the value placed by the Chinese on respect for etiquette, respect for age and hierarchy is the most enduring, with Faure and Fang (2008, p. 202) contending that "seniority and respect for the customs remain the impassable norm". Parallels can be drawn with African culture where elders are held in high regard and rules for living are dictated by customs and tradition (Ani, 2013; Narh, 2013, Maomeka, 1989; Myers, 1987). Other features that continue to underlie social interactions, particularly in the organisational setting in Chinese culture, include group orientation, face (*mianzi*) and the importance of relationships (*guanxi*). Such features help distinguish Chinese organisations from those in other cultures, particularly in the West (Lockett, 1988; Chen & Chung, 1994).

Despite a focus on what could be termed core Western, African and Chinese values, the fact is that value systems are constantly changing. This reality is a limitation in the discussion of findings based on consideration of purely indigenous perspectives. Nonetheless, basing initial investigations on indigenous perspectives is useful as it provides an opportunity for the generation of hypothesis and research questions.

While the preceding discussion has presented a comparison of cultural values in general, the next section delves into the different worldviews and paradigmatic assumptions of different cultures in relation to communication. Worldview is the "perception of the world that helps the individual locate his or her place and rank in the universe" and "it influences nearly every action in which the individual engages" (Skow & Samovar, 2015, p. 144). This includes communication.

Self-perceptions (2): comparison and implications for communication

Subheading 2 in Figure 5.2 represents the consideration of the self-perceptions of people in Western, African and Chinese cultures, because how people see themselves influences how they communicate (Huang, 2010, p. 100).

While in Western cultures the self is viewed as individualistic, ego-driven, self-sufficient and complete (Kim, 2007; Miike, 2002; Eaton & Louw, 2000; Gao & Ting-Toomey, 1998), in African culture the self is interdependent and self-perception is flexible – varying between contexts and relationships (Faniran, 2014; Eaton & Louw, 2000; Myer, 1987). In Chinese culture, Confucian tradition defines the self from a group per-spective and places self at the centre of relationships and the social roles they play (Miike & Yin, 2015, p. 458; Miike, 2002; Gao & Ting-Toomey, 1998). The value placed on an individual's self-perception and association with their community in African and Chinese culture is quite similar. They do not completely overlap, however, as differences are apparent in the manner in which communication takes place.

In African cultures, communication is largely consensual and community-centred with a strict following of the rules and norms of the community as well as the maintenance of respect (Faniran, 2014; Maomeka, 1989). Comparatively in Chinese cultures, communication is adaptive to the role and hierarchy of relationships (Chen, 2015; Yum, 1988). Maintaining harmonious relationships, saving face and giving face are central to com-munication in Chinese culture. In addition, whereas African people will use any means possible to share information, be it loud or subtle, the Chinese have a preference for subtlety and succinctness. In Western cul-tures, on the other hand, communication is explicit, assertive and geared towards controlling and differentiating one's self from others (Chen, 2015).

Nature of communication (3): comparison and implications for communication

Essentially Western cultures are dominated by the theme of individualism (Chen, 2015; Narh, 2013; Higgs, 2010; Hofstede, 1980) while African culture emphasises the interrelationship between the human and spiritual networks (Narh, 2013; Igboin, 2011; Myers, 1987). Chinese culture, sim-ilar to African culture, emphasises interrelationships of all across space and time (Miike, 2002; Chen & Starosta, 2003). In addition, the Chinese theme of circularity provides "a sense of relatedness of the present to the past and the future, and life to nature" (Miike, 2002, p. 6). All is viewed as being in transition and communication is seen as always being in a state of change and transformation (Chen & Starosta, 2003). This partly parallels African culture where the universe is viewed as "a composite blend of divine, spiritual, human, animate and inanimate beings constantly interacting with one another" (Igboin, 2011, p. 98; Myers, 1987). In African culture, no reality exists without a spiritual inclination (Narh, 2013). Consequently, because of the different views held on the nature of existence across the cultures, different values are displayed in interaction. In Western cultures, people display the value of individualism in interaction while in African and Chinese cultures, people display a more collectivistic and holistic orientation (Chen, 2015; Maomeka, 1989).

On the basis of what has been learnt of the different ontological assumptions, one can infer that communication in Western cultures is a matter of free will, and although polite, it may not necessarily show concern for others' feelings. In addition, preferred communication in Western culture is likely to present a situation of either "black or white" with no grey areas. On the other hand, communication in Chinese and African cultures may require extra care in ensuring the comfort of all interactants owing to their communal and holistic orientations.

Degree of interaction (4): comparison and implications for communication

By virtue of their individualistic and atomistic assumptions, Western cultures are characterised by a reductionist way of knowing (Chen, 2015). This has led to them being termed "truth-orientated cultures" (Metz, 2015; Hofstede & Bond, 1988). A reductionist view is dependent on dichotomising and simplification of complex phenomena through rational and logical thinking (Chen, 2002). As a result, the values of independence, the sense of "*I*", equality, free will and achievement in the process of interaction are seen to come through (Chen, 2015). This Western reductionist view differs from the Chinese and African interconnected way of knowing.

The Chinese way of knowing is intuitive, interconnected and holistic (Chen, 2015, 2011). Interconnectedness between the knower and known is seen as the centre of genuine knowledge (Chen, 2015; Miike, 2002, p. 6). As such, human communication is seen as a relational process in which interactants constantly adapt to and relocate each other in a network of interdependence (Chen & Starosta, 2003; Ding, 2006). Mutual dependence dominates Asian existence (Chen & Starosta, 2003) and interconnectedness in communication is demonstrated by behavioural characteristics such as "*we*" group sense, reciprocity, hierarchy and associative and ascribed relationship (Chen, 2015).

In African culture, on the other hand, community and ancestry lie at the centre of knowing (Narh, 2013) with individual knowledge being dictated by symbolic knowledge and participation in the social context of the community (Ani, 2013). As in Chinese culture, the highest value is placed on interpersonal relationships between people (Myer, 1987), and communication is, "a matter of human inter-relationships conducted strictly according to norms and mores of the community" (Maomeka, 1989, p. 5). Communication is therefore interdependent, prescribed and "*we*" centred. In this study, what remains to be determined is the potential impact of the different epistemological assumptions on the process of communication when people from the different cultures interact, and how these differences can be reconciled.

As a result of the perceived ways of knowing in each of Western, African and Chinese cultures, assumptions can be made about interaction between people from those cultures. It can be hypothesised that in Chinese cultures, because adapting to requirements of a context or relationship comes naturally, it may be possible to adapt to communication requirements in other cultures where cultural distance is not too large. In the case of Chinese and African cultures, there is a similarity in the value placed on the community and the need to follow rules and guidelines in communication, maintain relationships and preserve harmony. Through proactive knowledge-seeking and intercultural awareness, perhaps a third culture – an intercultural communication culture – can be established for people engaged in this type of communication. While creating an intercultural communication culture may be a possibility, this would need to be underpinned by an acknowledgment, understanding and incorporation of the broader perceived communication goals of all the cultures in interaction.

Objective of communication (5): comparison and implications for communication

While the goal of existence in Western cultures is to solve problems, control and influence (Chen, 2015; Trompenaars & Hampden-Turner, 1993; Miike, 2002), in African culture, the goal is to promote social order and harmony (Maomeka, 1989). In both African and Chinese cultures, harmony is the ultimate goal (Chen, 2015; Chen & Starosta, 2003; Miike, 2002). Harmony, as the core of Asian culture, has ethical appeal and is seen as an end rather than a means of human communication (Chen & Starosta, 2003). People communicate with dignity and influence in a mutual and interdependent network on the basis of cooperation (Chen & Starosta, 2003). Harmony thus regulates the process of communication in Asian culture. The goal of communication in Chinese culture, however, differs starkly from that of Western culture where there is an innate desire by interactants to exert power and direct interaction in their own favour (Chen, 2015; Chen & Starosta, 2003; Miike, 2002). In Chinese society, harmony is sought within the in-group and with the universe at large while in African society, it is largely directed at the community at large.

In addition, because collectivism is emphasised in both Chinese and African cultures, a quest for relationship and maintenance of social order is evident in the communalism and Ubuntu of African society, and in harmony and *guanxi* of Chinese society. It could be worthwhile investigating whether these seemingly related factors could be harnessed to develop unified goals in intercultural communication.

Process and style of communication (6): comparison and implications for communication

According to Chen (2015), the Chinese preference for intuitive problem-solving indicates that many paths can reach the same destination and that all paths are complementary and equally appropriate (Chen, 2011, 2015). Western cultures, on the other hand, follow structured logical thinking in their problem-solving (Littlejohn & Foss, 2008, 2010; Chen, 2015). Objectivity, linearity, analysis, justification and manipulation are Western approaches to interaction (Chen, 2015). In African culture, methods are potentially a blend of prescription, ritual and semi-objectivity aimed at gaining consensus. Overall, interaction styles could be described as accommodative in African cultures, adaptive in Chinese cultures and confrontational in Western cultures.

Furthermore, while Western cultures use speech to get their points across in communication, people in Chinese and African cultures are instead mutually concerned with cooperation (Chen, 2015, p. 468; Chen & Starosta, 2003). In Western culture, people will speak as they see fit based on their personality and socioeconomic position (Miike, 2002). What they say and how they say it is unpredictable as it is self-determined. In both African and Chinese cultures, on the other hand, what is said and how it is said is largely predictable owing to the prescriptive nature of African culture and the rule- and ethic-honouring nature of Chinese culture (Faniran, 2014; Maomeka, 1989; Chen & Starosta, 2003; Miike, 2002). Complications in intercultural communication can arise when the different cultures have different communicating rules.

This section has demonstrated an exploratory theoretical application of the multi-view approach in a Sino-African context. While other models and theories in communication science may well be useful in future investigations, it is evident at this point that this exploratory application has implications for both management practice and theory development.

Implications for management and theory development

A theoretical framework for conceptualising and understanding ICE in Sino-African interactions has the potential to make a significant contribution to improving communication effectiveness in Chinese organisations in Africa. Intercultural insights are particularly useful in the area of training, which has long been identified as a key area for dealing with many of the challenges emerging in the Sino-African relationship (Feng & Mu, 2010). The multi-view approach, encouraging mutual and reciprocal knowledge acquisition, can potentially mitigate the effects of ignorance-related barriers and challenges to intercultural communication such as ethnocentrism, stereotyping, prejudice, language differences, ambiguity and non-verbal misinterpretations (Okech, Pimpleton, Vannatta, & Champe, 2015; Washington, 2013; Beebe, Beebe, & Redmond, 2011; Martin & Nakayama, 2010; Phatak, Bhagat, & Kashlak, 2005).

If those engaged in intercultural communication have a proactive and accommodative knowledge-seeking attitude, an integrated communication culture may result, which can improve the effectiveness of the encounter. A multi-view approach provides another way to understand ICE, particularly in the Sino-African context. Applied practically, an understanding of communication in each culture can be sought in terms of the identified enablers of ICE. The resulting frameworks can then be verified by means of qualitative in-depth interviews based on a series of questions designed to capture communication nuances according to the identified enablers. A juxtaposition of findings would then illuminate gaps and synergies and point to potential training areas and to insights in need of sharing.

It is also anticipated that insights gained from a comparison of the different cultures will clarify what "effectiveness" means in ICE. Indeed, the different theoretical perspectives on communication in different cultures suggest that the state of effectiveness in intercultural communication is far less relevant than is congruence – where the multiple perspectives are taken cognisance of.

Finally, the multi-view approach to intercultural interaction can help to minimise misunderstandings and challenges in different organisational aspects of life. It does this through a process of simultaneous and reciprocal knowledge production and sharing by the cultural interactants. This in turn informs the nature and content of interventions aimed at enhancing ICE. If left unchecked, the challenges of ICE may have negative implications for integration between the Africans and Chinese, both inside and outside the organisation. On the other hand, culturally informed Africans and Chinese coming together are productive, as they interact effectively and appropriately while getting on with business.

Conclusion

This comparative theoretical framework for understanding ICE in Sino-African interactions points to potential similarities and differences in communication culture. However, subtle differences exist, even at the level of similarities, which means that appearances must not be taken at face value. This points to the need for empirically validating the insights gained. Finally, it is suggested that a multi-view approach is appropriate in seeking to understand ICE in intercultural interactions, such as those between African and Chinese people. This is because it allows for the identification of synergies and/or gaps in order to make communication potentially more acceptable to the interacting parties. It is also proposed that the focus of intercultural interaction in general could shift from effectiveness to congruence.

References

Ajei, M. O. (2007). *Africa's development: The imperatives of indigenous knowledge and values*. Ph.D. thesis. University of South Africa. Retrieved March 2, 2016, from http://uir.unisa.ac.za/bitstream/handle/10500/1266/thesis.pdf?Sequence=1

Ani, N. C. (2013). Appraisal of African epistemology in the global system. *Alternation*, 20(1), 295–320.

Asante, M. K. (1999). Afrocentric theories of communication. In J. L. Lucaites, C. M. Condit, & S. Caudill (Eds.), *Contemporary rhetorical theories: A reader* (pp. 552–562). New York: The Guilford Press.

Asante, M. K. (2012). Maat and human communication: Supporting identity, culture and history without global domination. *Communication: South African Journal for Communication Theory and Practice*, 38(2), 127–134.

Asante, M. K., & Miike, Y. (2013). Paradigmatic issues in intercultural communication studies: An afrocentric-asiacentric dialogue. *China Media Research*, 9(3), 1–20.

Baah, A. Y., & Jauch, H. (Eds.). (2009). *Chinese investments in Africa: A labour perspective*. African Labour Research Network. Retrieved October 18, 2017, from https://www.fnv.nl/site/over-de-fnv/internationaal/mondiaal-fnv/documenten/english/publications/Chinese_investments_in_Africa_final_report1.pdf

Beebe, S. A., Beebe, S. J., Redmond, M. V., & Geerinck, T. (2011). *Interpersonal communication: Relating to others* (6th ed.). Toronto: Pearson Canada.

Bell, D. A. A., & Metz, T. (2011). Confucianism and Ubuntu: Reflections and a dialogue between Chinese and African traditions. *Journal of Chinese Philosophy*, 38, 78–95.

Berger, M. (1987). Building bridges over the cultural rivers. *International Management*, 42, 61–72.

Brautigam, D. (2011). China in Africa: What can western donors learn? Oslo: Norwegian Investment Fund for Developing Countries (Norfund). [Online]. Retrieved October 16, 2012, from www.norfund.no/getfile.php/Documents/Homepage/Reports%20and%20presentations/Studies%20for%20Norfund/Norfund_China_in_Africa.pdf

Chen, G. M. (2002). The past, present, and future of Chinese communication study. *China Media Reports*, 2, 4–12.

Chen, G. M. (2011). An Introduction to key concepts in understanding the Chinese: Harmony as the foundation of Chinese communication. *China Media Research*, 7(4), 1–12.

Chen, G. M. (2015). Seeking common ground while accepting differences through tolerance: U.S. – China intercultural communication in the global community. In L. A. Samovar, R. E. Porter, E. R. McDaniel, & C. Sexton Roy (Eds.), *Intercultural communication: A reader* (14th ed., pp. 465–471). Boston, MA: Cengage Learning.

Chen, G. M., & Chung, J. (1994). The impact of Confucianism on organizational communication. *Communication Quarterly, 42*(2), 93–105.

Chen, G. M., & Starosta, W. J. (2003). Asian approaches to human communication: A dialogue. *Intercultural Communication Studies, 12*(4), 1–15.

Chigwendere, F. B. (2016). *Towards intercultural communication congruence in Sino-African organisational contexts.* Unpublished Doctoral thesis. Rhodes University, South Africa.

Collier, M. J., Ribeau, S. A., & Hetch, M. L. (1986). Intracultural communication rules and outcomes within three domestic cultures. *International Journal of Intercultural Relations, 10,* 439–457.

Dean, O., & Popp, G. E. (1990). Intercultural communication effectiveness as perceived by American managers in Saudi Arabia and French managers in the U.S. *International Journal of Intercultural Relations, 14,* 40–424.

Dietz, M. C., Orr, G., & Xing, J. (2008, May). How Chinese companies can succeed abroad. *McKinsey Quarterly.*

Ding, D. D. (2006). An indirect style in business communication. *Journal of Business and Technical Communication, 20*(1), 87–100.

Eaton, L., & Louw, J. (2000). Culture and self in Africa: Individualism-collectivism predictions. *The Journal of Psychology, 140*(2), 210–217.

Fang, T. (2011). Yin Yang: A new perspective on culture. *Management and Organization Review, 8*(1), 25–50.

Faniran, J. O. (2014). Toward a theory of African communication. In C. Christian & K. Nordenstreng (Eds.), *Communication theories in a multi-cultural world* (pp. 146–159). New York: Peter Lang.

Faure, G. O., & Fang, T. (2008). Changing Chinese values, Keeping up with the paradoxes. *International Business Review, 17,* 194–207.

Feng, G., & Mu, X. (2010). Cultural challenges to Chinese oil companies in Africa and their strategies. *Energy Policy, 38*(11), 7250–7256.

Francesco, A. M., & Gold, B. A. (2005). *International organisational behaviour: Texts, cases and exercises.* New Jersey: Prentice Hall.

Gan, S. (2014). *How to do business with China: An inside view on Chinese culture and etiquette.* Bloomington: AuthorHouse.

Gao, G., & Ting-Toomey, S. (1998). *Communicating effectively with the Chinese.* Thousand Oaks, CA: Sage.

Giese, K. (2014). Perceptions, practices and adaptations: Understanding Chinese – African interactions in Africa. *Journal of Current Chinese Affairs, 43*(1), 3–8.

Grunig, J, E., & Grunig L. A. (1992). Models of public relations and communication. In J. E. Grunig, D. M. Dozier, L. A. Grunig, F. C. Repper, & J. White (Eds.), *Excellence in public relations and communication management* (pp. 285–325). Hillsdale, NJ: Lawrence Erlbaum Associates.

Gudykunst, W. B., Matsumoto, Y., Ting-Toomey, S., Nishida, T., Kim, K., & Heyman, S. (1996). The influence of cultural individualism-collectivism, self-construal's, and individual values on communication styles across cultures. *Human Communication Research, 22*(4), 510–543.

124 *Fungai Chigwendere*

Guliwe, T., Mkhonta, S., & Vickers, B. (2009). Chinese investments in South Africa. In Y. Baah, & H. Jauchi (Eds.), *Chinese investments in Africa: A labour perspective* (pp. 300–332). African Labour Research Network. Retrieved October 18, 2017, from https://www.fnv.nl/site/over-de-fnv/internationaal/mondiaal-fnv/documenten/english/publications/Chinese_investments_in_Africa_final_report1.pdf

Hall, E. T. (1959). *The silent language.* Garden City, NY: Doubleday.

Hall, E. T. (1976). *Beyond culture.* New York: Doubleday.

Hammer, M. R., Gudykunst, W. B., & Wiseman, R. L. (1978). Dimensions of intercultural effectiveness: An exploratory study. *International Journal of Intercultural Relations, 2*(4), 382–393.

Higgs, P. (2010). Towards an indigenous African epistemology of community in education research. *Procedia Social and Behavioural Sciences, 2,* 2414–2421.

Hofstede, G. (1980). *Culture's consequences.* Beverly Hills, CA: Sage.

Hofstede, G. (1991). *Cultures and organizations: Software of the mind.* London: McGraw-Hill.

Hofstede, G. (2011). Dimensionalizing cultures: The Hofstede model in context. *Online Readings in Psychology and Culture, 2*(1). http://doi.org/10.9707/2307-0919.1014.

Hofstede, G., & Bond, M. H. (1988). The confucius connection. From cultural roots to economic growth. *Organisational Dynamics,* 5–21.

Huang, Y. H. (2010). Theorising Chinese communication research: A holistic framework for comparative studies. *Chinese Journal of Communication, 3*(1), 95–113.

Igboin, B. O. (2011). Colonialism and African cultural values. *African Journal of History and Culture, 3*(6), 93–106.

Jackson, T. (1999). Managing change in South Africa: Developing people and organizations. *International Journal of Human Resource Management, 10*(2), 306–326.

Khoza, R. J. (2011). *Attuned leadership: African humanism as compass.* Cape Town: CPT Printers.

Kim, M. S. (2007). The four cultures of cultural research. *Communication Monographs, 74*(2), 27–285. https://doi.org/10.1080/03637750701393063

Ladegaard, H. J., & Jenks, C. J. (2015). Language and intercultural communication in the workplace: Critical approaches to theory and practice. *Language and Intercultural Communication, 15*(1), 1–12, https://doi.org/10.1080/1470 8477.2014.985302

Laryea, S. (2010). Challenges and opportunities facing contractors in Ghana. In S. Laryea, R. Leiringer, & W. Hughes (Eds.), *Paper delivered at the Procs West Africa Built Environment Research (WABER) conference,* 27–28 July 2010, ACCRA, Ghana, pp. 215–226.

Leung, K. (2008). Chinese culture, modernization and international business. *International Business Review, 17,* 184–187.

Littlejohn, S. W., & Foss, K. A. (2008). Theories of human communication. [e-book] Belmont, CA: Thomson/Wadsworth. Retrieved December 21, 2015, from https://www.nelsonbrain.com/content/littlejohn95877_0495095877_02.01_chapter01.pdf

Littlejohn, S. W., & Foss, K. A. (2010). *Theories of human communication* (10th ed.). Long Groove, IL: Waveland Press.

Liu, S., Volcic, Z., & Gallois, C. (2011). *Introducing intercultural communication: Global cultures and contexts*. London: Sage.

Lockett, M. (1988). Culture and the problems of Chinese management. *Organisational Studies*, 9(4), 475–496.

Maomeka, A. A. (1989). Communication and African culture: A sociological analysis. In S. T. Boafo Kwame (Ed.), *Communication and culture: African perspectives*. Nairobi: Africa Church Information Services.

Martin, J. N., & Nakayama, T. K. (2010). *Intercultural communication in contexts*. New York: McGraw Hill.

Martin, J. N., & Nakayama, T. K. (2015). Reconsidering intercultural (communication) competence in the workplace: A dialectical approach. *Language and Intercultural Communication*, 15(1), 13–28, https://doi.org/10.1080/1470847 7.2014.985303

Matondo, M. J. P. (2012). Cross-cultural value comparisons between Chinese and Sub-Saharan Africans. *International Journal of Business and Social Science*, 3(11), 38–45.

McFarlin, D. B., Coster, E. A., & Mogale-Pretorius, C. (1999). South African management development in the twenty-first century. Moving toward an Africanized model. *Journal of Management Development*, 18(1), 63–78.

Men, T. (2014). Place-based and place-bound realities: A Chinese firms embededness in Tanzania. *Journal of Current Chinese Affairs*, 43(1), 103–138.

Metz, T. (2015). Values in China as compared to Africa. In H. Du Plessis, T. Metz, G. Raza, R. Poplak, D. Cisse, M. Davies, Y. Zhao, G. Le Pere, A. Ross, & M. Lauzon-Lacroix (Eds.), *The rise and decline and rise of China: Searching for an organizing philosophy*. Johannesburg: Real African Publishers.

Miike, Y. (2002). Theorising culture and communication in the Asian context: An assumptive foundation. In Chen, G. M., (ed.), Culture and communication an East Asian perspective [Special Issue]. *Intercultural Communication Studies*, 11(1), 1–21.

Miike, Y. (2007). An Asiacentric reflection on Eurocentric bias in communication theory. *Communication Monographs*, 74(2), 272–278.

Miike, Y., & Yin, J. (2015). Asiacentricity and shapes of the future: Envisioning the field of intercultural communication in the globalisation era. In L. A. Samovar, R. E. Porter, E. R. McDaniel, & C. Sexton Roy (Eds.), *Intercultural communication: A reader* (14th ed., pp. 449–465). Boston, MA: Cengage Learning.

Myers, L. J. (1987). The deep structure of culture: Relevance of traditional African culture in contemporary life. *Journal of Black Studies*, 18(1), 72–85.

Nair-Venugopal, S. (2015). Issues of language and competence in intercultural business and contexts. *Language and Intercultural Communication*, 15(1), 29–45.

Narh, P. (2013). Philosophical foundation of knowledge creation on Africa. *Discussion study NR*. Farafina Institute's Discussion Study Series, 3 June 2013.

Nussbaum, N. C. (1992). Human functioning and social justice: In defence of Aristotelian essentialism. *Political Theory*, 20(2), 205–246.

Okech, J. E. A., Pimpleton, A. M., Vannatta, R., & Champe, J. (2015). Intercultural communication: An application to group work. *The Journal for Specialists in Group Work*, 40(3), 268–293. https://doi.org/10.1080/01933922.2015.105656.

Ono, K. A. (2013). Reflections on problematizing 'nation' in intercultural communication research. In T. K. Nakayama & R. T. Halualani (Eds.), *The*

126 Fungai Chigwendere

handbook of critical intercultural communication (pp. 84–97). Oxford: Blackwell Publishing.

Park, Y. J., & Alden, C. (2013). 'Upstairs' and 'downstairs' dimensions of China and the Chinese in South Africa. In *State of the Nation, 2012. Tackling poverty and inequality* (pp. 611–630). Pretoria: HSRC Press.

Phatak, A. V., Bhagat, R. S., & Kashlak, R. J. (2005). *International management: Managing in a diverse and dynamic global environment.* New York: McGraw Hill.

Salo-Lee, L. (2006). *Introduction to intercultural communication.* Retrieved February 4, 2016 from https://moniviestin.jyu.fi/ohjelmat/hum/viesti/en/ics/

Samovar, L. A., & Porter, R. E. (1995). *Communication between cultures* (2nd ed.). Belmont, CA: Wadsworth.

Schein, E. H. (1990). Organisational culture. *American Psychologist, 45*(2), 109–119.

Schwartz, S. H. (1992). Universals in the content and structure of values: Theoretical advances and empirical tests in 20 countries. *Advances in Experimental Social Psychology, 25,* 1–65.

Schwartz, S. H. (1994). Are there universal aspects in the structure and content of human values? *Journal of Social Issues, 50*(4), 19–45.

Schwartz, S. H. (2012). An overview of the Schwartz theory of basic values. *Online Readings in Psychology and Culture, 2*(1). Retrieved November 18, 2015 from http://doi.org/10.9707/2307-0919.1116

Shonhiwa, S. (2008). *The effective cross-cultural manager: A guide for business leaders in Africa.* Cape Town: Zebra Press.

Skow, L., & Samovar, L. A. (2015). Cultural patterns of the Maasai. In L. A. Samovar, R. E. Porter, E. R. McDaniel, & C. Sexton Roy (Eds.), *Intercultural communication: A reader* (14th ed., pp 141–149). Boston, MA: Cengage Learning.

Ting-Toomey, S. (1988). Intercultural conflict styles: A face negotiation theory. In Y. Y. Kim & W. B. Gudykunst (Eds.), *Theories in intercultural communication* (pp. 213–238). Newbury Park, CA: Sage.

Ting-Toomey, S., & Kurogi, A. (1998). Facework competence in intercultural conflict: An updated face-negotiation theory. *International Journal of Intercultural Relations, 22,*187–225.

Traber, R. (1989). African communication: Problems and prospects. *Africa Media Review, 3*(3),86–97.

Trompenaars, F., & Hampden-Turner, C. (1993). *Riding the waves of culture: Understanding diversity in global business.* London: Nicholas Brealey Publishing.

Van Der Colff, L. (2003). Leadership lessons from the Africa tree. *Management Decision Journal, 41*(3), 257–261.

Von Schirach, P. M. (2012). *China's Point man for Africa in an interview admits that Chinese companies operating in the continent follow unorthodox practices to get business – "Bags of money on the table, and bribes"* [Online]. Retrieved May 11, 2012 from http://schirachreport.com/index.php/2012/04/07/chinas-point-man-for-africa-in-an-interview-admits-that-chinese-companies-operating-in-the-continent-follow-unorthodox-practices-to-get-business-bags-of-money-on-the-table-and-bribes

Washington, M. C. (2013). Intercultural business communication: An analysis of ethnocentrism in a globalized Business environment. *Journal of Business & Management, 1*(1), 20–27. Online issue.

Westropp, S. (2012). Cultural comparison of China and Sub-Saharan Africa. *Otago Management Graduate Review, 10,* 67–87.

Xu, K. (2013). Theorizing difference in intercultural communication: A critical dialogic perspective. *Communication Monographs*, *80*(3), 379–397. https://doi.org/10.1080/03637751.2013.788250

Yum, J. O. (1988). The impact of Confucianism on interpersonal relationships and communication patterns in East Asia. *Communication Monographs*, *55*, 374–388.

Part II
Countries and themes

6 Cross-cultural communication and knowledge transfer in China–Africa joint ventures

Anglophone versus francophone experiences

Abdoulkadre Ado

Scholars continue to raise questions about what Africa is gaining from its increasing cooperation and partnerships with China (Brautigam, Xiaoyang, & Xia, 2018; Geda, Senbet, & Simbanegavi, 2018; Mohan, Lampert, Tan-Mullins, & Atta-Ankomah, 2019). Meanwhile, knowledge transfer is a topic that is gaining increasing attention when it comes to China–Africa relations. Indeed, following the 2018 FOCAC meeting, the expression "knowledge transfer" emerged multiple times in the official narrative of Chinese and African governments and organizations while the 2015 FOCAC report almost ignored this topic. In fact, following the FOCAC (2018), just the terms "knowledge or experience sharing" and "technology transfer" were mentioned more than 28 times in the official document published by the Forum on China-Africa Cooperation Beijing Action Plan (2019–2021). This is partly because Africans now increasingly see China as a source for gaining expertise in multiple areas to boost business, innovation, and development (Ado, Su, & Wanjiru, 2017; Chrysostome, Munthali, & Ado, 2019; Jackson & Horwitz, 2018).

Africa is a diverse continent, with major differences across its national cultures, colonial legacies, institutions, and languages, and these characteristics contribute to the labelling of some countries as English-speaking (anglophone), French-speaking (francophone), Arabic speaking, Spanish-speaking, or Portuguese-speaking. In this study, we are interested in an analysis of anglophone and francophone Africans' experiences at the crossroads of knowledge transfer and national official languages within China–Africa joint ventures (JVs) settings. JVs are entities that are used to access knowledge from a foreign partner, often a multinational company. For JVs to become successful, it requires managers with significant expertise in cross-cultural management and strategic skills (Beamish & Lupton, 2009). To access knowledge and technologies, Africans are increasingly using such entities when partnering with Chinese. However, accessing knowledge through JVs has challenges and many organizational and human factors are crucial for effective knowledge transfer to take place (Ado, 2018; Haas & Cummings, 2015; Inkpen &

Beamish, 1997) especially when employees have multiple cultural backgrounds. China–Africa JVs are places characterized by significant multicultural aspects, with increasing numbers of Chinese being posted in African countries.

According to Chinese official data obtained by the China–Africa Research Initiative at Johns Hopkins University (SAIS-CARI, 2017), there were a total of 202,689 Chinese nationals working in Africa, with Algeria, Angola, Nigeria, Ethiopia, and Zambia topping the list of hosting countries representing 57% of all Chinese workers in Africa. The 12 countries included in this study were hosting all together 36,724 Chinese workers in 2017. Figure 6.1 shows the number of Chinese workers in those twelve countries from 2010 to 2017.

Figure 6.1 indicates that there is still a significant number of Chinese people working in Africa. Such presence has not yet been studied sufficiently by scholars and even the studies conducted on the subject remain theoretically and empirically inadequate. Indeed, Jackson (2012) suggested the need for new theoretical lenses to understand and research China's presence in Africa. Not only did the author point to the lack of empirical knowledge at various levels, but he also raised questions like – Is there reverse diffusion whereby Chinese organizations in Africa take back to China knowledge gained through the interaction of Chinese and indigenous knowledge, values, and practices? Are Western practices being introduced into organizations in Africa by Chinese managers?

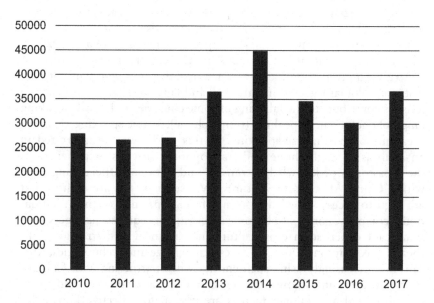

Figure 6.1 Number of Chinese nationals working in the 12 countries

Indeed, such questions are still in search of answers because, despite the increased Chinese presence in Africa and the specificity of China's practices in Africa, there is only a limited volume of serious international management literature in the area, leading to anecdote-based decision-making within organizations in Africa as well as weak research evidence (Jackson, 2014; Jackson, Louw, & Zhao, 2013).

Whether Chinese managers are introducing Western practices into Africa is an interesting question for debate. Moreover, what Chinese are introducing into Africa may actually be very different from what most people would expect. Since Chinese are already present in the majority of African countries, with significant investments in both anglophone and francophone regions, it is legitimate to inquire how Chinese companies and managers navigate such different national environments and multicultural organizational contexts. Conversely, it is also timely to investigate how Africans manage their relationship with Chinese partners in Africa. The Chinese presence on the African continent is clearly noticeable across multiple regions and sectors, but studies that help us understand the dynamics of that presence vis-à-vis host countries and communities are still scarce. Such scarcity becomes even more intense in terms of studies that highlight the differences between anglophone and francophone Africans in the context of China–Africa cooperation.

Background: anglophone vs. francophone Africa

In this section, we present a general overview of the twelve African countries that are included in this study. We define anglophones as those nations that have been colonized mostly by England while francophone countries are those colonized mostly by France and Belgium. So far, from a general literature standpoint, there have been more studies on anglophone than francophone countries, particularly in the field of politics and institutions in Africa (Briggs, 2017), making the anglophone environment more informed when it comes to international relations and business decisions. There are certainly major institutional differences between anglophone and francophone African countries. Those differences exist mainly in terms of political, economic, cultural, and social considerations. One should therefore refrain from generalizing research findings generated in anglophone Africa to francophone Africa, because most of the research does not in fact draw on evidence from the francophone countries (Briggs, 2017), especially when there are on average only five publications per francophone country while there are 27 for anglophones. Table 6.1 portrays some social and economic characteristics of the 12 countries, ranked in alphabetical order, included in this chapter.

Often, English-speaking countries are portrayed as economically performing better than their French-speaking counterparts. In fact, reports like the World Bank's ease of doing business (2019) have suggested several

Table 6.1 Countries' profiles

	Population (millions)	Local currency	GDP (millions)	Main trade partner	Former colony of	Official language
Benin	11.2	XOF	9236	India	France	Francophone
Burundi	10.9	BIF	3155	UAE	Belgium	
Chad	14.9	XAF	10717	USA	France	
Congo	5.3	XAF	11292	China	France	
Congo DRC	81.3	CDF	37642	China	Belgium	
Côte d'Ivoire	24.3	XOF	38055	Netherlands	France	
Niger	21.5	XOF	8120	France	France	
Togo	7.8	XOF	4786	Cameroon	France	
Cameroon	24.1	XAF	34924	China	England	Anglophone
Ghana	28.8	GHS	58996	India	England	
Nigeria	190.9	NGN	375770	India	England	
Rwanda	12.2	RWF	9136	UAE	Belgium	

Source: Adapted from UNCTAD (2019)

times that English-speaking African countries offer better business environments than French-speaking African countries. An article from *The Africa Report* highlighted that the lack of infrastructure, poor corporate culture, and bad governance are the issues that keep French-speaking Africa lagging behind its English-speaking counterpart. Additionally, a former President of the French Council of Investors in Africa (CIAN) stated in an interview with Jeune Afrique that "Countries with the Anglo-Saxon culture are more oriented towards business and entrepreneurship, and people in those countries are less inclined to yearn to become civil servants than their counterparts with the French culture".

Moreover, according to UNDP's latest report (2018), French-speaking countries in Africa also lag behind on the human development index compared to their English-speaking counterparts. In fact, Commonwealth countries are among the highest performing nations in the Ibrahim Index of African Governance (IIAG) and make up 7 of the top 10 nations according to the Mo Ibrahim Report (2018). So, from an economic standpoint, the evidence often suggested that English-speaking Africa does better overall. Table 6.2 shows how the 12 African countries represented in this study's sample are ranked by the World Bank (2019) with regards to the overall ease of doing business index and two of its components (starting a business and enforcing a contract). The ranking following instantly captures only the progress of countries in the previous year, in this case 2018, and therefore does not represent comprehensibly the countries' business climate and progress over the last decade. Indeed, although countries like Rwanda, Ghana, and Nigeria do not show a leading progress on some indicators, they remained among Africa's most emerging economies and promising places for business over the past few years with a high rate of economic growth.

Table 6.2 World Bank's ease of doing business index

Rank	Overall ease of doing business	Ease of starting a business	Ease of enforcing a contract
1	Rwanda	Burundi	Rwanda
2	Ghana	Côte d'Ivoire	Nigeria
3	Côte d'Ivoire	Niger	Côte d'Ivoire
4	Togo	Rwanda	Ghana
5	Niger	Benin	Niger
6	Nigeria	DRC	Togo
7	Benin	Togo	Chad
8	Cameroon	Cameroon	Congo, Rep.
9	Burundi	Ghana	Burundi
10	Congo, Rep.	Nigeria	Cameroon
11	Chad	Congo, Rep.	Benin
12	DRC	Chad	DRC

There are currently more than 300 million people worldwide who speak French, including more than 180 million Africans, according to the 2018 report of the Organisation Internationale de la Francophonie (OIF), and there are 32 countries which have French as one of their official languages. OIF has 31 member countries in Africa. This is certainly less compared to the people who speak English worldwide including in Africa. In fact, according to The Commonwealth statistics, there are 2.4 billion people who speak English worldwide with 53 official member countries within the organization. Nineteen of those member countries are in Africa, representing a population of nearly 576 million Africans, although some nations like Zimbabwe are no longer part of The Commonwealth. From an economic outlook, Commonwealth countries had a total GDP of US$10.4 trillion in 2017 with predictions for US$13 trillion by 2020. Additional statistics from The Commonwealth show that bilateral costs for trading partners in Commonwealth countries are on average 19 percent less than between those in non-member countries. Half of the top 20 global emerging cities, like Nairobi and Johannesburg, are in the Commonwealth.

These statistics expose some major differences between anglophone and francophone Africa. Such differences are certainly contributing to shaping how both parties handle their relations with China.

What we were looking for in this research

This chapter aims to answer the following question: How do anglophone and francophone Africans communicate with their Chinese counterparts with regards to knowledge transfer? The question is investigated through a comparative analysis between anglophones and francophones in Africa. The study seeks to highlight the key differences and similarities in the way(s) anglophone Africans interact and gain knowledge from Chinese JV partners in comparison with francophone Africans. The objective is to draw some patterns based on Africans' experiences from the intercultural communication and cross-cultural management perspectives. Based on a review of descriptive studies and sociological perspectives (Abernethy, 1971; Simbiri, Hausman, Wadenya, & Lidicker, 2010; Vigouroux, 2008), Table 6.3 highlights our preliminary conception of comparing

Table 6.3 Comparative conceptual frameworks of anglophone vs. francophone Africans

	Personality	*Mindset*	*Attitude*	*Institution*	*Legacy*
Anglophone	Diplomatic	Entrepreneurial	Learning	Adaptative	England
Francophone	Confrontational	Employable	Knowing	Bureaucratic	France/ Belgium

anglophones and francophones in Africa as derived from the prior studies. Indeed, according to Simbiri et al. (2010), there are fundamental social and cultural differences between anglophone and francophone African immigrants when they settle overseas. Francophone Africans demonstrated less acculturation and more adaptation problems, thus face greater challenges than anglophone Africans, who had a higher level of acculturation and adapted faster, thus perceiving fewer barriers than francophone Africans.

How we conducted the research

This study investigated several cases of JVs, commonly known as partnerships, between Chinese and Africans. The chapter is using data mainly gathered from interviews with Africans who were working in (or on) those China–Africa JVs.

Interviews with 75 participants who worked with Chinese colleagues took place in 2014. All participants were recruited based on the following requirements: the person had worked for/on a China–Africa JV for at least 3 years; the JV must have been in existence for more than 3 years; the person had daily interactions with Chinese colleagues. The recruited African participants individually answered open-ended questions during an hour-long semi-structured interview. The initial interviews occurred in 12 African countries that hosted the 29 joint ventures that we were interested in. Countries represented in this study were simply a reflection of the nationalities of the JVs under study. Amongst those countries, we categorized Cameroon, Ghana, Nigeria, and Rwanda as anglophones. The reason we categorized Rwanda as anglophone was because the country joined the Commonwealth a few years ago, although it still uses French in many public and private business communications. In this study, Cameroon was also considered as anglophone because English is the government's official language besides French, and most of our Cameroonian respondents preferred English for the interview. The remainder of the countries, namely Benin, Burundi, Chad, Congo, Cote D'Ivoire, DRC, Niger, and Togo, were categorized as francophones. This categorization was also reflected in the fact that we interviewed most participants in French or English based upon their language preference. Then, we translated the interview transcripts into English, doing our best to keep the original meaning of the texts. We have not done any back translation as meanings were carefully checked to ensure accuracy of our translations vis-à-vis the original transcript.

In total, we interviewed 43 francophones, 27 anglophones, and 5 indigenous Africans. Here, by indigenous, we mean Africans who spoke neither English nor French but only local languages. We should mention that although some participants identified as francophones, their interviews took place in English because they spoke both languages fluently and it was easier for this research to avoid translating their transcripts from French. However, our classification of anglophone and francophone participants was based on the category in which the interviewees identified themselves with, not the language in which the interview took place. Although all participants who were interviewed in French were francophones, in the case of interviews in English, a similar statement was not always true.

For the purpose of this chapter and its research question, we decided to focus only on parts of the interview transcripts that relate to our conceptual and theoretical perspective, namely aspects related to intercultural communication and knowledge transfer management. Our analysis mostly consisted of identifying excerpts of transcripts that related to the categories of participants we were dealing with. We went through the transcripts of anglophone participants and those of francophone participants as well as indigenous ones while identifying similarities and differences across those groups in terms of personality/profile, behavior/action and strategy/management particularly regarding intercultural communication.

We categorized those three groups of Africans (anglophones, francophones, and indigenous) by highlighting their specificities in profile, action, and management practices in the context of their joint ventures with Chinese partners. Also, from the descriptions that African participants offered based on their experiences with Chinese counterparts, we propose a portrait of Chinese people working in those joint ventures in terms of language skills. Such description will first help us understand the type of Chinese people that Africans are dealing with in those joint ventures in Africa.

What we found in our research

In this section, we highlight similarities and differences in terms of management practices and interpersonal relations regarding knowledge transfer among African anglophones vis-à-vis francophones within those JVs. The analysis of these two specific groups sought to reveal some insights regarding the effectiveness of the management practices in anglophone vs. francophone settings within those JVs. But first we present an overview of Chinese people working with Africans in those partnerships.

Chinese people working in Africa

Based upon our data, it appears that Chinese colleagues occupying top positions tend to display strong English or French language skills.

Those Chinese often work at top levels of the company as executives and managers, while engineers and workers are less likely to have language skills in either English or French. Table 6.4 presents a snapshot of the perceptions of interviewed Africans toward the likelihood that their Chinese colleagues possess strong language skills, be it English, French, or indigenous languages. For the French skills, we compiled perceptions (based on Africans' experiences of interacting with Chinese colleagues within the JVs) from 16 francophone Africans, and for the English skills, descriptions came from 13 anglophone transcripts. For the African language skills, our transcripts, especially those from the five indigenous respondents included in this study, indicate that it almost never occurred that Africans worked with a Chinese colleague who spoke indigenous language except rare mentions during two of our interviews where some Chinese workers in Congo were identified as speaking basic Lingala.

The following statement highlights very clearly some of the sentiments (described in Table 6.4) that Africans have regarding working with their Chinese colleagues.

> The Chinese sent to Africa are not qualified for the positions they occupy, especially when it comes to their language proficiency, it is very poor. Sometimes, even the engineers have difficulty expressing themselves in English which is shocking to me since they have been sent here to teach us. Therefore, a way for us to adapt to them is simply we stop asking questions. [Chad 43]

Overall, our results also indicate that anglophone and francophone Africans have different characteristics in their ways of dealing with Chinese people. Table 6.5 displays some of the major trends that our data suggest in terms of differences in behaviors and strategies as well as how Chinese describe their African counterparts, as reported by the participants in this study.

Understanding Sino-Africa communication

When Africans are dealing with Chinese colleagues who do not speak English or French, they tend to adopt specific solutions to cope with the communication challenge. While some tend to ask fewer questions or avoid interactions, some try to develop their Mandarin skills, initiate the Chinese to the English language, bring in people/software to translate or ultimately reduce their collaborations with Chinese colleagues. Table 6.6 presents a glimpse of Africans' practices and strategies.

Table 6.4 Profiling Chinese employees in Africa

	Executives	Managers	Engineers	Laborers/workers
Strong English skills Perception by Africans	Extremely likely "Our executive team has good command of English" [Ghana 53]	Very likely	Unlikely "China sends technicians that must improve their language skills" [Cameroon 15]	Very unlikely
Strong French skills Perception by Africans	Very likely "Only the CEO speaks French, the rest are beginners" [Niger 31]	Likely	Very unlikely "I promise you, you will not meet a Chinese who speaks French here" [Cote d'Ivoire 59]	Extremely unlikely
African language skills Perception by Africans	Extremely unlikely "One Chinese has managed to learn Lingala" [Congo DRC 28]	Very Unlikely	Unlikely "My Chinese co-workers show no interest in learning our local language" [Rwanda 60]	Likely

Table 6.5 Francophone vs. anglophone way of doing business with Chinese

	Francophone employees	Anglophone employees
Title of respect	Refer to their Chinese supervisors as "My Boss, My colleague"	Refer to their Chinese supervisors as "My Master, My superior"
Action	Behave in a rebellious, defensive way with sentences like "I force them to answer my questions", "I challenge their dictatorship", "I need an explanation from my director"	Behave in a submissive, cooperative way with sentences like "I kindly ask Chinese for help", "We suggest changes", "I propose my ideas at meetings"
Loyalty and conflict management	Complain more, often leaving the unit or even company is a first option, confrontation as conflict management strategy	More patient, leaving the unit or company is only a last resort, dialogue/cooperation as conflict management strategy
Reaction to change within organization	Resist more frequently, form unions, strike or protest is often considered by union as a viable first action for solving an issue	Adapt and negotiate more often. Form/use unions less, strike is unlikely to be a union's first decision
Chinese perception (as reported by Africans)	Ask too many questions, do not act very disciplined and miss to follow clear instructions	Are respectful to hierarchy and act very disciplined, follow instructions carefully

The characteristics in this table were based on the analysis of transcripts of mostly lower-level African employees.

Table 6.6 African communication strategies

	Socialization (best-case scenario)	Isolation (worst-case scenario)
Anglophones	Teach English – Learn Mandarin	Use technology – Translation Apps
Francophones	Learn Mandarin – Teach French	Use interpreter – Reduce collaboration
Indigenous	Use signs – Body language	Avoid communication – Separate station

The following statement describes how Africans perceive their interactions and collaborations with Chinese:

> Chinese refuse to attend language training; They avoid speaking French or English, and if they do not understand what you say, they simply dismiss you and move on like nothing happened; When you ask for document translations, you get incorrect or partial translation from Mandarin to English, though French is our official language.
>
> [Togo 10]

Such comments indicate that collaboration between Africans and their Chinese colleagues is not always easy especially when some workers are not willing to improve their language skills.

Anglophone Africans and Chinese people

Anglophone Africans dealing with Chinese colleagues who can speak English often described their interactions as easy and collaborative. Communication was not identified as a regular challenge, especially at the executive levels, thus making learning and knowledge transfer experiences smoother and even quicker in those JV settings. Indeed, when the Chinese have excellent professional English skills, they tend to be more receptive and responsive to Africans' questions and requests. This also makes anglophone Africans more comfortable, and more frequently they put forward their requests and questions regarding ways to gain more opportunities to access knowledge and reduce challenges.

In contrast, when anglophone Africans are dealing with Chinese colleagues who cannot speak English, the interactions are often described as unpleasant and uncollaborative especially at the managerial levels. Indeed, the top and middle management are contexts in which oral communication skills are key to successful collaborations, particularly for knowledge transfer. Chinese who lack English skills are described as avoiding requests and questions that may lead to long conversations. Thus, Africans often choose to (1) help and empower Chinese to learn English or (2) use technologies or translation Apps to stay on track during intercultural communication. This scenario was often reported with lower level Chinese employees.

> They always keep using Chinese English that is difficult to understand for us; Instructions are in Chinese although most Africans here do not understand Chinese. And when you state that you need information in English, they simply ignore your request.
>
> [Nigeria 50]

Ultimately, when Chinese refuse to learn English, some Africans try to learn Mandarin instead to improve interpersonal communication.

Francophone Africans and Chinese people

Francophone Africans dealing with Chinese colleagues who can speak French often describe their interactions as still challenging. Not only do Africans state that only a few Chinese speak French, but even those who do so are not always fluent in the language. Thus, Africans commented that whenever they must interact in French with their Chinese colleagues at positions lower than management level, they mentally prepare themselves to have fumbled communication through which misunderstandings are common and tacitly forgiven.

In contrast, when francophone Africans are dealing with Chinese who cannot speak French at all, the interaction often becomes tough and has negative consequences. As a result, Africans often choose to reduce their communication expectations from their Chinese colleagues, leading to less opportunities for knowledge transfer for Africans. A respondent highlighted this:

> Even though we are in a French speaking country, Chinese have informally imposed English as the official language despite the founding by-laws that require by default that all documents and communications take place in French. They clearly disregarded French as the official language of business here.
>
> [Niger 55]

In either case (whether Chinese speak French or not), francophone Africans have mentioned the need to improve their own Mandarin skills or use interpreters to be able to communicate efficiently with their Chinese colleagues because pronunciation often appeared to be another issue. The ultimate option as mentioned by many francophone Africans who could not learn Mandarin was to simply avoid oral communication with the Chinese or decline, whenever possible, invitations for collaborative assignments that involved Chinese employees who do not speak French. Also, getting posted to a different workstation was mentioned by some respondents as a solution.

Indigenous Africans and Chinese people

We consider this context to be the one where the Chinese speak neither English nor French although the Africans may understand one of these two languages. Another indigenous scenario is when an African speaks neither English nor French and has no knowledge of Mandarin either. In such a case, the indigenous context becomes entirely exploratory to both parties, creating a situation of deaf communication. Here, in any of the scenarios described previously, in the best case, the communication involves the use of signs and body language, and in the worst case, it ends up being cut with Africans and Chinese employees each working independently without oral communication, especially when the work is mostly manual and physical.

Looking into all three preceding configurations, an interesting and emerging phenomenon in the JVs context is that while Chinese investors in Africa often sent anglophone Africans to China for training, many francophone Africans were sent to France for training. According to some francophone Africans, since it is already hard for Chinese to train them in China in French or Mandarin, sending them to France is a way for Chinese partners to address the language challenges that francophones specifically face regarding knowledge transfer in those JVs.

Study highlights

Poor language as a significant obstacle to knowledge transfer

Although most studies on China–Africa have so far focused on macro-analysis with a focus on trade and other economic outcomes (Ado & Su, 2016), our findings bring a micro-level contribution and indicate that language barriers have been reported as a major obstacle to effective knowledge transfer for Africans within those JVs with Chinese partners. Although existing literature has documented that language plays an important role in the success of international JVs, the case of China–Africa JVs reveals that language barriers do not stop the JVs from performing with good profit overall, but rather affected the effectiveness of interorganizational knowledge transfer from the Chinese to the Africans. The language barriers were present on both sides because many Chinese could not speak English or French while many Africans could not speak Mandarin.

> Chinese trainers are beginners who speak neither English nor French perfectly, facing Africans who speak no word of Mandarin; Chinese

cannot speak a single local language; To cope with this issue, we bring in our local translators, but Chinese prefer their translators even when African translators are well qualified.

[Cameroon 58]

Such communication challenges were exacerbated by the fact that some Africans could speak only indigenous languages which the Chinese do not understand.

Anglophones like teaching English, francophones like learning Mandarin

Often, Anglophones who encountered language challenges during Sino-African collaborations considered teaching English to their Chinese colleagues first before trying to learn Mandarin themselves. A Ghanaian stated:

> My strategy is to encourage them improve their English by telling them for example that if you want to marry a beautiful Ghanaian lady, you must perfect your English. They often laugh at my jokes, but I think it works with a few of them. One of my colleagues is now much better compared to when he arrived in Accra.
>
> [Ghana 52]

This indicates that Anglophones' prioritized English as the preferred communication language and try consistently to maintain it as the standard official language of business within the JVs. For anglophone Africans, the use of technology and translation apps also appear to be common in coping with communication challenges. Those tools included instant Google translator and other apps such as iTranslate and Jibbigo.

In contrast, when facing language challenges, francophones often chose to learn Mandarin first before trying to teach French to their Chinese colleagues.

> I would rather please them and learn Chinese than force them to learn our language. My understanding is that the more you show them you like their language, the more they are willing to teach you new stuff. I do not want to waste my time and miss learning opportunities because of language preference. So, I rock with them in Chinese.
>
> [Congo 19]

Although Mandarin and French are often described as difficult languages, francophones display more interest in learning the Chinese language then in teaching French for the sake of maintaining it as the official language of business in the JVs. We should also mention that from a knowledge transfer perspective, one francophone employee indicated that because Chinese JV partners want to protect their strategic knowledge "It is not in Chinese advantage that locals learn Mandarin, therefore the Chinese do not encourage us to learn their language".

As to the indigenous Africans, there was no clear preference of either English or French when facing language challenges. Rather, those Africans who cannot speak or write often strengthened sign and body language to cope with their lack of English, French, and Mandarin communication skills.

> Since I cannot speak Chinese, my preferred solution is to enhance my sign language, I am so good at it now that I teach it to my coworkers. It is the only way we can survive here because Chinese people love their language, but it is tough for us to learn it.
>
> [Congo 40]

Sometimes, cutting the communication and choosing a separate workstation space were preferred as coping solutions for communication challenges. Whenever sign and body language did not work, their ultimate choice was to isolate themselves as often as possible from situations that could potentially require verbal communication with the Chinese. Finally, in DRC, one participant at a construction site reported that indigenous Africans and Chinese co-workers created a useful hybrid language that they called "Chingala", a mix of Chinese and Lingala.

The highlight regarding the fact that anglophones like teaching English while francophones like learning Mandarin allows us to speculate whether JVs in Africa are inadvertently helping the Commonwealth by contributing to the expansion of the English language among Chinese workers in Africa. Indeed, as counterintuitive as it sounds, the JVs we studied appear to contribute to anglicizing Chinese employees in Africa. Indeed, our findings suggests that anglophone Africans prefer to teach English to their Chinese colleagues rather than learn Mandarin. It is often argued that Mandarin is a difficult language to learn and even in Chinese culture this argument is widely well accepted. Plus, Chinese are increasingly realizing the advantage and necessity of speaking English to succeed in international business. Taking this into account, Chinese people tend to become more receptive to the idea of learning English instead of imposing Mandarin on their African counterparts. Considering these new developments, it is fair to speculate that through China–Africa JVs, English could be gaining additional adherents and territories outside the Commonwealth's regular population.

In contrast, JVs may not be contributing to the use of French language among Chinese people, but rather JVs are becoming a means to spread Mandarin across francophone Africans. This is apparently an unexpected spillover of China–Africa partnerships on the continent where not only French is losing ground but also Mandarin is gaining more African adherents across the continent. Besides, some francophone Africans who do not want to learn Mandarin stated that they would rather use interpreters to cope with communication challenges than teach French to their Chinese colleagues. As a last resort, some francophones reduce their collaboration with Chinese whenever they realize that their potential colleague does not speak French and is not interested in learning it and that language interpreters are not available.

Towards hybrid languages in Sino-African joint ventures: Chinglish and Frenchnese

Communication between African and Chinese people within China–Africa JVs has multiple dimensions. It mainly happens in English first, then to a lesser frequency in French, then in Chinese (mostly with Africans who lived/studied in China). Once these language options are exhausted, then a cohabitation of two languages emerges (Chinese and English or Chinese and French) within the JVs with both parties mixing them. These two combinations of languages sometimes become the common practice as neither of the two parties involved can speak both languages in a fully understandable manner. Indigenous languages, although rare, are spoken in those JVs mostly among Africans only. Figure 6.2 identifies the main

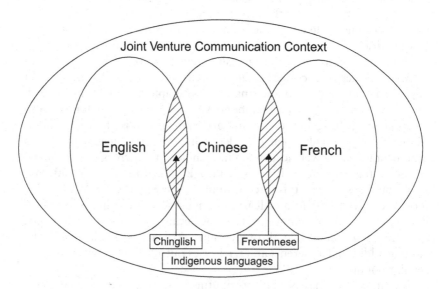

Figure 6.2 China–Africa intercultural communication configurations

configurations of the intercultural communication within China–Africa contexts.

At the intersection of English and Mandarin emerges what is nowadays being called **"Chinglish"** , a mix of the two languages whereby Chinese and Africans mobilize/mix words from both languages to communicate with one another.

> Our preferred jargon here is to mix English and Chinese. It is beneficial to both of us. No one masters other person's language perfectly, so one way to balance the communication is to combine English and Chinese at the same meeting; We call it Chinglish, I'm sure you have heard of it since you lived in China.
>
> [Nigeria 27]

> We all use Chinglish here, no one can escape it. It is a very useful language; We always invent words during the workshop. It also helps relax the work stress because people laugh at every invention of a Chinglish word; Soon, we will have a Chinglish dictionary!
>
> [Ghana 34]

This phenomenon has emerged as a common practice by both parties in the context of anglophone Africa, especially when the communication involves Africans who have studied or lived in China. Similarly, at the intersection of French and Mandarin emerges a concept of *"Frenchnese"*, a mix of both languages.

> My Chinese skills are not good, so I have to use French during some of my interactions with Chinese. There is no other way because my English is not good either. At least having studied in China, I know most of the basic words in Mandarin, but sometime, Frenchnese is my only way-out.
>
> [Burundi 1]

> With Chinese here, you either use Frenchnese or you go home. There is no other alternative.
>
> [Cameroon 16]

Although, "Frenchnese" appears to be less used than "Chinglish" but more used than "Chingala", all these trending phenomena have been mentioned by some participants in this study.

> I'm a very manual person, I like doing physical work. And since I did not go to China, here we often mix Chinese and Lingala for technical things. We call it Chingala; everybody on this site knows what

it stands for. It is a good way to avoid communication trouble with Chinese; as you keep repeating it, they end up absorbing it for good.

[Congo DRC 29]

This reality of hybrid languages is increasing and can lead toward a reconfiguration of communication styles in China–Africa JVs and relations. According to some respondents, such hybrid languages become even more appealing to both Africans and Chinese in situations of trial and error (or experiments) where neither of the parties has a name for new practices like a new technique, an innovative solution, or a do-it-yourself breakthrough.

Conclusion

This chapter seeks to develop theory in communication management and provide new insights to scholars, practitioners, firms, and governments in Africa and beyond. It identifies profiles, behavior, practices of Africans and Chinese at the intersections of intercultural communication, cross-cultural management, and knowledge transfer in the context of intensifying China–Africa economic ties and cooperation.

This chapter also offers some insights to scholars. Yes, language is identified in this chapter as a barrier to communication and to knowledge transfer, but this barrier has also become a conduit for innovative communication practices. Indeed, Africans and Chinese were able to develop a new set of hybrid languages that transcended English, French, and Mandarin to create a common ground for better mutual understanding between Africans and Chinese people. Cross-cultural management is not only about challenges but also about opportunities, and it appears that in the context of China–Africa collaborations, the parties took language challenge as an opportunity to improve and learn a new language (often the case for Chinese people) or to abandon a language (often the case of francophone Africans). While navigating such linguistic frontiers, individuals on both sides were able to address communication challenges in unique ways that are not yet extensively discussed in management theories.

Another takeaway is that as Chinese companies become more and more present in Africa, will this dynamic of language exchange and Sino-African communication phenomenon grow toward a more systematic linguistic practice across African countries? As the Chinese business community grows in Africa, so does the need for better communication with Africans. What language will or should take the language lead in African businesses: Mandarin, English, French or a set of hybrid languages? This research area could be an interesting topic to explore for China–Africa scholars. Indeed, Sino-African cooperation has a lot to gain in ensuring that cross-cultural communication is improved between Chinese and African people.

From a practical standpoint, the main recommendation this chapter offers is that more language training is needed for both Chinese and Africans if China–Africa partnerships are to become more beneficial, especially regarding knowledge transfer. Indeed, on one hand, more Africans learning Mandarin, and on the other hand, more Chinese learning English, French, or even indigenous languages will contribute toward increased learning and knowledge transfer for Africans during Sino-African JVs.

Contrary to more negative academic and journalistic reporting, the findings from the study reported in this chapter suggest that the increased Chinese presence in Africa appears to be contributing to the expansion of English language. Chinese working in Anglophone Africa are becoming increasingly interested in learning the language. This opportunistic spill-over among anglophones does not exist however among francophone Africans and the French language may be even losing ground over Mandarin in these countries. There is an important takeaway in this finding for both the Commonwealth and the Francophonie if African countries want to plan into their future. The Commonwealth has an opportunity to expand its reach to China not necessarily directly in China but rather through Africa to China as more and more Chinese people visit or settle in Africa for job, business, or permanent residency. This chapter shows that often those Chinese are potential anglophones as many of them end up learning and adopting English in Africa. For the Francophonie, the takeaway from this chapter is a more challenging issue as not only Chinese people are avoiding French but even the francophone Africans are abandoning French during their interactions with Chinese colleagues. This suggests that for the Francophonie to keep expanding, it has to create new incentives to encourage both Chinese and francophone Africans to use French more often in business.

References

Abernethy, D. B. (1971). Bureaucracy and economic development in Africa. *African Review*, *1*(1), 93–107.

Ado, A. (2018). Improving Africa's competitiveness through knowledge transfer: Lessons from partnerships with China and the way forward. In I. Adeleye & M. Esposito (Eds.), *Africa's competitiveness in the global economy* (pp. 249–283). Basingstoke and New York: Palgrave Macmillan.

Ado, A., & Su, Z. (2016). China in Africa: A critical literature review. *Critical Perspectives on International Business*, *12*(1), 40–60.

Ado, A., Su, Z., & Wanjiru, R. (2017). Learning and knowledge transfer in Africa-China JVs: Interplay between informalities, culture, and social capital. *Journal of International Management*, *23*(2), 166–179.

Beamish, P. W., & Lupton, N. C. (2009). Managing joint ventures. *Academy of Management Perspectives*, *23*(2), 75–94.

Briggs, R. C. (2017). Explaining case selection in African politics research. *Journal of Contemporary African Studies*, *35*(4), 565–572.

Brautigam, D., Xiaoyang, T., & Xia, Y. (2018). What kinds of Chinese 'geese' are flying to Africa? Evidence from Chinese manufacturing firms. *Journal of African Economies*, 27(1), 129–151.

Chrysostome, E., Munthali, T., & Ado, A. (2019). Capacity building in Africa: Toward an imperative mindset transformation. In *Capacity Building in Developing and Emerging Countries* (pp. 7–41). Cham: Springer.

FOCAC. (2018). *Forum on China-Africa cooperation Beijing action plan (2019–2021)*. Retrieved July 2, 2019 from www.focac.org/eng/zfgx_4/zzjw/t1594399.htm

Geda, A., Senbet, L. W., & Simbanegavi, W. (2018). The illusive quest for structural transformation in Africa: Will China make a difference? *Journal of African Economies*, 27(suppl_1), i4–i14.

Haas, M. R., & Cummings, J. N. (2015). Barriers to knowledge seeking within MNC teams: Which differences matter most? *Journal of International Business Studies*, 46(1), 36–62.

Inkpen, A. C., & Beamish, P. W. (1997). Knowledge, bargaining power, and the instability of international joint ventures. *Academy of Management Review*, 22(1), 177–202.

Jackson, T. (2012). Postcolonialism and organizational knowledge in the wake of China's presence in Africa: Interrogating South-South relations. *Organization*, 19(2), 181–204.

Jackson, T. (2014). Employment in Chinese MNEs: Appraising the dragon's gift to sub-Saharan Africa. *Human Resource Management*, 53(6), 897–919.

Jackson, T., & Horwitz, F. M. (2018). Expatriation in Chinese MNEs in Africa: An agenda for research. *The International Journal of Human Resource Management*, 29(11), 1856–1878.

Jackson, T., Louw, L., & Zhao, S. (2013). China in sub-Saharan Africa: Implications for HRM policy and practice at organizational level. *The International Journal of Human Resource Management*, 24(13), 2512–2533.

Mohan, G., Lampert, B., Tan-Mullins, M., & Atta-Ankomah, R. (2019). The (im)possibility of Southern theory: The opportunities and challenges of cultural brokerage in co-producing knowledge about China-Africa relations. In E. Mawdsley, E. Fourie, & W. Nauta (Eds.), *Researching South-South development cooperation: The politics of knowledge production*. Rethinking Development. Routledge (In Press).

Mo Ibrahim Report. (2018). *Ibrahim index of African governance*. Retrieved June 27, 2019 from http://s.mo.ibrahim.foundation/u/2018/11/27173840/2018-Index-Report.pdf?_ga=2.257620617.349146652.1562371008-1443862361.1562371008

SAIS-CARI. (2017). *Data: Chinese workers in Africa*. Retrieved June 15, 2019 from www.sais-cari.org/data-chinese-workers-in-africa

Simbiri, K. O. A., Hausman, A., Wadenya, R. O., & Lidicker, J. (2010). Access impediments to health care and social services between Anglophone and Francophone African immigrants living in Philadelphia with respect to HIV/AIDS. *Journal of Immigrant and Minority Health*, 12(4), 569–579.

UNCTAD. (2019). *General profile*. Retrieved June 15, 2019 from https://unctadstat.unctad.org/CountryProfile/GeneralProfile/en-GB/204/index.html

UNDP. (2018). *Human development indices and indicators*. Retrieved June 24, 2019 from www.hdr.undp.org/sites/default/files/2018_human_development_statistical_update.pdf

Vigouroux, C. B. (2008). "The smuggling of La Francophonie": Francophone Africans in Anglophone Cape Town (South Africa). *Language in Society*, 37(3), 415–434.

World Bank. (2019). *Doing business report*. Retrieved June 17, 2019 from www. doingbusiness.org/content/dam/doingBusiness/media/Annual-Reports/English/ DB2019-report_web-version.pdf

7 Chinese organisations and management in Zimbabwe

An analysis of press representation

Zindiye Stanislous

Introduction

The modern-day relationship between Zimbabwe and China developed from the liberation struggle with nationalist political parties, the Zimbabwe African National Union–Patriotic Front (ZANU–PF) and the Zimbabwe African Peoples Union (ZAPU) adopting a Maoist ideology (Prew, 1993). The Chinese taught the liberation movements guerrilla warfare in earnest and appeared to have no ambitions to conquer the economies of the third world. During the liberation war, the Chinese provided weapons thus becoming endeared to the nationalists. The victory against colonialism in Zimbabwe is therefore attributed partly to the contributions of both Chinese ideology (Mpofu, 2009) and their more practical help. It is from this background that the relations between the two countries are called 'all-weather friends' since the Chinese are perceived as having been there during the fight for self-determination and also when Zimbabwe came under attack from the West from the year 2000 to date. This laid the foundations for the current relationship between China and Zimbabwe's government (Zhang, 2014).

Chinese companies are operating in a wide range of industrial sectors in Zimbabwe including retail, mining, manufacturing and construction. On the construction side, they are focusing on power plants, dam construction and water works. The main companies involved are Sino-Hydro, China Machinery and Engineering Company focusing on power generation and Zhejiang Hailiang Company Limited of China from the mining side.

There are contradictory views about China–Zimbabwe relations. According to Zhang (2014), the media portrays the relationship between the two countries as 'a microcosm of China – Africa relations' especially in terms of China's economic engagement and resource-seeking activities in Zimbabwe.

Chinese relations with Zimbabwe

One view is that China and Zimbabwe appear not to operate on the same wavelength, with indications that the relations are of the rider and the horse with China riding and Zimbabwe being the horse. This is a view drawn by Maunganidze, Chiyadzwa, and Tobias' (2016) review of media relations between China and Zimbabwe where the purported friendship is seen not as symbiotic but rather as parasitic in nature. Taken in this context, such relations need to be revisited by policymakers. The open-door policy of China of ever accommodating Zimbabwe has always and continues to raise eyebrows leading to questions such as, what is in it for the Chinese and whose best interests are they serving?

As in the liberation struggle, the all-weather friend always was accommodative and supportive, pledging interest-free loans and investment and not interfering with Zimbabwe's politics (Zhang, 2014). From this perspective, the relations between China and Zimbabwe, though claimed to be equal, are heavily tilted in favour of the Chinese. They have used economic incentives, diplomacy and provision of arms and military hardware as a means at their disposal to secure the world for their own investments. State-controlled media always portrays the relationship between the two states as mutual, complementary, trusting and respectful. China is commended for supporting Zimbabwe materially and morally on one hand, whilst on the other hand Zimbabwe openly and strongly supports the sovereignty and territorial integrity of China. The national sports stadium, Magamba hockey stadium and Chinhoyi Hospital were all built with the help of technical cooperation from China. Schools, roads, agricultural demonstration centres and humanitarian programmes were and still continue to be put in place (Maunganidze, Chiyadzwa, & Tobias, 2013).

Bilateral trade between the two countries totalled US$205 million for the first half of 2007 (Matahwa, 2007). Yet despite the seemingly endless stream of goodwill from China, the cost to Zimbabwe has continued to rise over the years as the economic crisis deepens and the government continues to mortgage the country's resources to China to escape international isolation. According to Matahwa (2007), economic analysts predict that Zimbabwe will ultimately pay a high price for its government's appetite for cheap foreign 'loans' from so called 'friendly' countries like China in the near future. Zimbabwe has nowhere to go for financial support owing to being shunned by the rest of the world for its governance track record, and therefore the government has unreservedly accepted assistance from China. However, this may come with disastrous consequences for the Zimbabwean economy. The bulk of such deals usually take the form of barter trade (Matahwa, 2007). This is evidenced by Zimbabwe accepting the assistance from China whilst in return ceding control of certain minerals or agricultural crops to the Chinese firms and foregoing future foreign currency earnings.

Ever since the adoption of the Look East Policy, the government has been issuing business permits to Chinese shopkeepers, with an estimated 100 large- and medium-sized Chinese firms reported to have projects in

Zimbabwe according to a report in the *Global Times* (2016). Matahwa (2007) suggests that the government does not seem to realise, or they do not care, that its policies have pushed many locals into bankruptcy. He further argues that Chinese investment tends to be focused on Chinese companies on the ground and does little for long-term development or assistance in Zimbabwe. Further, attempts to dilute Chinese influence appear to have been thwarted. More and more delegations have been flocking in with the same end-effect: the Chinese promise but they do not deliver; they invest less money and spend less. Even in tourism, where Zimbabwe has the status of an authorised destination, Chinese tourists are reported to travel in large groups and always pay a group rate. In the meantime, *CNBC Africa* (2016) report that ordinary Zimbabweans have been complaining about working conditions in Chinese companies, the low quality of cheap Chinese imports (Zhing Zhongs) and the destruction of jobs in the small-scale manufacturing sector.

According to one report in *News Day*, Zimbabwe's economy continues to be flooded with Chinese materials and these products in most cases are very cheap and severely affect the locally manufactured ones (Zvinoira, 2015), attracting the greater market drawn mainly from the poor and the low-income earners. As a result, the local industries have been adversely affected by losing their market base (Matahwa, 2007). Some industries, especially clothing and textiles products, have encountered stiff competition from Chinese firms (Zvinoira, 2015). Because of such challenges, some decided to close down therefore making the relations fail to produce the desired results (Matahwa, 2007).

It would appear from these reports that Zimbabwe entered into bilateral trade agreements with China out of desperation. The West had imposed sanctions and the economy was having a downturn. Therefore, to emerge from this isolation, the government adopted the Look East Policy to break and neutralise the West's economic dominion on Zimbabwe. Thus according to Matahwa (2007), Zimbabwe has no choice but to accept a better devil, that is, China. Even the late Gaddafi, president of Libya, a champion of anti-Western African government had reduced his association with Zimbabwe. This further isolated Zimbabwe and it could only turn to China for help for capital at the expense of resources like minerals, especially diamonds, gold and chrome. Zimbabwe's resources appear to no longer be used to enhance Zimbabwe's industrialisation, economic growth and infrastructural development. It could be opined that this makes China an imperialist, because she is focusing on tapping the resources of Africa for her own advantages.

Chinese firms and the local community

China has played an important role in the training of Zimbabwean journalists. Several journalists from *Zimpapers* and the *New Ziana* have been sent to China for training. During the training in China, the journalists are made aware of the Chinese heritage and cultural sites. It appears to be a marketing exercise for the Chinese. The training by its nature appears to be ideological. Hence the other reason for the Chinese government to sponsor such training is to influence content and news gathering in a manner that is consistent with their expectations. This is witnessed by the change of perceptions about China relations with Zimbabwe. As Zimbabweans have warmed up to the presence of Chinese products, the word 'Zhing Zhong' is no longer as widely used to describe the Chinese as it used to be in the early years when the government adopted the Look East Policy.

The term 'Zhing Zhong' was used to refer to dumped cheap substandard products from China which had flooded the Zimbabwean market. Chinese investments in Zimbabwe were portrayed as the selling of the country to the Chinese. Bilateral treaties signed between China and Zimbabwe at the early stages of the adoption of the Look East Policy were likened to concessions signed by Lobengula, King of the Ndebeles in Zimbabwe in the 1880s (Matahwa, 2007). Just like the concessions signed by Lobengula after the bilateral treaties between the two countries, the period that followed was characterised by many Chinese coming to dominate the economy and controlling the media terrain. The government was accused of making Zimbabwe a dumping ground for textile and electronic products, hence the word 'Zhing Zhong' became part of journalism lexicon. This resulted in the collapsing of the textile sector in Zimbabwe (Mambondiyani, 2019).

Many Chinese business women and men were also accused of making a quick buck and swiftly shipping it back to their country. A number of them were reported to flagrantly contravene labour regulations which included subjecting workers to work under extreme conditions without safety shoes and paying them slave wages and salaries (Smith, 2012). Hence, they were painted as using cheap labour and mechanisation to compete with other businesses, illustrating that 'Zhing Zhong' products were not welcomed by the Zimbabwean community (Mambondiyani, 2019).

However, a few years later, the media, especially the private media, has changed its stance on how it portrays China's existence and relations with Zimbabwe. The term 'Zhing Zhong' has gradually disappeared in Zimbabwe given China's continued support to the comatose economy in the past three years by pouring huge investments and its promise to cancel Zimbabwe's US$40 million debt and introduce the yuan (Dzirutwe, 2015). The Chinese business people now hold the same high esteem which was once accorded to the Europeans. Chinese investments in Zimbabwe have increased by more than 5000% over the past years. This has changed and led to a positive perception of Chinese relations with Zimbabwe by the media with some media houses going to the extent of banning the use of the word 'Zhing Zhong.' The relations between Chinese firms and Zimbabwean employees have improved significantly, with most of these firms (90%) now being regarded as equal opportunity employers on a par with European firms.

The impact of the Chinese on the local job market

According to Hodzi, Hartwell, and Jager (2012), the increased economic and development relations between China and many African nations have elicited hope around the continent that Beijing would increase employment prospects. While the greater part of the media purport to believe that Chinese organisations do not hire local employees in Africa, new research suggests that the vast majority of workers are locally hired (Yating, 2016).

In Zimbabwe, Chinese organisations have admitted that there has been a problem and are trying to substitute Chinese employees with Zimbabweans mostly through two methods: first, by offering training to the local workforce in order to raise their level of skills; and second, by utilising more local managers to incorporate enterprises and to increase productivity. This is because in most cases the inefficiency of the local workers appears to be because of improper management as well as miscommunication emanating from language barriers that hinder efficiency (Hodzi et al., 2012). This had resulted in many Chinese organisations bringing their own employees.

Besides directly offering employment to Zimbabweans, the Chinese organisations' business activities are incidentally influencing the local job market as well (Honke & Thauer, 2014). Especially when the organisations arrive in Zimbabwe in such large numbers and in a controlled manner, their business patterns have massive impact on the market environment. The increase in the number of locals employed by some Chinese organisations operating in Zimbabwe appears to have led to the transfer of adequate skills to the local work force.

Not only are skills being transferred on the job, Chinese organisations operating in Zimbabwe are making efforts to even equip students in institutions of higher learning with advanced technical skills. According to *China Daily* (2016), Chinese telecoms firm Huawei Technologies recently signed a Memorandum of Understanding with the University of Zimbabwe (UZ) for the establishment of an information and communications technology (ICT) training and practicing centre at the country's oldest institution of higher learning. Also a prominent Chinese jewellery manufacturer, Harvest Way Group, is in the process of recruiting prospective students to undergo a year-long specialised diamond cutting training programme in China (Zimbabwe Daily, 2015). This will complement Harvest Way Group's plans of setting up a diamond cutting and polishing factory in Zimbabwe. Mr Teddy Cheung, the managing director of Harvest Way Group, indicated that China prioritise investing in skills transfer as evidenced by the diamond cutting scholarship programme. Harvest Way Zimbabwe managing director, Dr Edwin Gwenzi, said that the training programme gives the country the necessary foundation to become the regional hub for diamond processing (Zimbabwe Daily, 2015).

However, while some technical and engineering skills might have migrated out of Zimbabwe, there is still an abundance of general and lower skills that can be employed. There is a pool of unemployed graduates and semi-skilled in the country. One of the biggest impediments to skills transfer again appears to be the language barrier. This occurs even at the senior level where the reports of translators are too simple in the technical sense. Even where there are Zimbabweans who speak the languages, there are problems between the locals and official interpreters. There were concerns also at plants owned by a key Chinese firm, Sino-Steel, as only Chinese printed manuals are available. This raises questions about what will happen when, as the CEO indicated, Sino-Steel upgrades the equipment currently installed at ZIMASCO using Chinese blueprints. There is a real possibility that local know-how will not be available in the absence of training and technology transfer. It was reported that whenever Sino-Steel wanted mining developments, it sent for technical teams from China. This practice has a strong negative bearing on technology transfer, and it means that only Chinese nationals are benefiting in the process.

Chinese organisations and the management of Zimbabwe staff

The Zimbabweans who are mostly feeling the Chinese organisations' influence in their country are the workers. As Chinese firms take over business and Chinese managers increasingly run enterprises from billion-dollar mining companies to the downtown restaurants in capital Harare, Zimbabwean workers and labour unions are reportedly complaining of mistreatment and exploitation. In November 2016, construction workers went on strike over low pay of $4 per day and what they said were regular beatings by their managers. According to the spokesperson for the Zimbabwe Construction and Allied Trade Workers' Union, as reported by Fisher (2011) in *The Atlantic*,

> one of the most disturbing developments is that most of the Chinese employers openly boast that they have government protection and so nothing can be done to them. This clearly indicates that the issue has more serious political connotations than we can imagine.

Employee ill-treatment has been one of the main negative headlines about the activities of Chinese organisations in Zimbabwe. This appears to encourage locals to view the Chinese with suspicions. This results in a negative attitude towards the Chinese investing in Zimbabwe.

An investigation by *The Standard* newspaper (Mangirazi, 2016) recently exposed exploitation of workers and violation of labour and environmental laws in Zimbabwe by some of the Chinese firms. The Zimbabwe Diamond Miners Workers' Union (ZDMWU) has taken the Chinese-owned Detroop Mine near Chinhoyi to the National Employment Council (NEC) over its alleged abuse of employees (Mangirazi, 2016). Senior managers at the mine were allegedly abusing workers by demanding $50 from each of them every month as protection fees. Based on the preceding, the benefits of employment creation as a result of China investing in Zimbabwe may be overridden by such negative reports.

The construction site of the Zimbabwe National Defence College north of Harare as reported by Smith (2012) has also become a catalyst for another source of simmering resentment from the labour unions as a result of Chinese labour practices in Zimbabwe. Surrounded by a perimeter wall that runs for a kilometre through what was once farmland, the military academy was built by a Chinese contractor whose managers were accused of giving out physical punishments and providing miserable working conditions and insufficient pay according to Smith (2012) writing in *The Guardian*. Most workers cited unfair labour practices.

According to this report, a 26-year-old builder employed at the college, on his way to a nightshift, said:

> We tried to go on strike but the leader of it was beaten up and sacked. The government doesn't say anything, even though it knows people are beaten up. I saw them undress some workers and beat them with helmets. Some of them were crying with the pain.

A carpenter employed by the same Chinese contractor indicated that he typically woke up at 4 a.m. and worked from 7 a.m. to 9 p.m. every day and was paid just $4 a day. He had this to say: 'We don't have a choice because we need to survive. But if it was possible to chase all the Chinese away, I would.'

General issues, problems, positives and negatives

The positives

The relationship between Zimbabwe and China has resulted in several economic developments and initiatives. A discussion of some of the positives highlighted in the media follows next.

Funding the economy

Zimbabwe had not been able to obtain funds from Western governments and funding institutions such as the World Bank, as it had previously failed to repay billions of dollars in debt. This is a result of its being isolated from the world market through sanctions and having its lines of credit and borrowing powers cut. It could no longer access aid in any form mainly from the Western countries. Since 2005, this has resulted in its 'Look East' policy, relying increasingly on Chinese organisations to offset sanctions from traditional Western partners according to Song (2014) writing in the *International Business Times*. One organisation which has been most influential in funding the Zimbabwean economy is the China Exim-Bank. The bank has provided over US$1 billion worth of preferential, concessionary and commercial loans to Zimbabwe in recent years for projects including the National Defence College, Harare water project, medical equipment for hospitals, Victoria Falls Airport expansion and Kariba South hydropower station expansion, among others, as recorded by Lin (2014) in *The Herald*. From 2012 to 2014, the total amount of China's official assistance to Zimbabwe, namely grant and interest-free loans, amounted to over US$100 million (Lin, 2014), showing that China has done a lot for Zimbabwe thereby strengthening the relations between the two countries.

Positive reporting

The Chinese news media are seeking to compete with players such as *CNN* and *Al Jazeera*, but they are rolling out what they claim is a different approach to journalism. What Chinese media are offering to Africa is 'positive reporting,' a style of journalism that focuses on collective achievements rather than divisive issues like political crises or sensational negative news like famines according to Verhoeven and Gagliardone (2012) writing in CNN Online.

Zimbabwe has benefited from the Chinese media. Their message is that Zimbabwe, similar to China, has received too much negative publicity in the Western-dominated global media. In this view, Chinese and Zimbabwean voices are finally finding ways to tell their own stories which offer a healthy correction to stereotypes of Zimbabwe as the 'hopeless country,' with endless unemployment, HIV, political instability, poverty and hunger (Shonhiwa, 2014).

The Africa of today, while still consumed by many intractable problems, is no longer the Africa of the 1990s (Verhoeven & Gagliardone, 2012). Millions of Africans are seizing on unprecedented opportunities to build new lives. This optimistic message about Africa turning a corner has, however, faced criticism on different fronts. One of the most pertinent charges is that 'positive reporting' fails to deliver on one of the main mandates of journalism, which is acting as a watchdog and keeping those in power in check, rather than praising them for their successes (Verhoeven & Gagliardone, 2012).

Donations

The then Zimbabwean President, Robert Mugabe, has praised the Chinese for their non-interference approach to African affairs and their willingness to provide donations to Zimbabwe. China in November 2016 pledged to donate 90,700 tonnes of rice and construct 150 boreholes to help reduce the effects of the El Nino-induced drought that has occurred in most parts of the country, writes Dlamini (2016) in *CFUZ News*. In a major development in June 2016, during President Xi's visit to Harare, China decided to provide assistance to Zimbabwe for the construction of the new Parliament building of Zimbabwe, reports Gumbo (2016) in *All Africa News*; Gumbo quotes China's Zhang Ming as saying that the new building was a donation to Zimbabwe. Zhang Ming indicated that China has already completed the design of the Parliament building and submitted three design plans to the Zimbabwe side and China is waiting for confirmation from them for the early launch of the project (Dlamini, 2016).

The negatives

There has been a lot of negativism around Chinese activities in Zimbabwe reported in the press. Some of the allegations, as noted previously, range across poor working conditions, inferior goods or products, displacement and sexual and physical harassment. A discussion of some of the negatives reported in the media follows next.

Poor labour relations by the Chinese

Despite the statistics in a country with unemployment hovering at around 80%, the Zimbabwean government came out in favour of relaxing labour laws to make it easier to dismiss employees without following the current time-consuming procedures according to Muzulu (2014) writing in *News Day Zimbabwe*. The decision seems to have been driven by Zimbabwe's interest in luring more Chinese foreign direct investment, where the Chinese have a reputation for poor employment conditions and no respect for employees, according to the report. Zimbabweans at different levels have debated the conduct of Chinese companies and their treatment of employees in different meetings and even in Parliament. There have been accusations from employees at Chinese-owned companies, especially construction sites, about long working hours, poor working conditions, arbitrary dismissals, beatings at the workplace and low wages (Muzulu, 2014). These accusations paint a negative picture of Chinese organisations' operations in Zimbabwe. Hence the media, which is the private press, are replete with these allegations.

Mistrust

Hospitality is one of the main African values, which is still alive among Africans, and Zimbabweans are not an exception to this. Zimbabweans easily incorporate and accept strangers and strangers are always warmly welcomed into their country. However, the Chinese appear to be quite suspicious and cold toward strangers with whom relationships have not been established (Matondo, 2012). Nobody should be trusted except one's kinfolk in the form of the extended family. Consequently, the social network first consists of family members, relatives, friends, classmates and colleagues, which represent the immediate sphere on which trust is established and developed. This lack of trust in outsiders appears to define the behaviour of Chinese people in business, and why most important key positions within Chinese organisations are mainly supervised by Chinese nationals (Matondo, 2012).

Quality of products

One of the problems facing Zimbabweans is that most Chinese businesses appear to continue to engage in a practice referred to as 'quality fade' (Midler, 2013). This is the deliberate and secret habit of widening profit margins through a reduction in the quality of materials. Consumers usually never notice what is happening since the initial production sample is fine. Yet with each successive production run, a bit more of the necessary inputs are missing. Chinese businesses that engage in quality fade unfortunately subscribe to the view that business is about increasing one's share of the pie rather than growing the pie over time. They often focus on extracting profit through short-term schemes that inevitably militate against long-term development (Midler, 2013). Furthermore, they supply poor quality low-priced products usually referred to as 'Zhing Zhong' in Zimbabwe, as noted previously. They appear to use a general assumption that Zimbabwe is poor and the people cannot afford quality products commensurate with the price.

Environmental impact

The environmental impact of China–Africa engagement is one of the top concerns of many who are critical of a rising China in Zimbabwe. If environmental concerns rise along with income, as many commentators believe, China should be approaching a time when sustainability becomes a real, genuine, and public concern for its leaders (Brautingam, 2016). In Zimbabwe, the worst negative environmental impacts appear to be caused by some Chinese organisations in the mining sector. For example, they appear not to maintain roads they use in their daily mining activities.

The inhabitants around Zimbabwe's Marange diamond mine believe their village would be a better place to live in had it not been for the discovery of enormous deposits of alluvial diamonds in 2006, according to a report in *The Africa Report* (2012). Since the commencement of commercial diamond mining activities in Marange in September 2009, villagers have watched with concern as the Save River has become heavily polluted by some Chinese mining companies.

A scientific study commissioned by the Zimbabwe Environmental Law Association and carried out by the University of Zimbabwe confirmed the fears of villagers and non-governmental organisations (NGOs) who have long suspected that Chinese companies were polluting the Save River (*The Africa Report*, 2012). The report concluded that the water in the Save River is heavily contaminated to such an extent that communities cannot use the water for drinking purposes anymore.

Apart from water pollution, Marange is also experiencing serious air and noise pollution. Villagers fear a rise in cases of diseases such as tuberculosis because of dust inhalation. The noise from the heavy trucks and equipment also causes distress to wildlife in addition to loss of natural habitat which has been their preferred territory. There appears to be no longer any sign of wildlife in the area measuring over 120,000 hectares (*The Africa Report*, 2012).

Conclusion

The aim was to evaluate the soundness of the press' views and establish the theory informing the press' perspectives and varying views. This is important as a number of things, both negative and positive, have been written about the Chinese presence in Zimbabwe. From the available literature, it seems that there is a divided opinion between the government-controlled press and the private press. From a government perspective, China and its organisations have done much for Zimbabwe. In contrast, the private press has consistently focused on the perceived negative aspects ranging from resource plundering, exploitative labour practices and the influx of Zhing Zhong products that result in the closure of local industries as they cannot compete with them, mainly on the basis of cost and price.

Having gone through the available various press views, it seems the Chinese are doing much more good than harm in the Zimbabwean economy. This conclusion is against the backdrop of the prevailing economic conditions in the country characterised by high unemployment rates and closure of many big companies. The Chinese presence has resulted in employment creation thereby helping to address some of the socio-economic challenges being faced by Zimbabwe. Understanding the role of Chinese companies in Zimbabwe is important for both locals and local companies. Local companies and managers can create synergies with Chinese-owned companies in order to create win–win situations that benefit both local and Chinese-owned entities. Furthermore, if mutual understanding prevails, coexistence will be possible as the various stakeholders will understand their different roles and contributions in the Zimbabwean economy. Future research can focus on the economic contributions of the Chinese companies per industry or sector. This will help to dispel some myths or misunderstandings about the Chinese role and presence in Zimbabwe.

References

The Africa Report. (2012). The story of Zimbabwe's marange diamonds: Pollution, politics, power. *The Africa Report* [Online]. Retrieved July 17, 2019 from www.theafricareport.com/news-analysis/the-story-of-zimbabwes-marange-diamonds-pollution-politics-power.html

Brautingam, D. (2016). Thoughts on China, Africa, per capita income, and the environment. *The China Africa Research Initiative.* [Online]. Retrieved July 17, 2019 from www.chinaafricarealstory.com/2016/08/thoughts-on-china-africa-per-capita.html

China Daily. (2016). China's Huawei signs ICT training pact with University of Zimbabwe. *China Daily.* [Online]. Retrieved July 16, 2019 from www.chinadaily.com.cn/business/tech/2016-11/23/content_27463130.htm

CNBC AFRICA. (2016). *How Africans view Chinese investment.* [Online]. Retrieved July 17, 2019 from www.cnbcafrica.com/news/special-report/2016/11/07/africa-chinese-investment/

Dlamini, N. (2016). China to help end food shortages, revamp agriculture: Ambassador. *CFUZ News* [Online]. Retrieved March 28, 2017 from www.newsday.co.zw/2016/11/china-help-end-food-shortages-revamp-agriculture-ambassador/

Dzirutwe, D. (2015). *Zimbabwe says China to cancel $40 million debt, increase yuan use.* [Online]. Retrieved August 20, 2019 from https://uk.reuters.com/article/uk-zimbabwe-china-debt/zimbabwe-says-china-to-cancel-40-million-debt-increase-yuan-use-idUKKBN0U40TO20151221

Fisher, M. (2011). *In Zimbabwe, Chinese investment with hints of colonialism: The Asian power is exerting greater influence over political and economic systems across Africa.* [Online]. Retrieved July 27, 2019 from www.theatlantic.com/international/archive/2011/06/in-zimbabwe-chinese-investment-with-hints-of-colonialism/240978/

Frey, L., Botan, C., & Kreps, G. (1999). *Investigating communication: An introduction to research methods.* Boston, MA: Allyn & Bacon.

Global Times. (2016). *Zimbabwe law to hit Chinese firms* [Online]. Retrieved July 17, 2019 from www.globaltimes.cn/content/976300.shtml

Gumbo, L. (2016). Zimbabwe: China envoy meets president on Deals. *All Africa News* [Online]. Retrieved July 17, 2019 from http://allafrica.com/stories/201606220124.html

The Herald. (2013). *Zimbabwe: Mwana Africa, Chinese sign pact* [Online]. Retrieved July 28, 2019 from https://allafrica.com/stories/201302080361.html

The Herald. (2016). *Zimbabwe: "Increased" cooperation boost for Zim, China Media Sect* [Online]. Retrieved July 17, 2019 from http://allafrica.com/stories/201610130799.html

Hodzi, O., Hartwell, L., & De Jager, N. (2012). "Unconditional aid": Assessing the impact of China's development assistance to Zimbabwe. *South African Journal of International Affairs, 19*(1), 79–103.

Honke, J., & Thauer, C. R. (2014). Multinational corporations and service provision in sub-Saharan Africa: Legitimacy and institutionalization matter. *Governance*, 27(4), 697–716.

Lin, N. (2014). China-Zim friendship built on mutual co-operation. *The Herald* [Online]. Retrieved July 17, 2019 from www.herald.co.zw/china-zim-friendship-built-on-mutual-co-operation/

Mambondiyani, A. (2019). *Cheap Chinese imports disrupt manufacturing in Zimbabwe, cost thousands of jobs* [Online]. Retrieved July 17, 2019 from www.theepochtimes.com/thousands-lose-jobs-as-cheap-chinese-imports-kill-zimbabwes-manufacturing-industry_2757793.html

Mangirazi, N. (2016). *Diamond mine workers sue Chinese employer over 'abuse'.* [Online]. Retrieved July 17, 2019 from www.newsday.co.zw/2016/10/15/diamond-mine-workers-sue-chinese-employer-abuse

Matahwa, O. (2007). *China and Zimbabwe: Is there a future?* [Online]. Retrieved July 17, 2019 from http://archive.kubatana.net/docs/econ/matahwa_china_zimbabwe_future_071101om.pdf

Matondo, M. (2012). Cross-cultural values comparison between Chinese and sub-Saharan Africans. *International Journal of Business and Social Science*, 3(11).

Maunganidze, G., Chiyadzwa, I. F., & Tobias, D. (2016). Reflections on emerging horse and rider relationship: Media relations between Zimbabwe and China. *IOSR Journal of Humanities and Social Science (IOSR-JHSS)*, 16. [Online]. Retrieved July 17, 2019 from www.iosrjournals.org/iosr-jhss/papers/Vol16-issue6/L01667278.pdf?id=8289

Midler, P. (2013). *Dealing with China's quality fade.* South Africa: Pearson.

Mpofu, T. (2009). *Total history, Southern African history.* Harare: Priority Projects Publishing.

Mudyanadzo, W. (2011). *Zimbabwe's diplomacy 1980–2008.* Gweru: Booklove Publishers.

Musanga, T. (2017). Perspectives of Zimbabwe – China relations in Wallace Chirumiko's "Made in China" (2012) and NoViolet Bulawayo's we need new names (2013). *Journal of African Cultural Studies*, 29(1), 81–95 [Online]. Retrieved July 22, 2019 from https://doi.org/10.1080/13696815.2016.1201654

Muzulu, P. (2014). The rise of Chinese sweatshops in Zimbabwe. *NewsDay Zimbabwe* [Online]. Retrieved July 17, 2019 from www.zimbabwesituation.com/news/zimsit_the-rise-of-chinese-sweatshops-in-zimbabwe/

Prew, M. (1993). *People making history.* Harare: Zimbabwe Publishing House.

Shonhiwa, J. (2014). *Looking at Zimbabwean relations with China.* Englewood Cliffs, NJ: Prentice-Hall.

Smith, D. (2012) Workers claim abuse as China adds Zimbabwe to its scramble for Africa. *The Guardian* [Online]. Retrieved July 17, 2019 from www.theguardian.com/world/2012/jan/02/china-zimbabwe-workers-abuse

Song, S. (2014). China to help fund Zimbabwe's infrastructure building plan to revive its economy. *International Business Times* [Online]. Retrieved July 17, 2019 from www.ibtimes.com/china-help-fund-zimbabwes-infrastructure-building-plan-revive-its-economy-1554891

Verhoeven, H., & Gagliardone, I. (2012). Opinion: China's positive spin on Africa. *CNN Online*. Retrieved July 17, 2019 from https://edition.cnn.com/2012/12/18/opinion/china-media-africa-verhoeven-gagliardone/index.html

Yating, L. (2016). Chinese companies employ a lot more African workers than you think. *The China Africa project* [Online]. Retrieved March 28, 2017 from www. chinaafricaproject.com/podcast-china-africa-kenya-labor-luo-yating-sace/

Zhang Chun. (2014). *China – Zimbabwe relations: A model of China – Africa relations?* Occasional Paper 205. Global Powers and Africa Programme. November 2014 [Online]. Retrieved July 23, 2019 from https://saiia.org.za/ research/china-zimbabwe-relations-a-model-of-china-africa-relations/

Zimbabwe Daily. (2015). *China begins skills transfer* [Online]. Retrieved July 17, 2019 from www.thezimbabwedaily.com/news/22522-china-begins-skills-transfer.html

Zvinoira, T. (2015). Textiles want Chinese products banned. *Newsday, 8.* [Online]. Retrieved July 17, 2019 from www.newsday.co.zw/2015/07/08/textilers-want-chinese-products-banned/

8 South African employees' commitment to a Chinese organisation

Steven Paterson and Lynette Louw

Chinese organisations are receiving increasing support from the Chinese government to enter into Africa (Corkin & Burke, 2006). In 2011, over 2,000 Chinese organisations were operational in Africa, contributing greatly to employment in Africa (Cissé, 2012; Latham, 2011). So much so, that bilateral trade between China and Africa rose from 10.6 billion US dollars in 2000 to over 160 billion US dollars in 2011 (Cissé, 2012; Bräutigam, 2011a; Bräutigam & Xiaoyang, 2011; Abkowitz, 2009).

Concerns have, however, been raised regarding China's reputation as being characterised by a lack of work, health and industry standards, often resulting in poor working conditions and a lack of basic worker rights (Bräutigam, 2011b; AccountAbility DRC-ERI, 2009). Concerns have also been expressed about the limited Chinese knowledge of local African culture and practices, which may result in a large number of imported Chinese human resources instead of focusing on local employment and training (AccountAbility DRC-ERI, 2009). If a lack of cultural understanding and cooperation between Chinese employers and African employees exists, together with a range of other possible factors, including poor employment standards, this could lead to a negative effect on the organisational commitment of local employees and therefore a negative effect on Chinese business interests in Africa. Organisational commitment of local employees is therefore an important factor for consideration.

Concept of organisational commitment used in this study

Organisations not only need to secure and appoint good employees, but more importantly need to create a committed workforce. Committed employees are believed to be one of the most important factors in determining the success of an organisation in a competitive market (Jafri, 2010). Organisations cannot therefore succeed without the efforts and commitment of their employees (Mosadeghrad, Ferlie, & Rosenberg, 2008). Committed employees will place high value on job performance and invest their personal resources in ensuring workplace success while accepting challenging work activities (Meyer & Allen, 1997).

The multiple definitions of organisational commitment within the literature share a common theme in that it is considered to be a psychological link between employees and their organisations. For the purposes of this study and in line with the accepted definitions of multiple authors (Yiing & Ahmad, 2009; Hart & Willower, 2001; Byrne, 1998; Porter, Steers, Mowday, & Boulian, 1974), organisational commitment will be defined as an individual's identification with, and a strong belief in, an organisation's goals. It includes a willingness to exert extra effort on behalf of the organisation and a desire to remain an employee of the organisation.

Organisational commitment is a complicated concept which can take various forms and dimensions (Vallejo, 2009). A three-component model proposed by Meyer and Allen (1991) has become the most widely accepted in recent literature (Batool & Ullah, 2013; João & Coetzee, 2012; Jonathan, Darroux, & Thibeli, 2013; Kaur & Sandhu, 2010; Fu et al., 2009). According to Meyer and Allen's (1991) three-component model, commitment can take three unique forms, namely; affective, normative and continuance commitment.

Affective commitment refers to an employee's identification with and emotional attachment to an organisation (Beukes & Botha, 2013; Yiing & Ahmad, 2009; Meyer & Allen, 1997). Employees with strong feelings of affective commitment will often remain with an organisation because they wish to do so (Colquitt, Lepine, & Wesson, 2013). Normative commitment relates to an employee's commitment based on a sense of obligation or duty to the organisation, even if the organisation is facing problems and challenges (Meyer & Allen, 1991). As a result, employees with a strong normative commitment may feel a moral duty to an organisation and continue their employment because they feel they ought to do so (Colquitt et al., 2013; Meyer & Allen, 1991). Continuance commitment, on the other hand, refers to an employee's commitment based on the costs and risks the employee associates with leaving the organisation (Yiing & Ahmad, 2009; Meyer & Allen, 1991). Employees with high levels of continuance commitment believe they must remain employed with the organisation because of the investment of time and effort already put into the organisation, or because of the belief that they may have difficulty in finding new employment elsewhere (Aamodt, 2004). Should continuance commitment dominate employees' commitment profiles, they may exhibit high levels of work-related anxiety and stress (Meyer, Kam, Goldenberg, & Bremner, 2013).

Factors influencing organisational commitment

In order to efficiently manage organisational commitment, it is important to understand the factors that contribute to its development (Meyer & Allen, 1997). Although other factors may exist, the researchers initially identified seven factors which were deemed appropriate for the context of the study.

Open communication

Business strategies, goals and performances should be clearly communicated to all employees, encouraging regular constructive feedback (Rego & Cunha, 2006). Open and regular communication with employees should therefore exist within an organisation (Venter, Farrington, & Finkelstein, 2010). Such communication with employees is deemed to have a positive influence on employee commitment and is deemed to assist in building trust, employee satisfaction and work place relationships (Rego & Cunha, 2006; Haugh & McKee, 2003).

Leadership

A significant body of literature has highlighted the link between leadership and organisational commitment (Jackson, Meyer, & Wang, 2013; Vallejo, 2009; Yiing & Ahmad, 2009; Lesabe & Nkosi, 2007; Pierce & Dunham, 1987). Leaders who demonstrate commitment to the organisation and serve as an example of the desired changes within the organisation are important for organisational success (Iqbal, 2010). If employees perceive leaders to be committed and dedicated, it will build employee commitment to the organisation and its vision (Chawla & Renesch, 2006).

Supervisory support

The primary goal of a supervisor is to provide employees with the direction and support required in order to achieve their goals, as well as those of the organisation (Yiing & Ahmad, 2009). The perceived level of supervisory support experienced by employees is deemed to have an influence on their organisational commitment (Venter et al., 2010; Aubè, Rousseau, & Morin, 2007). Recognition from superiors gives employees a sense of self-worth, importance and ultimately motivation to perform within the organisation (Döckel, 2003).

Job security

It is believed that many individuals have experienced job losses and sustained unemployment because of many organisations engaging in restructuring, mergers, downsizing and acquisitions (Hirsch & De Soucey, 2006). Employees who perceive their jobs to be insecure will often be less motivated to perform their work tasks (Klandermans, Hesselink, & Van Vuuren, 2010). Perceived job security has been found to play an important role in an employee's commitment to an organisation (Abdullah &

Ramay, 2012; Sweeney & Quirin, 2009; Buitendach & De Witte, 2005; Yousef, 1998).

Opportunities for training and development

The continual training and development of an organisation's employees is deemed to be important for organisational development, adaptability and success (Asche & Schuller, 2008). Meyer and Allen (1997) believe that the training and development of employees are important for providing opportunities for employee advancement and may be perceived as a demonstration of the value the organisation places on its employees, ultimately building commitment to the organisation (Van Dyk & Coetzee, 2012; Scheible & Bastos, 2013). It is believed that if organisations give employees the opportunity to be trained and later apply their skills, it may lead to a positive psychological attachment to the organisation (McElroy, 2001).

Compensation

Employee compensation is believed to be a fundamental factor in the commitment of employees (Kantor, 2013; Van Dyk & Coetzee, 2012). Compensation from an employer provides employees with a sense of security, recognition and self-worth. Compensation is therefore of great importance to most employees (Lesabe & Nkosi, 2007; Hoyt & Gerdloff, 1999). Higginbotham (1997) asserted that although high salaries are not essential, employees who perceive their compensation to be "good" or "fair" are more likely to be committed to the organisation.

Promotional opportunities

Promotions within an organisation are deemed to provide employees with opportunities for personal growth, increased responsibility and increased social status (Mezzinson, Mosley, & Pietrie, 1992). As a result, it has been asserted that an employee's perceived opportunities for promotion are likely to influence the level of commitment to the organisation (Van Dyk & Coetzee, 2012; Iqbal, 2010; Kipkebut, 2010; Giffords, 2009; Moorhead & Griffin, 1992; McCormick & Ilgen, 1985).

What we were looking for in our research

Despite the importance of Chinese organisations and their operations in Africa, very little research has been done on individual and organisational issues in Chinese organisations operating in Africa (Jackson, 2012), and more specifically the local employees' organisational commitment to such organisations. The organisational commitment of South African

employees within Chinese organisations in South Africa is important as
it promotes the success of Chinese business, which may promote further
investment into the country as well as the use of local human resources.
In an attempt to address the gap in the literature on organisational commitment of South African employees in foreign Chinese organisations,
the main aim of this research was to conduct an empirical study into
the levels of and factors influencing the organisational commitment of
South African employees in a selected Chinese organisation. Our objectives were to:

- Identify and describe key factors influencing local employee commitment.
- Identify and describe current commitment levels amongst local
  employees.
- Draw conclusion regarding local employee commitment and its
  implications for the current literature and future research within a
  Chinese organisation in South Africa.

How we conducted this research

A large Chinese organisation, which manufactures and distributes elec-
tronics and appliances in South Africa, agreed to participate in this study.
The organisation is actively investing in its operations in South Africa
and is aiming to enhance its current workforce with over a thousand new
South African employees over the next few years. With its current growth,
active investment in South Africa and expected growth in local employee
numbers, the organisation was an ideal case for this study. The research
made use of a descriptive case study design. The participants in this study
were selected using purposive sampling, a non-probability sampling
technique. Data were collected by means of in-depth, semi-structured
interviews with 20 participating local employees. Data were collected at
four organisational branches across South Africa. The interviews lasted
approximately 25 hours in total and varied in time depending on each
interview, as certain participants were more interactive and offered
greater detail than others. The semi-structured interviews included: four
miscellaneous open-ended questions in order to ease the participant into
the interview; research questions pertaining to the seven factors influencing organisational commitment identified in the literature; and questions
relating to the participants' levels of commitment.

Participants included six females and fourteen males, numbered P1–
P20 (where the suffix M denotes "manager", S denotes "supervisor", and
T denotes "technician"). Four of the participants were employed in man-
agerial positions (P1-M; P16-M; P18-M; P20-M), three in supervisory
positions (P5-S; P13-S; P17-S) and 13 in technical positions (P2-T; P3-T;
P4-T; P6-T; P7-T; P8-T; P9-T; P10-T; P11-T; P12-T; P14-T; P15-T; P19-
T). In order to balance between openness in reporting research findings

and maintaining confidentiality and anonymity of participants, we have chosen not to provide specific biographical details of each respondent. The interview transcripts were the primary source of data and were enriched with the use of organisational and participant observations in order to provide important details and insights into the research important for the triangulation of data (Remenyi, 2013).

The researchers analysed the data using content analysis. The qualitative data collected for this study were analysed manually, making use of Tesch's (1990) model of content analysis as well as the researchers' own understanding of qualitative data analysis. In assessing the quality of the analysis, the four criteria for reliability as identified by Lincoln and Guba (1985) were considered, namely confirmability, credibility, transferability and dependability.

What we found from our research

In order to address the first and second objectives of this study, this section presents the findings pertaining to the factors influencing commitment as well as the perceived levels of commitment amongst participants.

Open communication

Fifteen of the 20 participants believed communication in the organisation to be open, with the remaining participants having a neutral or mixed view on the matter. Three communication categories emerged from the data, namely: open-door policy (P1-M; P2-T; P3-T; P5-S; P12-T; P16-M), feedback (P7-T; P9-T; P10-T; P16-M) and irregular communication (P11-T; P13-S; P17-S; P19-T; P20-M). Participants generally described an open-door policy in the organisation and highlighted that they felt that they have the freedom to speak directly to managers and discuss any problems they may have. A technical employee emphasised this viewpoint:

> If I am having problems, I can be open with the management, and they will listen and hear the problems. They are very kind in that they will always take the time to listen to any employee. Even if it's not really their department, they will try help where they can.
>
> (P3-T)

The findings indicate that an open environment within the organisation is of great importance to its management and employees.

Participants demonstrated that the organisation's management provided feedback which gave the employees a sense of direction and motivation. It was evident that the feedback participants received from managers influenced their positive feelings regarding the organisation's open communication.

The findings indicate that a number (P11-T; P13-S; P17-S; P19-T; P20-M) of participants believed a lack of regular communication was, however, hampering effective open communication in the organisation.

Leadership

Participants generally had positive feelings regarding how knowledgeable the organisation's leadership were and demonstrated great faith in their leaders, describing them as "knowledgeable" (P2-T; P3-T; P6-T; P12-T; P13-S; P15-T), "skilled" (P1-M; P5-S; P12-T; P13-S; P14-T; P18-M), and "experienced" (P1-M; P4-T; P9-T; P16-M; P20-M). The Chinese managers' leadership style was generally seen in a favourable light, and Chinese managers were described as "diligent" (P5-S; P6-T; P10-T; P14-T; P16-M), "committed" (P12-T; P14-T; P16-M) and "stern" (P1-M; P2-T; P3-T; P5-S; P11-T; P12-T). Participants described the diligence with which they believed Chinese managers worked and described them as deeply committed to the organisation. A local supervisor shared this belief:

> They are so particular about their work, always working very hard and diligently. Very particular and diligent. But this rubs off on us, as more junior managers and then on the rest of the staff as well. We don't want to disappoint them, we want to match their level.
>
> (P5-S)

The South African managers were described as "relaxed" (P3-T; P5-S; P12-T; P17-S; P19-T), and "open" (P6-T; P10-T; P17-S; P19-T; P20-M). The findings indicate that the South African managers practice what may be best described as a participative and transparent leadership style. Their leadership style involves having a close, open and supportive relationship with the staff. The participants generally felt strongly about there being no need for a change in the organisation's leadership.

Supervisory support

Participants generally highlighted a positive relationship with their immediate supervisors, the majority of whom were South African. Certain participants indicated that they consider their relationship with their supervisors to be more than just a working relationship and to involve a level of mutual friendship.

A number of participants demonstrated the encouragement and support they felt from their supervisors while performing their work (P1-M; P2-T; P6-T; P14-T; P20-M). A local technician commented:

> My supervisor is very supportive of me, and the rest of the team. We can always talk to him about any problems that come up, and he will

guide us through the problem if he is able to help. Having a supervisor who is really willing to help you is good for the team.

(P6-T)

Certain participants, however, indicted that although their supervisors listened to their concerns and suggestions, they were slow to take action (P3-T; P12-T; P19-T). The findings suggest that the slow speed at which some supervisors were perceived to take action is an area of frustration for some of the employees. Participants further noted that regular communication is an area which can be improved upon (P1-M; P3-T; P8-T; P12-T; P15-T; P19-T).

Opportunities for training and development

The majority of the participants expressed clear negative views on their current training and development opportunities in the organisation (P1-M; P2-T; P3-T; P6-T; P7-T; P8-T; P9-T; P10-T; P12-T; P14-T; P15-T; P17-S; P19-T; P20-M). This viewpoint was supported by a local technical employee who noted: "Maybe the main guys in the head office get training and stuff, but we really don't get much. They don't invest in training from what I can see" (P2-T). The findings suggest that once an employee is appropriately trained to fill a particular position, future opportunities to be trained and develop into new positions were perceived by certain employees to "simply not be there" (P19-T). A number of participants (P1-M; P9-T; P19-T) believed that this situation is caused by the organisation as it hires employees who already hold the skills to do the job instead of training those who are already in the organisation to fill these positions. In this regard, P1-M described how the technicians at the smaller branches were only Chinese nationals, as it was deemed easier for the organisation to bring in qualified technicians from China, rather than training and employing South Africans.

Compensation

The majority of participants held negative views pertaining to the compensation received from the organisation (P1-M; P2-T; P6-T; P8-T; P10-T; P12-T; P14-T; P15-T; P17-S; P19-T; P20-M), although a number of participants believed that their compensation was fair and reasonable (P3-T; P4-T; P5-S; P9-T; P11-T; P13-S; P16-M). All participants who expressed negative views regarding their compensation believed the remuneration offered to simply be inadequate to meet their financial needs. One of the employees who felt dissatisfied with compensation offered by the organisation commented: "I think the pay can be better here. The company is doing well here, they need to put a bit more of the profits into the employees, instead of sending it all back to China"

(P8-T). Moreover, the findings indicated a number of employees were disgruntled with the fact that employee benefits are not offered to all employees.

Job security

Three participants (P1-M; P6-T; P14-T) expressed negative views relating to their sense of job security and felt that the organisation lacked solid foundations and roots within South Africa. Fourteen of the 20 participants, however, seemed to have a different view on their job security in the organisation (P2-T; P3-T; P4-T; P5-S; P7-T; P8-T; P9-T; P10-T; P11-T; P12-T; P13-S; P16-M; P18-M; P20-M). Participants seemed to feel confident in both their short- and long-term positions. It emerged that a possible explanation for this confidence was a result of the fact that the organisation is expanding both internationally and within South Africa. In this regard, a local employee explained:

> I have not seen many people leave here . . . if we happy to stay, they will keep us on . . . as long as we do our work. We are increasing our manufacturing output, so it is more time to take people on, than lose them. I think they are doing well in this country, and it opens doors to other countries in Africa to sell.
>
> (P12-T)

Promotional opportunities

Fifteen participants demonstrated a negative outlook on their promotional opportunities in the organisation (P1-M; P2-T; P3-T; P4-T; P6-T; P7-T; P8-T; P9-T; P10-T; P13-S; P14-T; P15-T; P16-M; P18-M; P19-T) with five expressing neutral feelings on the matter (P5-S; P11-T; P12-T; P17-S; P20-M). Two categories emerged from the data as causes for such feelings, namely: limited number of senior positions available (P1-M; P3-T; P6-T; P8-T; P9-T; P13-S; P19-T) and ambiguity surrounding employees' career paths (P2-T; P4-T; P10-T; P19-T; P20-M).

Participants asserted that the limited number of senior positions available in the organisation caused negative feelings relating to their promotional opportunities. A technical employee who held this perception noted:

> We can get promoted. But it doesn't happen often. There are lots of us here in technical . . . but how many positions are management? Not many at all. So this can be a problem, and something which worries me . . . because I want a change and I want to grow.
>
> (P9-T)

Participants employed in smaller branches of the organisation seemed to feel even more strongly on the matter and believed their career growth opportunities to be very limited or non-existent.

A possible reason for the lack of promotional opportunities in the organisation can be attributed to the fact that the organisation's top management are Chinese employees negatively impacting on the South African employees' perceptions regarding their possible career growth. A number of participants commented on the lack of clarity with regard to their future careers as being a cause of negative feelings relating to their promotional opportunities in the organisation.

Recognition (new factor)

Recognition, a factor which was not included in the theoretical framework, emerged as an important factor influencing the participants' commitment to the organisation. Participants (P3-T; P11-T; P15-T; P20-M) highlighted that any recognition or gratitude from the organisation and its management would stimulate their positive feelings towards the organisation and inspire them to work harder. In this regard, a technical employee remarked:

> They need to recognise employees who are doing well, and give them a chance. Sometimes I feel people go unnoticed here. It's not a good feeling when you work really hard on something, and get nothing for it. So some kind of recognition for the staff would make the staff work better, and I'm sure make them committed.
>
> (P9-T)

Recognition and associated rewards from the organisation were perceived by the researchers to be of great importance to these participants. Participants suggested that such recognition could be as simple as words of gratitude (P3-T) or could perhaps include non-monetary rewards such as additional paid leave (P15-T).

Trust (new factor)

Trust was another factor which emerged as influencing organisational commitment. Five participants (P1-M; P2-T; P3-T; P10-T; P13-S) highlighted that the trust they have in their co-workers and the management of the organisation influences their commitment. An employee remarked: "You need to be able to trust your co-workers and your managers. If you living in a world with no trust, there won't be much commitment" (P2-T). Although trust was not included in the theoretical framework, the factor was clearly of great importance to these participants. It was generally felt that as the employees all rely on one another to do their work effectively, doubt in the abilities of others to do their work would negatively affect the working environment and commitment in the organisation. Participants further believed that it is important for the leaders of the organisation to trust them to perform their jobs independently, as it assists in developing a sense of autonomy.

Levels of organisational commitment

The findings indicated that the large majority of the participants (P1-M; P2-T; P3-T; P4-T; P5-S; P6-T; P7-T; P8-T; P9-T; P10-T; P13-S; P14-T; P15-T; P16-M; P18-M; P20-M) demonstrated a clear and strong emotional attachment to the organisation, possibly demonstrating high levels of affective commitment (Meyer & Allen, 1991). The findings with regards to normative commitment were relatively mixed, with 11 participants highlighting that they, to some extent, felt an obligation to the organisation and/or their co-workers to continue working for the organisation (P1-M; P2-T; P4-T; P5-S; P8-T; P9-T; P13-S; P14-T; P15-T; P16-M; P20-M). Seven participants demonstrated they did not feel an obligation to continue working for the organisation (P3-T; P6-T; P7-T; P10-T; P12-T; P18-M; P19-T). Fourteen of the 20 participants demonstrated feelings of continuance commitment towards the organisation. Nine of these participants highlighted their concern of finding new employment (P2-T; P3-T; P4-T; P5-S; P6-T; P9-T; P12-T; P14-T; P19-T), while six of them highlighted they would miss their job (P1-M; P4-T; P10-T; P13-S; P16-M; P20-M).

When participants were asked to reflect on their own perceived levels of commitment, the large majority demonstrated a strong commitment to the organisation (P1-M; P2-T; P3-T; P4-T; P5-S; P6-T; P7-T; P8-T; P9-T; P13-S; P14-T; P15-T; P16-M; P18-M; P20-M) with four of the participants demonstrating a moderate commitment (P10-T; P11-T; P12-T; P17-S) and one a weak commitment (P19-T).

Conclusions and Implications

Communication in the organisation appears to be open, with employees being able to easily approach and receive feedback from managers. This is a positive finding for the organisation, as Rego and Cunha (2006) emphasise the importance of interaction with and feedback to employees. Moreover, open communication as described in the organisation may positively influence organisational commitment, as asserted by Haugh and McKee (2003) as well as Rego and Cunha (2006). However, communication appears to be irregular within the organisation, a matter which may lead to misunderstandings and lower levels of commitment (Devries, 2007; Rego & Cunha, 2006). A possible explanation for the lack of regular feedback and communication could be related to the Chinese culture placing importance on centralised power, lines of authority and positions within the organisational hierarchy (Pittinsky & Zhu, 2005). The culture promotes listening to one's superiors and not questioning decisions (Basabe & Ros, 2005; Hofstede, 2001). It is therefore possible that Chinese leaders may not place importance on regular communication with local subordinate employees.

With regards to leadership, the overall result seems to demonstrate that the employees trust in and are satisfied with the current leadership within the organisation. This is a favourable finding considering possible cross-cultural complexities and variations in management styles of South African and Chinese managers (Handley & Louw, 2016; Bräutigam, 2009). The literature suggests that the positive perceptions of leadership may aid in building local employees' commitment to their organisation (Kruger & Rootman, 2010; Rego & Cunha, 2006).

Another encouraging finding relating to Chinese activities at an organisational level relates to the generally positive feelings of supervisory support expressed by participants. This may positively influence employees' commitment, as the perceived level of effective supervisory support experienced by employees is deemed to have an influence on their organisational commitment (Venter et al., 2010; Aubè et al., 2007; Bagraim, 2004).

As the training of Africa's work force is deemed vital to its development, China has committed to many training, learning and development programmes throughout Africa. In 2006, China expressed its intentions to train and develop 15,000 African experts and managerial personnel (Asche & Schuller, 2008). The importance of training and development opportunities was highlighted by certain participants who stated that it directly influences their commitment to the organisation. Such a finding concurs with the literature which highlights opportunities for training and development as having an influence on organisational commitment (Lesabe & Nkosi, 2007; McElroy, 2001; Meyer & Allen, 1997). The organisational-level findings, however, suggest strong negative feelings from participants and point to few training and development opportunities for local employees.

The importance of compensation was highlighted as it was the factor most frequently mentioned during the interviews as having an influence on organisational commitment. Such a finding concurs with the literature, as compensation is believed to be of great importance to most employees (Lesabe & Nkosi, 2007; Hoyt & Gerdloff, 1999) and deemed to influence organisational commitment (Chen, 2009; Kochanski & Ledford, 2001; Farris, 2000; Hoyt & Gerdloff, 1999; Higginbotham, 1997). The negative perceptions of employee compensation found in this study are aligned with previous concerns regarding poor remuneration packages for African employees within Chinese organisations (Butts & Bankus, 2009). Monetary compensation is clearly important to the participants, but non-monetary recognition is evidently also of importance.

If the organisation is not in a position to offer increased compensation to employees, Kochanski and Ledford (2001) assert that recognition in the form of non-monetary rewards, such as time off, could promote employee commitment. Zaitouni, Sawalha, and Sharif (2011) assert that recognition is required in an organisational environment in order to motivate employees and encourage favourable work outcomes. Moreover, praise and appreciation from managers and co-workers have been found to positively influence organisational commitment (Kruger & Rootman, 2010; Park, Erwin, & Knapp, 1997).

There were conflicting opinions amongst the participants regarding their sense of job security within the organisation. Although the participants who expressed negative views were in the minority, they may have been exposed to certain aspects in the organisation others might not have been, or could themselves be falsely guided by the often-negative perceptions of Chinese organisations in the media. The findings indicate that the growth and success that the organisation is currently experiencing plays an important role in the majority of the participants' positive feelings regarding their job security. As the majority of participants expressed favourable perceptions of their short- and long-term job security, this study sheds new light on literature which has previously alluded to local employees feeling insecure because of the temporary nature of many Chinese projects within Africa (Baah & Jauch, 2009, p. 100). Despite varying opinions on their job security, it was found to be an important aspect influencing commitment within the organisation, concurring with the literature (Buitendach & De Witte, 2005; Yousef, 1998).

The findings suggest that promotional opportunities are important to the participants and may have a strong influence on their commitment, which concurs with the literature (Chen, 2009; Moorhead & Griffin, 1992; McCormick & Ilgen, 1985). Perceptions of promotional opportunities in the organisation were however generally negative, concurring with researchers such as Bräutigam (2011b) who have suggested that managerial, supervisory and skilled positions may often be reserved for Chinese employees.

The findings suggest that trust is a factor which has an influence over employees' commitment. The finding concurs with Zaheer and Zaheer (2006) who note that feelings of trust are vital for international or intercultural business, with high levels of trust often leading to high levels of employee commitment (Kwon & Suh, 2005; Wong & Sohal, 2002). Handley and Louw (2016) also found that workplace relationships built on trust and respect are culturally significant for leaders and subordinates within South Africa and China.

With regards to the findings relating to employees' current perceived levels of commitment, the large majority of the participants demonstrated favourable levels of affective commitment, with more than half the participants demonstrating feelings of normative commitment. The majority of participants further stated that their ability to find new employment, or missing their job, is a possible implication for them leaving the organisation. This may be perceived to be a possible indicator of high levels of continuance commitment amongst these participants. When directly asked to rate their commitment, the findings concurred with the above perceptions relating to high commitment levels, with the large majority of participants demonstrating strong commitment to the organisation.

The general findings relating to the levels of commitment in the organisation were thus positive for the organisation. Despite certain issues being raised by the participants during the in-depth interviews, the large majority of the participants seem to remain committed and loyal to the organisation; a favourable finding which provides fresh insights into organisational-level research within Chinese organisations

Because of the qualitative nature of this study, the findings cannot be generalised. It is recommended that future researchers consider a quantitative study, with a large representative sample across multiple Chinese organisations in South Africa. It would additionally be of interest for future research to address the perceptions of Chinese employees in similar Chinese organisations operating in Africa. A comparative analysis between Chinese and South African employees can then be done to shed greater light on potential cultural differences and associated expectations from employers.

References

Aamodt, M. G. (2004). *Applied industrial/organizational psychology* (4th ed.). Belmont, CA: Thomson Wadsworth.

Abdullah, A., & Ramay, M. I. (2012). Antecedents of organizational commitment of banking sector employees in Pakistan. *Serbian Journal of Management, 7*(1), 89–102.

Abkowitz, A. (2009). China buys the world. *Fortune Magazine, 160*(7), 57–59.

AccountAbility DRC-ERI. (2009). *Responsible business in Africa: Chinese business leaders' perspectives on performance and enhancement opportunities.* Retrieved February 22, 2015 from www.iisd.org/pdf/2011/responsible_business_in_africa.pdf

Asche, H., & Schuller, M. (2008). *China's engagement in Africa: Opportunities and risks for development.* Retrieved June 30, 2014 from http://s3.amazonaws.com/zanran_storage/www2.gtz.de/ContentPages/19176160.pdf

Aubè, C., Rousseau, V., & Morin, E. M. (2007). Perceived organisational support and organisational commitment: The moderating effect of locus of control and work autonomy. *Journal of Managerial Psychology, 22*(5), 479–495.

Baah, A., & Jauch, H. (Eds.). (2009). *Chinese investments in Africa: A labour perspective.* Windhoek, Namibia: African Labor Research Network.

Bagraim, J. (2004). *The improbable commitment: Organizational commitment amongst South African knowledge workers.* Unpublished doctoral dissertation. University of Warwick, Coventry, UK.

Basabe, N., & Ros, M. (2005). Cultural dimensions and social behavior correlates: Individualism-collectivism and power distance. *International Review of Social Psychology, 18*(1), 189–225.

Batool, M., & Ullah, R. (2013). Impact of job satisfaction and organisational commitment in banking sector: Study of commercial banks in District Peshawar. *International Review of Basic and Applied Sciences*, *1*(2), 12–24.

Beukes, I., & Botha, E. (2013). Organisational commitment, work engagement and meaning of work of nursing staff in hospitals. *SA Journal of Industrial Psychology*, *39*(2), 1–10.

Bräutigam, D. (2009). *The Dragon's gift: The real story of China in Africa*. New York, NY: Oxford University Press.

Bräutigam, D. (2011a). *Testimony to the senate committee on foreign relations subcommittee on African affairs, dirksen senate office building*. Retrieved February 16, 2012 from www.foreign.senate.gov/imo/media/doc/Deborah_Brautigam_Testimony.pdf

Bräutigam, D. (2011b). *China in Africa: What can Western donors learn?* Oslo: Norwegian Investment Fund for Developing Countries (Norfund). Retrieved February 20, 2012 from www.norfund.no/getfile.php/Documents/Homepage/Reports%20and%20presentations/Studies%20for%20Norfund/Norfund_China_in_Africa.pdf

Bräutigam, D., & Xiaoyang, T. (2011). African Shenzhen: China's special economic zones in Africa. *Journal of Modern African Studies*, *49*(1), 27–54.

Buitendach, J. H., & De Witte, H. (2005). Job insecurity, extrinsic and intrinsic job satisfaction and affective organisational commitment of maintenance workers in a parastatal. *South African Journal of Business Management*, *36*(2), 27–37.

Butts, K. H., & Bankus, B. (2009). *China's pursuit of Africa's natural resources*. Center for Strategic Leadership, US Army War College. [Online]. Retrieved May 17, 2013 from www.csl.army.mil/usacsl/publications/CCS1_09_ChinasPursuitofAfricasNaturalR esources.pdf

Byrne, C. S. (1998). *An investigation into the relationship between organizational commitment and the employees' perceptions regarding leadership practices and success*. Unpublished doctoral dissertation. Claremont Graduate University, Claremont, USA.

Chawla, S., & Renesch, J. (2006). *Learning organisations: Developing cultures for tomorrow's workplace*. New York, NY: Productivity Press.

Chen, H. (2009, June). *A comparative study of organisational commitment of bank employees in Ireland and China*. Paper presented at the Academy of International Business Conference, Santiago, USA.

Cissé, D. (2012). *FOCAC: Trade, investments and aid in China-Africa relations*. Retrieved February 22, 2015 from The Centre for Chinese Studies website: www.ccs.org.za/wp-content/uploads/2012/05/FOCAC_Policy-Briefing_tradeinvest_final.pdf

Colquitt, J. A., Lepine, J. A., & Wesson, M. J. (2013). *Organisational behaviour: Improving performance and commitment in the workplace*. New York, NY: McGraw-Hill/Irwin.

Corkin, L., & Burke, C. (2006). *China's interest and activity in Africa's construction and infrastructure sectors*. Retrieved February 19, 2015 from The Centre for Chinese Studies website: www.ccs.org.za/downloads/DFID%203rd%20Edition.pdf

Devries, S. (2007). Is your family business treating non-family staffers fairly? *National Jeweler*, *101*(10), 42.

Döckel, A. (2003). *The effect of retention factors on organisational commitment: An investigation of high technology employees*. Unpublished master's dissertation. University of Pretoria, Pretoria, South Africa.

Farris, G. F. (2000). Rewards and retention of technical staff. *Proceedings of the IEEE International Engineering Management Conference.* Albuquerque, NM, 13–15 August.

Fu, F., Bolander, W., & Jones, E. (2009). Managing the drivers of organizational commitment and salesperson effort: An application of Meyer and Allen's three component model. *Journal of Marketing Theory and Practice, 17*(4), 343–358.

Giffords, E. D. (2009). An examination of organisational commitment and professional commitment and the relationship to work environment, demographic and organisational factors. *Journal of Social Work, 9*(4), 386–404.

Handley, R. C., & Louw, M. J. (2016). *The similarities and differences between South African and Chinese definitions and descriptions of leadership style: A mining joint venture case study.* Proceedings of the 28th Annual Conference of the Southern African Institute of Management Scientists. Pretoria, South Africa, 4–7 September.

Hart, D., & Willower, D. (2001). Principals' organisational commitment and school environmental robustness. *Journal of Educational Research, 87*(3), 174–179.

Haugh, H., & Mckee, L. (2003). It's just like a family – Shared values in the family firm. *Community, Work and Family, 6*(2), 142–145.

Higginbotham, J. S. (1997). The satisfaction equation. *Research & Development, 39*(10), 1–9.

Hirsch, P. M., & De Soucey, M. (2006). Organizational restructuring and its consequences. *Annual Review of Sociology, 32*, 71–189.

Hofstede, G. H. (2001). *Culture's consequences: Comparing values, behaviors, institutions and organizations across nations* (2nd ed.). Thousand Oaks, CA: Sage.

Hoyt, J., & Gerdloff, E. A. (1999). Organisational environment, changing economic conditions and the effective supervision of technical personnel: A management challenge. *Journal of High Technology Management Research, 10*(2), 275–294.

Iqbal, A. (2010). An empirical assessment of demographic factors, organisational ranks and organisational commitment. *International Journal of Business and Management, 5*(3), 16–27.

Jackson, T. A. (2012). Postcolonialism and organizational knowledge in the wake of China's presence in Africa: Interrogating South-South relations. *Organization, 19*(2), 181–204.

Jackson, T. A., Meyer, J. P., & Wang, X. H. (2013). Leadership, commitment, and culture: A meta-analysis. *Journal of Leadership and Organizational Studies, 20*(1), 84–106.

Jafri, M. H. (2010). Organisational commitment and employee's innovative behavior. *Journal of Management Research, 10*(1), 62–68.

João, T. F., & Coetzee, M. (2012). Job retention factors, perceived career mobility and organisational commitment in the South African financial sector. *Journal of Psychology in Africa, 27*(2), 69–76.

Jonathan, H., Darroux, C., & Thibeli, M. (2013). Exploring the effect of job satisfaction and demographic factors on affective, normative and continuance commitment: An empirical evidence of public secondary school teachers in Tanzania. *Journal of Education and Practice, 4*(23), 85–96.

Kantor, R. L. (2013). *Pay Satisfaction, organisational commitment, voluntary turnover intention, and attitudes to money in a South African context.* Unpublished master's thesis, Johannesburg, South Africa: University of the Witwatersrand.

Kaur, K., & Sandhu, H. S. (2010). Career stage effect on organizational commitment: Empirical evidence from Indian banking industry. *International Journal of Business and Management*, 5(12), 141–152.

Kipkebut, D. J. (2010). *Organisational commitment and job satisfaction in higher educational institutions: The Kenyan case*. Unpublished doctoral thesis, London: Middlesex University.

Klandermans, B., Hesselink, J. K., & Van Vuuren, T. (2010). Employment status and job insecurity: On the subjective appraisal of an objective status. *Economic and Industrial Democracy*, 31(4), 557–577.

Kochanski, J., & Ledford, G. (2001). How to keep me – Retaining technical professionals. *Research Technology Management*, 44(3), 31–38.

Kruger, J., & Rootman, C. (2010). How do small business managers influence employee satisfaction and commitment? *Acta Commercii*, 10(1), 59–72.

Kwon, I., & Suh, T. (2005). Trust, commitment and relationships in supply chain management: A path analysis. *Supply Chain Management: An International Journal*, 10(1), 26–33.

Latham, D. (2011). *China shifts focus in Africa*. Retrieved February 22, 2012 from www.businessday.co.za/articles/Content.aspx?id=147520

Lesabe, R. A., & Nkosi, J. (2007). A qualitative exploration of employees' views on organisational commitment. *SA Journal of Human Resource Management*, 5(1), 35–44.

Lincoln, Y. S., & Guba, E. G. (1985). *Naturalistic inquiry*. Newbury Park, CA: Sage Publications.

McCormick, E. J., & Ilgen, D. R. (1985). *Industrial and organisational psychology* (8th ed.). London, UK: Allen and Unwin.

McElroy, J. C. (2001). Managing workplace commitment by putting people first. *Human Resource Management Review*, 11(3), 327–335.

Meyer, J. P., & Allen, N. J. (1991). A three-component conceptualisation of organisational commitment. *Human Resource Management Review*, 1(1), 61–89.

Meyer, J. P., & Allen, N. J. (1997). *Commitment in the workplace: Theory, research and application*. Thousand Oaks, CA: Sage Publications.

Meyer, J. P., Kam, C., Goldenberg, I., & Bremner, N. L. (2013). Organizational commitment in the military: Application of a profile approach. *Military Psychology*, 25(4), 381–401.

Mezzinson, L. C., Mosley, D. C., & Pietrie, P. H. (1992). *Management: Concepts and applications*. New York, NY: Harper Collins.

Moorhead, G., & Griffin, R. W. (1992). *Organizational behavior* (3rd ed.). Boston, MA: Houghton Mifflin Company.

Mosadeghrad, A. M., Ferlie, E., & Rosenberg, D. (2008). A study of the relationship between job satisfaction, organizational commitment and turnover intention among hospital employees. *Health Services Management Research*, 21(4), 211–221.

Park, R., Erwin, P. J., & Knapp, K. (1997). Teams in Australia's automotive industry: Characteristics and future challenges. *International Journal of Human Resource Management*, 8, 780–796.

Pierce, J. L., & Dunham, R. B. (1987). Organisational commitment: Pre-employment propensity and initial work experiences. *Journal of Management*, 13(1), 163–178.

Pittinsky, T. L., & Zhu, C. (2005). Contemporary public leadership in China: A research review and consideration. *The Leadership Quarterly*, 16(6), 921–939.

Porter, L. W., Steers, R., Mowday, R., & Boulian, P. (1974). Organizational commitment, job satisfaction and turnover among psychiatric technicians. *Journal of Applied Psychology, 59*, 603–609.

Rego, A., & Cunha, M. (2006). *Perceptions of authentizotic climates and employee happiness: Pathways to individual performance.* Retrieved May 20, 2012 from http://fesrvsd.fe.unl.pt/WPFEUNL/WP2006/wp499.pdf

Remenyi, D. (2013). *Field methods for academic research – Interviews, focus groups and questionnaires* (3rd ed.). Reading, UK: Academic Conferences and Publishing International.

Scheible, A. C. F., & Bastos, A. V. B. (2013). An examination of human resource management practices' influence on organizational commitment and entrenchment. *Brazil Administration Review, 10*(1), 57–76.

Sweeney, J., & Quirin, J. (2009). Accountants as layoff survivors: A research note. *Accounting, Organizations and Society, 34*(6), 787–795.

Tesch, R. (1990). *Qualitative research: Analysis types and software tools.* New York, NY: The Falmer Press.

Vallejo, M. C. (2009). Analytical model of leadership in family firms under transformational theoretical approach. *Family Business Review, 22*(2), 136–150.

Van Dyk, J., & Coetzee, M. (2012). Retention factors in relation to organisational commitment in medical and information technology services. *South African Journal of Human Resource Management, 10*(2), 1–11.

Venter, E., Farrington, S., & Finkelstein, C. (2010, September). *An exploratory study of the factors influencing non-family employee commitment to the family business.* Paper presented at the 22nd Annual Conference of the South African Institute of Management Scientists (SAIMS), Port Alfred, South Africa.

Wong, A., & Sohal, A. (2002). An examination of the relationship between trust, commitment and relationship quality. *International Journal of Retail and Distribution Management, 30*(1), 34–50.

Yiing, L. H., & Ahmad, K. Z. B. (2009). The moderating effects of organizational culture on the relationships between leadership behaviour and organizational commitment and between organizational commitment and job satisfaction and performance. *Leadership and Organization Development Journal, 30*(1), 53–86.

Yousef, D. A. (1998). Satisfaction with job security as a predictor of organisational commitment and job performance in a multicultural environment. *International Journal of Manpower, 19*(3), 184–194.

Zaheer, S., & Zaheer, A. (2006). Trust across borders. *Journal of International Business Studies, 37*(1), 21–29.

Zaitouni, M., Sawalha, N. N., & Sharif, A. (2011). The impact of human resource management practices on organizational commitment in the banking sector in Kuwait. *International Journal of Business and Management, 6*(6), 108–123.

9 The influence of organisational culture on a high-commitment work system

The case of a Chinese multinational corporation in South Africa

Linda Mabuza and Mattheus J. Louw

China's presence in and involvement with Africa has been an increasing phenomenon, with China recently becoming Africa's largest trading partner (Chatelard, 2012; The Economist, 2013). According to the Chinese Ambassador to South Africa, Chinese investment in Africa has exceeded US$110 billion in accumulative terms. He further reiterated that China and Africa need to synergise their development strategies in order to achieve win–win solutions in their trade and economic cooperation (Lin, 2019). The reasons for China's presence in Africa have been outlined by Gill, Huang, and Morrison (2007, cited in Jackson, Louw, & Zhao, 2011, p. 3) as those of seeking resources to fuel China's development goals, seeking political alliances to support its aspirations to be a global influence and seeking markets to sustain its growing economy.

Shambaugh (2012, p. 1) states that the 'Achilles' heel of Chinese multinational corporations (MNCs) is human resources. Chinese organisations in Africa and South Africa have thus been confronted with human resource (HR) challenges which include, inter alia: poor working conditions, inadequate safety standards for workers, local labour practice requirements and conflict with labour unions (Brautigam, 2009; US Congress, 2011). These HR challenges are further exacerbated by the language and cultural differences between Chinese and African workers (Chatelard, 2012; Horwitz, Hemmant, & Rademeyer, 2008). This chapter specifically examines the case of a Chinese multinational sales organisation operating in South Africa in the personal computer (PC) industry, assessing how its organisational culture contributes to the organisation's performance and its influence on high-commitment work system (HCWS).

Organisational culture and HCWS in a Chinese MNC

Despite successful growth, Chinese MNCs are facing challenges that could impede their ability to be competitive. These challenges include dealing with unfamiliar cultural, legal and political landscapes, perceptions of unethical practices, and an inability to separate from their national organisational culture and business practices (Boulton, 2013; KPMG, 2013, p. 4; Shambaugh, 2012).

In this regard, organisational culture is a powerful and stabilising force within organisations (Schein, 1996) with important implications for organisational performance (Kotter & Heskett, 1992, cited in Øgaard, Larsen, & Marnburg, 2005, p. 24). Additionally, given the importance of organisational commitment for employee and organisational performance (Guest & Conway, 2011, p. 1691; Samgnanakkan, 2010, p. 56), a HCWS has been defined as a system of HR practices that aim to elicit employees' commitment to the organisation (Walton, 1985 cited in Xiao & Bjorkman, 2006, p. 403).

A narrative of organisational culture

Schein (1990, p. 113) defines organisational culture as 'a pattern of basic assumptions, invented, discovered, or developed by a given group, as it learns to cope with its problems of external adaptation and internal integration'. Schein's (1990) definition was used in the research as it was found to be consistent with Cameron and Freeman's (1991) framework of organisational culture types. Tsui, Wang, and Xin (2006, p. 369) corroborate this view. Cameron and Freeman's (1991) framework proposes four elements which are considered to be core attributes of different forms of organisational culture: prominent features; values bonding people; the role of leadership; and the organisation's strategic focus (Cameron & Freeman, 1991, p. 28). The first culture type described by Cameron and Freeman (1991, p. 29) is that of the clan culture and includes cohesiveness, participation, team work, a sense of family and the organisation being seen as a personal place (Lund, 2003, p. 221; Cameron & Freeman, 1991, p. 29).

The second culture type, adhocracy culture, has flexible processes with a focus towards its external environment. An organisation with this type of organisational culture will therefore emphasise creativity, innovation and adaptability (Lund, 2003, p. 222; Cameron & Freeman, 1991, p. 30).

An organisation that exhibits the third type of culture, market culture, is competitive and goal-driven (Louw, 2012, p. 521; Lund, 2003, p. 221; Cameron & Freeman, 1991, p. 29). Employees in these organisations would therefore be rewarded based on their achievement of goals set by the organisation (Den Hartog & Verburg, 2004, p. 60).

Lastly, the defining features of hierarchy culture include formal rules, procedures, coordination and structure (Louw, 2012, p. 518; Den Hartog & Verburg, 2004, p. 60). As a result of the bureaucratic nature of these formal control processes, however, such organisations may tend to be ineffective (Louw, 2012, p. 518).

HCWS and employee commitment

Given the importance of organisational commitment for employee and organisational performance (Guest & Conway, 2011, p. 1691; Samgnanakkan, 2010, p. 56), a HCWS has been defined as a system of HR practices that aims to elicit employees' commitment to the organisation (Walton, 1985 cited in Xiao & Bjorkman, 2006, p. 403). Hence, the HR practices included in the measure of a HCWS, as proposed by Xiao and Bjorkman (2006), include the following: promotion from within, careful selection, extensive training and socialisation, job security, enlarged jobs and job rotation, appraisal team, appraisal behaviour, appraisal development, high remuneration, extensive ownership, egalitarianism, participation, information sharing and communication, overarching goals, and teamwork.

When implemented, each of the above mentioned 15 HCWS practices are theoretically expected to lead to greater organisational commitment of employees, especially as part of a system of integrated practices (Xiao & Bjorkman, 2006, p. 406). Furthermore, Xiao and Bjorkman (2006, p. 412) propose that the antecedents of a HCWS would be employee job levels and job functions. Similarly, Boxall and Macky (2007, p. 262) state that

> large organisations typically have one kind of HR system for managers and another for their main group of production or operations workers. Where professionals, technical specialists and administrative support staff are employed, it is commonplace to have distinctive HR models for these groups as well.

According to Xiao and Bjorkman (2006, p. 412), employees in higher job levels and more technical/specialised functions within an organisation are more likely to be the recipients of HCWS practices.

What we wanted to achieve in our research

With strategic Chinese–African partnership relations expected to strengthen even further in the coming years (Brautigam, 2009; SAFPI, 2012), it is imperative to undertake studies that address the HR issues within Chinese MNCs so that their long-term performance in the African context is successful and sustainable. The main purpose of this research was to describe how the organisational culture of a Chinese MNC's South African subsidiary has shaped the nature of its HCWS.

In order to achieve the abovementioned research purpose, the following research objectives were formulated:

- To identify and describe the subsidiary's dominant type of organisational culture.

- To describe the nature of the subsidiary's HCWS.
- To explain how the organisational culture has shaped the nature of the HCWS.

How we conducted this research

In order to achieve the purpose of the research, a case study approach, which is located within the interpretive research paradigm, was used (Collis & Hussey, 2009). As previously mentioned, our research case was a Chinese multinational PC manufacturing and sales organisation operating in South Africa. The South African branch of the Chinese organisation is also the headquarters of the multinational's operations in the African region. Specifically, the organisation's operations in the South African market are mainly sales-oriented and therefore the core group of employees are salespeople. The South African office has a total of 40 employees including sales and support staff and managers across frontline, middle and top management levels. Purposive sampling (Sekaran & Bougie, 2009, p. 276; Cooper & Schindler, 2006, p. 424; Zikmund, 2003, p. 382) was used to sample research participants at the organisation. The 12 research participants were chosen because of their knowledge, which was deemed to be useful for the study. They were selected from the core sales and support departments across all managerial levels. For the research, we chose to primarily use semi-structured interviews to collect data pertaining to administrative questions (Cooper & Schindler, 2006, p. 364) covering descriptive biographical data and target questions (Saunders, Lewis, & Thornhill, 2000, p. 244) to gain an in-depth understanding of the organisational culture and the nature of the Chinese MNC's 15 HCWS practices. We analysed the data using content analysis which is 'a research technique for making replicable and valid inferences from texts to the contexts of their use' (Krippendorff, 2004, p. 18). The four quality criteria for qualitative research – credibility, transferability, dependability and confirmability – as identified by Lincoln and Guba (1985) were used to establish the trustworthiness of the research. A total of 12 participants were thus interviewed, as can be seen in Table 9.1, with research participants coming from different departments and job levels in order to give multiple perspectives on the researched phenomena.

Our findings from the research

In order to address the research objectives, this section presents and discusses the findings pertaining to the organisational culture of the subsidiary and the nature of the Chinese MNC's HCWS. In terms of the first objective, the interpreted data were assessed according to the four main categories considered to be the core attributes of different forms of

Table 9.1 Profile of research participants

Participant	Department	Job level
P1	Support	Top management
P2	Sales	Top management
P3	Support	Top management
P4	Support	Line management
P5	Sales	Employee
P6	Sales	Employee
P7	Sales	Line management
P8	Sales	Middle management
P9	Sales	Employee
P10	Support	Top management
P11	Support	Top management
P12	Sales	Employee

organisational cultures, namely prominent features, values bonding people, role of leadership and strategic focus. To address the second objective, questions pertaining to a HCWS examined each of the HR practices included in Xiao and Bjorkman's (2006) measure of a HCWS. The third objective of the research relates to how the subsidiary's organisational culture has shaped the nature of the HCWS.

Organisational culture of the MNC (Objective 1)

Prominent features

Participants were asked to give keywords that they would use to describe the prominent features of their organisation's culture and to also explain the reason for their choice. Analysis of the data showed that participants felt that the most prominent features of their organisation's culture were that it was: performance driven (P1, P4, P5, P8, P9, P10); global (P1, P2, P3, P12); Chinese (P2, P10, P11); and entrepreneurial and innovative (P7, P11, P12).

PERFORMANCE DRIVEN

Participants felt that their organisational culture was 'very performance-oriented' (P4). With regard to this performance orientation, one participant explained, 'it's a sales organisation; we're all about um, selling of course' (P1). Achievement was therefore linked to this performance orientation, where participants felt that they had to constantly achieve the goals of the organisation (P1, P8, P9). Hard work also characterised this performance orientation (P8, P10) in that the organisation emphasises 'recognising hard work, but also very firm in terms of managing poor performance' (P1). In this regard, one participant felt that the organisational culture was 'demanding and not very people-focused' but about 'achieving numbers' and 'if you don't perform consistently then they'll get rid of you' (P9).

GLOBAL

With the organisation 'being a multinational' (P2), four of the participants felt that the organisational culture of the South African operation was that of a global culture. This global culture, inherited from the headquarters of the organisation, was described by one participant as being 'comprehensive, thought-through, being implemented correctly also' (P2) and another as 'brought down from a global version all the way down and then carried throughout the entire organisation' (P12). The global nature of the organisational culture is described as prevailing in all operations of the organisation worldwide – 'so whether you're in Nigeria, in the US, or in China, we speak the same language' (P1). Additionally, one participant stated, 'we inherit the global cultures but we use them from a local standpoint . . . adapting a global culture to local conditions' (P3).

CHINESE

Some participants felt that because of the Chinese origin of the organisation, as well as the presence of Chinese managers in the top global management team, the local organisation's culture had been influenced by elements of the Chinese culture (P2, P10, P11). One participant stated that 'it's a Chinese-owned company so a lot of the cultural aspect would be driven by, you know, the way they do things in China. The work ethic – you know the Chinese work quite hard and there isn't that, you know, mentality that, you know, "tomorrow's still another day" type of thing' (P10). This participant perceived that Chinese culture embodied the ethic of hard work and that this aspect of the Chinese culture had filtered through to the rest of the organisation's operations, even in South Africa. In contrast, another participant pointed out that 'efficiency' (P11), as an element of the Chinese culture, had filtered through to the organisation's culture. Efficiency was viewed by this participant as a feature of the organisational culture because the organisation manufactures its own products and efficiency was therefore important for their production.

ENTREPRENEURIAL AND INNOVATIVE

Due to the dynamic nature of the organisation and its environment, some participants felt that the organisational culture also had entrepreneurial and innovative features. One participant expressed the view that 'it's not a slow-paced environment. But anyway that's what IT is all about because you know, technology changes all the time so you need to be always on your toes' (P10). This view was supported by another participant who felt that, as a result, the organisational culture was 'quite energetic', 'fast' and 'ever changing' (P7). In addition, due to 'no real proper processes and systems in place; no defined process on everything' (P11), employees needed to be 'innovative' (P11, P12) and 'think out the box, setting your own grounding' (P11). Specifically, one participant also believed that this entrepreneurial and innovative feature existed because the organisation is fairly new in its operations in South Africa and that the nature of their business is dynamic (P11).

Values bonding people

In order to ascertain which organisational values bond people within the organisation, participants were asked to give examples of prevalent values and how they have seen them enacted. Participants felt that they were mainly bonded by the organisation's value statement (P1, P3, P4, P9, P11, P12).

ORGANISATION'S VALUE STATEMENT

The organisation has an explicitly communicated culture statement (P3) that outlines the values upheld by the organisation. As a result, half of the participants interviewed believed these values created bonding amongst organisational members. Speaking of these values, one participant stated, 'we have them around and not just on the walls but, uh it's our ethos, it's what drives us; it's not just lip service, you know, because it's what drives our behaviour, it's what drives our culture' (P1). This view was supported by another participant who stated that 'it's the way that we define the way we do everything . . . no matter whether you're in segment A or segment Z within our organisation' (P3). Furthermore, these values are displayed in the meeting rooms and serve both as a reminder to employees and as information for everyone who interacts with the organisation (P1, P4). These values specifically pertain to performing excellently and with integrity, being committed to the organisation, continually growing through new challenges, and by being innovative. These values are 'highlighted in everything' (P12) employees do and employees are 'measured on' (P4) these values. Finally, those employees seen to embody these values in their daily work are recognised and rewarded both formally and informally (P1, P8) – 'the informal recognition programme really is about just catching people doing the right things at that time and just recognise them informally. You know, 'thank you' . . . so formal recognition is, you know, we have a quarterly award where an employee that has demonstrated not just the performance side of things which is more quantitative, but also the qualitative behaviours, you know, um, without having to sell, but having demonstrated the values that we stand for, where we recognise them' (P1).

Role of leadership

Participants described the roles that they have seen leadership playing in the organisation as: sharing the vision and strategy (P1, P2, P3, P4, P5, P7, P11, P12); setting performance expectations (P1, P4, P6, P7, P9, P10, P12); and diversity of roles (P1, P2, P3, P7, P10).

SHARING THE VISION AND STRATEGY

For more than half of the participants, sharing the vision appeared to be the major key role that they have seen the leadership at their organisation playing. One participant stated, 'I think there's a lot of focus on strategies that have been put in place so I think there's a lot of strategic views in terms of how we're going to move forward' (P5). Sharing the vision and strategy was seen to be done by both the global leadership team as well as by local leadership teams (P1, P2, P3). However, local leadership teams were seen to not only share the vision but also to ensure that it is executed in a manner that suited local conditions (P3). Sharing the vision and strategy was seen to be done by leadership through 'presenting where the company is going' (P4) and 'sharing information and aligning the business units' (P5). Participants therefore felt that the result of sharing the vision and strategy was that it 'helped the organisation a lot in terms of where we want to go in the future' (P5) and that they now 'all speak the same language, all understand what [the organisation] is looking at growing' (P12). There was, however, one participant who expressed that generally employees felt that although the vision and strategy had been clearly communicated, the individual part each employee played in achieving that vision was unclear: 'I think a lot of us are sitting in limbo with, "Well, what's my part in this" – kind of thing. We know where the direction is, but the execution of what the strategy is, is the problem' (P7). This led the participant to therefore feel that the leadership is 'disconnected' (P7).

SETTING PERFORMANCE EXPECTATIONS

Leadership was seen to be setting performance expectations for employees to achieve. 'There's a definite plan and you're expected to be achieving that plan . . . you've got to hit the ground running' (P6). In this regard, the global leadership team was thought to be 'more autocratic, coming from the top' (P10) in setting performance expectations for the organisation's local operations. This generally perceived autocratic approach was not viewed favourably as employees felt that local leadership teams should be given more leeway in setting performance expectations. Participants felt that as they know and understand the local market best, they should therefore not be just given targets that need to be achieved (P9, P10). Employees are also viewed as 'leaders in their own right' (P1) so when employees are given performance targets to achieve, managers should not be 'peering over employees' shoulders for them to do their jobs' (P1).

DIVERSITY OF ROLES

Finally, participants also expressed the belief that leadership fulfilled a diversity of roles simultaneously. In addition to communicating the vision, leaders were seen to trust and empower employees to run with the vision (P1, P3), manage the mentorship and development of employees (P3), lead decisively by giving options of solutions to be implemented (P2), and employ different personal leadership styles (P10). For example, with regard to mentorship and development, it was expressed that, 'so more of the team leads manage a full ecosystem of development, as well as promotion and all of those things. But I wouldn't be able to put it in a sentence just because the roles are so diverse and um your team leads would do way different things and their different tactics in order to drive their team' (P3).

Strategic focus

The final question asked participants to describe what they understood to be of strategic (long term) importance to their organisation. It is evident that participants believe that it is of strategic importance for the organisation to maintain current markets and grow new markets (P1, P2, P3, P6, P7, P11, P12).

MAINTAIN CURRENT MARKETS AND GROW NEW MARKETS

Globally, the strategic focus of the organisation is deemed to be 'two-fold' (P3) – to maintain its leading position in its current market, while also growing its market share in markets where it is still 'a new entrant' (P3). The organisation was mentioned as having experienced success by being among the top global players in the PC industry and having secured a position as one of the leaders in the market (P1, P3, P10). Maintaining this lead in the market was seen to be equally important to the organisation's operations in China (P3). Looking to the future, the organisation was described as having an ambition to break into the detachable devices sector of the PC industry. 'Innovation' (P2, P7, P12), 'new products' (P11), 'an established brand name' (P2), 'channel capability' (P1, P2) and 'staff talent' (P1, P2) were all described as key factors that will help the organisation execute its strategy. Overall, therefore, the organisation was said to be focused on 'profitability and growth' (P12) and was 'market share driven' (P6).

The nature of the Chinese MNC's HCWS (Objective 2)

In line with the second objective of the research, this section presents the findings concerning the nature of the Chinese MNC's HCWS. Research participants were specifically asked to describe the nature of the MNC's individual HCWS practices.

Promotion from within

Just over half of the participants (P1, P2, P3, P6, P8, P11, P12) felt that when a vacant position arises within the MNC, the MNC prefers to promote a capable (P1, P2, P3, P6, P8) employee to fill the vacancy. In this regard, two participants (P2, P6) said that they had been recently promoted. The MNC was thus viewed as 'pro on developing your career path' (P6).

Careful selection

A majority of participants (P1, P3, P5, P6, P8, P10, P12) felt that the selection process applied by the subsidiary was quite intense. Recruitment was done by advertising internally and externally (P1). The process involved screening applications based on qualifications and experience (P1, P10), shortlisting possible candidates (P1, P12), conducting multiple panel interviews where candidates are asked pre-set questions to determine their competency for the position (P1, P3, P5, P6, P10), reference checks (P1), and psychometric assessment for certain job levels (P1, P3, P8, P10). Consequently, it was believed that the most suitable person is appointed for the position (P6, P12), with the long-term view of employee retention (P3).

Extensive training and socialisation

Socialisation at the MNC was described as 'very comprehensive' (P2), involving the HR department (P1, P10, P11, P12), all other departmental managers (P1, P3, P6, P8, P10, P11), other employees (P1, P6), the MNC's business partners (P1), and regional leaders in Dubai for local top leadership positions (P1). An orientation workshop is also conducted whereby the HR department provides information on the Chinese MNC's history, strategy, culture, structure, code of conduct, global policies and procedures (P1, P5, P9, P11).

The MNC is viewed as a 'learning' and 'not a teaching environment' (P2) and training is demand- and not supply-led (P1). When the organisation conducts performance appraisals, any identified gaps in terms of what employees are expected to deliver with their current capabilities are regarded as development opportunities (P1, P2, P6). In addition, employees can also motivate for training and development based on what they perceive to be personal learning opportunities (P5, P7, P8, P10, P11, P12).

Job security

The MNC was described as implementing a performance improvement programme that provides employees who fail to achieve their targets with the opportunity to improve. This is achieved through a process of seeking assistance from their team leaders, managers and other mentors (P1, P3, P6). Seven of the 12 participants (P1, P2, P3, P5, P6, P11, P12) felt that the way the MNC conducts its performance appraisal system helps employees feel more secure in their jobs. Additionally, employee wellness initiatives and support given to employees helped some participants feel that the MNC cares for their overall well-being.

Enlarged jobs

Participants (P1, P2, P3, P4, P5, P6, P8, P9, P11, P12) mentioned that, although the main purpose of their job descriptions was quite specific about achieving targets and only selling to the designated target market or customers (P5, P10, P12), job descriptions are quite broad and flexible as the 'job description is not necessarily everything' (P11) that employees do. This indicates that in order to meet their performance targets and objectives, employees are required to go beyond the scope of their job descriptions (P4, P5, P9, P11).

Performance appraisal

The MNC's performance appraisal system is conducted 'biannually' (P1, P2, P3, P4, P10, P11). Employees are given the opportunity to rate themselves in the appraisal process before being assessed by their managers (P1, P2, P3, P6, P7, P8, P10, P11, P12). Outcomes of the performance appraisal process were described as both evaluative and developmental. The evaluation determines the performance-based employee remuneration (P1, P2, P5, P7, P10, P11). Development-focused appraisal (P1, P3, P6, P9, P10, P11, P12) identifies development opportunities to improve employees' job performance (P3, P6).

High remuneration

Salespeople were remunerated differently to support employees (P10). Both groups, however, are given basic pay and incentivised pay. Whereas salespeople's incentive is sales commission (P1, P2, P4, P5, P6, P8, P9,

P10), incentivised pay for support employees is a performance bonus based on the accomplishment of key performance indicators (P3, P4, P10). Employees mentioned various other benefits received by employees. These include, medical aid (P1, P2, P5, P6, P7, P8, P11, P12), pension and provident fund (P1, P5, P7, P8, P11, P12), traveller's allowance (P1), car allowance (P5, P11), phone allowance (P1, P5, P11), unemployment fund contributions (P1, P2), death and disability cover (P1, P8) and maternity benefits (P6). Additionally, access is provided to an employee wellness company that provides professional help to employees in need (P6),

Extensive ownership

The majority of participants stated that either the MNC had no form of ownership practices implemented at the local level (P3, P4, P12) or that they were not aware of any ownership practices that were implemented (P6, P8, P9, P10). One participant speculated that perhaps ownership practices were implemented 'at a higher level' (P6).

Egalitarianism

A majority – nine out of 12 – of the participants (P1, P2, P3, P4, P5, P6, P8, P11, P12) felt that the MNC treated all employees equally and fairly. For example, the MNC was described as a place where 'whether you're the receptionist or the CEO' (P11), you would be treated with the same level of respect. In addition, employees at the subsidiary said that remuneration was fair 'across all employees' (P3) and was guided by a market index.

Participation

Employee participation at the MNC was facilitated in various ways including the global MNC's online employee morale survey (P3, P4, P5, P7, P10, P11), approaching managers (P1, P2, P4, P6, P7, P8, P10), going to the HR department (P1, P2, P5, P6, P7, P8, P10), and voicing questions and suggestions during staff meetings (P1, P2, P3, P8). Employees are actively encouraged to develop open relationships with their managers so that any problematic issues can be resolved promptly.

Information sharing and communication

The MNC typically shared information and communicated by means of face-to-face meetings (P2, P3, P4, P5, P6, P7, P8, P9, P10), email and telephone (P2, P6, P8, P10, P11) and one-on-one interactions (P2, P8, P10). The method of information sharing depended largely on the nature of the information to be communicated (P1, P12). In addition, employees were regularly updated on matters regarding what is currently happening in the industry (P3, P4, P5, P6, P7), any changes in the MNC (P2), the MNC's performance targets (P4, P9) and the Chinese MNC's future global strategy (P3, P5, P7).

Overarching goals

The MNC was described as emphasising its goals by holding meetings (P2, P4, P5, P7, P8, P9, P11, P12), quarterly update sessions (P8, P10, P12) and by online communication (P3, P6, P11). Since the MNC is 'target-oriented' (P2), performance targets are one of the overarching organisational goals. Regular meetings serve to communicate and remind employees of the global performance strategy of the MNC (P5, P11). The Dubai-based regional director visits South Africa quarterly (P8, P10) and engages with the MNC on issues such as the region's performance targets, major announcements, the Chinese MNC's global strategy and any other key concerns (P10).

Teamwork

Participants felt that the MNC promoted teamwork by holding team-oriented events (P2, P4, P5, P6, P9, P10, P11, P12), offering team rewards (P1, P2, P3, P6, P8, P10, P11, P12) and by promoting a culture that supports teamwork (P1, P2, P4, P5, P8). The MNC was described as having 'regular events where teaming is a part of the event' (P4) which help to promote a 'team spirit' (P10) amongst employees. Teams are also recognised and rewarded for their successful performance on a quarterly (P1, P3) and annual basis (P3). Furthermore, management allows for the formation of temporary cross-functional teams formed by 'different people from different business units' (P5), and provides support to teams to resolve any team conflicts that may arise (P1).

Discussion and conclusions relating to our findings on culture and HCWS

The findings relating to Objective 1 of the study indicate that market culture is the organisation's dominant organisational culture type. The most prominent feature of the culture was described primarily in terms of 'performance'. Performance was driven by communicating the strategy, setting performance targets, rewarding performing employees and managing poor performance. The organisation's culture is therefore goal-driven, which is characteristic of market cultures (Lund, 2003, p. 221). Employee achievement is highly valued by the organisation and is rewarded, thereby further reinforcing the market culture (Den Hartog & Verburg, 2004, p. 60). As the South African operation of the MNC is primarily a sales organisation, employees are given performance objectives in the form of sales targets. Performance targets indicate that processes in the organisation tend to be more mechanistic and controlled (Lund, 2003, p. 221) with the only flexibility being how employees achieve their goals in prospecting new clients and how they maintain customer relationships. Employees are not only rewarded for achieving their sales targets but are also rewarded for demonstrating the values upheld by the organisation in their work behaviours. Competitiveness was also found to be another feature of the organisation's market culture, aligning with the organisation's goal of attaining market superiority over its competitors. Performance and achievement are thus key criteria for fulfilling and maintaining the vision of being a market leader (Cameron & Freeman, 1991, p. 29). Leaders in the organisation, consistent with the market culture, were seen as decisive by setting achievement targets for employees (Lund, 2003, p. 221). In addition, in this market culture, the role of leadership was seen to be geared towards communicating the strategy and culture by tying it to organisational performance. The organisational strategy was driven by the global leadership team who set performance objectives for the organisation and empowered local leadership teams to implement the strategy in their respective territories.

As the market culture is externally oriented with the objective of being a market leader (Øgaard et al., 2005, p. 25), market culture therefore best serves the organisation in its endeavours to achieve and maintain its position as the leading PC manufacturing and sales organisation worldwide.

Finally, the dynamic and competitive nature of the PC industry, both globally and locally (IDC, 2013; Niemond, 2013), means that the organisation has had to prioritise innovation and be externally oriented in order to survive, adapt and remain a market leader in the industry. The organisation's objective to be a market leader aligns with elements of the market culture discussed earlier.

With the exception of ownership practices and the performance appraisal system, findings related to Objective 2 of the study indicate that HR practices are consistent with the existence of a HCWS at the MNC. Ownership practices at the MNC seem to be limited because of the global nature of the organisation and the fact that its shares are not listed on the South African stock exchange. Ownership practices have the benefit of contributing to employee retention (Azfar & Danninger, 2001, p. 619) and, in cases when share options were deployed, it was stated that this was done to reward and retain specific employees who were considered to be high performers. As the MNC is primarily a sales organisation, employees receive feedback that informs them of their performance levels and the areas in which they can improve (Lim & Ling, 2012, p. 111). At the MNC, individual performance appraisal was results-oriented and the main purpose was evaluation. Because of the organisational context of the MNC, these two practices – extensive ownership and performance appraisal – did not measure up to the HCWS practices descriptions proposed by Xiao and Bjorkman (2006, p. 419). However, as the premise of the practices included in HCWSs lies in their theoretical ability to lead to enhanced organisational commitment (Xiao & Bjorkman, 2006, p. 407), the overall descriptions given by participants of the subsidiary's HCWS practices seem to suggest that the subsidiary's HCWS has the potential to promote organisational commitment of employees.

The third objective of the research was to explain how the subsidiary's organisational culture has shaped the HCWS. Bowen and Ostroff (2004, p. 205) state that 'organisational culture shapes HRM practices, which in turn reinforce cultural norms that can shape individual and organisational performance'. The findings of the research appear to corroborate the claim of Bowen and Ostroff (2004, p. 205) as the subsidiary's dominant market culture was discovered to have had the greatest effect in shaping the nature of the HCWS. The subsidiary's dominant market culture appears to have led to the implementation of HCWS practices that have emphasised the performance orientation of the subsidiary. The market culture has had a direct influence in shaping the majority of the subsidiary's practices. Only four practices – job enlargement, egalitarianism, participation and team work – were not found to have been shaped by the subsidiary's market culture. Cameron and Quinn (2006, pp. 39–40) proposed that the market culture 'is focused on transactions with (mainly) external constituencies such as suppliers, customers and contractors' and that for an organisation with a dominant market culture, 'outpacing the competition and market leadership are important'. The subsidiary therefore values and places a great emphasis on performance to enable it to satisfy customer needs and achieve market leadership. In this regard, Gong, Law, Chang, and Xin (2009, p. 264) mention that HR systems with performance-oriented practices serve to motivate employees to achieve organisational goals. Furthermore, as stated by McKenzie (2010, p. 63), 'given a certain strategic goal, a set of HRM practices should be implemented to help the organisation attain these goals'. It thus appears that the majority of the practices implemented aim to facilitate performance achievement at the subsidiary and that the practices are aligned with the subsidiary's externally focused market culture. Den Hartog and Verburg (2004, p. 60) also conclude that 'high performance work practices emphasising progress towards targets such as performance measurement and performance-related pay seem relevant' to the goal of performance-orientated organisational culture.

The findings of the third objective of the research relating to how the organisational culture has shaped the nature of the HCWS suggest that the most dominant organisational culture type at the subsidiary had the greatest effect in shaping the nature of the subsidiary's HCWS. Specifically, the subsidiary's dominant market culture led to the implementation of the performance-orientated nature of most of the subsidiary's HCWS practices.

Managerial implications and recommendations

Given the nature of the organisational culture and HCWS of the organisation, the following observations and recommendations are made:

- From the research it is evident that employees of the MNC had certain expectations related to labour practices and supervision and that miscommunication of these issues sometimes led to a cultural misunderstanding with the Chinese MNC. It is therefore essential for Chinese managers to understand local culture and, equally, to ensure that local workers are apprised of the culture of the MNC and that the culture is understood and accepted.
- It is also important that Chinese managers are not only aware of the organisational culture but also have the ability to maintain and influence the organisational culture (Kerr & Slocum, 2005, p. 130). The managers' thorough understanding of and commitment to the organisational culture will set the organisation apart from its competitors (Smith, 2003, p. 249). In this research, the organisation's dominant market culture and performance-oriented HCWS practices appear to be well-aligned. Chinese managers should also be able to entrench the desired organisational culture by implementing appropriate management practices. The reward system currently based on the achievement of set targets is an example of how leaders in the organisation can effectively reinforce the performance, the ethos of hard work, and the competitive values of the organisation's market culture.
- Because of the organisational context of the organisation, 'extensive ownership and performance appraisal' did not meet the HCWS best practice descriptions as proposed by Xiao and Bjorkman (2006, p. 419). It is thus imperative for other HCWS best practice criteria to be met to avoid employee dissatisfaction (Amos, 2012). It is, therefore, recommended that the organisation continues to implement those practices which were found to align with descriptions of ideal HCWS practices, namely promotion from within, careful selection, extensive training and socialisation, job security, enlarged jobs and job rotation, high remuneration, egalitarianism, participation, information sharing and communication, overarching goals, and teamwork. These practices can enhance the effective commitment and desired performance of employees (SamGnanakkan, 2010, p. 43).
- It is important that managers address the issue of the HCWS practices with which employees were dissatisfied (e.g. perceptions regarding a lack of career-focused training and inequitable remuneration). As explained by the social exchange theory (Whitener, 2001, p. 522), it is the employees' perceptions of HCWS practices rather than the simple existence of the HCWS practices that affects organisational

commitment. Managers, therefore, need to engage with employees about these practices, making any possible changes and communicating the subsidiary's goodwill in order to change any negative perceptions that may affect employee commitment and, ultimately, their performance.

- Chinese managers would be wise to consider other management practices to determine whether they serve to further reinforce the organisational culture and to create clarity as to what is expected of the employees. It is also important for Chinese managers to understand the cultural differences in South Africa regarding the concepts of loyalty to your employer, communication with employees, and the questioning of authority. South African employees frequently question why a decision is being taken and may possibly offer their own viewpoint, both of which are in stark contrast to the decision-making style of the Chinese.

- Finally, the extent of the dissatisfaction expressed by some employees regarding the organisation's culture being too performance-driven at the expense of people-focused issues indicates that managers should examine how these issues can be addressed in order to improve employee satisfaction. It is suggested that Chinese organisations should invest more money and resources in cultural training in order to ensure that they understand the local labour laws and customs, especially when Chinese managers are supervising local workers. This would serve to enlighten Chinese supervisors when they are working in a different cultural environment and would hopefully lessen the potential for cultural conflict between the supervisors and local employees.

Limitations and further research

The limitations of the research related to the absence of Chinese managers or employees at the South African operations of the Chinese organisation. The findings of the research could have been enriched by the participation of Chinese employees to shed further light on any other possible influencers from Chinese culture. The generalisability of the research is also limited by this specific and other similar contexts, and it is therefore recommended that the results are used cautiously for other contexts. It is suggested that future research could more rigorously explore the organisational cultures of other Chinese multinational organisations in South Africa and the rest of Africa to determine which other factors have a specific and significant influence on the formation of their organisational cultures in the African context. Given some of the similarities between Chinese and South African cultures, future research could investigate how new synergies can be formed from the two cultures that could enhance management practice in the South African and, possibly, the greater African context.

This research has attempted to contribute to the still growing knowledge of Chinese organisations in Africa by specifically considering the case of a South African subsidiary of a Chinese MNC. The research thus explored the phenomena of organisational culture and HCWS at the Chinese MNC, phenomena which are all essential in effectively managing the human resources of organisations towards successful organisational performance.

References

Amos, T. (2012). Motivating for performance. In D. Hellriegel, S. E. Jackson, J. W. Slocum, G. E. Staude, T. Amos, H. B. Klopper, L. Louw, M. J. Louw, T. Oosthuizen, S. Perks, & S. Zindiye. *Management: Fourth South African Edition* (pp. 404–437). Cape Town: Oxford Press. ISBN: 9780195995602.

Azfar, O., & Danninger, S. (2001). Profit-sharing, employment stability, and wage growth. *Industrial and Labor Relations Review, 54*(3), 619–630.

Boulton, P. (2013). *Africa booms and multinationals take notice.* Retrieved April 4, 2014 from http://ftijournal.com/article/africa-booms-multinationals-take-notice

Bowen, D. E., & Ostroff, C. (2004). Understanding HRM-firm performance linkages: The role of the "strength" of the HRM system. *Academy of Management Review, 29*(2), 203–221.

Boxall, P., & Macky, K. (2007). High-performance work systems and organisational performance: Bridging theory and practice. *Asia Pacific Journal of Human Resources, 45*(3), 261–270.

Brautigam, D. (2009). *The dragon's gift: The real story of China in Africa.* New York: Oxford University Press.

Cameron, K. S., & Freeman, S. J. (1991). Cultural congruence, strength and type: Relationships to effectiveness. *Research in Organisational Change and Development, 5*, 23–58.

Cameron, K. S., & Quin, R. E. (2006). *Diagnosing and changing organizational culture: Based on the competing values framework.* San Francisco, CA: Jossey-Bass.

Chatelard, S. G. (2012). *Africa must do more to profit from China.* Retrieved March 28, 2014 from www.bbc.com/news/world-africa-18143515

Collis, J., & Hussey, R. (2009). *Business research: A practical guide for undergraduate and postgraduate students* (3rd ed.). Houndmills, Basingstoke: Palgrave.

Cooper, D. R., & Schindler, P. S. (2006). *Business research methods* (9th ed.). New York: McGraw-Hill.

Den Hartog, D. N., & Verburg, R. M. (2004). High performance work systems, organisational culture and firm effectiveness. *Human Resource Management Journal, 14*(1), 55–78.

The Economist. (2013). China and Africa: Little to fear but fear itself. Retrieved March 28, 2014 from www.economist.com/news/middle-east-and-africa/21586583-slowing-demand-raw-materials-will-not-derail-african-economies-little-fear

Gill, B., Huang, C.-H., & Morrison, J. S. (2007). Assessing China's growing influence in Africa. In T. Jackson, L. Louw, & S. Zhao (Eds.) (2011). *Chinese organisation and management in sub-Saharan Africa: Towards a cross-cultural research agenda. The seventh international symposium on multinational business* management – Enterprise management in a transitional economy and post financial crisis. Nanjing, China, June 5–6.

Gong, Y., Law, K. S., Chang, S., & Xin, K. R. (2009). Human resources management and firm performance: The differential role of managerial affective and continuance commitment. *Journal of Applied Psychology*, 94(1), 236–275.

Guest, D., & Conway, N. (2011). The impact of HR practices, HR effectiveness and a "strong HR system" on organisational outcomes: A stakeholder perspective. *International Journal of Human Resource Management*, 22(8), 1686–1702.

Horwitz, F., Hemmant, R., & Rademeyer, C. (2008). Chinese business negotiations: South African firm experiences and perspectives. *South African Journal of Business Management*, 39(1), 1–13.

IDC. (2013). *East Africa PC market shrinks in Q1 2013*. Retrieved November 8, 2013 from www.biztechafrica.com/article/east-africa-pc-market-shrinks-q1-2013/5970/

Kerr, J., & Slocum, J. W. (2005). Managing corporate culture through reward systems. *Academy of Management Executive*, 19(4), 130–138.

Kotter, J. P., & Heskett, J. L. (1992). Corporate culture and performance. In Øgaard, T., Larsen, S. & Marnburg, E. (2005). Organisational culture and performance – Evidence from the fast food restaurant industry. *Food Service Technology*, 5, 23–34.

KPMG. (2013). *The emergence of Chinese multinational corporations (MNCs): Local and global implications*. Retrieved June 10, 2014 from www.kpmg.com/CN/en/IssuesAndInsights/ArticlesPublications/Newsletters/China-360/Documents/China-360-Issue13-201310-emergence-of-Chinese-MNCs-Local-and-global-implications.pdf

Krippendorff, K. (2004). *Content analysis: An introduction to its methodology* (2nd ed.). Thousand Oaks, CA: Sage.

Lim, L. J. W., & Ling, F. Y. Y. (2012). Human resource practices of contractors that lead to job satisfaction of professional staff. *Engineering, Construction and Architectural Management*, 19(1), 101–118.

Lin, S. (2019, June 21). Chinese Ambassador: No empty talks but actions for China-South Africa and China-Africa cooperation. *The Star*, p 16.

Lincoln, Y. S., & Guba, E. G. (1985). Naturalistic inquiry. In E. Babbie & J. Mouton (Eds.), *The practice of social research*. Cape Town: Oxford University Press.

Louw, M. J. (2012). Organisational cultures and workforce diversity. In *Management* (4th ed., pp. 503–535). Cape Town: Oxford University Press.

Lund, D. B. (2003). Organisational culture and job satisfaction. *Journal of Business and Industrial Marketing*, 18(3), 219–236.

McKenzie, K. (2010). Organizational culture: An investigation into the link between organizational culture, human resource management, high commitment management and firm performance. *Otago Management Graduate Review*, 8, 57–68.

Niemond, G. (2013). *Industry analysis: Computer and peripherals*. Retrieved November 8, 2013 from www.valuline.com/Stocks/Industry_Analysis_Computer_And_Peripherals

SAFPI. (2012). *Beijing declaration of the fifth ministerial conference of the forum on ChinaAfrica cooperation* [Online]. Retrieved July 24, 2012 from www.safpi.org/news/article/2012/beijingdeclaration-fifth-ministerial-conference-forum-china-africa-cooperation

Samgnanakkan, S. (2010). Mediating role of organizational commitment on HR practices and turnover intention among ICT professionals. *Journal of Management Research*, 10(1), 39–61.

Saunders, M., Lewis, P., & Thornhill, A. (2000). *Research methods for business students* (2nd ed.). Harlow: Pearson.

Schein, E. H. (1990). Organisational culture. *American Psychologist*, 45(2), 109–119.

Schein, E. H. (1996). Culture: The missing concept in organisation studies. *Administrative Science Quarterly*, 41, 229–240.

Sekaran, U., & Bougie, R. (2009). *Research methods for business: A skill building approach* (5th ed.). West Sussex: Wiley.

Shambaugh, D. (2012). *Are China's multinational corporations really multinational?* Retrieved April 4, 2014 from www.brookings.edu/research/articles/2012/07/10-china-multinationals-shambaugh

Smith, M. E. (2003). Changing an organisation's culture: Correlates of success and failure. *Leadership and Organization Development Journal*, 24(5), 249–261.

Tsui, A. S., Wang, H., & Xin, K. R. (2006). Organisational culture in China: An analysis of culture dimensions and culture types. *Management and Organisation Review*, 2(3), 345–376.

US Congress. (2011). *Congressional testimony. China's role in Africa: Implications for U.S. policy*. David H. Shinn, Adjunct Professor, Elliott School of International Affairs, George Washington University, November 1, 2011. [Online]. Retrieved February 20, 2012 from http://allaffrica.com/stories/201111021445.html

Walton, R. E. (1985). From control to commitment in the workplace. In: Xiao, Z. and Bjorkman, I. (2006). High commitment work systems in Chinese organisations: A preliminary measure. *Management and Organisation Review*, 2(3), 403–422.

Whitener, E. M. (2001). Do "high commitment" human resource practices affect employee commitment?: A cross-level analysis using hierarchical linear modeling. *Journal of Management*, 27(5), 515–535.

Xiao, Z., & Bjorkman, I. (2006). High commitment work systems in Chinese organisations: A preliminary measure. *Management and Organisation Review*, 2(3), 403–422.

Zikmund, W. G. (2003). *Business research methods* (7th ed.). Mason, OH: South-Western.

10 Experiences of Chinese and Tanzanian cooperation in a Chinese organisation in Tanzania

Claude-Hélène Mayer and
Christian Martin Boness

In globalised work environments, organisations are characterised by diverse workforces – in terms of culture, ethnicity, gender, age and social class (Holvino, 2010; Mayer, 2011). Research in critical management studies suggests that demarcation lines, across which identity definitions within organisations and conflict occur, are not predefined, but rather occur and are constructed based on the context and the situation (Prasad, Pringle, & Konrad, 2006; Wells, Gill, & McDonald, 2015; Marfelt, 2016). At the same time, macro-, meso-, and micro-levels influence how individuals relate towards each other in organisational settings (Syed & Özbilgin, 2009).

In management research, according to Zanoni, Janssens, Benschop, and Nkomo (2010, p. 13), the "white, heterosexual, western, middle/upper class, able man" remains the norm of management and organisation studies in theory and in practice. However, the authors of this chapter intend to close a gap in research by studying Chinese and Tanzanian employees' experiences in management and organisation in a selected African context. Through presenting the particularities of the described context and its relevance, the chapter contributes to opening new perspectives by exploring Chinese and Tanzanian business interaction, management and organisation in a selected Chinese organisation in Tanzania. It expands the body of knowledge on Chinese and Tanzanian cooperation and management, as previous studies (Mayer, Boness, & Louw, 2016; Mayer, Boness, Louw, & Louw, 2016) recommended that more in-depth qualitative research on the interrelationship of Chinese and Tanzanian employees be conducted in different organisational contexts. Therefore, for this study, a governmental Chinese organisation was chosen as a research context.

Contextual insights

Chinese organisations have increasingly been investing in emerging markets with tremendous momentum (Power & Mohan, 2008). With the growing cooperation networks between China and the African continent, Tanzania has become one of China's most attractive trading and cooperation partners (Ni, 2015). The cooperation between Chinese and

Tanzanian traders dates back to the 15th century – probably more than 100 years before the first contact between Tanzanians and Europeans (New African Magazine, 2015).

In 2012, for example, Tanzania received huge amounts of investment funds from China; job creation and the number of private Chinese organisations investing in Tanzania have grown constantly (Pigato & Tang, 2015). Whilst the Tanzanian government welcomes investments from China in Tanzania (Majani, 2013), potential Tanzanian employees welcome new job opportunities which are offered by Chinese companies who recruit large numbers of employees at job fairs in Dar-es-Salaam (Kazoka, 2016).

Despite increases in research within African management contexts (Kamoche, 2002; Kamoche, Debra, Horwitz, & Muuka, 2004), with some research focusing on managing intercultural management interactions (Vorster, Kipnis, Bebek, & Demangeot, 2019) and conflicts in organisations (Mayer, 2008, 2011), research in Chinese Human Resource management (HRM) in African countries is still scarce (Xing, Liu, Tarba, & Cooper, 2016; Mayer, Louw, & Boness, 2016). An urgent need to identity factors of HRM and cooperation has been highlighted (Jackson, Louw, & Zhao, 2013).

Managing Chinese organisations in African contexts

Cooperating and managing in African contexts require a complex, multi-faceted knowledge of historical, socio-economic and political complexities (Jackson, 2004) as well as the exploration of management and value concepts relating to participation, decision-making and human interactions (Dutton, Frost, Worline, Lilius, & Kanov, 2002; King, Kruger, & Pretorius, 2007). Cooperation in particularly intercultural contexts needs to take account of employees of different origins (Mayer, Boness, Louw, & Louw, 2016), not least because of the perception that management in African contexts requires strong contextual knowledge to deal with challenges such as high levels of administration and bureaucracy, political instability, lack of personal security, transparency and business confidence and challenging labour relations (Humphreys & Bates, 2005).

Recently, research on Chinese organisational contexts (Zheng & Lamond, 2009; Chan & Wyatt, 2007; Wang & Walumbwa, 2007; Mayer, Boness, & Louw, 2017a, 2017b) and interactions in African countries have increased owing to increasing intercultural work cooperation and interactions (Alden, 2006; Alden & Davis, 2010; Alden, Large, & Soares de Oliviera, 2008) and based on the assumption that effective international leadership is imperative for cooperation and international success (Weinberger, 2009).

Chinese organisations have experienced challenges in international management and cooperation and therefore appear to be aiming for improved international cooperation (Wang, Freeman, & Zhu, 2013). Therefore, research on Chinese cooperation in African countries has increased (Lee, Melber, Naidu, & Taylor, 2007; Alden et al., 2008;

Lindberg, 2015). For example, research is focusing on cooperation in particular African countries, such as Tanzania or South Africa, and on intra- and inter-group perceptions of Chinese and Tanzanian employees in private organisations (e.g. Mayer, Boness, Louw, & Louw, 2016). Research has also been undertaken on perspectives of Chinese and Tanzanian employees on intercultural cooperation (Mayer, Boness, & Louw, 2016) and views regarding leadership styles of South African and Chinese employees (Handley & Louw, 2016).

African leadership is often portrayed negatively with authoritarian, bureaucratic, ineffective and conservative leadership styles (Handley & Louw, 2016). However, Nkomo (2011) contends that African leadership is often based on consensus, stewardship, morals and value concepts, such as Ubuntu, which is defined as leadership based on trust and family bonds (Bolden & Kirk, 2009).

Chinese leadership styles have been described as relational – aiming at harmony, moral behaviour and Confucian belief in which the relationship-building component is the most important (Bird & Fang, 2009; Handley & Louw, 2016). Other scholars (Chen, Eberly, Chiang, Farh, & Cheng, 2014) have suggested that Chinese organisational contexts and Chinese leadership are often strongly influenced by hierarchical values and relationalism as well as by authoritarian and paternalistic leadership styles.

Chinese HRM practices need to focus on the cooperation of employees across cultures. Cultural factors influence the way Chinese manage African employees at the meso- and micro-levels and how African employees react to the management and leadership styles. It has been pointed out that adaptation from Chinese managers needs to increase to manage African employees well (Xing, Cooper, Liu, & Tarba, 2014). Further on, Xing, Liu, Tarba, and Cooper (2016) emphasise that Chinese managers' crossvergence HRM practices are a blend of divergent local contextual factors and convergent cultural factors, taking cultural proximity between Chinese Confucianism and African "Ubuntu" concepts into account. A mix of cultural factors, Chinese and African, therefore influence Chinese management and leadership in African countries. Jackson et al. (2013) emphasise that Chinese organisations in African countries need to take power dynamics and cultural crossvergence into account. By taken these into account, new forms of cultural hybridity within Chinese organisations in African countries can be built. These new cultural forms can then lead to new forms of hybrid cultures and cultural "third spaces" which consist of a new (organisational) culture which is based on the fusion of two previous cultures.

How we did the research

It was important to our research aims to understand the experiences of cooperation between Chinese and Tanzanian employees of a Chinese governmental organisation working in Tanzania by gaining new insights into the views of Chinese and Tanzanians working for the organisation. We focused on three research questions.

1   What do Chinese and Tanzanian employees experience regarding cooperation in a governmental organisation?
2   How do Chinese and Tanzanian employees see their societal and organisational work environment?
3   Which cultural values are important for Chinese and Tanzanian employees?

In this research study, a hermeneutic research design was used to explore the complex phenomenon of the Chinese and Tanzanian experiences within the selected governmental Chinese organisation. The hermeneutical design uses Dilthey's modern hermeneutic which focuses on "Verstehen" (understanding) of experiences described whilst applying the self-reflection of the researcher. Hermeneutics thereby uncover the uniqueness of employees' experiences, with an emphasis on the employee's socio-historical, as well as social-cultural background (Gadamer, 1997; Heidegger, 1962). To date, there appears to be a void in hermeneutic research in this area of Chinese–Tanzanian cooperation in Tanzania.

Utilising the theoretical principles and practices of hermeneutics, this study aimed to explore the experiences of employees of different cultural origin as a phenomenon that is often subconscious and that stays unexplored in daily life interactions. To understand the nature and meaning of the employees' lived experiences, this hermeneutic phenomenology was followed and Dilthey's (2002) approach of modern hermeneutics was applied to create "Verstehen" (understanding) of the experiences described. As according to Ratner (2002), the researcher used a self-reflective attitude throughout the research process.

The context of the study is the building and construction industry. Shortly after Tanganyika's independence in 1961, the foreign aid department of the Ministry of Railways of China invested in railway lines between Tanzania, Zambia and other countries through the TAZARA railway project (1968–1976). This project was its first Chinese project of this dimension, based in Tanzania, and was soon to be followed by other projects.

This research study was conducted in a Chinese governmental organisation which has been active in the building and construction industry in Tanzania for several decades with many construction projects following the original TAZARA project. The organisation at hand supplies consulting services to the Tanzanian government and Tanzanian organisations. However, the main products of the organisation include railway construction, real estate development, trading and industrial investment, civil engineering design and hotel management, bridge construction, road construction and maintenance, water supply and irrigation systems. The organisation employs approximately 2000 employees and is ranked amongst the 70 top international contractors in the world. The

208 Claude-Hélène Mayer et al.

organisation was chosen as a research context because of several research criteria, such as: the long-standing tradition of work relationships of the Chinese organisation and Tanzanian partners in Tanzania, the willingness of the organisation and its management to be a key player in this research, and access to the organisation.

The research team for this study consisted of four researchers – two German, one Tanzanian and one Chinese-Tanzanian researcher with a dual citizenship. There were three male researchers and one female researcher. All the researchers were fluent in English, whilst three were also fluent in Kiswahili and one in Mandarin (Chinese). All of the four researchers were strongly familiar with the Tanzanian context, whilst one had lived in China for about eight years and was very familiar with the Chinese organisational context of this study.

In accordance with the interpretive research paradigm, and in line with the need to explore employees' experiences of the "phenomenon" under inquiry, snowball sampling strategies were used to select the participants (Denzin & Lincoln, 2000; Woodley & Lockard, 2016). Altogether eight interviewees agreed to voluntarily participate in the study. Three employees were female and five were male, whilst four were managers and four were working at a subordinate employee level.

Data were collected through semi-structured interviews within the governmental Chinese organisation. The interviews were conducted in a face-to-face interview situation. The duration of the interviews ranged between 30 and 90 minutes. The interviews were either conducted in English, Kiswahili or Mandarin, according to each participant's language preference. Interviews in Kiswahili and Mandarin were translated by the dual national researcher who is fluent in English, Kiswahili and Mandarin. Observations made by the researchers in the organisation were captured in field notes and used to interpret the interview data (Graham & Bell, 2016; Walsh, Fleming, & Enz, 2016).

The interview questions focused on the employees' experiences in the organisation, in the sociocultural context of the Chinese organisation in Tanzania, on the organisational culture, leadership style experiences, the cooperation between Chinese and Tanzanian employees and their work attitude and work values. Questions included, for example: "What are your experiences in terms of Chinese and African employees' cooperation within the organisation?" "What is the leadership style like in this organisation?" "Please describe the organisational culture" or "Please describe your experiences with work attitudes and work cooperation within the organisation".

Data were transcribed and (where necessary) translated verbatim and were stored according to ethical guidelines. Generalised findings were returned to the participating organisation (management), and in particular to the employees who participated, through presentations and discussions. This procedure was part of the ethical considerations regarding the research collaboration and particularly for the organisation to become aware of issues of intercultural collaboration.

How we analysed and interpreted our data

Data were analysed through the five-step process of content analysis (Terre Blanche, Durrheim, & Kelly, 2006, pp. 322–326) – step 1: familiarisation and immersion; step 2: inducing themes; step 3: coding; step 4: elaboration; and step 5: interpretation and checking. Throughout the process, intersubjective validation processes were used (Yin, 2009). These processes included reflections and discussions about experiences and their interpretations to validate the perceptions and interpretations of the researchers. The data and findings were discussed and interpreted from the researchers' perspectives, which were expected to yield rich, complex and detailed descriptions and interpretations (Chan, Walker, & Gleaves, 2015; Creswell, 2015).

Qualitative research criteria included rich rigor, sincerity, credibility, resonance, the significant contribution, ethical considerations and the construction of meaningful coherence in the context of creating a worthy research topic (Tracy, 2010). As according to Charmaz (2014), data quality was further ensured through informed consent, anonymity, rigorous analysis and constant comparison of the data and of the research topic throughout the analysis. For protection of the participants, informed consent and anonymity were guaranteed by the researchers. As according to Lincoln and Guba (1985), the internal coherence of the research product was checked through the intersubjective validation processes of the researchers as well as through the logical structure of the research process and description to guarantee a rigorous data analysis. Rigor was further on established through the transparent research process description, the clear reporting style and description of the analysis and evaluation and the confirmation of the findings by four researchers with different sociocultural and language backgrounds, as emphasised by Poggenpoel (1998).

The research study followed clearly defined research ethics. Participants voluntarily participated in the study and informed consent was provided in writing by the organisation as well as orally by all of the voluntarily participating employees. Participants were assured of anonymity, confidentiality and the freedom to withdraw at any stage during the research process. The research was conducted in the name of Rhodes University in Grahamstown, South Africa with Rhodes University providing the ethical approval through their research committee.

We were aware of the limitations of our study, being based on a single organisational case study (Yin, 2009). It is therefore limited to a very specific context, selected theories and methodologies. This study's findings are not generalisable, but rather provide the readers with an in-depth insight into the experiences of selected individuals.

The findings contribute in-depth knowledge of a single case which can be taken as a point of entry into similar case studies in the Chinese–African organisational context.

What we found from our research

The biographical details of the employees who participated in the study are shown in Table 10.1. We present our findings next as they address our research questions.

Experiences of Chinese and Tanzanian employees within the organisation

Firstly, the research question: 1. "What do Chinese and Tanzanian employees experience regarding cooperation in a governmental organisation?" is explored.

Findings show that the intercultural collaboration between Chinese and Tanzanian employees mainly relates to: 1. Strategy, 2. Structure, decision-making and participation, 3. Leadership styles, 4. Staff and managers, 5. Recruitment, 6. Qualifications and training, 7. Knowledge sharing, 8. Working conditions and atmosphere, and 9. Motivation, benefits rewards. These are dealt with in detail following, as far as possible using the words of the respondents

Table 10.1 Biographical data of employees in a Chinese state-owned organisation

Inter-view code	Managerial position in organisation	Nationality and mother tongue of employees*	Age in years	Sex**	Work duration in organisation
17 C-E	PERSONAL SECRETARY	TZ SU	35	F	24
18 C-E	COMMUNICATIONS EMPLOYEE	RC CH	40	M	6
19 C-E	SECRETARY IN TRADE	RC CH	30	F	24
20 C-M	PROCUREMENT MANAGER	RC CH	50	M	12
21 C-M	ENGINEER	RC CH	45	M	6
22 C-E	LOGISTICS AND PROCUREMENT DEPARTMENT	TZ SU	30	F	18
23 C-M	SENIOR QUANTITY SURVEYOR	TZ SU	40	M	24
24 C-M	ADMINISTRATOR – HR	RC CH	50	M	8

*RC (Republic of China), CH (Chinese language), TZ (United Republic of Tanzania), SU (Kiswahili language)
**M (male), F (female)

Source: authors' own construction

Strategy

A Chinese communications employee highlights the organisational strategy with the following words:

> Right now our department is mainly focused on real estate developing and we need to go through some clause before purchases and we need to go to different ministries like Ministry of Lands and sometimes it knows the GPS for the plot so that when we come back we can mark it out on Google Earth.
>
> (18C-E)

The employee displays the departments strategy focusing on the purchase of properties and the development of collaboration with Tanzanian authorities. Others define the strategy as "getting suppliers and quality-material" (20C-M) or looking for investment opportunities to make money from the market, and "focusing on buildings" (21C-M). A Chinese HR administrator emphasises the strategy of keeping the organisation at number one in competition in construction (railway, water supply, buildings and roads (24C-M)), whilst highlighting the organisation's strategy within the socio-historical context of Chinese, Tanzanian and Zambian relationships since the 1960s (24C-M).

A Tanzanian employee describes the strategy rather as a way to improve the country through the organisational impact:

> to upgrade this country – but the main focus is with this company's construction.
>
> (22C-E)

A Tanzanian personal secretary reports that there is no official information of the organisation's strategy (17C-E), whilst the statement of a Tanzanian senior quantity surveyor points out that strategy means "getting projects for the company" (23C-M).

Structure, decision-making and participation

Further on, Chinese and Tanzanian employees refer to the issues of structure, decision-making and participation. A Chinese procurement manager points out:

> If it is a big decision, I can make the decision. All the people, even the boss, say "we can discuss it" and everyone gives advice and the boss will make the final decision.
>
> (20C-M)

This Chinese employee sees the decision-making process as a consensual, mutual process of discussion and advising between the boss and the employees. The discussion finally informs the decision of the leader. Another Chinese employee (18C-E) reports similar experiences, emphasising that the decision-making process lies in the hands of the department which results in the decision-making of the leader (18C-E).

An interviewee (21C-M), relates participation in decision-making to Chinese work ethics: if you "work hard", you are promoted, which increases the influence in decision-making processes.

According to a Chinese manager (24C-M), major decisions are made by the organisation's head office in China or the regional office in East Africa. Local expertise is always included in decision-making processes; however, the final decision always lies with the government (24C-M).

A Tanzanian manager (23C-M) explains his view of decision-making:

> Chinese have principles, but to know which principles they employ is not easy, because even in the monthly and weekly meetings they do not involve Africans, they just have meetings for Chinese. They never have meetings with local staff, unless there is a critical issue.

This Tanzanian manager feels excluded from Chinese decision-making processes. To him, Chinese decision-making principles are not transparent and are also exclusive. He does not experience participation, only when there are "critical issues" to solve. Similarly, another Tanzanian employee states: "No, we do not have that opportunity for participation" (22C-E), whilst yet another Tanzanian employee (17C-E) agrees: "There are no meetings and sharing of information". All Tanzanian employees and managers feel excluded from decision-making and participation and experience a strong hierarchical organisational structure in which Chinese employees are included and involved in decision-making, whilst Tanzanians are not. However, one Tanzanian manager (23C-M) explains that the departments seem to have a full mandate in decision-making processes.

Leadership styles

A Chinese manager reflects on leadership styles applied in the organisation (18C-E):

> And Chinese right now from the private companies, they are just using the way Westerners use, because the leadership all comes from Western influence and people studying the leadership, study the Western leadership, because it is the most efficient way for the company

to run. But, for us, it is a little bit different, because we are controlled by the government. Somehow, it is like the military, like the government. But then it changes into the company, but then it is still controlled by the government and the head office of our company has a relationship with the government.

This Chinese manager emphasises the differences between private and governmental Chinese organisations in Africa. Private organisations are associated with Western leadership styles, whilst governmental organisations refer to Chinese leadership which is associated with military structures and applications, including guiding principles of command, obedience and control. Other Chinese employees also refer to private Chinese organisations and Western leadership (21C-M) or define Chinese leadership as a mix of Western and Chinese applications (24C-M). One Chinese procurement manager highlights that he uses African leadership methods to lead local staff by "pushing" and "face-to-face talks" (20C-M).

One Tanzanian employee (22C-E), working in the logistics and procurement department, describes the leadership styles as follows:

It is Chinese-oriented. We have a difference with the regulations: so the Chinese have their regulations and their policy and Tanzanians, we have our regulations and working policy; that is the main difference.

This Tanzanian employee identifies a main difference between regulations and policy applied in Chinese and Tanzanian organisations. However, he does not explain further what exactly the difference means to him. Another Tanzanian employee (23C-M) feels that the organisation is based on a mix of Western and Chinese leadership styles.

Staff and managers

A Chinese procurement manager explains the relationship between Tanzanian employees and Chinese management (20C-M):

The Tanzanian employees they do not operate. We have a boss who tells us every day which time we should be here and which time we should go home. Tanzanians are always late and you can't punish them, because the Tanzanian government will help them. They come and think the Chinese have money, so they should give our people jobs. However, they deal badly with the jobs and you can't fire them. This is a big problem for me, because I am in charge of the drivers.

This Chinese manager struggles with disparate expectations between the Chinese managers and Tanzanian staff. Tanzanians expect jobs, money and freedom of time management, which collides with the Chinese expectations of punctuality and fulfilling the duties of the job.

The support of the Tanzanian government is regarded as problematic, because it interferes with the work ethics of the Chinese manager who experiences Tanzanian employees as unreliable. Another Chinese employee (18C-E) complains about Tanzanian employees being uneducated and unable to meet the operational standards (18C-E), whilst another Chinese HR manager is stressed about the task to educate Tanzanians to be punctual. This manager therefore suggests interlinking punctuality with salary payment, so that Tanzanian employees lose money when they arrive late at work. However, this manager highlights that Tanzanians enjoy entertainment, poker, football, chess and watching movies together (24C-M).

A Tanzanian senior manager presents his view of Chinese employees in the organisation (23C-M):

> Chinese are many in numbers in the organisation when you compare it to the local employees. But the number depends on the levels of employment; semi-skilled and professionals. Normally the project manager will be a Chinese, the assistant project manager is Chinese . . . maybe the second assistant could be Tanzanian. But it is from the fourth level that you usually find the local.

This Tanzanian manager describes the inequality in the organisation with regard to national belonging and hierarchical rank within the organisation, pointing out that Chinese are found in the higher ranks. "Tanzanians are only a few guys", highlights another Tanzanian employee (22C-E) in the logistics and procurement department, whilst a female PA (17C-E) describes the ratio between Chinese and Africans in the organisation as being adequate.

Recruitment

Recruitment is an important issue in the organisation and a Chinese manager (18C-E) refers critically to recruitment of labour in the organisation (18C-E):

> It is quite difficult to find educated people here. So sometimes we need to send people from China here and that costs much more than if we had local staff. We need time to adjust and sometimes maybe . . . Chinese employees are not quite fit in this environment . . . this makes it less efficient.

This Chinese manager describes the difficulties of recruiting Chinese into positions in Tanzania, the economical disadvantages and the challenges of international labour migration. At the same time, other Chinese employees highlight that Tanzanian employees are "dishonest" and "not good, because they steal" which makes cooperation difficult (20C-M, 21C-M, 24C-M). One manager defines Tanzanian employees as "disobedient" and "not listening" (20C-M).

From Tanzanian perspectives, recruitment is also a "difficult" topic. A Tanzanian manager expresses his opinion as follows (23C-M): "Opportunities are minimal when you try to check . . . there are very few." Tanzanians mainly find work in Chinese organisations through informal communication and personal relationships with Tanzanian employees who already work in the organisation.

Qualifications and training

Chinese and Tanzanians comment on qualifications, training and development within their organisations. A Chinese employee highlights (19C-E):

> It is hard to bring African colleagues to the same level as Chinese. Their language is much better than ours, but the technical jobs, the Chinese people will do better than the locals. Some of them study hard, but some are not. . . . We can't control that.

This employee emphasises the language competencies of Tanzanian employees with regard to English where she sees advantages; however, she emphasises that Chinese employees have advantages with regard to technical skills. She also highlights that Tanzanian employees are not controllable with regard to self-development and education and she seems to be critical about the Tanzanian way of dealing with self-development.

Other Chinese agree with this employee that it is difficult to train Tanzanian employees and bring them to the "Chinese level" (19C-E). Chinese employees focus on development through training (20C-M), and also on practical training on construction sites (21C-M). Chinese employees highlight that they all have at least bachelor's degrees (24C-M) whilst there are only "two Tanzanian educated managers in the office" (20C-M).

A Tanzanian personal assistant comments: "I have not been chosen to get training" (17C-E). She is very disappointed that only a few employees are selected in the organisation to be trained. Other employees highlight that there is no training within the organisation for "unskilled labourers" (22C-E) Training always depends on "the profession an employee brings to the organisation" (23C-M).

Knowledge sharing

A Chinese procurement manager expresses concern regarding knowledge sharing (20C-M):

> We employ the local workers, but if the project is finished and we will move and maybe the workers in that area, . . . they don't want to move to Dar es Salaam. They just go to the other Chinese company . . . it is very hard to give long term planning to the training.

This Chinese manager highlights the problem of job hopping with regard to Tanzanian employees and thereby expresses why Tanzanians are not trained in the organisation. However, if people are trained, they are trained during spare time, through the internet and training videos (24C-M). But one Chinese assumes that Tanzanian employees do not discuss or question Chinese during training sessions, because they are afraid of them (18C-E).

A Tanzanian manager provides his view on knowledge sharing (23C-M):

> When they come to Tanzania, you find that the Chinese come to learn English gradually. And the normal language they have is the English; but when it comes to the professional jargon, they cannot really cope with it, because there are some words that belong to engineering . . . so it becomes difficult to share knowledge. They have the knowledge, but how to share it with the other part becomes difficult because of the medium of communication.

The Tanzanian manager highlights that knowledge sharing is particularly difficult owing to the Chinese lacking language competencies. Another Tanzanian employee is more positively inclined, convinced that "knowledge sharing" needs to happen through mutual cultural learning (22C-E).

Working conditions and atmosphere

With regard to working conditions and work atmosphere, a Chinese communications employee points out:

> Firstly, hard working is (important) . . . in China, but we work even much more and we have fewer staff, but more work. We should work hard, but for the atmosphere we need to work hard, but I think the atmosphere is happy.
>
> (18C-E)

This employee emphasises a few key aspects: working hard is important and expected; the way people work creates the organisation's atmosphere which is described as "happy". Other Chinese employees agree (19C-E) or add that there are problems regarding truck blockades and Saturday meetings on top of long work-shifts (18C-E). However, unfriendly treatment and stealing may disturb the work atmosphere and create bad feelings (19C-E).

A Chinese engineer thinks that the work atmosphere is reserved when he fires an employee because of bad performance or theft (21 C-M).

A Tanzanian employee experiences the work conditions and atmosphere as difficult:

> In most Chinese companies, we local people work for their company without contracts. I do not have a contract. I want it, yes.
>
> (22C-E)

This Tanzanian employee does not have a contract and 23C-M agrees that most Tanzanians work without contracts, without agreements on sick leave, holiday leave and family care (23C-M). These working conditions are not valued: "The trust is not good, because they normally say that most of the local workers are not faithful" (23C-M). A Tanzanian employee describes the inequality regarding working conditions in which the Chinese have two hours whilst the Tanzanians only have a one-hour break per shift. The Chinese usually blame the Tanzanians regarding their behaviour (17C-E) which diminishes the work atmosphere (17C-E).

Motivation, benefits and rewards

A Chinese manager explains how motivation, benefits and rewards work:

> With Chinese employees . . . your manager will see on your performance for the year and give you your bonus. But for local people it is very different: if you can do your job fast and good, you will get your bonus.
>
> (21C-M)

Another Chinese employee regards his salary, one month's leave, improvement of his English competency, and travelling the country as being benefits of his work in the organisation (19C-E). An increase in salary, savings because of canteen food and other opportunities are also motivating (20C-M). Likewise, a bigger salary and bonuses are motivating and benefitting (21C-M, 24C-M). Benefits like coffee and telephone vouchers and gifts like wine (24C-M) also contribute to keeping employees motivated.

A Tanzanian interviewee reflects on rewards:

> I remember one day, a reward was given for the best work done, but when you compare what you have done and what you are being

rewarded, it does not really sound like a reward. So, the culture of rewarding and motivations they do not have.

(23C-M)

This Tanzanian is critical of Chinese rewards and reward systems, which he experiences as low (22C-E, 23C-M). However, a secure job makes one happy and new experiences in the organisation might motivate some (23C-M).

Conclusion on the experiences of Chinese and Tanzanian employees within the organisation

Throughout our interviews, employees mainly emphasised differences between Chinese and Tanzanians working in the organisation.

Chinese employees see the organisational strategy as being connected to the socio-historical context of Chinese–African relations, whilst Tanzanians complain about a lack of information regarding organisational strategy. This might be based on the fact that Tanzanians mainly work at lower levels of the organisation and are not being included in the information system that provides insights into strategic decisions. Furthermore, Chinese employees emphasise "discussion", "advising" and "consultations" as major interactions between Chinese and Tanzanians. However, Tanzanian employees feel excluded from decision-making processes. They feel that they are not part of participative management practices and expect more communication between the hierarchical ranks in the organisation.

Both Chinese and Tanzanian employees emphasise that within the organisation, a mixture of Chinese and Western leadership styles are being used. However, the Chinese employees differentiate between leadership styles in governmental and private organisations and emphasise that the organisation is more Chinese and military-like than Western, whilst Tanzanians experience Chinese and Western management approaches.

Tanzanian employees are irritated that a Tanzanian is unlikely to be promoted into higher management levels in the organisation, whilst the Chinese usually occupy the leadership positions. Tanzanians and Chinese differ with regard to their expectations and attitudes concerning the way the job should be done, and they have developed different strategies to deal with it (e.g. Chinese – "pushing", Tanzanians – "gaining protection from the government").

In recruitment processes, Tanzanian employees feel "left out" and "uninformed", whilst the Chinese complain about the "lack of education" of Tanzanian employees who do not meet the required standards and who are additionally regarded as "dishonest" and "disobedient". Both, however, agree that the best way of recruitment for the organisation is recruitment through "official information channels".

Chinese and Tanzanian employees see information sharing in the organisation as a difficult task owing to language difficulties. Both feel that employees with Chinese and Tanzanian backgrounds can hardly understand each other. Furthermore, they perceive differences with regard to work attitude: Chinese employees value the concepts of "working hard" and "happiness" as being interrelated and contributing to the organisational culture. They feel that Tanzanians do not comply with their values and do not treat Chinese employees respectfully. Tanzanians report that they feel insecure because of the lack of work security based on written work contracts which they are missing out on. This causes distrust and a feeling of injustice among the Tanzanians, who at the same time do not feel supported by the Tanzanian government and employment laws.

Finally, Chinese gain more benefits and bonuses in the organisation than Tanzanians since they understand how to be promoted within the Chinese organisational system, whilst Tanzanians feel "left behind" because of the fact that they do not understand the reward system and are not included in promotions. Members of both groups see value in their monthly salary with different visions: Chinese aim at saving their income, whilst Tanzanians aim at securing their daily life expenses.

We now move on to focus on how the Chinese and Tanzanians perceive the wider societal and work environment.

Chinese and Tanzanian employees' perceptions of their societal and organisational work environment

We focus on this aspect of the perceptions Chinese and Tanzanian employees through three specific aspects: interaction with community and local organisations; interaction with government and trade unions; and perceived benefits for Africa and Tanzania

Interaction with community and local organisations

A Chinese procurement manager refers to his experiences of collaborating with local entrepreneurs (20 C-M) as follows:

> Sometimes the Tanzanians are not honest. There is a small amount to pay regarding an order and we talk on the phone. They say that they want the money to be paid first. African people, they want the money first and they say they will give me the materials tomorrow. Then you just wait a while. After a while, they don't give you the material and that is a problem.

This Chinese manager criticises the reliability of Tanzanian businessmen and judges them as being "dishonest" and "not honouring agreements" in business interactions. One other Chinese manager reports on his partnership with electrical mechanics (21C-M) and another Chinese manager highlights a lack of communication with local communities and organisations (19C-E).

The Chinese interact with Tanzanians only through work-related relations (20C-M, 24C-M) and highlight their emphasis on social responsibility projects, such as the sponsorship of schools (library building sports equipment) to establish contact with local communities (24C-M).

A Tanzanian employee is satisfied with the organisation's relationship with the community, highlighting (17C-E): "There is good interaction with the community through job offers and school aids." This employee emphasises the job opportunities the Chinese create for the community. Another Tanzanian employee (23C-M) reports positive relationships between the organisation and the schools, referring to donations of sport items, books and the provision of teaching facilities.

Interaction with government and trade unions

One Chinese employee comments on the interaction with the government (20C-M):

> The big difference is: the government just talks – they should do their job quickly and harder. The government officer comes to the office at 9 o'clock and leaves at 4 pm. Their working time is so short. I do business with them. In the afternoon, I go there at 3 pm and they tell me: 'We don't work, come tomorrow!' So you waste one day.

This Chinese employee criticises the work ethics and effectiveness of governmental employees in the Tanzanian offices. In a later statement, this employee also criticises the police and their "senseless document probes" which just "cost time and money".

Another Chinese employee complains about the traffic chaos in Dar es Salaam, which "the government does not care about" (18C-E). Further constraints which Chinese employees highlight are the governmental visa policies and the issue of refusing visas (21C-M), particularly because of Chinese employees lacking English language skills (24C-M). However, other employees highlight that when a visa is provided, the investment policies in Tanzania are easy to meet (17C-E), far easier to meet than in Europe (19C-E). As an aside, despite issues with their perceived traffic chaos in the city, the Chinese are appreciative of the fact that "the air is not so polluted" (21C-M).

Although the Chinese see issues with government officials, one of the main issues raised by the Tanzanian employees is the lack of tolerance of trade unions in the organisation. For example, a Tanzanian senior manager reports that (23 C-M):

> Unions are not available, but we have tried our best to make those unions for the sake of our problems. But we have not yet succeeded with that, because there are several problems and we fail to solve them, because we do not have a union.

This Tanzanian employee emphasises the lack of the unions' power and impact with regard to the rights of the Tanzanian employees. He experiences a lack of labour rights, which the organisation does not make provision for.

Benefits for Africa and Tanzania

One important topic with regard to the societal development is that employees refer to the benefits of Chinese organisations investing in Africa. A Chinese manager points out (24C-M):

> Chinese contribute a lot, because we built a railway, there is construction work for the city. We make sure that this country is developed. We build railways, water supply, roads, benefiting the local people a lot. Maybe we will also build the central line. We have a project in Morogoro. Before, if people wanted to buy something in Morogoro, they would have to take a taxi which takes an hour and a half. After the road was finished, it took them twenty minutes. That is a difference.

Chinese employees value the impact their organisation has on the convenience of transport for the Tanzanian society. Other Chinese employees (19C-E, 18C-E) share this opinion and also emphasise their aid for schools. One Chinese manager, however, is irritated by "the loss of money and peoples' lives, corruption, the only interest in serving personal benefits, but not treating the railway as a whole" (24C-M). This manager is frustrated and expects more organisational commitment and social welfare through the organisation.

A Tanzanian logistics and procurement manager also refers to the example of TAZARA, critically assessing Chinese benefits in Tanzania (22C-E): "TAZARA – they took cheap materials and you know even cheap labour; so you know, if you use cheap labour: obviously they will not do the work seriously." This statement is backed up by another Tanzanian manager who feels that Chinese projects, such as TAZARA, lack funds for maintenance, spare parts and technicians (23C-M). Others, such as the personal secretary (17C-E), emphasise the great benefit of railway construction, roads and construction of schools contributing to employment options and development in Tanzania.

Conclusion on the Chinese and Tanzanian views on the societal and organisational work environment

Comparing Chinese and Tanzanian views on Chinese engagement in the society and organisational environment, both members report very good relationships between the organisation and local organisations, such as schools. Only one Chinese employee is concerned about the "dishonesty" of local entrepreneurs.

Cooperation with government and trade unions is experienced differently by Chinese and Tanzanian employees: Chinese employees focus on governmental activities in a critical manner, whilst a Tanzanian manager is concerned about the missing influence of trade unions in the organisation which leads to a lack of applied labour laws and problems for Tanzanians in Chinese organisations.

The views on benefits for Tanzania and Africa regarding the influence of Chinese organisations highlight the positive effects of infrastructural development in general. However, regarding the TAZARA project, members of both groups blame each other for the deplorable status of the transnational railway, emphasising corruption, environmental dangers and loss of funds (Chinese) and "cheap Chinese material", low payments, lack of spare parts and technicians (Tanzanian).

Chinese and Tanzanian views on culture

Finally, we focus on our findings addressing the research question: "Which cultural values are important for Chinese and Tanzanian employees?" Responses to this research question include three main aspects, namely: Chinese views on African and Chinese values; Tanzanian views on African and Chinese values; and ideas for future collaboration.

This section differentiates between Chinese and Tanzanian views on cultural values regarding their own culture and the "other culture". Chinese employees use the terms "African culture", "Swahili culture" and "Tanzanian culture" synonymously and they refer to the "Han culture" as a major, dominant culture in Chinese contexts.

Chinese views on Chinese and African values

Chinese employees comment particularly on work, personal and family values as well as religion and work ethics. One Chinese manager (24 C-M) draws a contrast between Chinese and African cultural core values as follows:

> Oh, a Chinese couple works very hard to buy a big house, but because they are working so hard, they have got to find someone to take care of the house, right? So they find a house girl to keep that house clean and whatever. So, basically it looks like this young couple works from eight AM to midnight every day and their house girl sitting on the couch playing with the pet. And she sees the sunrise and sundown.

This Chinese manager explains the work ethic and at the same time explains the misfalls of the Chinese lifestyle which leads to the fact that the Chinese cannot enjoy what they are working for, because they only work. The manager concludes that because of the work ethic, Chinese managers miss out on enjoying life. Lower paid and lower status jobs, however, provide the workers with freedom and the opportunity to enjoy the life the hard-working people should have.

The same manager (24 C-M) comments further that:

> When you have a chance, you should enjoy the life and you should have like a very open attitude. Local workers do not make very good money, but when they get their salary, they go to the bar and enjoy themselves, and do not worry about next week. But they do enjoy themselves.

Besides the highly valued loyalty towards country and company, the Chinese emphasise work ethics, the high prevalence of efficiency, and chance-taking regarding investment (18C-E).

Further, the Chinese see Tanzanian employees as not displaying control (21C-M) and as "slow workers" because of the threat of dehydration (24 C-M). They are seen as cherishing family values; putting family, parents, and children first. Chinese perceive that truth-telling (24 C-M), honesty, parental care, respect for elderly and "not lying to others" are also seen in Tanzanians (21C-M).

Chinese see family values in Tanzanians as the highest values, followed by enjoying life, creating a better life, enjoying good food, having a place to live, kindness and patience (20C-M). Tanzanians appear to be "simple people" who entertain good relationships (21C-M). They are kind, they love personal safety, they treat people with respect and respect minorities (24 C-M). However, there are also Tanzanian robberies which Chinese people fear (24 C-M). The Chinese enjoy the fact that African food is fried to kill germs and therefore healthy (24 C-M).

For Chinese employees, the religious orientation is not important, highlighting that religion is "a story": 18 C-E comments:

> We believe in something like God. God only helps the people who help themselves. God is a thing that, in Chinese, I translate directly into 'Sky'.

Another Chinese employee (19C-E) highlights: "Chinese have no faith, they believe in Buddha, and do not enjoy self-belief and not God-belief, because of the 'socialist government socialization'." However, the Chinese see that Tanzanians believe strongly in God (24 C-M).

Tanzanian views on Tanzanian and Chinese values

A Tanzanian manager emphasises the necessity of equality and advantages in relationships between Chinese and Swahili cultures (23 C-M):

> Chinese should know that the Swahili culture is a good culture; it is like the other cultures, like the Chinese culture. And if they work

with people based on their culture they can get more output from them than just trying to force them to cope with the Chinese culture.

Tanzanians want Chinese employees to learn about the Tanzanian culture and respect it, without judging it in a biased, dominating and forceful way to comply with Chinese expectations. Mutual respect and equality are expected of both cultures to achieve an equilibrium of respect, work ethics and personal values. The manager feels that "what they do take from us is that spirit of hard work and tolerance" (23 C-M). He tries to balance the conflicted fields of work ethics and general tolerance towards human differences.

Tanzanians see Chinese as holding "materialistic values", keeping and using money properly (17 C-E). They see that the Chinese are "fair and committed", holding "a culture that nothing is impossible for them, any problem can be solved" (23C-M). Another Tanzanian employee has learnt to "follow the Chinese and what they like to be done" (22C-E), to be successful and in peace.

Conclusions on the Chinese and Tanzanian views on cultural values

Comparing Chinese views on Chinese and African values, Chinese work ethics and values are characterised by "working hard", materialism and "successful achievements". Chinese emphasise efficiency, timeliness and taking opportunities and loyalty towards the organisation and their home country. Some Chinese employees emphasise family values, such as respecting elders and parents. Chinese value honesty and truth-telling and do not believe in God, but some Chinese employees refer to Buddha, self-belief and self-confidence.

As main values of Tanzanians, Chinese identify joy of life, kindness, socialising and entertaining. Tanzanians are seen as "simple" and "slow", "uncontrolling" and "respectful". "Family values" and a "safe home" appear to be valued by Tanzanians, as well as spiritual values and the belief in God.

Tanzanians feel that their own cultural values are "good" in comparison to Chinese values. They see Chinese as "hard working" and "tolerant" whilst defining themselves as "not working hard", but also as "unequal to Chinese" and "subordinate". Chinese people appear to be "fair and committed" and responsible regarding spending money, materialistic. Tanzanians like regarding Chinese values as the successful "problem-solving attitude".

Chinese and Tanzanian ideas of future collaboration

Our findings also focus on Chinese and Tanzanians' ideas of future mutual collaboration.

The Chinese indicated that in future they aim at putting more emphasis on work–life balance (19C-E):

> I leave my parents in China and I come here for work. I just go back once per year. African people they will not have to leave their family, but Chinese people always do like that and this is not good. The better life situation is to be with our families and to share time with them. So I think Chinese should focus more on family and learn from African people.

Through intercultural cooperation and experience, the manager reflected on his lifestyle and his values and came to a conclusion that family values are also important to him and more important than work and live "just for the purpose is money". However, for the future, Tanzanians should learn how to work faster to succeed with their business (18C-E):

> In future: efficiency and to take care of the cost. I think, this is something of the Western . . . we are doing the investment, because it is Chinese money. If you take a long time, the money will disappear. Future is about taking a chance and in the shortest time you will succeed.

Another Chinese manager (19C-E) mentions that the Tanzanians should learn what authority in China means, being based on the person and on the laws. They should "follow strict laws, be fair and treat others equally". The statement shows that the person and the law should always be taken into account to manage intercultural relationships and cooperation well.

Management of organisations is essential for the Chinese engineer, who focuses in the future on skills development (21C-M): "I think local people can learn management from China, but they can also learn how to manage the company in Africa in future." Additionally, the same Chinese manager recommends learning English and Swahili, making friends, learning about the "last hundred years of history and local culture" and to "respect Confucius, to start understanding Chinese people" (21C-M).

Furthermore, the Chinese have to learn to understand the "Swahili lifestyle and tribal culture in dressing and food habits, respect the local people and take care of nature", according to a Chinese manager (24C-M). This manager expects Tanzanians to learn "time management, learn field operating and efficiency, and to keep deadlines. They should learn to work efficiently and not to lose time in 'African palaver'." He (24C-M) continues that

> Chinese language courses should be pushed by the local government and Tanzanians should learn of the long lasting Chinese culture, that

> Chinese culture is like a centripetal ball, absorbing other cultures and mixing them with Chinese culture until it feels like being part of the Chinese culture.

A Tanzanian interviewee perceives that the Chinese tend to stick to

> their own Chinese lifestyle. But Chinese have to adjust to African lifestyle in future to learn about African dressing, the importance of greetings, such as bending to greet respectfully, and the specific African communication style.
>
> (17C-E)

Another Tanzanian manager (23C-M) suggests that "Chinese should not intervene in Swahili culture, but learn from it". He adds that Tanzanians should in future "not be forced in labour and decision-making processes." He proceeds then to talk about spirituality, religion and God (23C-M):

> Another thing is that these people do not have faith. They do not know that God exists. So the issue of religion is a big problem, because they want you to work on Sunday. If you are a Muslim, they want you to work on Friday, there is no ample time to worship. They have to adopt that people need freedom of worship; so they should be considerate. However, they say they do not have time for worship, but because they work with the communities that have belief, they have to respect their faith.

Further on, "basic human dignity should be respected" (23C-M), whilst Tanzanians should learn from Chinese employees "to work hard and to work on time" (17C-E). Sticking to these points will bring "peace and good cooperation" (22C-E) in future.

Summary of Chinese and Tanzanian ideas towards future collaboration

Comparing Chinese and Tanzanian ideas on future collaboration, it can be said that for Chinese employees the most important in understanding and adopting is the compliance of family values and work ethic in the Swahili culture and that these should be at least reflected upon, whilst for Tanzanians, embracing the work ethic regarding efficiency and punctuality of the Chinese can be helpful in the future.

Regarding the field of work ethics, Chinese need to learn that the authority of law should dominate and limit the power of individuals from a Tanzanian perspective. Chinese also need to learn to respect the Tanzanian belief in God and their respect for human dignity.

Chinese expect Tanzanians in future to learn about Chinese time management, culture and history and Confucianism. The Tanzanians recommend that the Chinese adjust more to the African lifestyle with regard to respect, greeting, dressing, food and communication. Additionally, they should learn not to force Tanzanians to disrespect their spiritual culture of worship and faith, which affects Sunday work duties.

Reflections on our findings

This chapter addresses the need to increase research which considers other viewpoints besides Westernised ideas and perceptions of management (Zanoni et al., 2010). It also responds to the need to focus on the HRM and organisational aspects of Chinese organisations in Africa (as previously emphasised by Kamoche, 2002; Kamoche et al., 2004) and the need for exploring differences and similarities in the perceptions of both local and Chinese employees in Chinese organisations operating in Tanzania (Mayer, Boness, & Louw, 2016; Mayer, Boness, Louw, & Louw, 2016).

Although the critical management literature highlights that globalised work environments and organisations are characterised with regard to culture, ethnicity, gender, age and social class (Holvino, 2010; Mayer, 2011), findings show that Chinese as well as Tanzanian employees in this study reduce their experiences to national/cultural ascriptions of experiences. That means: experiences with Chinese and Tanzanian employees, regardless of attention to other categories, such as gender, age or social class. Findings further show that the experiences of Tanzanian and Chinese employees often refer to specific contextual and situational aspects experienced within the organisation (e.g. strategy, decision-making, leadership style, job expectations, language use in certain situations and working conditions). This supports the idea of Prasad et al., 2006; Wells et al., 2015; Marfelt, 2016, that experiences (including conflictual and identity-based experiences) are constructed in relation with the situation and context.

This study shows that Tanzanian employees basically welcome new job opportunities which are offered by Chinese organisations (as in Kazoka, 2016); however, both Chinese and Tanzanian employees narrate on experiences of (cultural) differences, misunderstandings and even conflicts.

This research takes socio-historical influences into account (Jackson, 2004) to understand the complexities. However, at the same time, it reduces the experiences of the participants to their core experiences within the organisation. As explained by Dutton et al. (2002) and King et al. (2007), employees' experiences are associated with their value concepts (participation, decision-making, differences in perception).

Chinese employees have a broad view and understanding of the strategy applied in their Chinese organisation. They have a deep understanding of the processes and occupy higher ranked positions in the management levels of the organisation. Tanzanian employees, on the other hand, emphasise that they do not understand the strategy behind the organisation and feel not part of the management ranks. Furthermore, Chinese and Tanzanian employees experience differences in decision-making processes and concepts of participation. Whilst Chinese employees define "discussion", "advising" and "consultations" with Tanzanians as majorly important, Tanzanian employees feel excluded from decision-making processes and they feel that their idea of "transparency and business confidence" (Humphreys & Bates, 2005) is not achieved.

Chinese employees highlight that they aim at improving their management, leadership and cooperation (as in Wang et al., 2013). Our findings show that Chinese managers see the leadership style within their organisation as a mixed style of Chinese and Western leadership approaches, whereby one leader emphasises that the Chinese leadership style in governmental organisations is more a "military style" in contrast to privately owned organisations. It might be related to the perception of African management and leadership being portrayed as negative and related to negative stereotypes such as authoritarian, bureaucratic, ineffective and conservative (as described in Handley & Louw, 2016); that Chinese employees do not refer to African leadership within their organisation at all. Tanzanian and Chinese employees therefore might feel that there are strong divergences in how to do the job, how to manage and how to lead.

Chinese employees highlight their feelings of being reprimanded by the Tanzanian government because of employment laws according to which they cannot "punish" or "fire" Tanzanian employees. Meanwhile, Tanzanians talk about their experiences of missing trustful relations and bonds, as well as loyalty towards the Chinese organisation. This might be because of the lack of value-concepts such as consensus, morals and stewardship, or even Ubuntu (see Bolden & Kirk, 2009; Nkomo, 2011) within the organisation. At the same time, Chinese employees do not see Tanzanian employees as compliant towards the organisation – they even describe them as dishonest, disobedient and unskilled, whilst Tanzanian employees feel excluded and unknowledgeable of the information channels within the organisation. They feel excluded from the hierarchies and feel that Chinese employees relate to a strongly authoritarian and paternalistic leadership style (as described in the literature by Chen et al. (2014), whilst excluding Tanzanians from training opportunities in the organisation because of language, learning and motivation constraints.

Language problems, however, do not only impact on self-development and training opportunities within the organisation, but on all intercultural communication and cooperation experiences within the organisation: Chinese and Tanzanian employees feel that communication is very difficult because of restrictions in language ability.

Finally, focusing on the way Chinese and Tanzanian employees relate to the work conditions and the atmosphere within the organisation, Chinese employees see themselves as hard-working and happy within a good work atmosphere. In contrast, Tanzanian employees report their concerns about their mostly illegal work status, working for the organisation without a work contract and therefore on a "hire-and-fire" basis, unprotected by the labour law, whilst Chinese employees all hold legal work contracts.

Neither Chinese nor Tanzanian employees have described the possible similarities between Chinese Confucianism and African Ubuntu (as described by Xing et al., 2016). Also, Chinese and Tanzanian employees seem to be far from ideally constructing cultural hybrid forms of organisation or cultural "third spaces" as proposed by Jackson et al. (2013). However, the first steps to create "third spaces" could be made by taking the mutual wishes for future collaboration into account.

Concluding remarks and recommendations

The purpose of this chapter was to provide insights into the experiences of Chinese and Tanzanian employees working in a governmental Chinese organisation in Tanzania. The aim was to respond to the three research questions which focused on the experiences of Chinese and Tanzanian employees in cooperation within the organisation; on the views regarding the societal and organisational work environment; and on the cultural values involved, from the viewpoint of the employees.

Findings show that Chinese and Tanzanian employees encounter differences with regard to understanding the organisation's strategy, decision-making, leadership styles, and expectations regarding the organisation; and the position, recruitment and recruitment procedures, training opportunities and self-development within the organisation; the use of language as well as the organisational culture, atmosphere and working conditions. The differences between members of the two groups are associated with misunderstandings, insecurities and emotions which are experienced as negative, such as frustration or fear. It can be assumed that intercultural training and mentorship with regard to an improved mutual, intercultural understanding could lead to an improved work atmosphere and culture, improved learning and working opportunities for all employees and an increase in effectiveness, leadership and production.

Future research should focus on the macro-, meso- and micro-levels of cooperation whilst exploring the views, perceptions and concrete behaviours of employees with regard to the cooperation of Chinese and Tanzanian employees. Furthermore, future research should take different intersectionalities into account, such as culture, gender, age and social class, to differentiate the experiences of employees not only with regard to national belonging, but also referring to other sociocultural categories and their influences on the employees. The possibilities of creating a hybrid "third space" culture could be studied through research, and its implementation should be explored.

As highlighted in previous research (Xing et al., 2014; Xing et al., 2016), this research also points out that intercultural training should be offered in Chinese organisations investing in African countries to prepare Chinese as well as African/Tanzanian employees to deal with culture-specific phenomena in Chinese organisations and create an improved and in-depth cultural understanding. Intercultural training should focus on cognitive levels (knowledge about culture and working cultures), affective levels (dealing with emotions) and behavioural levels (ways of behaving in certain situations and contexts). The intercultural training should be accompanied by language courses in Chinese (Mandarin) and Kiswahili, one of the major African languages spoken in Tanzania and East Africa.

Acknowledgements

This work is based on the research supported in part by a Research Grant of Rhodes University, Grahamstown, South Africa. We thank our interviewees, the participating organisation and Rhodes University for their support.

References

Alden, C. (2006). China in Africa. *Survival, 47*(3), 147–164.
Alden, C., & Davis, M. (2010). A profile of the operations of Chinese multinationals in Africa. *South African Journal of International Affairs, 13*(1), 83–96.
Alden, C., Large, D., & Soares de Oliviera, R. (2008). *China returns to Africa: A rising power and a continent embrace.* New York: Columbia University Press.
Bird, A., & Fang, T. (2009). Editorial: Cross-cultural management in the age of globalization. *International Journal of Cross Cultural Management, 9*(2), 139–143.
Bolden, R., & Krik, P. (2009). African leadership: Surfacing new understandings through leadership development. *International Journal of Cross Cultural Management, 9*(1), 69–86.
Chan, K. W., & Wyatt, T. (2007). Quality of work life: A study of employees in Shanghai, China. *Asia Pacific Business Review, 13*(4), 501–517.
Chan, N. N., Walker, C., & Gleaves, A. (2015). An exploration of students' lived experiences of using smartphones in diverse learning contexts using a hermeneutic phenomenological approach. *Computers and Education, 82*, 96–106.
Charmaz, K. (2014). *Constructing grounded theory* (2nd ed.). Los Angeles, CA: Sage.
Chen, X.-P., Eberly, M. B., Chiang, T.-J., Farh, J.-L., & Cheng, B. S. (2014). Affective trust in Chinese leaders: Linking paternalistic leadership to employee performance. *Journal of Management, 40*(3), 796–819.
Creswell, J. W. (2015). *Essential skills for the qualitative researcher.* New York: Sage.

Denzin, N. K., & Lincoln, Y. S. (Eds.). (2000). *Handbook of qualitative research* (2nd ed.). Thousand Oaks, CA: Sage Publications.

Dilthey, W. (2002 [1910]). The formation of the historical world in the human sciences. In R. A. Makkreel & F. Rodi (Eds.), *Wilhelm Dilthey selected works: The formation of the historical world in the human sciences* (Vol. III). Princeton, NJ: Princeton University Press.

Dutton, J. E., Frost, P., Worline, M., Lilius, J., & Kanov, J. (2002). Leading in times of trauma. *Harvard Business Review, 80*(1), 54–61.

Gadamer, H. G. (1997). *Truth and method* (2nd rev. ed.). New York: Continuum.

Graham, C., & Bell, A. (2016). *The career advancement experiences of female faculty of color in athletic training education programs.* Kansas State University Libraries. New Prairie Press. Adult Education Research Consortium, 2016 Conference Proceedings, Charlotte, NC. [Online.] Retrieved December 1, 2017 from http://newprairiepress.org/cgi/viewcontent.cgi?article=1005&context=aerc

Handley, R. C., & Louw, M. J. (2016). *The similarities and differences between South African and Chinese Definitions and descriptions of leadership style: A mining joint venture case study.* Proceedings of the 28th annual conference of the Southern African Institute of Management Scientists [Online.] Retrieved September 20, 2016 from www.up.ac.za/media/shared/643/ZP_Files/2016/Papers/hrl19_full.zp97858.pdf

Heidegger, M. (1962). *Being and time.* New York: Harper & Row.

Holvino, E. (2010). Intersections: The simultaneity of race, gender and class in organisation studies. *Gender, Work & Organization, 17*(3), 248–277.

Humphreys, M., & Bates, R. (2005). Political institutions and economic policies: Lessons from Africa. *British Journal of Political Science, 35*, 403–428.

Jackson, T. (2004). *Management and change in Africa: A cross-cultural perspective.* London: Psychology Press.

Jackson, T., Louw, L., & Zhao, S. (2013). China in sub-Saharan Africa: Implications for HRM policy and practice at organizational level. *The International Journal of Human Resource Management, 24*(13), 2512–2533.

Kamoche, K. N. (2002). Introduction: Human resource management in Africa. *International Journal of Human Resource Management, 13*(7), 993–997.

Kamoche, K. N., Debra, Y. A., Horwitz, F. M., & Muuka, G. N. (2004). *Managing human resources in Africa.* London: Routledge.

Kazoka, L. (2016, June 16). Tanzania: Chinese companies to recruit en masse at job fair in Dar. *Tanzania Daily News* [Online.] Retrieved November 13, 2017 from http://allafrica.com/stories/201606160394.html

King, N., Kruger, N., & Pretorius, J. (2007). Knowledge management in a multicultural environment: A South African perspective. *Aslib Proceedings, 59*(3), 285–299.

Lee, M. C., Melber, H., Naidu, S., & Taylor, I. (2007). *China in Africa.* Nordiska Afrika Institutet, Uppsala [Online]. Retrieved October 11, 2016 from www.divaportal.org/smash/get/diva2:240876/FULLTEXT02

Lincoln, Y. S., & Guba, E. G. (1985). *Naturalistic inquiry.* Beverly Hills, CA: Sage.

Lindberg, H. V. M. (2015). *China in Africa.* Thesis. Roskilde University Digital Archive [Online]. Retrieved August 10, 2017 from http://Rudar.ruc.dk/handle/1800/24010

Majani, F. (2013, October 4). China drops anchor in Tanzania. *Mail and Guardian* [Online]. Retrieved December 1, 2017 from http://mg.co.za/article/2013-10-04-00-china-drops-anchor-in-tanzania

Marfelt, M. M. (2016). Grounded intersectionality. *Equality, Diversity and Inclusion: An International Journal, 35*(1), 31–47.

Mayer, C.-H. (2008). *Managing conflict across cultures, values and identities: A case study in the South African automotive industry.* Marburg, Germany: Tectum Publishers.

Mayer, C.-H. (2011). *The meaning of sense of coherence in transcultural management.* Münster, Germany: Waxmann.

Mayer, C.-H., Boness, C. M., & Louw, L. (2016). *Perspectives of Chinese and Tanzanian employees on intercultural cooperation in a private Chinese organisation in Tanzania.* 10th China Goes Global Conference, University of Macerata, Italy, 26–28 July 2016.

Mayer, C.-H., Boness, C. M., & Louw, L. (2017a). *Chinese managers' views on cooperating with Tanzanian employees in a Chinese organisation in Dar-Es-Salaam, Tanzania.* Poster presentation at the European Congress of Psychology, Amsterdam, The Netherlands, 11–14 July 2017.

Mayer, C.-H., Boness, C. M., & Louw, L. (2017b). Perceptions of Chinese and Tanzanian employees regarding intercultural colloboration. *South African Journal of Human Resource Management, 15,* 11 pages. https://doi.org/10.4102/sajhrm.v15i0.921

Mayer, C.-H., Boness, C. M., Louw, L., & Louw, T. (2016). *Intra- and inter-group perceptions of Chinese and Tanzanian employees in intercultural cooperation.* 28th SAIMS (The Southern Africa Institute for Management Scientists) conference "Managing in Resource Restricted Times: Make Everyday Matter", University of Pretoria, Pretoria, South Africa, 4–7 September 2016.

Mayer, C.-H., Louw, L., & Boness, C. M. (2016). *Managing Chinese-African business interactions: Growing intercultural competence in organizations.* Cham, Switzerland: Palgrave Macmillan.

New African Magazine. (2015). *China's long history in Africa* [Online]. Retrieved October 16, 2016 from http://newafricanmagazine.com/chinas-long-history-africa/

Ni, Y. (2015, December). Gaining momentum: Johannesburg summit to consolidate China-Africa partnership. FOCAC Johannesburg Summit, 26. November 2015. *Special Issue Beijing Review,* 20–23.

Nkomo, S. M. (2011). A postcolonial and anti-colonial reading of "African" leadership and management in organization studies: Tensions, contradictions and possibilities. *Organization, 18*(3), 356–386.

Pigato, M., & Tang, W. (2015). *China in Africa: Expanding economic ties in an evolving global context. Investing in Africa Forum: Partnering to accelerate investment, industrialization and results in Africa.* Conference Addis Ababa, Ethiopia, March 2015 [Online]. Retrieved October 15, 2017 from www.worldbank.org/content/dam/Worldbank/Event/Africa/Investing%20in%20Africa%20Forum/2015/investing-in-africa-forum-china-and-africa-expanding-economic-ties-in-an-evolving-global-context.pdf

Poggenpoel, M. (1998). Data analysis in qualitative research. In A. S. de Vos (Ed.), *Research on grass roots: A primer for the caring professions.* Pretoria, South Africa: Van Schaik.

Power, M., & Mohan, G. (2008). Good friends & good partners: The new face of China-African co-operation. *Review of African Political Economy, 35*(115), 5–6.

Prasad, A., Pringle, J. K., & Konrad, A. M. (2006). Examining the contours of workplace diversity. In A. M. Konrad, A. Prasad, & J. K. Pringle (Eds.), *Handbook of workplace diversity* (pp. 1–22). London: Sage.

Ratner, C. (2002). Subjectivity and objectivity in qualitative methodology. *Forum Qualitative Social Research*, *3* [Online]. Retrieved October 15, 2016 from http://nbn-resolving.de/urn:nbn:de:0114-fqs0203160

Syed, J., & Özbilgin, M. (2009). A relational framework for international transfer of diversity management practices. *International Journal of Human Resource Management*, *20*(12), 2435–2453.

Terre Blanche, M., Durrheim, K., & Kelly, K. (2006). First steps in qualitative data analysis. In M. Terre Blanche, K. Durrheim, & D. Painter (Eds.), *Research in practice. Applied methods for the social sciences* (pp. 321–344). Cape Town, SA: University of Cape Town Press.

Tracy, S. J. (2010). Qualitative quality: Eight "big-tent" criteria for excellent qualitative research. *Qualitative Inquiry*, *16*(10), 837–851.

Vorster, L., Kipnis, E., Bebek, G., & Demangeot, C. (2019). Brokering intercultural relations in the Rainbow Nation: Introducing intercultural marketing. *Journal of Macromarketing*, *40*(1), 51–72.

Walsh, K., Fleming, S. S., & Enz, C. A. (2016). Give and you shall receive: Investing in the careers of women professionals. *Career Development International*, *21*(2), 117–143.

Wang, D., Freeman, S., & Zhu, C. J. (2013). Personality traits and cross-cultural competence of Chinese expatriate managers: A socio-analytic and institutional perspective. *The International Journal of Human Resource Management*, *24*(20), 1–9.

Wang, P., & Walumbwa, F. O. (2007). Family-friendly programs, organizational commitment, and work withdrawal: The moderating role of transformational leadership. *Personnel Psychology*, *60*, 397–427.

Weinberger, L. A. (2009). Emotional intelligence, leadership style, and perceived leadership effectiveness. *Advances in Developing Human Resources*, *11*(6), 747–772.

Wells, C. C., Gill, R., & McDonald, J. (2015). "'Us foreigners'": Intersectionality in a scientific organization. *Equality, Diversity and Inclusion: An International Journal*, *34*(6), 539–553.

Woodley, X. M., & Lockard, M. (2016). Womanism and snowball sampling: Engaging marginalized populations in holistic research. *The Qualitative Report*, *21*(2), 321–329.

Xing, Y., Cooper, C. L., Liu, Y., & Tarba, S. Y. (2014). Managing African employees of Chinese firms in Africa: Chinese managers' HRM practices. *Academy of Management Proceedings 2014* [Online]. Retrieved October 15, 2016 from http://proceedings.aom.org/content/2014/1/14342.short

Xing, Y., Liu, Y., Tarba, S. Y., & Cooper, C. L. (2016). Intercultural influences on managing African employees of Chinese firms in Africa: Chinese managers' HRM practices. *International Business Review*, *25*(1), Part A, 28–41.

Yin, R. K. (2009). *Case study research: Design and methods* (4th ed.). London: Sage.

Zanoni, P., Janssens, M., Benschop, Y., & Nkomo, S. (2010). Editorial: Unpacking diversity, grasping inequality: Rethinking difference through critical perspectives. *Organization*, *17*(1), 9–29.

Zheng, C., & Lamond, D. (2009). A Chinese style of HRM: Exploring the ancient texts. *Chinese Management Studies*, *3*(4), 258–271.

11 Chinese firms in Uganda

The important role of the mediator

Charles Mbalyohere

This chapter focuses on Uganda as a country context to offer insights into the little understood HRM practices deployed by Chinese firms in the region. As has been noted in other chapters, the entry of these firms into this fast-growing and dynamically evolving region in the last decade has taken on unprecedented levels, with the volume of Chinese inward FDI steadily rising from less than US$3 billion in 2003 to over US$30 billion in 2013 (e.g. Gandhi, 2018). This decisively upward trend is evident in the whole region and reflects a Pan-African trajectory. While the trend is welcome, in light of Africa's development needs, there is concern about the quality of FDI (Tutor2U, 2019). As an example, the job creation rate (1.78 people per $1 million of Greenfield FDI into Africa) is significantly lower than in other regions receiving Chinese FDI (2.24 people per $1 million of Greenfield FDI) (Garcia-Herrero & Xu, 2019). One of the key reasons why the mediator role discussed in this chapter is important, as part of strategies to improve the quality of Chinese FDI in Africa, is rooted in exactly this observation.

Uganda's case is especially interesting as the country has developed a reputation as a good springboard for entry into the generally more fragile markets in countries like the DRC and South Sudan (e.g. Mbalyohere, Lawton, Boojihawon, & Viney, 2017). This can be traced back to the locational advantages that have been established over the past 30 years in which relative political stability and economic progress have been restored. The country has boasted an average GDP growth of 6%–7% per annum (World Bank, 2019). In addition to the continuing development of the agriculture/agro-processing sector, which is the main base of the economy, as well other sectors like tourism, small- to medium-scale industry and international labour export, the country is at an advanced stage of preparing for oil and gas production (e.g. Kjaer, 2015). Notwithstanding the challenges that other African countries have experienced in managing their extractive resources, as a reflection of what is commonly referred to as the 'resource curse' (Polus & Tycholiz, 2016; Badeeb, Lean, & Clark, 2017), all eyes are now set on Uganda to establish whether it will emerge as a new reference for constructive exploitation of extractive resources that are in rich abundance in Africa. There is however lots of concern given levels of corruption and graft, especially in the public sector (Tradingeconomics, 2018).

What we were looking for in this study

In this chapter, we assess evidence in Uganda that can contribute to our understanding of HRM in the region in view of the Chinese influence. Specifically, we investigate what Chinese firms are doing to attempt to succeed using hybrid HRM strategies. There is also evidence of a growing intensity of competition between key Asian countries, for example China, India and Malaysia, in the various country markets on the continent (Cheru & Obi, 2011). This might benefit the continent as it gets exposed to diverse models of doing business and HRM. It is hence a far cry from the times in most African countries when making such choices was unheard of, since there was most times only one option which was state sponsored.

Contrary to the assumptions in extant literatures that the effects from the home markets might be the decisive factor surrounding HRM and wider strategic patterns, some researchers suggest that it is actually the host market dynamics that are critical (e.g. Brewster, Wood, & Brookes, 2008). Insights into how this host country influence practically plays out remain sparse. Perceptions of the collective public in the recent past have generally been influenced by some bad apples that have exposed an alarming level of unscrupulousness, especially regarding working conditions and basic health and safety standards (Cooke, 2014). Cooke attributes some of this behaviour to still low levels of experience by Chinese managers in operating in international markets. The mediators that are identified in this study could be one of the ways in which this lack of experience can be compensated for. Some researchers have in fact suggested that such mediators are not only important to MNEs for their operational and market value, but also for their institutional value, such as access to local knowledge and local social capital (e.g. Berger, Choi, & Kim, 2011; Kamoche & Siebers, 2015). The informal institutions underlined in this study constitute a key element of this knowledge and capital. In light of MNE activities across cultures, this emerges as a critically important function of mediators in enabling successful operations in new market contexts. Mediators also emerge as key agents in assessing the performance of MNE subsidiaries, thus constituting a major consideration in formulating and implementing successful international strategies (e.g. Lazarova, Peretz, & Fried, 2017). A major international debate has been about how local employees are generally treated in such subsidiaries. The generally negative perception about how Chinese firms treat local employees has been recently questioned by some research, however (e.g. GCR, 2019). This may point to some quiet organisational learning and adaptation on the part of Chinese firms in the face of increased scrutiny.

We now turn to an explanation of the methodology of the study that informs this chapter. This is then followed by a discussion of the key findings of the study, locating them in extant literatures and identifying elements that can make a contribution to knowledge among the still limited research-based evidence in the area.

How we conducted this research

The assessment of the situation in Uganda is based on an in-depth case study of a Chinese firm that deals in machinery for agriculture and agro-processing, construction, carpentry and welding, among others. There is particular interest in an African manager who emerges as a mediator between his Chinese managers and the employees over whom he is given extensive power. He appears to be the core person in helping the Chinese managers to understand the host communities in which the firm has to get embedded and the formal and informal institutions that it has to deal with.

The firm entered Uganda around 2008 and so had been in the country for about a decade at the time of publishing the findings of this study. The Chinese founder originally intended to be based in Tanzania or Mozambique, but was persuaded by Chinese associates already established in Uganda that it was a strategically better place, especially given its central location in the Great Lakes Region. The firm started off with a team of five (three Chinese managers and two local Africans, including our focal manager) but has since grown to over 30 (eight Chinese and over 22 local staff), with two subsidiaries in the capital of the host country. It has increasingly not only established itself in the host country, but also started expanding into the neighbouring and generally more fragile countries, including South Sudan and DRC.

While the lead African manager at the firm was the main interest in our study, the views of the local employees were considered important too and they helped place the observations about the local manager in a broader emerging HRM context. Twelve of these employees were hence interviewed. They ranged from technicians to salespersons and hence constituted the full range of activities at the firm. They in addition reflected a balanced gender mix. An African lead manager of a competing Chinese firm and the Chinese manager of a smaller firm in the same sector were also interviewed to corroborate what the focal manager was saying. The core manager was interviewed twice, thus offering an opportunity to discuss various issues at length and to follow up on some others. In addition to two face-to-face interviews, the lead researcher had the opportunity to hold multiple short phone conversations with him. These conversations served to further deepen understanding of his role in the firm, especially the mediator role that is highlighted in the study. The qualitative data was further supported by various documents, including newspaper articles, that addressed the presence of Chinese firms in Uganda and other African countries, with particular attention to human resource management.

In effect, the study therefore relied on a mix between elements of a narrative qualitative approach (to accommodate the experience and stories of the individual in question) and case study method (to accommodate the broader context of the firm(s) in question). Some of the researchers that have extensively explained the use of such methods include Eisenhardt (1989), Yin (2017) and Stake (2013).

What we found from our research

The mediator role

The most important finding in the study was the identification of a pattern of mediation by the lead African manager, who was the link between the Chinese managers and groups of other stakeholders, especially the African employees, the hosting communities and the regulatory institutions. From the moment the founding Chinese managers entered the Ugandan market, they appeared fully dependent on the resourcefulness of a carefully chosen local manager to guide them in adapting to the market. Here is how the manager recalls those early times:

> The biggest challenge when they come to Uganda is that they don't speak English. So they didn't know basics like where to drive when you are going anywhere. Lucky enough, we were staying together in one area. Going to buy food, I drove together with them. So, which food they need, I speak for them. We buy, we go to park, we drive together home. I kept moving them around town.

While there was support and advice from a network of other Chinese investors, active not only in Uganda but also in neighbouring countries like Tanzania and Kenya, the identification and recruitment of a committed local manager emerged as critical to the strategy of adapting to the new market. The local manager recalls thus further:

> They wanted to invest in Madagascar but a few of the Chinese who were in Uganda gave the founding manager interest. Uganda basically is connecting many countries. So like Eastern Congo, it depends on Uganda. Same for Rwanda, it depends on Uganda. South Sudan is not a country without Uganda.

In making choices here, nuanced contextual factors that qualitatively differ in various countries might act as an important influence (e.g. Child & Marinova, 2014). The general openness of the host economy since pro-market reforms were initiated in the early 1990s was conducive (Kuteesa, Tumusiime-Mutebile, Whitworth, & Williamson, 2010). In fact, it was this ease of entry and the freedom to do business that played a critical role in finally deciding to enter Uganda.

An important observation was that this identification of a local manager and the negotiations that followed with him were generally informal, characterised by a high dependency on developing trust, mutual confidence and an appreciation of the cultural challenges involved. The manager went far beyond what would be expected in such a situation in traditional circumstances to make his case. In regularly accompanying the Chinese managers to help them with their shopping, negotiating possibilities of car parking with local authorities in an otherwise restricted area of the city or explaining the importance of key public holidays to the managers, he emerged as an all-rounder who was needed to understand and practice the managerial role even outside contemporary boundaries. There were no benchmarks and no references to draw on. Instead there was the possibility to explore new possibilities and to experiment with a new business relationship. It is the opportunity to do this that partly motivated the local manager and contributed to the intrinsic value he derived from the effort. Here is how he reminisced:

> One thing I like about the Chinese is that if they have given that respect for you, they will always do it. And once they have given that trust for you, they will always live to trust. And once they have failed to trust you, it is very hard for them to convert their minds back to you.

The comments indicate that the manager was also carefully studying and observing human behaviour that would be critical to establishing a good working relationship. This also involved going deeper to understand values and the home country cultural orientations that informed them. In a way, it was an example of cross-cultural communication taking place, and letting it inform managerial views.

Table 11.1 summarises the key mediatory roles that were identified and their characteristics. These are discussed in detail in the following sections. There are also sample excerpts to represent the body of data that was gathered.

In developing an integrated understanding of the preceding roles and establishing their strategic importance, the following model (Figure 11.1) emerged as the proposition for the mediatory interaction of the mediating manager with various other stakeholders. It was a co-developed synthesis of understanding and sense making by the respondents to the semi-structured interviews, supported by the probing of the researchers. The iterations that were a core ingredient of the data analysis enhanced the rigour that led to the emergence of this explorationary model. Srivastava and Hopwood (2009) propose that such an

Table 11.1 Mediator roles

Mediator role	Key characteristics	Sample excerpts	Broader comments
Mediating between Chinese managers and African employees	Able to bridge values-based differences Ability to be trusted by both sides Able to represent the broader purpose of the firm	*He gave me that authority to employ staff. And he gave me that authority to disqualify someone who is not performing.* >(local Manager)	All these characteristics depended on being able to explore the possibilities that the situation offered, while realising what was realistic or not
Mediating between Chinese managers and hosting communities	Able to think of the broader issues affecting communities Able to gradually dismantle often negative perceptions in the communities Able to act as an accurate cultural interpreter	*While we are not against investment in the area, we do ask that these things . . . do not cause harm to our people and environment.* >(local community leader talking to an African manager)	Effective mediation here would help the firm to get strongly embedded in the hosting community and to play a constructive role as a corporate citizen
Mediating between Chinese managers and regulatory institutions	Able to advise on regulatory law Able to explain informal aspects of the law	*We have decided that workers temporarily stop working until Thursday as we engage the managers of the company.* >(Town clerk of a city division after discussions with worker representatives/mediators)	This form of mediation was a contribution to developing a shared understanding of emerging institutions and how they could be approached
Mediating between Chinese managers and the market	Able to explain the dynamics of the national market, especially the preferences of the clients and the business culture Able to help the senior managers to identify and exploit cross-border opportunities Able to interpret trends in the region	*I have been in this business for long and I travel around for the firm . . . So I think David (Chinese manager) looked far and that is why he came to do all those investments.* >(local manager commenting on opportunities in the region)	In essence, this would ultimately be the most important measure of success of the mediation model.

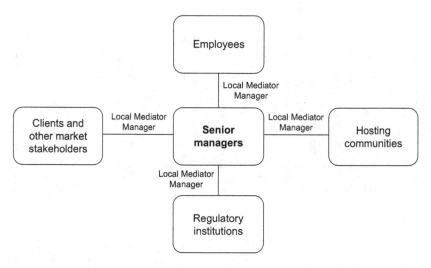

Figure 11.1 Mediatory influences in emerging Asian–African HRM systems

iteration, when approached as a reflexive and not a repetitive, mechanical process, translates into continuous meaning-making and progressive focusing of the findings of qualitative analysis. The model depicts the central role of the mediator and therefore the potential to exert significant influence on the dynamics surrounding the emerging version of Sino-African HRM.

Mediation between Chinese managers and African employees

This mediation was at the heart of an emerging Sino-African HRM strategy with some chance of working fairly well. The key element was that the managers from China had only an elementary understanding of the employee situation in the host market. All they depended on was what they had heard from their friends and fellow Chinese investors. This observation is in line with the findings of some researchers who have highlighted the network- and informal-based approaches to gathering information and making decisions by Chinese managers (e.g. Giese & Thiel, 2015; Peng, Wang, & Jiang, 2008). In developing into an effective mediator, the African manager needed to accumulate several skills, some of which are summarised in Table 11.1. One of the most important of such skills was the capability to adapt to evolving market circumstances, including regionalisation, and to grow with the needs of the firm. The manager was hence able to understand his bosses well with time. This in turn put him in a much better position to explain decisions to the rest of the employees. Having recruited them and knowing their circumstances in the host country, he was then also in a good position to, as much as possible, represent them before the bosses. It was consequently a constant to and fro between the two sides as he tried to bridge often seriously different views. Here is how he comments about his handling of the employees:

I always sit them down and advise them.

All the employees interviewed in this study appeared to deeply acknowledge this supportive role.

Initially, it was very hard to align the two positions and he at one time opted to walk away. It was only the quick realisation by his bosses that they badly needed him that made them soften up. Here is how he further recollects:

One day I got a misunderstanding with K (the senior Chinese manager). He got mad at me, he gave me my salary, he told me to leave. I accepted. I told him it is fine. I got my things and left. I was leaving actually, then they called and brought me back. He asked why and indeed I explained it to him. 'My work is very clear, you saw my papers, I have no reasons why you should tell me to go and start cleaning the floor, start cleaning the toilets'.

With time, it became relatively easier. Both sides developed trust in him and he felt motivated to give his best as part of developing the hybrid HRM system. His confidence and his sophistication at managing the situation grew with time too. In a sense, his development as part HRM manager was a mix of informally designed contributions from his bosses and his own proactive initiative and creativity. The latter aspect seemed to dominate in the mix though. This observation depicts the self-initiative and the drive that such managers need in order to succeed in this largely uncharted territory. The confident and hopeful note that the manager struck, when he summarised the advantages of Chinese engagement in Africa when juxtaposed on the challenges he faced, underscores the intrinsic value of the empowerment of sorts that he had. Here are some of his thoughts:

Still I see China as the 'only' country doing something to really develop Africa . . . . All that I am saying is not because I have a job with them but because I have seen with my own eyes and had experience. . . . I am not decampaigning, but that is what is on the ground.

I now even have potential to be employed by big projects like Karuma (the largest dam project being constructed by Chinese in East Africa).

Mediation between Chinese managers and the hosting communities

An equally important role for the African manager was to mediate between the Chinese senior managers and the hosting communities (Figure 11.1). This was a significantly more challenging, but important role, in light of the sub-cultural and institutional diversity common in the region (Kamoche, Siebers, Mamman, & Newenham-Kahindi, 2015). With hardly any understanding of the details of the local culture, including the language, rituals and, more specifically, the business culture by his bosses, he was effectively their main means of explanation and interpretation of what was right and what was wrong. It all depended on the accuracy, consistency and comprehensiveness with which he could do this. Yet he realised that his bosses would crosscheck with their fellow bosses in their circles to verify his views. By being accurate, consistent and comprehensive, the ground was set for trust and confidence to grow (Horwitz, 2012). It apparently then became ever less necessary for his managers to verify his advice and analyses. This is what he observed:

> So, I kept realizing that with Chinese, it is all about trust and all about confidence. Where there is challenge, you don't sit and challenge yourself. Face them and explain the situation, it is like this, like this. There they understand.

With time, one would expect the Chinese managers to make an effort to directly interact with the communities themselves. But this was still far in the future. For one, they needed to become more fluent with the official language of the country – English, not to mention the basics of some of the local languages, not least Luganda which was unofficially the local business language. Cultural acceptance depended, to a significant level, on evidence of efforts to master these basics. In turn, it also depended on the effectiveness with which the mediator laid a good foundation on which to build this deeper cultural engagement or crossvergence as some scholars have increasingly called it (e.g. Jackson, 2011; Jackson, Louw, & Zhao, 2013).

An interesting observation was that the local manager was also increasingly being given responsibility to mediate the interaction with local communities in neighbouring countries where the firm was finding new markets. The skills of mediation were apparently now reaching a regional, cross-border perspective. As an example, the manager severally referred, during the interviews, to new clients in South Sudan where he had to take the lead in negotiations and in explaining expectations from both sides. He observes thus:

> You can't understand how much Uganda is participating in South Sudan. . . . Actually South Sudan is not a country without Uganda.

Sino-African cultural mediation and HRM development is therefore increasingly assuming a Pan-African dynamic as the mediators share experiences and as they help shape coherence, alignment and synergies across borders. This might play an important role in the future in making it much easier for Asian firms to do business across African borders. It might also make it easier for labour to move across these borders (e.g. Cross & Cliffe, 2017) as regional economic integration becomes placed high up on the political agendas of African countries. South Sudan, for example, got admitted to the East African Community not too long ago and the DRC has made a widely publicised and excitedly debated application to be admitted (New Vision, 2016; Mutambo, 2019). With all indication that more firms from Asia, especially China and India, are set to contribute to increased Asian FDI in the region (Gandhi, 2018), these early experiences with HRM-oriented mediation can play an important role in improving the quality of the FDI. The market entrants that will constitute this new wave of FDI are consequently bound to find a much larger pool of local managers with some experience in working in Chinese firms and playing the mediating role. Conversely, there will be a larger population of Chinese managers and employees who could be recruited by the new entrants. Ultimately, the extent of what is generally referred to as 'liability of foreignness' will have a less negative effect on the activities of these firms (Gorostidi-Martinez & Zhao, 2017). In such a case, a differentiation might increasingly become evident on the African continent with some countries emerging with stronger locational advantages than others, by virtue of how efficiently they manage this skills development process (e.g. Mbalyohere et al., 2017).

But as noted in the introduction to the chapter, there are still some serious question marks about the proportionality of benefit by China compared to the hosting African countries (e.g. Ado & Su, 2016). A point of particular concern is the extent to which Chinese firms bring in Chinese workers to work in these firms at all levels rather than extensively training local employees to perform the jobs in question (e.g. Kamoche & Siebers, 2015). The room for high-skilled knowledge transfer gets therefore narrowed with the exception of the mediators that are highlighted in the study. Given that such mediators are only individuals in the firms, the rate at which a critical level in numbers of such managers can be attained is low. It would significantly enhance skills development and HR resource profiles if the commitment to train comprehensively was extended to lower levels of the employee structure. This calls for a more proactive stance by the hosting government in negotiating terms and rules governing Asian FDI, without making it terminally difficult to do business. A united African Union stand is a possible strategy, as the numbers would put pressure on the Chinese and other Asian home governments to in turn put pressure on their firms to cooperate more and support higher local participation. But there are some suggestions that this ability to control their firms might be exaggerated (Albert, 2017).

Mediation between Chinese managers and regulatory institutions

The mediation between the Chinese managers and various regulatory institutions was one of the most critical roles that the local manager played (Figure 11.1). From his narration, he repeatedly literally stood between the two sides to bring about an understanding. It is also here that the Chinese managers depicted most unease and looked very vulnerable. The lack of understanding of the details of regulation created a situation in which a good local mediator was of existential importance to them. Such a mediator conversely needed to be well versed with the regulations of the host market. While there was a company lawyer who occasionally paid a visit and was approached whenever an emergency arose, the operational reference was the mediator who was at hand effectively every day. Under normal circumstances, the manager actually needed to do a training course in regulatory law in order to give more solid advice and to make the right decisions. With more Asian, especially Chinese firms, set to enter African markets, more such regulatory law-oriented mediation would be needed. Deeply grounded local mediators would hence be in high currency. It is though also important to be aware of the political dimensions of stakeholdership, especially in this stakeholder category (Mbalyohere & Lawton, 2018). As more and more Chinese firms enter the continent and as African and the Chinese governments figure out how to shape the new partnership, these elements might play an even more important, yet still thinly understood role. Here is how one of the mediating agents commented to a Chinese manager:

> We can be your eyes, and ears on the ground to monitor and handle labour issues.

The imagery of eyes and ears is strong and points to the extent of engagement that is possible once there is commitment from and trust by both sides.

Mediation between Chinese managers and clients/market stakeholders

In essence, the satisfaction of clients and other key market stakeholders was the most important measure of performance by the firm. It would ultimately affect referrals that would culminate in new clients, let alone repeat business. Effective mediation was hence of critical importance here too (Figure 11.1). While many of the issues raised under mediation for local communities are applicable here too, this was a more specific mediation and it went to the heart of the survival of the firm. The under-standing of the specific needs of the clients and the market at large by the senior managers depended on there being very good explanations by the mediator. Conversely, the clients needed to understand the business and the advantages they would accrue in not searching elsewhere. To this end, the mediator observes:

I had to drive him all over Uganda.

This was effectively a market orientation tour and an induction into the market. Given that most of the purchases constituted a substantive invest-ment by the clients, the mediation could not be taken lightly. The media-tor therefore needed to not only have a comprehensive understanding of the different machines on offer, but to also be able to explain the techni-cal details with a fitting level of simplicity. The interviews suggested that such a manager needed both a good technical background and the capa-bility to translate this into persuasive propositions from a market view point. An article in one of Uganda's two leading newspapers underlines his competence at explaining technical details and the level of autonomy he was meantime being given to do this (Nasasira, 2018). There was also an indication of the need for the opportunity to spend lots of time learn-ing about the machines and testing out usage as a preparation for facing the potential clients.

Another outstanding feature was that the mediator many times took the initiative to search for potential clients, for example by visiting agri-cultural machinery shows and making cold calls to farmers who could potentially afford to purchase. The Uganda Manufacturers Association, which is a leader in the whole region, registered him as the lead person at the firm. Ultimately, the early market presence meant that extra care needed to be taken to set positive precedent. All this was happening in the context of lack of extensive formal market research data. There was therefore a disproportionate dependence on informal data and its equally informal interpretation. Once again, the local manager played a critical role in making interpretations that would have far-reaching implications for the firm.

Integrated perspectives about the mediatory role

In bringing all the preceding roles together, an all-round picture emerges. For a more established firm, this would be too much responsibility del-egated to one person. In this case, there were some advantages of doing this at this early stage of market entry. Above everything, it focused the attention of both the mediator and his bosses. As long as the manager delivered on expectations and he felt motivated to continue, the Chinese managers had no good reason to change the situation. Their increasing dependence on him was reflected in the almost desperate effort to make him change his mind when at one time he was annoyed and decided to quit, as was noted earlier.

However, it would be hard to continue like that as the market grew and demands from clients intensified. The managers would need to either empower more local managers to achieve some level of specialisation or they would need to get more involved themselves by acting on their learning. Ultimately, the sustainability of the emerging Sino-African HRM model depended on openness to widening responsibility and accommodating more mediators. In light of regional economic integration dynamics and the new opportunities that were arising in the market to enable growth, managerial vision would need to look much farther than focusing on a single individual. There was a need for more systematic, formal and well-resourced training programs in which the key aspects of the model would be addressed and managerial capabilities developed. As noted by most participants in the study, language was a major obstacle in the interactions in the firm. In recognition of the increasing participation of Chinese firms in the economy and the importance of addressing the language-related communication issues, the host government has initiated a policy to teach Chinese in schools (Daily Monitor, 2018). Here is what a government minister says at passing out a contingent of Chinese tutors:

> We have received materials such as textbooks and illustrations. We have also received some tutors from the Chinese government.

To a large extent, the mediator role was an ongoing learning experience for all parties, not least the stakeholders highlighted in this section. It was in fact a mix of individual, organisational and national learning dynamics in light of the relatively short duration of massive Chinese FDI into the continent. It is noteworthy that research to date has tended to address these learning dimensions separately rather than as a combined and interrelated whole. There is therefore a gap in understanding how this mixed dynamic expresses itself and how the firms in question can best adapt. Some of the ingredients of the mix were a significant departure from observations about HRM in extant literatures and therefore required an exploratory research approach in order to extract insights. The observation that Chinese managers were generally reluctant to talk about their experiences (Siebers, 2012) made it even more important to use mediator managers, as exemplified in this study, to gather evidence.

Suggestions to enhance the mediatory role

Having demonstrated the importance of the mediator role within this one organisation and the internal and external circumstances under which it expressed itself, it would be useful to make some suggestions about how the role can be improved, in order to inform this important role within other firms. These suggestions are outlined following:

1   It would be useful to develop a training course for such local managers. Such a course, perhaps based at an institution of higher learning, could then take a deeper look at the key issues involved and develop learning modules around them. Bringing together the local managers and, eventually, some of their bosses in a training environment would offer an opportunity to share experiences and to apply solid analyses to them. The body of experiences and diverse cases would ultimately provide a basis for theorisation about the hybrid HRM models in question (e.g. Horwitz, 2012).
2   The training suggested prior could benefit from government support, especially in the introductory stages, to facilitate an enabling institutional environment. The ministries of labour and education could work together to develop a framework in which such courses could be developed, including their location in the wider skills development in the country.
3   Chinese managers can be encouraged to accommodate more arrangements that depend on more formal systems and approaches. In effect, the balance between informal and formal approaches to HRM needs reconsiderations to make the outcomes more effective. While there should generally be freedom to make managerial choices about the mix, it is in the best mid- to long-term interests of the host country to negotiate for more local content and local participation. But this in turn depends on more formalised and therefore accessible systems. It further depends on having a policy framework that resonates well with emerging HRM models and the supportive environment in both the home and host markets. In light of the fact that many of the Chinese firms entering African countries are either directly state-owned or very close to the state (e.g. Fowler, 2019), the state is therefore in a position to influence certain decisions. A key criticism is that a disproportionate number of Chinese employees are brought in with the investments. This therefore decreases the opportunities that local managers have to grow and to develop their managerial capabilities more comprehensively.
4   In the interests of deeper cross-cultural understanding (Jackson, 2012), the lead local African managers would be more strongly equipped if they spent part of the training suggested prior as a learning trip to China.

Conclusions

In conclusion, the chapter has demonstrated how an African mediator manager can play a strategically important role in an emerging

Sino-African HRM model. The role is based on acting as a bridge between senior Chinese managers and various stakeholder groups, not least African employees, hosting communities, regulatory institutions and clients on the market. It ends up being an all-rounder role requiring a rich mix of skills and capabilities to fulfil it well. In light of increasing Chinese FDI inflow into the African continent and its ever more Pan-African dimension, the further development of the role could significantly contribute to strengthening the enabling environment for higher quality Chinese and generally Asian FDI on this fast-growing continent. At a broader level, the role offers an opportunity to develop the early forms of an emerging Sino-African HRM model that is an alternative and, better still, a compliment to traditional models. One of the most important strengths of the model is that it introduces local African elements, for example the views and interpretations of the local manager as reported in this study, into HRM practices to synergise with external ones. This might be a more sustainable model than others that have historically been imposed without consideration of local preferences. An ironically important ramification is that it would potentially catalyse a rethink of these more traditional models to make them more compliant with local cultural needs. Such competition for the best models can only be healthy for the continent.

Limitations of the study and implications for future research

While the advantages and the strengths have been extensively explained, it is also important not to forget that there are some limitations. First of all, there is a need to increase the sample of firms through which to understand the mediator role. The chapter depended on one firm and one local manager, albeit supported by employees and another local manager and a Chinese manager in two other firms. A wider interaction with more local managers working for Chinese firms would corroborate the findings and add richer insights from which eventual generalisations can be made. Second, it would be important to study the role in both other industry sectors and in other African countries. It is this wider understanding that would enable more generalisation of the findings. However, the study has contributed to laying the foundation for these future studies. It could also form the basis for a methodological extension into a quantitative study, benefiting from the exploratory, qualitative findings. Not least, there is a need to talk to more Chinese managers and assess what they think. While they are generally reluctant to directly talk, ways have to be found in the future to engage them and to make them realise that such research is actually to their advantage too because it contributes to helping them understand the African markets better.

References

Ado, A., & Su, Z. (2016). China in Africa: A critical literature review. *Critical Perspectives on International Business, 12*(1), 40–60.

Albert, E. (2017). *China in Africa: Council on foreign relations* [Online]. Retrieved August 30, 2019 from www.cfr.org/backgrounder/china-africa

Badeeb, R. A., Lean, H. H., & Clark, J. (2017). The evolution of the natural resource curse thesis: A critical literature survey. *Resources Policy, 51*, 123–134.

Berger, R., Choi, C. J., & Kim, J. B. (2011). Responsible leadership for multinational enterprises in bottom of pyramid countries: The knowledge of local managers. *Journal of Business Ethics, 101*(4), 553–561.

Brewster, C., Wood, G., & Brookes, M. (2008). Similarity, isomorphism or duality? Recent survey evidence on the human resource management policies of multinational corporations. *British Journal of Management, 19*(4), 320–342.

Cheru, F., & Obi, C. (2011). Chinese and Indian engagement in Africa: Competitive or mutually reinforcing strategies? *Journal of International Affairs,* 91–110.

Child, J., & Marinova, S. (2014). The role of contextual combinations in the globalization of Chinese firms. *Management and Organization Review, 10*(3), 347–371.

Cooke, F. L. (2014). Chinese multinational firms in Asia and Africa: Relationships with institutional actors and patterns of HRM practices. *Human Resource Management, 53*(6), 877–896.

Cross, H., & Cliffe, L. (2017). A comparative political economy of regional migration and labour mobility in West and Southern Africa. *Review of African Political Economy, 44*(153), 381–398.

Daily Monitor. (2018). *Uganda to now teach Chinese* [Online]. Retrieved August 31, 2019 from www.theeastafrican.co.ke/news/ea/Ugandan-schools-set-to-teach-Chinese/4552908-4905436-4rwtsbz/index.html

Eisenhardt, K. M. (1989). Building theories from case study research. *Academy of Management Review, 14*(4), 532–550.

Fowler, J. (2019). China's multi-faceted economic development strategy in East Africa. *Orbis, 63*(2), 172–186.

Gandhi, D. (2018). *Figures of the week: Trends and determinants in Chinese FDI in Africa* [Online]. Retrieved August 1, 2019 from www.brookings.edu/blog/africa-in-focus/2018/07/25/figures-of-the-week-trends-and-determinants-in-chinese-fdi-in-africa/

Garcia-Herrero, A., & Xu, J. (2019). *China's investments in Africa: What the data really say, and the implications for Europe* [Online]. Retrieved August 2, 2019 from www.forbes.com/sites/aliciagarciaherrero/2019/07/24/chinas-investments-in-africa-what-the-data-really-says-and-the-implications-for-europe/#2dd4a259661f

GCR. (2019). *Chinese construction firms deserve better press in Africa, study suggests* [Online]. Retrieved August 1, 2019 from www.globalconstructionreview.com/news/chinese-construction-firms-deserve-better-press-af/

Giese, K., & Thiel, A. (2015). The psychological contract in Chinese-African informal labor relations. *The International Journal of Human Resource Management, 26*(14), 1807–1826.

Gorostidi-Martinez, H., & Zhao, X. (2017). Strategies to avoid liability of foreignness when entering a new market. *Journal of Advances in Management Research, 14*(1), 46–68.

Horwitz, F. M. (2012). Evolving human resource management in Southern African multinational firms: Towards an Afro-Asian nexus. *The International Journal of Human Resource Management, 23*(14), 2938–2958.

Jackson, T. (2011). From cultural values to cross-cultural interfaces: Hofstede goes to Africa. *Journal of Organizational Change Management, 24*(4), 532–558.

Jackson, T. (2012). Cross-cultural management and the informal economy in sub-Saharan Africa: Implications for organization, employment and skills development. *The International Journal of Human Resource Management, 23*(14), 2901–2916.

Jackson, T., Louw, L., & Zhao, S. (2013). China in sub-Saharan Africa: Implications for HRM policy and practice at organizational level. *The International Journal of Human Resource Management, 24*(13), 2512–2533.

Kamoche, K., & Siebers, L. Q. (2015). Chinese management practices in Kenya: Toward a post-colonial critique. *The International Journal of Human Resource Management, 26*(21), 2718–2743.

Kamoche, K., Siebers, L. Q., Mamman, A., & Newenham-Kahindi, A. (2015). The dynamics of managing people in the diverse cultural and institutional context of Africa. *Personnel Review, 44*(3), 330–345.

Kjær, A. M. (2015). Political settlements and productive sector policies: Understanding sector differences in Uganda. *World Development, 68*, 230–241.

Kuteesa, F., Tumusiime-Mutebile, Whitworth, A., & Williamson, T. (2010). *Uganda's economic reforms: Insider accounts.* Oxford Scholarship. Retrieved August 2, 2019 from www.oxfordscholarship.com/view/10.1093/acprof:oso/9780199556229.001.0001/acprof-9780199556229

Lazarova, M., Peretz, H., & Fried, Y. (2017). Locals know best? Subsidiary HR autonomy and subsidiary performance. *Journal of World Business, 52*(1), 83–96.

Mbalyohere, C., & Lawton, T. C. (2018). Engaging stakeholders through corporate political activity: Insights from MNE nonmarket strategy in an emerging African market. *Journal of International Management, 24*(4), 369–385.

Mbalyohere, C., Lawton, T. C., Boojihawon, R., & Viney, H. (2017). Corporate political activity and location-based advantage: MNE responses to institutional transformation in Uganda's electricity industry. *Journal of World Business, 52*(6), 743–759.

Mutambo, A. (2019). *DR Congo applies for admission to East African community* [Online]. Retrieved August 1, 2019 from www.theeastafrican.co.ke/news/ea/DR-Congo-seeks-to-join-East-African-Community/4552908-5157244-rld-jtsz/index.html

Nasasira, R. (2018). *Shelling maize need not be a tough task* [Online]. Retrieved September 1, 2019 from www.monitor.co.ug/Magazines/Farming/Shelling-maize-need-not-be-tough-task/689860-4614096-mcutqdz/index.html

New Vision. (2016). *Eala congratulating South Sudan on EAC admission* [Online]. Retrieved August 1, 2019 from www.newvision.co.ug/new_vision/news/1419259/eala-congratulating-ssudan-eac-admission

Peng, M. W., Wang, D. Y., & Jiang, Y. (2008). An institution-based view of international business strategy: A focus on emerging economies. *Journal of International Business Studies, 39*(5), 920–936.

Polus, A., & Tycholiz, W. (2016). Why is it taking so long? Solving the oil extraction equation in Uganda. *African and Asian Studies, 15*(1), 77–97.

Siebers, L. Q. (2012). Foreign retailers in China: The first ten years. *Journal of Business Strategy, 33*(1), 27–38.

Srivastava, P., & Hopwood, N. (2009). A practical iterative framework for qualitative data analysis. *International Journal of Qualitative Methods, 8*(1), 76–84.

Stake, R. E. (2013). *Multiple case study analysis*. London and New York: Guilford Press.

Tradingeconomics. (2018). *Uganda corruption rank* [Online]. Retrieved August 2, 2019 from https://tradingeconomics.com/uganda/corruption-rank

Tutor2U. (2019). *Study notes: Foreign direct investment in Africa* [Online]. Retrieved August 2, 2019 from www.tutor2u.net/economics/reference/foreign-direct-investment-in-africa

World Bank. (2019). *GDP growth (Annual)*. Uganda [Online]. Retrieved August 2, 2019 from https://data.worldbank.org/indicator/NY.GDP.MKTP.KD.ZG?locations=UG

Yin, R. K. (2017). *Case study research and applications: Design and methods*. London: Sage Publications.

Part III

Implications

12 How can we help to develop Chinese and African managers? Building synergies through hybrid practice-based management partnerships

Dev K. (Roshan) Boojihawon

In 2018, a Chinese manager in Kenya was filmed calling an employee a 'monkey', and his remarks extended to Kenyans and their president (Agence France-Presse, 2018). The video went viral, sparking outrage and condemning the blatant racist attitudes of some Chinese bosses in Africa. Unfortunately, these are not isolated cases (Adisu, Sharkey, & Okoroafo, 2010; Mbamalu, 2018; Dahir, 2019; Feng & Pilling, 2019a), for Chinese management behaviour and styles have been questioned on several occasions. In the literature, the real reasons underpinning such behaviour and incidents are still unexplored and might be emblematic of deeper differences in perceptions, attitudes and expectations between Chinese managers and African employees (Geldart, 2014).

To some extent, such sentiments are fuelled by the fact that Africans are still unclear and concerned about the impact of Chinese engagement, given the paucity of research and data (Alden & Davies, 2006; Jackson, Louw, & Zhao, 2013; Jackson, Louw, Zhao, Boojihawon, & Fang, 2014; Osundu-Oti, 2016; Jayaram, Kassiri, & Yuan Sun, 2017). Africans are aware of the risks of Chinese engagement on their continent. Politicians and boutique consultancies may be the ones who are benefitting the most, but influential voices, such as those of Nigeria's former finance minister Ngozi Okonjo-Iweala, have warned of the harm in promoting China's state-led growth model, arguing it can fuel corruption and resource overconsumption (Patey, 2018). Undoubtedly, Africa needs to be more conscious of the benefits of its relations with China and learn how to better leverage its position with Chinese investors when negotiating more rewarding trade and financial deals. It should also consider more meaningful transfers of knowledge, skills and technology to improve the competitiveness of domestic firms and the competences of African employees. The latter, in particular, demands thinking about more radical ways to train and develop managers or enact management education approaches that better address the particular situations and needs in Africa in a post-China–Africa context. They may also determine Africa's absorptive capacity (Jackson et al., 2013, 2014; Jayaram et al., 2017; Xing, Liu, Tarba, & Cooper, 2016).

Indeed, 'poor management' is a common complaint across business sectors in Africa (Pfeffermann, 2008), to illustrate:

> African managers are ill-equipped. Large companies are forced to import expats; smaller companies become overly dependent on a small group of senior managers; NGOs struggle to execute their vision on the ground; and investors have to get operationally involved, which limits deal-flow. We need more well-trained and competent managers. . . . The management development ecosystem is woefully inadequate to develop the quantity and quality of managers that we need. There are roughly 90 business schools in Africa – one per 11 million people. Fewer than 10 of them meet international standards. Another 40 offer reasonable quality, but usually fail to translate theory into useful, practical knowledge, and too often have poor links with business. The training market for middle managers is fragmented and low quality. There are a few good SME programmes but they have struggled to find scalable and sustainable business models.
>
> (AMI, 2013, p. 77)

The concept of Africa-centred management education is still premature, lacks support and voice and is unable to keep pace with the increase in business activities across Africa. For instance, the emergence of regional conglomerates across the continent, the growth of small businesses and the expansion of multinational companies all point to an urgent need for more managers with the requisite skills and know-how to realize the continent's growth potential. To keep up, several business schools and management education providers have mushroomed throughout the continent, but their expansion and provisions are still deemed inadequate or not grounded enough on African experiences (Kiggundu, 1991; Dia, 1996; Jackson, 2002, 2004, 2015; Brotheridge & Long, 2007; Kamoche, 2011; Kamoche, Chizema, Mellahi, & Newenham-Kahindi, 2012; Muriithi, 2017; Amankwah-Amoah, Boso, & Yaw, 2018).

This management shortfall manifests its impact in various ways: for instance, in international businesses, shortage of local talent is a constant complaint and shows in how they are run by Chinese enterprises or projects. For example, Standard Bank flies in senior staff from South Africa to make significant decisions. The same applies to Chinese MNEs, which rely on the entrepreneurial and decision-making abilities of senior managers to steer African projects (Feng & Pilling, 2019b; Mbewa, 2019). Even established businesses struggle to recruit and retain capable staff. Good managers are quick to jump ship: they want to go to the West, perhaps for further training, and many do not return (Samir, Selvarajah, Meyer, & Dorasamy, 2014). In the experience of non-profit consultancies (like Wellspring, Whitehead, 2015), many of their problems are not because of a lack of local company or NGO ideas, but lie in the implementation of those ideas. Everyone is aware of the issues around getting skilled managers, staffing and teams right, but this is precisely what is so difficult. The partners they work with are increasingly aware of this, but no immediate solution is available. To them, the main challenges now are no longer the need for technical solutions (for example, in science, crops and vaccines), but poor management and 'institutional' problems in the public and private sector. Sometimes NGOs pay excessively to draw in the best talent, but NGOs also lack managers with private sector skills or management knowledge and experience. Yet these NGOs are the conventional players now being funded to 'develop' African markets. In the public sector, a very similar complaint arises. The phrase 'the missing middle' (Kirchhoff, 2013) has come to describe the apparent disconnect when top officials try to make things happen, even when they are very capable and well-intentioned. However, as noted before, it is increasingly evident that managing a business in Africa requires not only knowledge of management practices but also an understanding of the peculiarities of doing so in that context, and this issue has become a dilemma challenging the curriculum relevance of many African-based business schools.

This chapter suggests a possible way of reconciling this dilemma by furthering the concept of hybridization in management education and development through a practice-based lens. The chapter is organized as follows. The next section reviews current debates and discussions on the failings of effective management education in Africa. Section 3 makes the case for a hybrid practice-based African management approach. Section 4 reviews extant research and debates capturing Chinese management approaches and its implication for African management. Section 5 discusses the implementation of hybrid practice-based African management education using the China–Africa hybrid practice-based management development (CAHPMD) framework.

The failings of management education in Africa

The preceding observations and experiences of 'poor management' are not controversial. Indeed, they are quite commonplace. They challenge the roles of business schools and their contributions in sub-Saharan Africa. Taken at face value, they might seem to indicate a need for more business schools. Indeed, The African Management Initiative (AMI) recently led an in-depth study surveying both the gaps and the excellence in African management, illustrating that parts of the continent are now awash with business schools. These schools have some value, for example in training accountants, but too often they are a distraction from more urgently needed professional studies or from more practice-based or work-based forms of learning and engagement that seriously consider the African context. In short, management education and pedagogy are still overwhelmingly knowledge-based and didactic, and the teaching resources used rarely address the needs of African contexts. When they do they almost always concern multinationals' issues operating in Africa (Jackson, 2002; Kuada, 2006; Muriithi, 2017). In consequence, training and qualifications are often inadequate or deemed irrelevant. Successful African professionals are abandoning local universities and prefer to send their children abroad, who in most cases do not return to exercise their skills and expertise in and for Africa.

But, so far, all efforts to raise awareness of these issues and develop management education has made some contributions (Zoogah & Nkomo, 2013). It is understood that 'Good managers are the engines of growth and development. They build globally competitive companies and vibrant SMEs which create jobs, they execute on development strategy and they drive national economies forward' (AMI, 2013, p. 77). Overall, whether from university courses, short executive workshops or project-based training, African managers have largely been exposed to normative Western-based, Anglo-American models and they have become skilled in using the right language in contexts where this is deemed beneficial (Jackson, 2002, 2004). Indeed, African managers have to do this because their roles often involve holding together and trying to reconcile the conflicting requirements of transplanted and indigenous institutions. Arguably, when managers in Africa succeed, it is because they find ways to do this creatively. The reality is that although they perform well superficially, they are unable to learn and reapply these ideas or combine them with local meanings and values in order to deliver what is needed. As a result, in development contexts, the concepts and meanings associated with terms like 'strategy', 'leadership', 'entrepreneurialism' and 'innovation' are often misused or stretched with little or no cultural relevance or significance (AMI, 2017, Amankwah-Amoah et al., 2018; Andrew, 2019).

African management experience does not appear to be taken seriously. None of this should be surprising: the major issue, reconciling transplanted and indigenous institutions, generally goes undiscussed or unchallenged. Where it does appear, it tends to be in terms of African ways versus Western ways (Anyansi & Chiekwe, 2001; Zoogah & Nkomo, 2013). Arguably, raising this as an alternative indicates a vital divide, one where Africa is lagging behind, which leads to nostalgic idealization of past times. In any event, this 'reconciliation paradigm' (Dia, 1996) is certainly not a focus of business school teaching, to say nothing of research (Jackson, 2015). African management research reflects the same problem: it has been assimilated into a transplanted discourse, further promoting 'modernization' without tackling the equally urgent need for Africanization (Chizema, Nyathi, Amaeshi, Okupe, & Idemudia, 2018). The deeper understanding of the issues that is required might usefully start by recognizing the wide differences in values, perceptions and business practices that are masked by the use of a common language. For many upcoming African managers, the local values of the village or tribe are still the bedrock of the world on which their thinking is based and in which they find refuge when under pressure (Beck & Cowan, 1992, 1996). By comparison, the concepts and values that managers acquire in professional contexts are usually only of surface relevance or are adapted to serve these underlying governing needs. Likewise, the necessity of engaging with informal systems of power and patronage in order to get things done needs to be recognized. This is compounded by the 'big man' syndrome (Houeland & Jacobs, 2016) that haunts African politics and business, feeding inequality and corruption, and is both a constant concern and an endemic burden. These realities are here to stay. They are ingrained in African business and politics, and they raise important questions around when and how one can operate or navigate effectively within such systems (Lutz, 2009). These issues need to be explored and reflected upon if they are ever to be made part of credible management pedagogy and research connecting with practice in Africa.

Refusing to play the game: the case for a hybrid practice-based approach for African Management

The practice-based approach to management education is still a new form of scholarship that fundamentally relies on the idea that management and success in business are interdependent. Therefore, management training should always critically and constructively align with business practice. This view argues that management education is a central feature of business schools everywhere, but that its provision is often biased by political agendas, perceived ideologies about business and what matters in it and institutional and educational divides and drivers (Higgins, 2018). Traditional and didactic forms of management training and teaching, such as lectures, examinations and papers, for the most part adopt a 'teach about' approach and are often inadequate and counterproductive for supporting business practice or in dealing with the complexities of running modern businesses (Brotheridge & Long, 2007; Datar, Garvin, & Cullen, 2010). Proponents of the practice view emphasize the need to nurture innovating ways of thinking, designing curriculums and new modes of pedagogy to fully enhance and develop approaches to management education and learning. These make more sense to business practice, thereby exhibiting greater connectivity to the issues and challenges of now and the future, and avoid de-marginalizing or devaluing the broader social context in which the manager functions (Datar et al., 2010; Locke & Spender, 2011; Samir et al., 2014). 'The current demand to develop proficient managers requires methods for enhancing and stimulating the learning experiences of the manager which enhance aspirations, critical thinking skills, capabilities and behaviour' (Higgins, 2018, pp. 87–88).

This focus on practice emphasizes the manager's need to become aware of and develop their cognitive skills to support them when they deconstruct and make sense of their own actions and practices (Perriton & Reynolds, 2004). It values pedagogical approaches interested in methods of upskilling and reflection as a means of understanding how management works. It creates real-time management learning processes by permitting, supporting and encouraging managers to explore their judgements and critique their means of inquiry, calling into question the knowledge, images and assumptions behind their actions and stories that relate to their experiences of themselves and others (Antonacopoulou, 2007, 2008; Trehan & Rigg, 2015). Higgins (2018) argues that such notions of management practice sought to establish a focus towards methods which enables one to gain a real insight into the natural practices of what it means to be a practicing manager, where experience and learning is gained through the natural process of action, and within this process the use of action learning and reflexive methods as a means of critiquing practice are key methods.

Following similar arguments, Burger and Trehan (2018), exploring action learning in an African context, examine how as a cultural product it 'is biased towards Western values and practices'. Their paper draws attention to the political, cultural and social encounters of internationalizing action learning that are often taken lightly in current debates on practice-based approaches to management education. In particular, they argue that:

> knowledge in action learning is highly contextual. The source of knowledge is the action learners' own experience, the vehicle the reflective engagement with the specific situation' (Weinstein, 1999; Bunning, 1997). If knowledge is derived from practice, then it is bound to the social, cultural and historical context of this practice.
> (Burger & Trehan, 2018, p. 132)

Against this backdrop, it is therefore important to understand and acknowledge what does and does not work within the African context. We must also consider how and why we enable management development approaches that centre on the active professional engagement of the African manager or employee as the learner within business practices across Africa. Scholarly management research is greatly needed in order to understand this further, and anecdotal evidence from practice suggests that where this does work it leads to positive results. For example, boutique consultancies like Wellspring have achieved results with a practice-based approach to securing major projects, funding and government involvement across pan-African projects. Its founder, Mike Shaw, does not work independently of his clients (Cambieri, 2011). He involves them so that they understand what is happening on the ground and see it for themselves. As such, Wellspring tends to attract clients that are willing to be more flexible and open-minded and are less restricted by their funders. Mike Shaw also emphasizes the importance of recognizing the value systems and local power dynamics at work and of not being sentimental about the lives of subsistence village communities if the plan being devised is not feasible because of management shortfalls. Other small-scale collaborative lab-based formats like the 'Innovation Labs' in Kampala, and elsewhere, adapt to the needs of a young, determined Ugandan population. These labs connect academia from the US, Europe and Kampala, and create system change at a national scale. Similarly, the CCORE lab in Zimbabwe takes best practices from the world of operational research and applies them to pressing programmatic issues addressing specific local issues, and, importantly, allows the solutions that are created to move to a global scale (UNICEF, 2013). These examples are physical spaces that allow for collaboration between the private sector, academia and civil society

Arguably, the management know-how coming out of these lab format approaches cannot be reduced to a neat set of 'tips' or 'tool kits', not least because the local differences between different culture groups, policies and other comparative factors are often hugely important. Each situation and business challenge they address is unique and needs to be tackled on the ground, starting from where the people or issues lie. Beginning bottom-up with an open mind, accepting that one cannot know in advance what is needed, is crucial. Nevertheless, sooner or later it becomes apparent to those working on the ground, be they technicians, project managers or local business partners, that there is a need to acquire new 'tools for thinking through how to assist in addressing unfamiliar challenges in ways that will last', which is a continuous challenge. The question really is what sort of management education and training might equip Africa to address this challenge. Currently, the state of management research there falls short of providing an answer to this question, and none of the answers we are aware of are convincing. A form of management education, grounded in and for African settings, has yet to be devised or discovered. And if such learning processes were conceived, how might they be made accessible at scale for managers across Africa? Can we gain any insights by examining Chinese management approaches? The next section explores this possibility.

Tapping into Chinese management approaches

Today, China is Africa's biggest economic contributor, driving and stretching its engagement across trade, investment, infrastructure financing and aid more than any other foreign investor in Africa (Jayaram et al., 2017). Over the past two decades, Chinese firms of all sizes and sectors have been investing in Africa, bringing capital investment, management know-how and entrepreneurial energy to the continent. Yet, to date it has been challenging to understand the true impact of the Africa–China economic relationship on management development because of a paucity of research in this area (Tang, 2010; Shen, 2015; Zoogah & Nkomo, 2013; Acquaah, Zoogah & Kwesiga, 2013).

Africa-China workplaces are flourishing. Notably, when setting up their shops, Chinese investors have carved their own path to and within Africa, driven by the quest for resources and commodities, African market opportunities or simply to get away from competition within China (Wang, Fan, Freeman, & Zhu, 2017). Undoubtedly, the leadership of most of these companies is characterized by a strong entrepreneurial spirit, bringing with it a wealth of experience, technologies, skills and know-how (Lee, 2009; Gu, 2009), but how these elements are absorbed with African experiences and contexts has largely been underestimated and misunderstood (Kragelund, 2009; Leavy, 2018). For instance, Yuan Sun, Jayaram and Kassiri report that of the companies they researched, 89% of employees were African, adding up to nearly 300,000 jobs for African workers. 'Scaled up across all 10,000 Chinese firms in Africa, this suggests that Chinese-owned businesses employ several million Africans. They also noted that nearly two-thirds of Chinese employers provided some kind of skills training' (Yuan Sun, Jayaram, & Kassiri, 2017, p. 13). They also note that levels of African employee engagement vary for different business sectors. For companies engaged in construction and manufacturing, where skilled labour is a necessity, half offered apprenticeship training but most managerial jobs were taken by Chinese employees.

Undoubtedly, capacity is being built and up-skilling is taking place, particularly through Chinese government-funded teaching and medical, technical and agricultural training institutions, but where firms are taking on unskilled local labour there is currently little evidence of up-skilling or knowledge transfer (Muriithi, 2017). The extent to which Chinese MNEs may be contributing directly to the up-skilling of predominantly unskilled labour, if there is a tendency to import skilled Chinese labour, needs also to be investigated in view of a lack of evidence in this area. In a more general sense, Brautigam and Xiaoyang (2011) reports a commitment by China to provide short-term training to 15,000 Africans over three years in poverty reduction, new leather technologies and other areas not specifically linked to projects, and to train 1,500 principals and teachers and 1,000 doctors, nurses and health sector managers in the 30 countries receiving new hospitals. Vocational training also figures highly in China's aid-financed construction, with centres being opened in Ethiopia, Uganda and Angola. Yet the extent to which Chinese MNEs are directly involved in this capacity building (a clear strategic goal of China's overall engagement with Africa) remains largely uninvestigated.

Looking at the similarities and differences between African and Chinese management approaches, specifically, Muriithi (2017) argues that our notion of what constitutes Chinese management is very weak. He notes that there are major similarities between China and Africa, largely drawn from Confucian–Ubuntu principles, relating to culture and work expectations, but that Chinese management need to improve their inter-action with African managers and workforces in terms of language, eth-ics at work and poor working conditions. The Chinese presence in Africa continues to face challenges and accusations regarding poor working conditions, language-communication barriers and overall mistreatment of local workers by managers.

> An improvement in working relationship can be enhanced through good communication skills, hybrid management, talent management, creating conducive working climate and innovativeness. It is for both Africans and Chinese to work in collaboration as they stand to gain economically, socially and politically, all leading to development of stronger partners. It is a marriage that must be made to work.
>
> (p. 11)

Xing et al. (2016) add to this by arguing that this 'marriage' could work better if more effort were made to bring Chinese–African working prac-tices together through cross-cultural training and mutual learning, in order to enhance mutual understanding, but this has not been without controversy (Marsh, 2019; Ongiyo, 2019).

This supports earlier assertions by Jackson (2004), a major proponent of hybrid management approaches as effective ways of managing in Afri-can contexts. Valuing distinctly African (i.e. indigenous) management approaches, he emphasizes the need to integrate important aspects of African traditional values and other world cultures (including Chinese) in order to employ an approach that fits the African context and needs. No purely Western, African or Eastern style will work effectively in modern Africa, given the dynamic nature of cross-cultural diversity, needs and per-ceptions. This chapter argues that practice-based management approaches provide ample scope for such hybridization to occur. This has been well documented empirically and illustrated in management literature examin-ing the effectiveness of cross-functionality in innovation project teams. Hybridization through cross-functional team structures is acknowledged to be an important part of the innovation process, providing knowledge to new generations, overcoming barriers between functional departments and disciplines, developing trust and overcoming organizational, cultural and spatial barriers, and creating opportunities to enhance connectedness across the organization (Jassawalla & Sashittal, 1999; Love & Roper, 2009; Blindenbach-Driesse, 2009; Blindenbach-Driessen & van den Ende, 2014). With this in mind, the next section expounds a framework that reflects on the ways in which a practice orientation developing African managers now and, in the future, can be enabled.

Modelling hybridization for Africa: a China–Africa hybrid practice-based management development (CAHPMD) framework

For hybridization to occur in China–Africa workplaces, it needs to be supported by a vision, a common set of values, stakeholder engagement, appropriate financing, operational and spatial considerations and a strategy binding all of them together.

Figure 12.1 attempts to reconcile these essential elements by suggesting four key areas of parallel work and consideration underpinning the design, set-up and implementation of a China–Africa hybrid practice-based management development (CAHPMD) framework. It is important to understand that the relationships between these elements highlighted in each section are mutually-dependent and necessary in order to make hybridization work in China–Africa professional relationships. The framework describes the process in four sections, and argues that hybridization can occur in several forms, as shown in Area 4 of this framework. These learning and innovation formats are the end aims or results of the hybridization process. They could be structured physical locations, e.g. in terms of learning and innovation labs, or could simply be a space for creativity and collaboration that is aimed at practically solving significant China–Africa business and managerial problems through the application of dedicated resources. The process leading to the creation and success of such hybrid spaces needs to be actively managed, and this inevitably means bringing together, managing and sustaining all the other elements described in Areas 1, 2 and 3 through a unifying strategy (Park, Jong Won Lim & Birnbaum-More, 2009).

> Area 1: There is no ego in the concept of hybrid spaces, but a demand for methodologies of openness, collaboration and experimentation, which might necessarily start with a process of education and information for all parties likely to be involved in the process, and how it might work (Blindenbach-Driessen & van den Ende, 2014). Research shows that what makes a successful hybrid space, e.g. an innovation lab, involves a culture or common set of values that is defined and supported from the outset by the collaborating partners, setting the basis for a governance structure that leads and manages the hybrid space (Majchrzak, More, & Faraj, 2012). This may require openness to change in procedural and problem-solving approaches to achieve the desired goals. Such an atmosphere embraces experimentation and emphasises the need to constantly evaluate and recognize failure as a learning process, something with which Chinese partners might not necessarily agree (Mayer, Boness, & Louw, 2017). In fact, failure viewed in the proper light often leads to novel solutions that can be beneficial

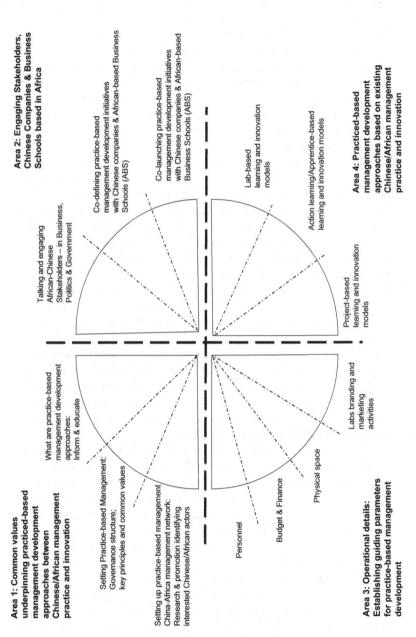

Figure 12.1 China–Africa practice-based management development framework

to all parties involved. Risk is managed by performing research and groundwork in advance of resource-intensive implementation and by continuing to test and evaluate as an integral process throughout the life cycle of a project or product. The argument here is that by making African employees part of this innovation and learning process, Chinese companies will be opening up to ideas and solutions at a grassroots level in Africa (Mbewa, 2019) and working with Africans on how to identify, adapt and upscale them. Management innovation and learning is embedded in every part of this process – from launching relevant projects, deployment of resources, to better monitoring the results – eventually leading to better management.

Area 2 highlights the need to bring all the relevant actors together and work strategically in defining and launching joint management development initiatives between Chinese companies and African-based Business Schools (ABS). For such hybrid ideas to work, it is crucial that they are primarily seen as collaborative undertakings. Besides Chinese and African workforces, this can usefully involve politicians, government bodies, academic and NGOs, all contributing to help start, support and sustain the progress of this hybridization process (Sethi, Smith & Park, 2001; Rogers, 2019). The framework emphasizes that ABSs can be the more proactive and distinct actors, the launch pads or platforms for China–Africa hybrid collaborations. They can position themselves as orchestrators of the whole process and its strategy, extending their own capabilities for teaching and research, and facilitate open or mutually agreed exchanges between Chinese and African managers. In enabling a mutual exchange of skills and professional know-how between these parties, the African employee or manager, seeking experience, will stand to benefit the most.

Area 3 gives a sense of what a lab or a hybrid space might contain, from providing specific, operational parameters and costs needed to get a lab up and running, to providing examples of current models of this, and finally to providing the technical documents (terms of reference, partnership agreements, etc.) that can be adapted for multiple use. Most importantly, there needs to be reflection here on how hybrid ideas and spaces can be designed so they can be extended effectively.

Area 4 delineates the different types or formats of learning and innovation models that can support hybridization, i.e. laboratory-based, action learning/apprentice-based and project-based learning and innovation models. In the China–Africa workplace scenarios, what is needed is a collaborative laboratory in which business learning can take place. Arguably, the lab can be tailored for specific purposes, and it carries the potential to generate project models that can be adapted by other labs. Every implementation can be a proving ground for potential results that seek to address pervasive China–Africa ventures or related organizational or operational problems. If there are several such labs set up, together they can constitute an optimized innovation network relevant to China–Africa businesses. One can envisage a suite of linked management learning and development projects, each an experiment addressing specific challenges in which China–Africa businesses are involved. These learning projects can be action learning oriented, apprentice-based, bespoke around projects and co-designed with the help or involvement of ABSs. Usually they would be, or be part of, a system intervention, e.g. working at several organizational levels or across a supply chain. Within these experimental projects, learning would be role- and organization-related, and the touchstone of success would be the contribution made in addressing the perceived problems. Some projects would probably be based on versions of existing ABS-taught management programmes (e.g. Apprentice-based MBAs, or Executive Management modules). This would be a quick way to get started and would immediately focus on the adaptation and use of the ideas and techniques in the workplace.

Other possibilities include:

- Devising bespoke training and drawing on ABS resources, presented through a series of workshops interspersed with private study and group activities.
- Starting with an appreciative/work-based inquiry of the problematic situation, and moving into an action learning mode, with support for Chinese managers in dealing with issues they face, including learning resources selected and provided on a need-to-know basis.
- 'Learning journeys' with group visits to other sites and facilities ('show don't tell') also designed to include opportunities for resource-based learning and group problem-solving, perhaps with participants encouraged to capture their reflections in journals.

Whatever the approach devised, much of the learning would focus on whether, why and to what extent it was actually being used and working or not, and how it needs to evolve in the next phase or in further application elsewhere.

Implications for African management education and research

Leaving hybrid spaces and achieving scale and reach is a central challenge of this model of management development. As sound knowledge of business learning with and for African managers is taking form in the hybrid spaces, it is time to consider how it can be made more widely available and to develop and test systems for doing this for the wider benefit of African management. Management learning cannot just be for those involved in China–Africa contexts, but must apply to wider African contexts. Likewise, it is reasonable to assume that appropriate African management will vary greatly between contexts. Chinese firms are not the same across Africa (Wang, Freeman & Zhu, 2013; Mayer et al., 2017, Ryder, 2018, Pilling, 2019), ABSs are different and institutional barriers and bureaucracies pose their own distinctive challenges, as do specific industries (agriculture, health, manufacturing, services). As more and more hybrid spaces and labs become a reality across these various sectors, identifying and adapting success models in one context and applying them to another situation can become much more streamlined. The implications for innovation are great, and this would be a blueprint for collaboration that could have a profound impact across Africa.

Africa is not a homogeneous place. The question, then, is what sort of mechanism or institution might make the hybrid forms of management learning rapidly and widely available, both directly through its own provision and indirectly by training and supporting a variety of ABSs working in a range of ways with different groups of African employees and managers. Potentially, ABSs can a play crucial role in helping to disseminate and reassimilate this knowledge across African contexts in the following ways:

- A locally-proven version of a supported online management learning portal for African managers, based on locally-developed resources and backed up by the testimony of successful experiences of working in hybrid spaces and their outcomes.
- The African-based business and management knowledge that would be created through the hybrid spaces would also feedback into UK/ Western management knowledge. China–Africa represents a unique context with the potential to advance management understanding globally.

Apart from scaling this model for impact, there is a lack of rigorous management research into what kinds of programme and intervention do result in better-managed organizations or better African managers, particularly in an African context (Bloom, Mahadran, McKenzie & Roberts, 2010). Academic research relevant to management education is greatly needed. We need a systemic approach to improving the quality of management across Africa, and learning from engagement with Chinese businesses can be a game changer (Blunt & Jones, 1997). African management research focusing on China–Africa ventures and relations in order to better understand their beneficial or detrimental impact at micro and macro organizational levels, and studying hybrid spaces and interactions within, can provide better lenses through which to explore and understand China–Africa workplace dynamics (Shen, 2015; Tan-Mullins & Mohan, 2013). It is essential that such research focuses on organizations as well as individuals, and that interventions start to build a network of African managers who exhibit the kind of behaviours, skills, qualities and competences we aspire to cultivate across Africa to support its next phase of growth and development.

Conclusion

Undoubtedly, there would be considerable benefits for Africa if Chinese investment and business activity accelerates, but with that comes an urgent need to reflect seriously on how Africa learns from these experiences and stands on its own to assert and develop its growth at all levels. Developing competent African managers will play a key role in this process, and it should be taken seriously. At the macroeconomic level, African economies are readier than ever to gain from greater capital investment and thus boost productivity, competitiveness and technological readiness, but with the current lack of good managers this will fail (Chen, Goldstein & Orr, 2009; Hongxiang, Rounds & Zhang, 2016). African managers need to dramatically improve their own productivity and efficiency in order to perform better and partner effectively when working with and learning from Chinese companies already established in their area.

The sketch of a practice-based management development framework in this chapter is no more than that, and as always, the test will be in the implementation. If only crudely pursued, these ideas, which themselves can be counter-cultural in important respects, could easily reproduce the kind of shortcomings discussed previously. Additionally, if a general approach of this sort is developed and agreed by stakeholders, then discussion of leadership and action must start on the ground at the centre of China–Africa relations. Hybrid spaces provide unique ways and systems, using which we can learn more, better and faster by getting on with the execution and reviewing with rigour, rather than by planning carefully on the basis of what will work in theory, which can quickly turn out to be well-meaning but irrelevant in terms of how the Chinese work.

References

Acquaah, M., Zoogah, D. B., & Kwesiga, E. N. (2013). Advancing Africa through management knowledge and practice: The way forward, African. *Journal of Economic and Management Studies*, 4(2), 164–176.

Adisu, K., Sharkey, T., & Okoroafo, S. C. (2010). The impact of Chinese investment in Africa. *International Journal of Business and Management*, 5(9), 3.

Agence France-Presse. (2018). Chinese man arrested after describing Kenyans as "monkey people". *South China Morning Post*. Retrieved from www.scmp.com/news/world/africa/article/2163086/chinese-man-arrested-racist-monkey-slurs-involving-kenyan

Alden, C., & Davies, M. (2006). A profile of the operations of Chinese multinationals in Africa. *South African Journal of International Affairs, 13*(1), 83–96.

Amankwah-Amoah, J., Boso, N., & Yaw, A. D. (2018). Africa rising in an emerging world: An international marketing perspective. *International Marketing Review, 35*(4), 550–559.

AMI. (2013). *Catalysing management development in Africa identifying areas for impact.* Retrieved July 29, 2014 from https://africanmanagersblog.files.wordpress.com/2016/04/ami-report-summarised-2.pdf

AMI. (2017). *AMI Blog.* Retrieved from https://africanmanagersblog.org/

Andrew, J. (2019, January 28). Demand for business education rises in Africa. *Financial Times.* Retrieved from www.ft.com/content/90afd37e-14ff-11e9-a168-d45595ad076d

Antonacopoulou, E. P. (2007). Actionable knowledge. In S. Clegg & J. Bailey (Eds.), *International encyclopaedia of organization studies* (pp. 14–17). London: Sage.

Antonacopoulou, E. P. (2008). On the practise of practice: In-tensions and extensions in the ongoing reconfiguration of practice. In D. Barry & H. Hansen (Eds.), *The SAGE handbook of new approaches to management and organization* (pp. 112–131). London: Sage.

Anyansi, A., & Chiekwe, B. (2001). Toward an African-oriented management theory. In F. M. Edoho (Ed.), *Management challenges for Africa in the twenty-first century: Theoretical and applied perspectives* (pp. 63–72). Westport, CT: Praeger.

Beck, D. E., & Cowan, C. C. (1992). *The values test overview basic guide for administration and interpretation.* National Values Centre Texas USA.

Beck, D. E., & Cowan, C. C. (1996). *Spiral dynamics – Mastering values, leadership and change.* Oxford: Blackwell Publishers Ltd.

Blindenbach-Driessen, F. (2009). The effectiveness of cross-functional innovation teams. *Academy of Management Proceedings, 2009*(1), 1–6. https://doi.org/10.5465/ambpp.2009.44252588

Blindenbach-Driessen, Floortje, and van den Ende, Jan. (2014). The locus of innovation: The effect of a separate innovation unit on exploration, exploitation, and ambidexterity in manufacturing and service firms. *Journal of Product Innovation Management, 31*(5), 1089–1105. https://doi.org/10.1111/jpim.12146.

Bloom, N., Mahadran, A., McKenzie, D., & Roberts, J. (2010). Why do firms in developing countries have low productivity? *American Economic Review, 100*(2), 619–623.

Blunt, P., & Jones, M. L. (1997). Exploring the limits of Western leadership theory in East Asia and Africa. *Personnel Review, 26*(1/2), 6–23.

Bräutigam, D., & Xiaoyang, T. (2011). African Shenzhen: China's special economic zones in Africa. *The Journal of Modern African Studies, 49*(1), 27–54.

Brotheridge, C. M., & Long, S. (2007). The "real-world" challenges of managers: Implications for management education. *Journal of Management Development, 26*, 1.

Burger, U., & Trehan, K. (2018). Action learning in East Africa: New encounters or impossible challenges? *Action Learning: Research and Practice, 15*(2), 126–138. https://doi.org/10.1080/14767333.2018.1462144

Cambieri, G. (2011). *MBA who built successful consulting business in Africa.* Retrieved May 31, 2019 from www.businessbecause.com/news/entrepreneurs/833/mba-who-built-successful-consulting-business-in-africa

Chen, C., Goldstein, A., & Orr, R. J. (2009). Local operations of Chinese construction firms in Africa: An empirical survey. *International Journal of Construction Management, 9*(2), 75–89.

Chizema, A., Nyathi, N., Amaeshi, K., Okupe, A., & Idemudia, U. (2018). *Foreign investors and Africapitalism: The case for Chinese foreign direct investment in Africa* (pp. 215–239). Cambridge: Cambridge University Press. https://doi.org/10.1017/9781316675922.010.

Dahir, A. L. (2019). Ethiopia's garment workers make clothes for guess, H&M and Levi's but are the World's lowest paid. *Quartz Africa*. Retrieved August 7, 2019 from https://qz.com/africa/1614752/ethiopia-garment-workers-for-gap-hm-lowest-paid-in-world/

Datar, S. M., Garvin, D. A., & Cullen, P. G. (2010). *Excerpt from rethinking the MBA: Business education at a crossroads*. Boston: Harvard Business Press.

Dia, M. (1996). *Africa's management in the 1990s and beyond: Reconciling indigenous and transplanted institutions*. Directions in Development. Washington, DC: World Bank.

Feng, E., & Pilling, D. (2019a, March 27). The other side of Chinese investment in Africa. *Financial Times*. Retrieved from www.ft.com/content/9f5736d8-14e1-11e9-a581-4ff78404524e

Feng, E., & Pilling, D. (2019b). How Chinese entrepreneurs are quietly reshaping Africa. OZY. Retrieved August 7, 2019 from www.ozy.com/fast-forward/the-chinese-entrepreneurs-quietly-reshaping-africa/93519

Geldart, J. (2014). How China's management style differs from the West. *Grant Thornton UK LLP*. Retrieved December 3, 2019 from www.grantthornton.co.uk/en/insights/how-chinas-management-style-differs-from-the-west/

Gu, J. (2009). China's private enterprises in Africa and the implications for African development. *The European Journal of Development Research, 21*(4), 570–587. https://doi.org/10.1057/ejdr.2009.21

Higgins, D. (2018). Management education in action – Observations, reflections and ways forward. *Action Learning: Research and Practice, 15*(2), 87–89. https://doi.org/10.1080/14767333.2018.1493175

Hongxiang, H., Rounds, Z., & Zhang, X. (2016). China's Africa dream isn't dead. *Foreign Policy* (blog). Retrieved August 7, 2019 from https://foreignpolicy.com/2016/02/18/africa-kenya-tanzania-china-business-economy-gdp-slowing-investment-chinese/

Houeland, C., & Jacobs, S. (2016). *The "big man" syndrome in Africa*, n.d. Retrieved December 14, 2019 from https://africasacountry.com/2016/03/the-big-man-syndrome-in-africa

Jackson, T. (2002). The management of people across cultures: Valuing people differently. *Human Resource Management, 41*(4), 455–475.

Jackson, T. (2004). *Management and change in Africa: A cross-cultural perspective*. London: Routledge.

Jackson, T. (2015). Management studies from Africa: A cross-cultural critique. *Africa Journal of Management, 1*(1), 78–88.

Jackson, T., Louw, L., & Zhao, S. (2013). China in sub-Saharan Africa: Implications for HRM policy and practice at organizational level. *The International Journal of Human Resource Management, 24*(13), 2512–2533.

Jackson, T., Louw, L., Zhao, S., Boojihawon, D. K. (R.), & Fang, T. (2014). Chinese organizations in sub-Saharan Africa: New dynamics, new synergies1. *AIB Insights, 14*(1), 11.

Jassawalla, A. R., & Sashittal, H. C (1999). Building collaborative cross-functional new product teams. *Academy of Management Perspectives*, 13(3), 50–63.

Jayaram, K., Kassiri, O., & Yuan Sun, I. (2017). The closest look yet at Chinese economic engagement in Africa. *McKinsey*. Retrieved December 7, 2019 from www.mckinsey.com/featured-insights/middle-east-and-africa/the-closest-look-yet-at-chinese-economic-engagement-in-africa

Kamoche, K. (2011). Contemporary developments in the management of human resources in Africa. *Journal of World Business*, 46(1), 1–4.

Kamoche, K., Chizema, A., Mellahi, K., & Newenham-Kahindi, A. (2012). New directions in the management of human resources in Africa. *The International Journal of Human Resource Management*, 23(14), 2825–2834.

Kiggundu, M. N. (1991). The challenges of management development in sub-Saharan Africa. *Journal of Management Development*, 10(6), 32–47.

Kirchhoff, C. (2013). The missing middle: Developing Africa's managers. *ReConnect Africa*. Retrieved August 8, 2019 from www.reconnectafrica.com/January-February-2013/africa/the-missing-middle-developing-africas-managers.html

Kragelund, P. (2009). Part of the disease or part of the cure? Chinese investments in the Zambian mining and construction sectors. *The European Journal of Development Research*, 21(4), 644–661.

Kuada, J. (2006). Cross-cultural interactions and changing management practices in Africa: A Hybrid management perspective. *African Journal of Business and Economic Research*, 1(1), 96–113.

Leavy, B. (2018, January). Will China's entrepreneurial migrant managers awaken Africa's dream of becoming the next factory of the world? *Strategy & Leadership*. https://doi.org/10.1108/SL-11-2017-0107

Lee, C. K. (2009). Raw encounters: Chinese managers, African workers and the politics of casualization in Africa's Chinese enclaves. *The China Quarterly*, 647–666. https://doi.org/10.1017/S0305741009990142

Locke, R. R., & Spender, J. C. (2011). *Confronting managerialism how the business elite and their schools threw our lives out of balance*. London: Zed Books.

Love, J. H., & Roper, S. (2009). Organizing innovation: Complementarities between cross-functional teams. *Technovation*, 29(3), 192–203.

Lutz, D. W. (2009). African Ubuntu philosophy and global management. *Journal of Business Ethics*, 84(3), 313.

Majchrzak, A., More, P. H. B., & Faraj, S. (2012). Transcending knowledge differences in cross-functional teams. *Organization Science*, 23(4), 951–970.

Marsh, J. (2019). *Employed by China*. Retrieved August 7, 2019 from www.cnn.com/interactive/2018/08/world/china-africa-ethiopia-manufacturing-jobs-intl/

Mayer, C.-H., Boness, C. M., & Louw, L. (2017). Perceptions of Chinese and Tanzanian employees regarding intercultural collaboration. *SA Journal of Human Resource Management*, 15, 11. https://doi.org/10.4102/sajhrm.v15i0.921

Mbamalu, S. (2018). Plight of African workers under Chinese employers. *African Liberty*. Retrieved December 9, 2019 from www.africanliberty.org/2018/09/27/plight-of-african-workers-under-chinese-employers/

Mbewa, D. O. (2019). Chinese companies create a scholarship for vocational training in Kenya. *CGTN Africa* (blog). Retrieved August 7, 2019 from https://africa.cgtn.com/2019/04/02/chinese-companies-create-a-scholarship-for-vocational-training-in-kenya/

Muriithi, S. (2017). The Chinese-African management and cultural relevancy, challenges and the future of Chinese business in Africa. *European Journal of Research and Reflection in Management Sciences, 5*(2), 1–14.

Ongiyo, J. (2019). China's strict work ethics the real cause of conflict in Africa. *The Standard.* Retrieved August 7, 2019 from www.standardmedia.co.ke/article/ 2001299347/china-s-strict-work-ethics-the-real-cause-of-conflict-in-africa

Osondu-Oti, A. (2016). China and Africa: Human rights perspective. *Africa Development/Afrique et Développement, 41*(1), 49–80. Retrieved from www. jstor.org/stable/90001834

Park, H., Jong Won Lim, M., & Birnbaum-More, P. H. (2009). The effect of multiknowledge individuals on performance in cross-functional new product development teams. *Journal of Product Innovation Management, 26*(1), 86–96.

Patey, L. (2018, August 26). The Chinese model is failing Africa. *Financial Times.* Retrieved from www.ft.com/content/ca4072f6-a79f-11e8-a1b6-f368d365bf0e

Perriton, L., & Reynolds, M. (2004). Critical management education: From pedagogy of possibility to pedagogy of refusal. *Management Learning, 35*(1), 61–77.

Pfeffermann, G. (2008, January 15) Bad management and sub-Saharan Africa. *The Globalist* (blog). Retrieved from www.theglobalist.com/bad-management-and-sub-saharan-africa/

Pilling, D. (2019, July 3). It is wrong to demonise Chinese labour practices in Africa. *Financial Times.* Retrieved from www.ft.com/content/6326dc9a-9cb8-11e9-9c06-a4640c9feebb

Rogers, C. (2019). How Hybrid teams are driving innovation. *Marketing Week* (blog). Retrieved July 10, 2019 from www.marketingweek.com/innovation-hybrid-teams/

Ryder, H. W. (2018). Are Chinese loans to Africa good or bad? That's the wrong question, n.d. Retrieved December 9, 2019 from https://thediplomat.com/2018/09/ are-chinese-loans-to-africa-good-or-bad-thats-the-wrong-question/

Samir, S., Selvarajah, C., Meyer, D., & Dorasamy, N. (2014). Exploring excellence in leadership perceptions amongst South African managers. *Human Resource Development International, 17*(1), 47–66.

Sethi, R., Smith, D. C., & Park, C. W. (2001). Cross-functional product development teams, creativity, and the innovativeness of new consumer products. *Journal of Marketing Research, 38*(1), 73–85.

Shen, X. (2015). Private Chinese investment in Africa: Myths and realities. *Development Policy Review, 33*(1), 83–106. https://doi.org/10.1111/dpr.12093.

Tang, X. (2010). Bulldozer or locomotive? The impact of Chinese enterprises on the local employment in angola and the DRC. *Journal of Asian and African Studies, 45*(3), 350–368.

Tan-Mullins, M., & Mohan, G. (2013). The potential of corporate environmental responsibility of Chinese state-owned enterprises in Africa. *Environment, Development and Sustainability, 15*(2), 265–284.

Trehan, K., & Rigg, C. (2015). Enacting critical learning: Power, politics and emotions at work. *Studies in Higher Education, 40*(5), 791–805.

UNICEF. (2013). *UNICEF innovation labs: DIY for solving global problems | Creative Huddle,* n.d. Retrieved December 24, 2019 from www.creativehuddle. co.uk/unicef-innovation-labs-diy-for-solving-global-problems

Wang, D., Fan, D., Freeman, S., & Zhu, C. J. (2017). Exploring cross-cultural skills for expatriate managers from Chinese multinationals: Congruence and contextualization. *Asia Pacific Journal of Management, 34*(1), 123–146.

Wang, D., Freeman, S., & Zhu, C. J. (2013). Personality traits and cross-cultural competence of Chinese expatriate managers: A socio-analytic and institutional perspective. *The International Journal of Human Resource Management, 24*(20), 3812–3830.

Whitehead, F. (2015, February 13). Creating a fertile future for smallholder farmers in Africa. *The Guardian.* Working in Development. Retrieved from www.theguardian.com/global-development-professionals-network/2015/feb/13/private-sector-africa-smallholder-farmers-training-diversification

Xing, Y., Liu, Y., Tarba, S. Y., & Cooper, C. L. (2016). Intercultural influences on managing African employees of Chinese firms in Africa: Chinese managers' HRM practices'. *International Business Review, 25*(1), 28–41. https://doi.org/10.1016/j.ibusrev.2014.05.003

Yuan Sun, I., Jayaram, K., & Kassiri, O. (2017). Dance-of-the-Lions-and-Dragons. *McKinsey & Company.* Retrieved December 7, 2019 from www.mckinsey.com/~/media/McKinsey/Featured%20Insights/Middle%20East%20and%20Africa/The%20closest%20look%20yet%20at%20Chinese%20economic%20engagement%20in%20Africa/Dance-of-the-lions-and-dragons.ashx

Zoogah, D. B., & Nkomo, S. (2013). Management research in Africa: Past, present and future. In T. R. Lituchy, B. J. Punnett, & B. B. Puplampu (Eds.), *Management in Africa: Macro and micro perspectives* (pp. 29–51). New York: Routledge.

Index

absorptive capacity 5, 6, 17, 36, 38, 59, 256
Adamolekun, W. 62
Adem, S. 61
adhocracy culture 185
Adisu, K. 95
Ado, A. 23, 64, 82, 82–83
affective commitment 167, 176
Africa 5, 7, 131; absorptive capacity 5–6; communalism 112; communication 117–118; development 3–4, 30; goal of communication 119–120; guiding philosophies 111–117; management approaches 262–263; motives for China's engagement with 9, 10, 11, 18; national culture 39; process and style of communication 120; resources 28; self-perceptions 117; trade unions 11–12, 42; *ubuntu* 15, 37, 41, 84, 85, 109, 111, 112, 113, 120, 206, 229; unemployment 13; ways of knowing 118–119; Zambia 13; *see also* anglophone Africa; francophone africa; Ghana; indigenous Africans; Mozambique; Nigeria
African Labour Research Network 12, 15
African Management Initiative (AMI) 257
African Union 10
African-based Business Schools (ABSs) 266, 267, 268
Agbebi, M. 30, 31, 32
Alden, C. 9, 63, 82, 104
Algeria 132
All-China Federation of Trade Unions (ACFTU) 10–11, 42

Allen, N. J. 167
all-weather friend 152, 153
Alves, A. C. 9
anglophone Africa 131, 133, 135, 136, 149; hybrid languages 146, 147–148; interactions with Chinese people 141–142; interviews 137–138; overcoming language barriers 144–146
Angola 14, 23, 57, 62, 132, 262
Ankomah, A. 12
Asian FDI in Africa 243
Ayodele, T. 24
A'Zami, D. 66

Baah, A. Y. 12, 15, 42–43
Bandara, A. 61
benefits 217–218
Benin 137
Benschop, Y. 204
Berry, J. W. 33
Bhabha, H. K. 6, 7
Bjorkman, I. 186, 198
Botswana 55
Bowen, D. E. 198
Boxall, P. 186
Bräutigam, D. 13, 262
Brewster, C. 90
BRICS 104
Buckley, J. P. 76–77
Burger, U. 260
Burundi 137
Busse, M. 61
Butterfield, W. 57

Cameron, K. S. 185
Cameroon 137
Carmody, P. 68
Chad 137

Printed in the United States
by Baker & Taylor Publisher Services